THE SĀHITYA-DARPAṆA

THE SĀHITYA-DARPAṆA

or

Mirror of Composition

of

VIŚVANĀTHA

A TREATISE ON POETICAL CRITICISM

Translated by

J.R. BALLANTYNE

and

PRAMADÁ DASÁ MITRA

MOTILAL BANARSIDASS PUBLISHERS
PRIVATE LIMITED • DELHI

2nd Reprint : 2016
First Published: Calcutta, 1875

ISBN : 978-81-208-1145-4

MOTILAL BANARSIDASS
41 U.A. Bungalow Road, Jawahar Nagar, Delhi 110 007
8 Mahalaxmi Chamber, 22 Bhulabhai Desai Road, Mumbai 400 026
203 Royapettah High Road, Mylapore, Chennai 600 004
236, 9th Main III Block, Jayanagar, Bengaluru 560 011
8 Camac Street, Kolkata 700 017
Ashok Rajpath, Patna 800 004
Chowk, Varanasi 221 001

Printed in India

by RP Jain at NAB Printing Unit,
A-44, Naraina Industrial Area, Phase I, New Delhi–110028
and published by JP Jain for Motilal Banarsidass Publishers (P) Ltd,
41 U.A. Bungalow Road, Jawahar Nagar, Delhi-110007

PREFACE

The translation of the Sâhitya-darpaṇa was commenced by the late lamented Principal of the Benares College, Dr. Ballantyne, whose memory, be it said in passing, will be ever cherished with gratitude and affection by his pupils as well as the pundits of that institution. The performance of that eminent scholar, however, extends little beyond a quarter, ending with page 128 of the present publication. At the particular instance and under the kind encouragement of his worthy successor and my honoured tutor, Mr. R.T.H. Griffith, M.A., I undertook to continue the work, which is now presented to the public in its completed form. The former portion has been revised and edited, and no pains have been spared in the task, wherein I had to compare the original and the translation word for word. I have, however, been particularly careful not to make in the learned Doctor's work any alterations not absolutely required by the text, and such sentences and passages only have been entirely re-written as misrepresented the original. I think I have sometimes been over-scrupulous in this direction, as, for instance, in adding only in a foot-note what evidently is the correct interpretation (see p. 78). As I am personally responsible for the alterations, I annex a list of references to the principal ones. I could wish Dr. Ballantyne had used the word 'taste' or 'relish' to render such an important term as *rasa*, denoting, as it does, the very essence of the essential subject-matter of the work. But I was asked to revise the former portion when the first two or three forms of my work had already passed through the press, so I could not help retaining the name 'flavour,' which will perhaps grate on the ears of better judges than myself as tasteless and gross. I should think it is the most unpoetical expression that could be used to denote the soul of poetry.

Our author, I think, has furnished a very apt definition of Poetry, viz., 'A sentence the soul whereof is Relish.' Now the question arises—What is it that constitutes relish itself? It is pleasure no doubt, but not the sort of pleasure which is felt, for instance, from hearing such words as simply convey a gratifying intelligence. It is a peculiar pleasure, it is a passion or emotion, it is love, or sorrow, or mirth, or wrath, or magnanimity, or terror, or wonder, or even disgust, or it may be pure and passionless joy,*—not excited by its ordinary causes but delightfully suggested by a representation of what are its causes, effects, and concomitant mental and bodily states in the theatre of life. These, as exhibited in Poetry, are respectively called Excitants (*vibháva*), Ensuants (*anubháva*) and Accessories (*vyabhichari*); and a combination of these, whether wholly expressed, or partially expressed and partially implied, developing the nine modes of sentiment mentioned above, constitutes Poetry which has thus a nine-fold character. It is clear from the above elucidation that the Indian Critics held the right view, that an exhibition of human passion or emotion alone is poetry. Where, it might at first be objected, is the element of passion in the description of inanimate nature, or of irrational creatures? A little reflection would show that, in order to be poetical, it must have the colouring of emotion; it must, to use Indian phraseology, call forth one of the permanent sentiments by an exhibition of a part at least of the three-fold cause of its manifestation. Thus, the Sublime and the Beautiful in nature must come under one or other of the Relishes enumerated.** First, the objects described may be contemplated with wonder as the prevailing sentiment, and the Marvellous will be the Relish of such poetry. Or, secondly, the poet may rise from the contemplation of Nature of Nature's God, reverence (bháva see text 245) being the prevailing sentiment in such a case. Or, thirdly, the scenes may be depicted as heightening some passion—love, for instance, or as ministering to that pure and passionless joy which constitutes the Relish of Holy Tranquillity (the Quietistic Flavour***). In the first case the objects form the Substantial Excitant, and in the rest the Enhancing Excitant of the Relish.+ The lower animals, however, may form the Excitants, Substantial or Enhancing, of almost all the varieties of Relish.++ Shelly's

* See Text 206, p. 109.

** P. 111. Text 209.

*** Text 238.

\+ Text 62.

++ Mill's remarks on the subject are so clear and impressive that I cannot help quoting them in extenso:—

Descriptive poetry consists, no doubt, in description of things as they appear, not as they are; and it paints them not in their bare and natural lineaments, but seen through

celebrated Hymn to a skylark, for instance, is throughout coloured with wonder or admiration, the other sentiments suggested by the varied and exuerant imagery serving only to minister to that main passion. We will select two or three stanzas for illustration:

Higher still and higher
    From the earth thou springest;
Like a cloud of fire,
    The blue deep thou wingest;
And singing still dost soar, and soaring ever singest.

What thou art we know not:
    What is most like thee?
From rainbow clouds there flow not
    Drops so bright to see,
As from thy presence showers a rain of melody.

Like a high-born maiden
    In a palace tower,
Soothing her love-laden
    Souls in secret hour
With music sweet as love, which overflows her bower.

It is remarkable that though wonder is evidently the leading sentiment of this short poem, the poet commits not even in a single instance the fault of bluntly naming it.* The Relish of the last stanza is 'love in separation,' here manifested in subordinate condition.+

The coincidence of this view of poetry and that of John Stuart Mill is so remarkable that I cannot resist the temptation of quoting here the

the medium and arrayed in the colours of the imagination set in action by the feelings. If a poet describes a lion, he does not describe him as a naturalist would, nor even as a traveller would, who was intent upon stating the truth, the whole truth, and nothing but the truth. He describes him by imagery, that is, by suggesting the most striking likenesses and contrasts which might occur to a mind contemplating the lion, in the state of awe, wonder, or terror, which the spectacle naturally excites, or is, on the occasion, supposed to excite. Now this describing the lion professedly, but the state of excitement of the spectator really. The lion may be described falsely or with exaggeration, and the poetry be all the better; but if the human emotion be not painted with scrupulous truth, the poetry is bad poetry, *i.e.*, is not poetry at all, but a failure." *Dissertations and Discussions*, Vol. I, p. 69.

* Text 577.

+ See Text 212 and 245.

words of that thinker which would indeed serve to throw some light on the third chapter of the present work, treating of the essentials of poetry. Let us first compare our author's definition of poetry. Let us first compare our author's definition of poetry, which, by somewhat unfolding the technical term *rasa*, may be more perspicuously rendered—'Words whose essence is emotional delight are Poetry' with the two approved by Mill, viz., 'Poetry is impassioned truth,' '(Poetry is) man's thoughts tinged by his feelings.' The Ensuants (*anubháva*), one of three sets of the essentials in the delineation of the Permanent or Principal Sentiment (*stháyi-bháva*), are very clearly recognised in the following remarks:—

"But there is a radical distinction between the interest felt in a story as such, and the interest excited by poetry; for the one is derived from incident, the other from the representation of feeling. In one, *the source of the emotion excited is the exhibition of a state or states of human sensibility*; in the other, of a series of states of mere outward circumstances."* *Dissert. and Disc.*, Vol. I. p. 65.

* The italics are ours. In spite of the distinction here drawn, it is impossible to deny that incident is often *inseparably* connected with feeling and indispensable to its greatest manifestation as in the epos. Mill indeed seems in a manner to admit this by saying 'Many of the greatest poems are in the form of fictitious narratives, and in almost all good serious fictions there is true poetry.' But we should humbly think that the author ought to have more distinctly asserted the indissoluble relation of the two elements in the highest development of poetry. It is also to be observed that Hindu critics could not consent to the above restricted application of the word poem which, in their opinion, is a generic name equally applicable to a poetical fiction in prose. They were, however, quite sensible of the distinction of incident and feeling, along with the fact of their mutual subserviency (see text, 316). In his zeal for a distinction between a poem and a novel, Mill indeed makes certain remarks not perhaps quite warranted by truth. He says, 'He (the novelist) has to describe outward things, *not the inward man*; actions and events, *not feelings*.' Perhaps the writer means to declare the *predominance* of incident over feeling in a novel, otherwise a novel without a sufficient depiction of passion would be hardly readable, and the fact of 'almost all good serious fictions' containing 'true poetry' is admitted by himself. The fact is that the terms 'poem' and 'novel' are vaguely used in English, and though the idea of a novel being written in verse is conceived by Mill, that of giving the designation of 'poem' to a work in prose never perhaps occurred to him, the latter being so entirely opposed to usage. The distinction between a poem and a novel may be thus stated : A poem, (at least, one of the higher order) is a work in which the feeling is principal and the incident is subordinate, though indispensable. A novel is its converse. Thus either of the elements is necessary in either, though in different proportions. It must not be forgotten that, though not a necessary element of poetry, metre, like music, assists considerably in the excitement of emotion. Where it is wanting, the defect has to be compensated

Nor have the Permanent Sentiments (Text 206), themselves, of Indian critics escaped the keen observation of the British thinker, and the nine principal feelings enumerated by the latter, strikingly correspond to, and differ but little from, the nine recognised by the former. He says:

"Every truth which a human being can enunciate, every thought, even every outward impression, which can enter into his consciousness, may become poetry when shown through any impassioned medium, when invested with the colouring or joy, of grief, or pity, or affection, or admiration, or reverence, or awe, or even hatred or terror: and unless so coloured, nothing, be it as interesting as it may, is poetry." (p. 70).

It will be observed that joy, except under the comic sentiment, or mirth, is not recognised by Indian critics as one of the leading emotions in poetry, but only as one of the concomitant moods. The reason is obvious. Joy is either pure or mingled with passion. In the former case it comes under that passionless and holy repose of the soul called Quietism (*śama* Text 238) and is hence counted as one of its Accessories. In the latter, its subordination need not be pointed out. The following noble lines of Coleridge, for instance, depicting joy, in a prominent manner, as forming the fountain of Creation's lustre, are a decided instance of the Quietistic Relish:

O pure of heart! thou need'st not ask of me
What this strong music in the soul may be!
What and wherein it doth exist,
This light, this glory, this fair luminous mist,
This beautiful and beauty-making power,
Joy, virtuous Lady! Joy that ne'er was given
Save to the pure, and in their purest hour,
Life and life's effluence, cloud at once and shower,
Joy, Lady, is the spirit and the power
Which wedding Nature to us gives in dower,
A new Earth and new Heaven,
Undreamt of by the sensual and the proud—

by an adequate addition of feeling. Of two poems, for instance, equal in other respects, the poetry of the one which avails itself of the assistance of metre will certainly be the more striking, for the feeling itself is heightened by the melody of the versification. Strip the Paradise Lost of its metre and it loses half its effect.

Joy is the sweet voice, Joy the luminous cloud:
  We in ourselves rejoice!
And thence flows all that charms our ear or sight
  All melodies the echoes of that voice,
All colours a suffusion from that light.

What is the Joy which glows in such a brilliant imagery? The poet himself tells us that it is the joy 'that never was given save to the pure and in their purest hour,' 'undreamt of by the sensual and the proud.' It has no admixture of earthly passion, though it may be associated with holy love—love that takes the name of universal benevolence (भूतदया), another concomitant of the Quietistic Relish. The above verses sound indeed as if they were a long-continued echo to the sublime strain of the Upanishad which exclaims—

को ह्येवान्यात् कः प्राण्यात् यदेष आकाश* आनन्दो न स्यात ।
(*Taittiríyopanishad*, p. 100, *Bib. Ind.*)
(Who indeed, would inhale, who exhale, if this ether were not Joy!)
Joy here, is the Deity himself, the Essential Excitant of the Relish.

The three essential merits (*guṇa*) of poetry, according to the later school of Rhetoric to which our critic belongs, are Sweetness, Energy and Perspicuity. To guard against misconception, it is to be mentioned that Dr. Ballantyne had inappropriately rendered to the term *guṇa* into 'style' by which name he refers to the subject of the eighth chapter, in his Advertisement. The proper equivalent of style is *ríti*, the subject of the ninth chapter.

It is with no ordinary pleasure that I have now obtained the long looked for opportunity of expressing publicly my gratitude to Mr. R.T.H. Griffith, M.A., who (not to mention my great obligations as a pupil) has kindly revised, in MS. or proof, a great portion of my work. From that distinguished scholar's paper on Indian Figures of Speech appended to his Specimens of Old Indian Poetry, I have borrowed some of the renderings of names in the tenth chapter. Deeply too do I feel myself indebted to the accomplished Professor A.E. Gough, B.A., for the kind help he has lent me, in my weak health, in the translation of the concluding portion of the seventh and of the eighth and ninth chapters.

* Sankaráchárya construes आकाश as आकाशे in the locative case, but we should prefer the nominative, as the natural and more forcible interpretation.

My hearty acknowledgements are also due to the distinguished antiquarian and scholar, Bábu Rájendralál Mitra, who has not only all along evinced a true interest in the work, but has actually urged me on to its completion.

PD. M.

List of references to the principal alterations made in Dr. Ballantyne's portion of the work.

Page.	Line.	Page.	Line.	Page.	Line.
1	20	39	11	85	4
2	16—18	41	25—26	87	28—29
4	31	45	7—8	92	28—29
5	5—6	46	23	93	20—22
6	2—13	47	4	95	21
7	13	48	8—12	97	30—31
12	10	48	34—35	98	2—5
12	28-31	49	13—14	100	2—3
12	35	51	13—15	102	36—38
13	2	55	11—12	103	32
22	14	56	11	106	2—3
25	17—20	56	19	106	24—26
26	19	56	22	111	16
29	32—33	59	9	111	17—19
30	1	60	17—18	116	12
35	15	60	23—24	120	11—12
36	12—14	61	31	123	12—18
36	20	67	22—24	123	23
38	22	74	17—20		
38	30—32	74	24—25		

ADVERTISEMENT

Some account of the work here offered to his notice may be not unacceptable to the reader.

Among the Sanskrit texts printed at Calcutta under the authority of the General Committee of Public Instruction, there are two works the titles of which are given in English as follows:—

"*Kávya Prakáśa*, a treatise on Poetry and Rhetoric by MAMMATA ÁCHÁRYA. (1829)."

Sahitya Darpaṇa; a treatise on Rhetorical Composition by VIŚWANÁTHA KAVIRÁJA.—(1828)."

The *Kávya Prakáśa*—the "Illustration of Poetry,"—consists of a number of metrical rules (*káriká*) interspersed with comments and illustrative examples. The rules are founded on the Aphorisms of VÁMANA, who owed his knowledge of the subject to the divine sage BHARATA. The *Sáhitya Darpaṇa*— the "Mirror of Composition"—also has memorial verses as its text; and the rules are frequently illustrated by the same examples as those employed in the earlier work. Both works are held in high esteem; but that of VIŚWANÁTHA—the more recent and the more copious of the two—is generally admitted as the standard of taste among the learned Hindús.

Of the etymology of the term *Sáhitya* two explanations are offered. According to the one, it is derived from *hita* 'benefit' and *saha* 'with,' because a knowledge of it is beneficial in all departments of literature. The other, with less appearance of reason, explains it as denoting the sum total of the various sections of which the system itself is made up.

The term Rhetoric as employed to denote the subject of a treatise of this description, is liable—according to our view of the division and denomination of the sciences—to an objection the converse of that to which we hold the term Logic liable, when employed to denote the all-embracing sphere of the Nyáya philosophy. In the *Sáhitya* we have but a part and the least important part of what, according to Aristotle,*

* The main consideration being that of Arguments–τὰ δ' ἄλλα προσθῆκαι– "but the rest mere out-work." *Rhet. B. 1. c.* I.

belongs to Rhetoric. In order to attain its specific end of convincing or persuading—between which we agree with Mr. Smart in thinking that there is more of a distinction than a difference*—Rhetoric does not hesitate to avail itself of the graces of language which gratify the taste; but in the *Sáhitya*, "taste" (*rasa*) is all in all. The difference between the political history of India and that of Greece or Rome so obviously suggests the reason why eloquence, in the two cases, proposed to itself ends thus different, that it would be idle to do more than allude to it in passing.

The *Sáhitya Darpaṇa* is divided into ten sections—of lengths varying from eight or nine pages to eighty or ninety. The first section declares the nature of poetry. The second treats of the various powers of a word. The third treats of taste. The fourth treats of the divisions of poetry. The fifth discusses more fully one of the powers of a word adverted to in section second. The sixth takes particular cognizance of the division of poetry into 'that which is to be seen,' and 'that which is to be heard'. The seventh treats of blemishes. The eighth treats of style. The ninth treats of the varieties of composition resulting from the blending of styles, and the predominance of one or other of them. The tenth and last treats of embellishment. To the subject of this tenth section the *Kuvalayánanda* of Apyayya Díkshita, with which the student usually commences, confines itself.

According to established custom the *Sáhitya Darpaṇa* opens with an invocation. The author then proceeds to say that as his work is ancillary to poetry, its fruits can be no other than those which poetry bestows. These are declared to consist in the attainment of the four great objects of human desire—viz. Merit, Wealth, Enjoyment, and Salvation—which, "by means of poetry alone, can be obtained pleasantly even by persons of slender capacity." Salvation, it is to be remembered, or liberation from the liability to being born again, is the reward held out to its followers by each of the various systems of Hindu doctrine. Even the

* "That common situation in life. *Video meliora proboque, deteriora sequor*, proves indeed that there are degrees of conviction which yield to persuasion, as there are other degrees which no persuasion can subdue: yet perhaps we shall hereafter be able to show that such junctures do but exhibit one set of motives outweighing another, and that the application of the term persuasion to the one set, and of conviction to the other, is in many cases arbitrary, rather than dictated by a correspondent difference in the things." *Sematalogy*—p. 175.

Grammarians claim for their own art (—more than was claimed for the kindred Grammarye of the Dark Ages—) the power of leading the soul to bliss;* and it is scarcely to be wondered at that the poets should contend that the goal might be gained, as surely as by any of the more rugged routes, and much more pleasantly, by the "primrose path" of Poesy. Poetry is to conduce to this by setting before its votary such examples for imitation as that of Ráma, and for avoidance as that of Rávaṇa, and so training him up to virtue. After showing, how all the four great objects sought after by the wise have been at various times obtained through conversancy with poetry, our author gravely disposes of the objection that the possession of the Vedas renders the study of poetry with such views superfluous, by asking, where is the wisdom of seeking to remove by means of bitter drugs an ailment that can be cured with sugar-candy?

Having established the importance of Poetry, he proceeds to determine what it is that poetry consists in; and this he decides is 'Flavour' (*rasa*).** Between this and the Vedántic conception of the Deity, he does his best (in his third section) to make out a parallel, which the reader will be the more likely to understand, if he have some previous acquaintance with Vedántic speculations.

It is worth noticing that the notion of reckoning *metre* among the circumstances that constitute poetry is not even hinted at by our critic. The fact that the learned of India are accustomed to put into verse almost all their driest treatises—on law, physic, divinity, &c.—affords a ready enough explanation why the accident of metre should not be mistaken by them for the essence of poetry. Their test of poetry, (under which title, as we shall see, they reckon "poetry in prose"—*gadya kávya*), coincides pretty closely with that specified by Whately as the test of "*good* poetry," when he says (Rhet. p. 344),—"The true test is easily applied: that which to competent judges affords the appropriate *pleasure* of Poetry, is *good* poetry, whether it answer any other purpose or not: that which does *not* afford this pleasure, however instructive it may be, is not good *Poetry*, though it may be a valuable *work*." The

* According to the Grammarians—"A single word, perfectly understood, and properly employed, is, alike in heaven and on earth, the *Kámadhuk*"—the marvellous cow from which you may "milk out whatever you desire"—including, of course, final emancipation, if you wish it.

** *Vákyam rasátmakang kávyam*—see p. 10.

Archbishop goes on to say, "Notwithstanding all that has been advanced by some French critics, to prove that a work, not in metre, may be a Poem, (which doctrine was partly derived from a misinterpretation of a passage in Aristotle's Poetics,) universal opinion has always given a contrary decision. Any composition in *verse*, (and none that is not,) is always called, whether good or bad, a Poem, by all who have no favourite hypothesis to maintain." The paṇḍits furnish apparently an exception to the universality of this dictum, for if you wish to *astonish* a paṇḍit, you have only to ask him gravely whether, for example, that terse *metrical* composition, the Nyáya compendium entitled the *Bháshá-parichchheda* is a *poem*. If, in holding it to be as far removed as anything well can be from poetry, he goes on a "favourite hypothesis," it is because the notion of an opposite hypothesis probably never occurred to him.

In the 2nd chapter (on the various powers of a word) the explanation of some of the terms is rather curious. "Let that 'Indication' (says the author) be 'Superimponent' which makes one think of the identity with something else of an object *not swallowed* (by that with which it is identified, but expressed along with it). That 'Indication' is held to be 'Introsusceptive' which makes one think of the identity with something else of an object *swallowed*—not expressed but recognised as it were within that with which it is identified." For example—"The horse—the white—gallops:" here "the horse" and "the white" mean just one and the same thing, and both terms are exhibited; but the same sense would be equally well understood (by a jockey, for example, to whom the horse was notoriously "the white"—or "the dun"—or "the chesnut"—) if the sentence were briefly. "The white gallops." Here the "white" has swallowed the "horse," and the case is one of "Indication inclusive introsusceptive founded on Notoriety" (*rúḍhávupádána-lakshaṇá sádhyavasáná*). This classification of phraseology may serve to illustrate a passage in the "Poetics" of Aristotle, which Mr. Theodore Buckley (of Christ Church) concurs with Dr. Ritter in condemning as spurious. The passage occurs in the 21st chapter, where, in speaking of metaphors, Aristotle, as rendered by Mr. Buckley, says "And sometimes the proper term is added to the relative terms." We incline to regard the caluminated passage as genuine. Let us see. Aristotle goes on to remark "I say, for instance, a cup has a similar relation to Bacchus that a shield has to Mars. Hence, a shield may be called the cup of Mars and a cup the shield of Bacchus." Now, it seems to us that if the following proportion—viz.

Cup : Bacchus : : shield : Mars

were not present to the mind of the hearer, then (to use Mr. Buckley's words—on a kindred passage in the 11th chapter 3rd Book of the Rhetoric—) "with a view to guard the metaphor from any incidental harshness or obscurity," the proper term may be advantageously added—making what our author calls a case of the "Superimponent" (*sáropá*). Thus, had Aristotle followed up his remark by a special example, we should have read, "The cup—the shield of Bacchus"—"The shield—the cup of Mars." According to the Hindú phraseology, when we omit the proper term and say, "The cup of Mars," then, (through Indication Introsusceptive) the cup has *swallowed* the shield—which latter, nevertheless, is discerned within the other by the eye of the intelligent.

From the chapter of the *Sáhitya Darpaṇa* which treat of Dramatic Poetry, many interesting extracts have been given by Professor H.H. Wilson in the Introduction to his "Select Specimens of the Theatre of the Hindus.".

J.R.B

Benares College,
5th January, 1851.

CONTENTS

THE MIRROR OF COMPOSITION.

SALUTATION TO GANES'A!

CHAPTER I.—*The Declaration of the Nature of Poetry.*

AT the beginning of his book, desiring the unobstructed completion of what he wishes to begin, he *i. e., the author—commenting on his own metrical treatise*—makes his address to the Goddess of Speech, because in the province of Eloquence it is she who is the constituted authority.

TEXT.

Invocation. 1.—May that Goddess of Language, whose radiance is fair as the autumnal moon, having removed the overspreading darkness, render all things clear in my mind!

COMMENTARY.

a. As this book is ancillary to Poetry, by the fruits of Poetry only can it be fruitful:—therefore he states what are the fruits of Poetry:—

TEXT.

The subject declared by implication. 2.—Since the attainment of the fruits consisting of the class of four *i. e., the four great objects of human desire—viz., Merit, Wealth, Enjoyment, and Liberation*—is pleasantly possible even in the case of those of slender capacity, by means of Poetry only, therefore its nature shall be now set forth.

COMMENTARY.

a. The allegation in the text is borne out by facts—for it is notorious that the fruits of the "class of four" have been attained by means of the counsels, as to doing and forbearing to do *respectively* what ought to be done and what ought not to be done, deduced from

Poetry—*to the effect* that "one ought to do as Ráma and the like, not as Rávaṇa and the like." And it has been said—"Addiction to good Poetry produces sagacity in regard to Merit, Wealth, Enjoyment, and Liberation, and *it produces also* fame and favour." Further—*to explain these assertions severally*—the attainment of Merit through Poetry *may take place*, for instance by means of the laudation of the lotus-feet of the divine Náráyaṇa. That this is the case is notorious, from such statements of the Vedas as this one, viz.;—"A single word, properly employed, and perfectly understood, is, in heaven and on earth, the *Kámadhuk—the cow from which you may 'milk out whatever you desire.'*" And *as for* the attainment of Wealth—*that this may take place by means of Poetry* is established by the evidence of the senses, *for we see men make money by it*:—and the attainment of Enjoyment *is possible* just by means of Wealth. And *finally—by means of Poetry* the attainment of Liberation *may take place* by not aiming at *or having no desire of* the fruits—*at best but transitory*—of Merit arising from it *i. e., arising from Poetry, as above explained*—or *Liberation may be attained* through the possession of conversancy with statements conducive to Liberation—*such as are to be met with in sacred poems like the Bhagavad Gítá.*

The praise of Poetry.

b. And justly may this pursuit be commended above others, for, from the Scriptures and the Institutes of Science, by reason of their insipidity *or dryness*, the attainment of the "class of four" (§. 2.) takes place painfully, even in the case of men of ripe understanding; whilst, from nothing but Poetry, by reason of its producing a fund of the highest delight, does the attainment take place pleasantly, even in the case of the very tender-minded.

An objection answered.

c. "But then—*some one may here object*—since there are the Scriptures and the Institutes of Science, why should men of mature minds take any pains about poems?"—this too is not proper to be said *in the way of objection—for, truly*, when a disease, curable by bitter drugs, happens to be curable by candied sugar,—in the case of what man, having that disease, would the employment of candied sugar not be most proper?

d. Further—the excellence of Poetry is declared also in the *A'gneya Puráṇa*—thus—"In this world to attain to be a man is hard, and there very hard to attain is knowledge; to attain to be a poet there is hard, and very hard to attain there is *poetic* power." And again—"Poetry is the instrument *in the attainment* of the 'class of three' —*viz., Merit, Wealth, and Enjoyment,—see* §. 2." And in the *Vishṇu Purána it is declared*—"And the utterances of Poetry, one and all, and all songs,—these are portions of Vishṇu, the great-souled, who wears a form *composed* of sound."

e. By the word "therefore" *in the text—see* §. 2—*is meant* "for that reason"—*and by the word* "its"—"of Poetry." The nature thereof—*or what it is that Poetry consists of*—is to be set forth:—and by this *i. e., by the statement, in the text, that the nature of Poetry is about to be set forth,* has the subject *of the treatise—viz., Poetry*—been *by implication, and hence all the more ingeniously* propounded.

The definition of Poetry in the Kávya Prakás'a objected to.

f. In regard, then, to the question—"of what—leaving everything else apart—does Poetry consist?"—a certain person *viz., the author of the Kávya Prakás'a*—says—"This—*i. e., Poetry*—consists of words and meanings faultless, with Excellence or Beauty (—*see Chapter* 8*th*)—*even though sometimes* undecorated." This requires some consideration—as thus:—if that only which is *faultless* be held poetry, then *look at the following speech of Rávaṇa, in Bhavabhúti's drama of the Víra-charitra.*—

"For this indeed is an utter contempt of me that there are foes *of mine at all,* and amongst these this anchoret too! He, too, even here *in my own island of Ceylon,* slaughters the demon-race! Ha! Doth Rávaṇa live? Fie, fie, *my son,—thou* conqueror of Indra! what *avail is there* from Kumbhakarṇa awakened *untimeously from his six months' slumber—gigantic ally though he be*—or what from these *my own score of brawny* arms that IN VAIN swelled with *the pride of carrying off* the spoils of the poor villages of Heaven?"—

First objection to the definition.

If faultlessness, I say, were essential to Poetry, then the nature of Poetry would not belong to these verses, by reason of their being tainted with the fault termed "non-discrimination of the predicate"—*see Chapter 7th :—for the expression* "*in vain*" *is faultily mixed up in a descriptive epithet applied to the subject—the* "*arms*"—*whilst the speaker really intended to say* "*how vain are now these arms that then did swell.*" On the other hand he—*the author of the Kávya Prakás'a* admits that the essence of the highest Poetry is Suggestion *which—see Chapter 2nd—the example above-quoted presents in abundance—for the speaker does not really entertain any doubt of his being himself "alive," whilst his making a question of it suggests in a lively manner his astonishment ;—nor is he speaking of a literal "anchoret" when he contemptuously indicates by that term the hero Ráma who had been dwelling in banishment in the forest ;* hence the definition has the fault of "not extending" *to cases which it unquestionably ought to include.*

A compromise rejected.

g. "But then," *some one may say,* "a certain PORTION is faulty here *i. e., in the example under* §. 2, *f.* but not, again, also the WHOLE ;"—*now* if *we were to apply the definition with this qualification* then *see what would happen*—in what portion there is a fault, that *portion* urges that the case is one of not-poetry ; in what *portion* there is Suggestion, that *portion* urges that the case is one of the highest poetry ; hence, being dragged in two opposite directions by its two portions, it would be neither one thing nor another—poetry nor not-poetry.

h. Nor do such faults as unmelodiousness (*see Chapter 7th*) mar only a certain portion of a poem, but quite the whole, *if any part of it*—that is to say—when there is no damage to the Flavour (*see Chapter 3rd,*) it is not admitted even that these are faults ; else there could be no distribution *such as the recognised and unquestioned one —see Chapter 7th—of faults* under the heads of "the invariably a fault" and "the not invariably a fault ;"—as it is said by the author of *the work called* the *Dhwani*—"And the faults, such as unmelodiousness, which have been exhibited, are not so *invariably :* they have been instanced as what must be invariably shunned when the sentiment of *Love* is the sole essence of what is poetically figured *or suggested.* Moreover, were it thus—(i. e., were it the case, as your view of the matter implies, that *none but a faultless piece is poetry*) then the nature of poetry would have very few objects *of which it could be predicated* —or *probably* would find place nowhere, from the exceeding unlikelihood of faultlessness in every respect.

A second compromise rejected.

i. "But then," *some one else may say,* "the negative particle is employed *in the definition* §. 2, *f.* *not absolutely, but* in the sense of 'a little.'" If it were so, then, as *on this interpretation* the statement would be this—that "Poetry consists of words and meanings A LITTLE faulty," *this absurdity would follow, that* the name of Poetry would not belong to what *words and meanings* are *absolutely* FAULTLESS.

Second objection—to a redundancy in the definition.

j. Should you, however, explain the expression to mean—'with a little fault, IF ANY,' *I reply* this too is not to be mentioned in the DEFINITION of Poetry; just as, in the definition of such a thing as a jewel, one omits such a circumstance as its being perforated by insects—*that circumstance not tending to constitute anything a jewel, though it may not cause it to cease to be regarded as such* :—for such circumstances as its perforation by insects are not able, *I grant you,* to repel a jewel's claim to the name of jewel, but *the effect thereof is* only to render applicable to the case the degrees of comparison. In like manner, here, such faults as unmelodiousness *render applicable such terms as "superior" and "inferior"* in the case of Poetry: And it has been said *by the author of the Dhwuni* : "The nature of Poetry is held to reside even in faulty *compositions* where taste &c. are distinctly recognised, in like manner as *the character of a jewel, or the like, is held to belong to* such a thing as a jewel perforated by insects."

A third objection.

k. Moreover *in the definition under* § 2. *f.* the application of the distinction *conveyed in the expression* "with Excellence" to words and meanings is inappropriate—*as is proved* by the fact of its having been declared by him—*the author of the Kávya Prakás'a* himself, that the Excellences are properties of the Flavour *or sentiment* alone *and hence not of words or their meanings,* by means of such *unmistakable expressions employed by him* as this—viz., "which *Excellences* are properties of the Flavour *or sentiment,* just as heroism and the like are *properties* of the soul."

A compromise in regard to the third objection rejected.

l. If *some one should yet argue, saying,* "This *employment of terms objected to in* § 2. *k.* is appropriate, because there is here a metaphor *the expression "words and meanings" standing for the Flavour,* since these *viz., the words and meanings* are what REVEAL the Flavour *or sentiment*;"—even that way it—*the definition* would be unfitting. To explain:—in these "words and meanings," which he chooses to regard as constituting Poetry, there either is Flavour or there is not. If there is not, then neither is there the possession of any excellence—since the excellences, *being properties of the Flavour*, conform—*as regards the being present or absent*—to the presence or absence thereof. If *on the other hand* there IS—then why did he not state that distinction thus—"*words and meanings* possessing Flavour." If *in reply to this, you contend* "That is UNDERSTOOD, since otherwise there is an unfitness in *predicating* the possession of Excellences *which are properties of Flavour*." Then *I repeat that* the proper course was to say "*words and meanings* with *Flavour*" and not "with Excellence;" for no one, when he has to say "The regions possess LIVING BEINGS," says "The regions possess HEROISM AND THE LIKE"—*although from the expression we infer that the regions possess living beings—in whom only can the properties of heroism and the like reside.*

A second compromise in regard to the third objection rejected.

m. But then *some one, in defence of the definition in the Kávya Prakás'a, may further contend*—"In saying 'words and meanings with Excellence,' the aim was to state this—that in Poetry there are to be employed those words and meanings which develope *some one of the three varieties of* Excellence"—if *any one does urge this—then I say* No,—*this defence will not avail*—for, in the case of Poetry, the presence even of words and meanings which develope Excellence, is a cause of its ELEVATION only—§ 5., but not the cause of its ESSENCE—*and we are not enquiring what* HEIGHTENS *Poetry, but what* IS *Poetry;*—for it has been said *by the author of the Dhwani, whose authority the author of the Kavyá Prakás'a never questions*—"Words and meanings are *merely* the body of Poetry; and Flavour and the like its soul *or essence*;" the Excellences *or qualities of Elegance, Energy, and Perspicuity,—see Ch. 8th—in respect of Poetry, as mentioned in* § 2. *k.* are like heroism and the like *in regard to men;* Faults (*see Ch. 7th*) are like one-eyedness and the like; Styles (*see Ch. 9th*) are like the particular dispositions of the members *of the body;* Ornaments (*see Ch. 10th*) are like bracelets, earrings, and the like.

A 4th objection.

Hence that also which he says—(see the definition of Poetry quoted under § 2 *f.*) viz., "and, again, *even though* undecorated"—I reject—for (—to state his meaning without ellipsis—) he means to say "Everywhere, when ornamented—and sometimes even when no ornament appears—*faultless* words and meanings constitute Poetry"—*and, I say, I must reject this,* because here, too, *as well as in the case referred to under* § 2. *m.*, embellished words and meanings, as regards Poetry, serve only to heighten it.

Another definition rejected.

n. For this reason I reject also the position of the author of the *Vakrokti-jívita*, viz., that "Equivoque is the life of Poetry," because equivoque is of the nature of ornament —*and hence not the body even—much less the soul or essence.*

o. And as for what he—*the author of the Kávya Prakás'a*— instances *as exemplifying his assertion that there may be Poetry* "sometimes when there is no obvious ornament"—*viz., these verses:*

"There is that very husband who gained me as a girl, and those same April nights, and the bold breezes *wafting perfume* from the Naucleas, and fragrant with *the odours* of the full-blown jasmine,— and I too am the same:—but still my heart longs for the sportive doings, in the shape of toyings, under the ratan-trees on the banks of the Reva:"—

—this requires some consideration—for here *where we were told that there was no obvious ornament* it is plain that there is that dubiously mixed ornament *to be described in Ch.* 10*th* which has its root either in the description of an effect without a cause—*the lady describing herself, not as regretting, but, as longing for what she had already possessed—whereas possession annihilates longing*—or in a cause without an effect—*the lady having sufficient reason for not longing—while she yet speaks of herself as doing so.**

Other similar definitions objected to.

p. For the same reasons I reject such definitions as *that involved in the following verse of the Rájá Bhoja in his Saraswatí Kanṭhábharaṇa,—viz.*, "The poet, making Poetry—i. e., what is faultless and possesses Excellence, embellished with ornaments, and having Flavour—wins fame and favour."

A definition admitted with a proviso.

q. And as for what the author of the *Dhwani* says —that "the soul of Poetry is Suggestion"—what does he thereby mean? Is it Suggestion in its three-fold

* It is but fair to mention that, in the *Kávya Pradípa*, a commentary on the work containing the definition which our author persecutes so perseveringly, it is remonstrated that if there be no other ornament in these verses than that which it required so much ingenuity to detect, then it was not so very great a mistake after all to instance the verses as being without "*obvious* ornament."

aspect—(1) as regards Matter, (2) as regards Embellishments, and (3) as regards the Flavour and the like,*—that is the soul of Poetry? Or is it only that which takes the shape of Flavour? Not the first—for then it—*i. e., the definition of Poetry*—would improperly extend to such things as *enigmas—where more, no doubt, is suggested than is uttered.* But if the second *is what he means to assert—then* we say "Agreed."

Objections to the proviso repelled.

r. "But then," *some one may object, to the definition with our proviso,*—"if Suggestion be the soul of Poetry only when it is in the shape of Flavour and the like—then, in such cases as *the following—viz.*,

"'My respected *mother-in-law* lies here; and here I myself. While it is day, observe this; and do not,—O traveller, since you get blind at night *like other people afflicted with night-blindness*—lie down upon my couch, *mistaking it for your own*'"—

—*in such cases as this—the objector may ask*—"As there is the suggestion of a matter simply—*the speaker here intending to suggest the traveller's doing the reverse of what she says*—how *on such terms* can you apply the name of Poetry to this?" If *any one asks this*—we say that here also—*whilst we admit that there is Poetry—we admit it* only because there is a *semblance* of Flavour *and the semblances of Flavour, as we shall have occasion to declare further on—see* § 3. *b.* —*are admitted to constitute Poetry;—and there is here the semblance of the Flavour of Love—a sentiment real only where legitimate*—for otherwise—*i. e., if we admitted the foregoing to be Poetry without shewing that it had any reference to Flavour* then there would *by parity of reasoning* be Poetry in the proposition "Devadatta goes to the village"—from its being understood that there is *here also* something suggested—in the shape, viz., of his being attended, *as a gentleman usually is*, by his followers. If *you say*, "Be it so"—*that the expression* "*Devadatta goes to the village*" IS *Poetry, on the strength of the unqualified definition given by the author of the* 'Dhwani'—*then I say*, No,—for I will allow the name of Poetry to that only which has Flavour.

Concurrent testimonies cited.

s. For the aim of Poetry is by means of giving a fund of delight *in the shape* of the relishing of

* See Ch. IV. § 255—56—57—58.

Flavour,—in the case of princes and the like, averse to the Scriptures and the Institutes of Science, with very tender minds, and proper to be taught,—to inculcate the practising of what ought to be done and the forbearing from what ought not to be done,—*and this it aims at effecting by inculcating* thus—"One ought to act like Ráma and not like Rávaṇa"—as has been declared even by the ancients. And so too it is stated in the Ágneya Purána—viz.,—"In this,—*Poetry*, which is rendered first-rate by skill in words, Flavour alone is the LIFE." Also by the author of the Vyakti-viveka it is said,—"*As to the fact* that the soul of Poetry—*meaning by the soul that in respect of which everything else is something subordinate*—is Flavour and the like—no one has any difference of opinion." So also the author of the 'Dhwani' says—as for instance,—"For not merely by narrating—'Thus it fell out'—is the soul of Poetry compassed;—for that—*viz., the mere narration of events* can be effected even through Histories* and the like *such as the Mahábhárata—which histories, though in verse, are not held to be poems.*"

Objections repelled.

u. "But," *some one may object*—"*if Flavour is the essence of Poetry*—then some flavourless—*e. g., simply narrative*—verses in the composition will not be Poetry—*and thus the difficulty will recur—see* § 2. *g.—as to whether the composition, as a whole, is poetry or not poetry;*"—if *any one argues thus, then I say*, No,—for, as we allow that words, themselves tasteless, have a flavour when included in tasteful verses, so *do we hold that* those *verses which may, in themselves, be insipid* have a flavour through the flavour of the composition itself *in which they are embodied.* And as for the customary application of the term Poetry to those *separate copies of verses* even that are without Flavour, in consideration of the presence of such letters (—see Ch. 8th—) as give rise to *some of the varieties of* Excellence, and the absence of faults, and the presence of ornaments—that is merely a secondary, *not a strictly technical* application of the term, *which has come into use* from the *superficial* resemblance *of such verses* to poetical compositions which do possess Flavour *and which alone are Poetry in the strict application of the term.*

* So Aristotle—Poetics, Ch. IX.—says, "the history of Herodotus might be written in verse, and yet be no less a history with metre than without metre," &c.

Other definitions objected to.

v. And as for what Vámana says *in his Aphorisms*—that "The soul of Poetry is the Style"—*or Diction—see Ch. 9th*—it is not so:—for a Style is a species of disposition—and disposition consists in the arrangement of parts—and the soul is something different from that. And as for what has been said by the author of the 'Dhwani'—that "A Sense commended by the man of taste—, which, it has been settled, is the soul of Poetry,—of this *i. e., of such Senses* two kinds are mentioned, named *respectively* the *expressed, or literal,* and the *understood otherwise than literally*"—*the allegation, I say,* here—that the soul *of Poetry* can consist of an expressed Sense—is to be rejected, by reason of its contrariety to his own declaration, *quoted under* § 2. *r.*—viz., that "The soul of Poetry is SUGGESTION"—*see* § 10.

The author's own definition of Poetry.

w. Then what, after all, IS Poetry? To this it is replied *as follows:*—

TEXT.

3. Poetry is a Sentence the soul whereof is Flavour.

COMMENTARY.

a. We shall declare (in Ch. 3rd) what it is that Flavour consists of. Flavour alone—*the text declares*—is the soul *of Poetry*—essentially the cause of its life—since it is not admitted that, without this, anything is Poetry.

Three degrees of emotion recognized in the definition.

b. The Sanskrit word for Flavour—viz., 'rasa,' by regular derivation *from the verb* ras "*to taste or relish,*" signifies "what is tasted, or relished." So in this—*i. e., under the term* rasa are included the incomplete Flavours, and the semblances, &c. thereof—*which will be treated of in Ch. 3rd.*

The first degree—or Flavour proper.

Among these, then, *we may have* Flavour *complete as well as real* as *exemplified in the following verses—viz.,*

"Perceiving that the house was empty, having arisen very gently from her couch, and having for a long time gazed upon the face of her husband counterfeiting sleep, having confidently kissed him,—then seeing his cheek quiver, the girl, with face downcast through modesty, was long kissed by her laughing lover."

For in this example there is the Flavour, *or Sentiment*, called, *to distinguish it from the love of separated lovers*, "love in union."

The second degree, or Flavour not attaining its full development.

c. Incomplete Flavour *is exhibited* for example *in the following verses* of the great minister, manager of the questions of peace and war, Rághavánanda:—

"To the limit *only* of whose *lowest* scales, *when incarnate as the Fish*, the ocean reached; on whose *tortoise* back *rested* the globe of the world; on whose *boar's* tusk the earth *was upheld;* on whose *man-lion* claws the lord of the sons of Diti *expired;* in whose footstep, *as the dwarf Vámana*, both worlds *found their measure as he traversed each at one step;* at whose rage *as, Parusaráma*, the bands of the Kshattras *melted away;* on whose arrow, *as Ráma*, the ten-headed *Rávaṇa met his death;* in whose hand, *as Krishṇa*, Pralambásura *expired;* in whose contemplation, *as Buddha*, the universe *melted into its proper nothingness;* on whose sword the race of the evil-doers *will perish when the tenth incarnation shall take place;* to Him, whoe'er he be, all hail!"

In this example *the Flavour of* love—its object being the Deity—is an incomplete Flavour—*seeing that the Deity is no fit object, for instance, of those tendernesses, &c., which belong to the Sentiment of Love proper—any more than a son, against whom one may feel angry for a moment, is a fit object of those hostile attacks in which Anger proper naturally vents itself, and the description of which conduces to reproduce, in Poetry, the Sentiment itself in its completeness.*

The third degree, or the semblance of Flavour whether fully developed or not.

d. The semblance of Flavour *is exhibited*, for example, *in the following verses*—

"Accompanied, in one flower-bell, by his loved mate, the honey-bee drank *nectar;* and the black deer, with his horn, scratched the doe, who, at the touch, bent down her eyelids."

For since, in this example, the Flavour of "love in union"—§ 3. *b.* is located in the lower animals, there is a semblance of that Flavour *which is regarded as real when it occurs in mankind;* and so of others —*for, having exemplified the three-fold variety of poetic emotion in the case of* one *of the passions, it is unnecessary to exemplify it in all.*

Faults defined generally.

e. Then, again,—in Poetry, of what nature are faults—*which we do not consent*—*see* § 2. *f.*—*to regard as destructive of Poetry?* To this it is replied *in the following half of a line which completes the half-line No.* 3.

TEXT.

4. Faults are depressers thereof.

COMMENTARY.

a. Unmelodiousness, incompleteness in the sense, &c., *operate depreciatingly on Poetry* through the words and meanings—as one-eyedness and lameness *operate depreciatingly on man* through the body; and *in the second place*, such *faults* as the mentioning of the Accessories or the like—*see* § 168—by their own names *bluntly, instead of suggestively,—these being faults* which depreciate the Flavour which is the soul of Poetry, *not mediately, like the former class of faults, but* directly, as idiocy *depreciates directly the* soul *of man—both of these classes*, are called *in the text* the depressers of Poetry. Special examples of these *various faults* we shall mention *in their proper place—viz., in Ch. 7th.*

Excellences, &c., defined generally. *b.* Of what nature are the Excellences, or Merits, &c., *which were alluded to under* § 2. *f.?* To this it is replied—

TEXT.

5. Excellences—*Ch. 8th*—ornaments—*Ch. 10th*,—and Styles—*Ch. 9th*—are called the causes of its elevation.

COMMENTARY.

a. Excellences, *or good qualities—as already remarked under* § 2. *k.*—are, *in regard to Poetry*, as heroism, &c., *in regard to the soul of man.* Ornaments are *to the language of Poetry* as bracelets, earrings, &c., *to the human figure.* Styles are a kind of arrangement of parts *leading to different varieties of Poetry*, as *different muscular arrangements may give a man the symmetry of a Hercules or that of an Apollo.* Elevating, *as they do*, through words and meanings, as through its body, the Flavour simply which is the soul of Poetry, these are *not incorrectly* called the heighteners of Poetry, *for this rises, of course, with the Flavour, of which it consists.*

b. Although the Excellences here—*spoken of in the text*—are properties of Flavour, *—and how—it might be asked—can they be heighten-*

ers of it through words and meanings to which they do not belong?—yet the word "Excellence" is employed here by synecdoche for "the words and meanings which develope Excellence or poetical merit;" and hence what is meant is this—that *words* which develope Excellence are heighteners of the Sentiment, as was said before—*see* § 2. *m.* Special examples of these—*i. e., of ornaments, &c.,*—we shall mention *in the proper place.*

c. So much for the "Declaration of the Nature of Poetry"—the first chapter of the "Mirror of Composition," the work of the illustrious Vis'wanátha Kavirája, that bee of the lotus-feet of the divine Náráyana, the pilot of the ocean of composition, the best of guides on the road of *ingeniously poetic* Suggestion, the jewel-mine of the poet's finest utterances, the lover of that nymph *embodied in* the Eighteen Dialects *employed in dramatic composition—see Ch. 6th—*, minister of the peace and war department.

CHAPTER II.

The Declaration of the Nature of a Sentence.

Having declared—§ 3—*that Poetry is a kind of Sentence, and the meaning of the term Sentence being as yet undefined,* he declares what a Sentence consists of.

Text.

A Sentence defined.

6. Let a Sentence mean a collection of words possessing Compatibility, Expectancy, and Proximity.

Commentary.

a. 'Compatibility' means the absence of absurdity in the mutual association of the things *signified by the words.* If the nature of a sentence belonged to a collection of words even in the absence of this *compatibility of the things signified,* then *such a collection of words as* "He irrigates with fire" would be a sentence, *which it is not here held to be;—fire—and everything but water—being incompatible with irrigation.*

b. 'Expectancy'—"*the looking out for*" *some other word in construction*—means the absence of the completion of a sense; and this *absence of a complete sense* consists in the listener's desire, *on hearing the word*, to know *something which the other words in the collection will inform him of—if the collection of words* is *a sentence.* If the nature of a sentence belonged even to that *collection of noninterdependent words* where this expectancy is wanting—then such *a collection of words* as "cow, horse, man, elephant" would be a sentence.

c. 'Proximity' means the absence of an interruption in the apprehension *of what is said.* If there could be the case of a sentence even when there is an interruption in the apprehension, then there would be a coalescence—*into one sentence*—of the word "Devadatta," pronounced just now, with the word "goes" pronounced the day after.

d. Since expectancy (§ 6. *b.*) and compatibility (§ 6. *a.*) are properties, the one, of the SOUL, and the other, of THINGS;—it is by a figure of speech that they are here—*i. e., in the text* § 6.—taken as properties of a collection of WORDS.

TEXT.

7. A collection of Sentences is a Great Sentence.

COMMENTARY.

a. Only if this *Great Sentence too* possess *the requisites mentioned in* § 6—*of* compatibility, expectancy, and proximity.

TEXT.

8. Thus is a Sentence held to be of two kinds.

COMMENTARY.

a. "Thus"—that is to say, inasmuch as it may be a Sentence (*see* § 6) and inasmuch as it may be a Great Sentence (*see* § 7).

b. And, *if a justification of this employment of terms be required*, it is said *by Bhartrihari in his Vákyapadíya:* "Of Sentences, completed as regards the conveying of their own meaning, when put together, there becomes further, through their being viewed under the relation of parts and whole, the nature of a single Sentence."

c. *To give examples* of these *two kinds of Sentences*, there is the Sentence simple—as *in the verses given at length under* § 3. *b.*

—*viz.*—"Perceiving that the house was empty, &c." The Great Sentence is such *a collection of sentences* as the Rámáyaṇa *of Válmíki,* the Mahábhárata *of Vyása,* and the Raghuvans'a *of Kálidása.**

d. It has been stated *in* § 6 that a collection of WORDS is a Sentence. *But the question remains* then what is the criterion of a WORD? Therefore he says:—

TEXT.

Definition of the term word. 9. A word means letters *so combined as to be* suited for use, not in logical connection *one part with another*—conveying a meaning, and only one.

COMMENTARY.

a. As—*for example*—"jar" *is a word.*

b. By *the expression employed in the definition* "suited for use" the crude form, *in which a vocable appears in the Grammar before receiving its inflection,* is excluded *from being regarded as a word.*

c. By *the expression employed in the definition* "not in logical connection" *the exclusion is effected* both of Sentences and Great Sentences *which*—§ 8—*consist of letters, and are suited for use,—but which, as their parts are connected in sense, are not to be denominated* "*words.*"

d. By *the expression employed in the definition* "only one" *the exclusion is effected* of sentences containing a plurality of words inter-dependent—*see* § 6. *b.*—*yet not excluded by the limitation under* § 9. *c., which refers only to words in logical connection, without ellipsis; while, by the present exclusion, a collection of words not in logical connection but yet, when the ellipses are supplied, inter-dependent, is debarred from being regarded as a* "*word.*"

e. By *the expression employed in the definition* "conveying a meaning" *the exclusion is effected* of *such unmeaning combinations of letters as* 'kachatatapa'—*which is an unmeaning combination of the first letters of the five classes of consonants.*

* Compare Aristotle—Poetics, Ch. xx.—"But a sentence is one in a two-fold respect; for it is either that which signifies one thing, or that which becomes one from many by conjunction. Thus the Iliad, indeed, is one by conjunction."

f. By "letters" *in* § 8 it is not intended to speak of a plurality, —*for a word may consist of a single letter.*

g. In that—*i. e., in a "Word"—what* meaning *may reside, is next to be considered.*

TEXT.

9. The meaning *that may belong to a word* is held to be threefold —viz., Expressed, Indicated, and Suggested.

COMMENTARY.

The three powers of a word—Denotation, Indication and Suggestion.

a. The nature of these *three Meanings* he next states :—

TEXT.

10. The Expressed meaning (váchya) is that conveyed to the understanding by the *word's* Denotation (abhidhá); —the *Meaning* Indicated (lakshya) is held *to be conveyed* by the *word's* Indication (lakshaná); the *meaning Suggested* (vyangya) *is held to be conveyed* by the *word's* Suggestion (vyanjaná). Let these be the three powers of a word.

COMMENTARY.

a. "These"—*i. e.,* Denotation and the others.

TEXT.

Denotation the leading power of a word.

11. Among these *three powers of a word* the primary one is Denotation, for it is this that conveys to the understanding the meaning which belongs to the word by convention *which primarily made it a word at all.*

COMMENTARY.

How the conventional force of words is learned.

a. How one learns the conventional meaning of words may be illustrated thus :—On the old man's saying—when giving directions to the middle-aged man—"bring the cow,"—the child, having observed him—*the man to whom the order was given by his senior,* employing himself in bringing the cow, determines, first that "the meaning of this sentence was the fetching of a body possessing a dewlap, &c." and afterwards, through the insertion and omission *of the portions of the sentence "bring the cow" which he as yet understands only in the lump,* in such *other sentences heard by the child* as "fasten the cow"—"bring the horse"—he ascertains the convention that the word "cow" shall mean "the thing with a dewlap, &c.," and the word "bring" shall mean "fetching."

b. And *this is not the only process by which the conventional meaning of a word may come to be known—for,* sometimes *the meaning of a word may be gathered* from the utterance of familiarly known words along with it—as in this example—viz., "In the bosom of the expanded lotus the honey-maker drinks honey"—*where the hearer, knowing that* bees *drink the* juices *of the lotus, infers that it is the bee that is here called the honey-maker, and that the juice of the lotus, extracted by the bee, is called honey.*

c. Sometimes *the conventional meaning of a word is learned* from the instruction of one worthy *of confidence*—as *when such a one declares* "This"—*pointing—suppose to the animal*—" is what is denoted by the word horse."

d. And it is that power of a word which conveys to the understanding the conventional meaning without the intermediacy of any other power of the word that is called here—*in the text* § 11—Denotation.

TEXT.

Four-fold Division of words in respect of what they denote.

12. A convention *whereby the expressed meaning of a word is settled* is accepted, *by men among themselves,* in regard to Kinds, Qualities, Things, and Actions.*

COMMENTARY.

Kinds.

a. By a "Kind"—*or genus—is meant* the nature of a cow and the like *which resides* in the *particular* body *called* cow and the like—*and in virtue of which the thing* is *a cow or the like.*

Qualities.

b. By "Quality" *is meant* a settled habit of a thing which is a cause of making a distinction *between one thing and other things of the same genus*:—for *the qualities* white, and the like, differentiate such a thing as a cow from its congeners—such as a black cow.

Things.

c. Names of "Things" are those that denote a single individual—as Hari—*the name of the god Vishṇu,* Hara—*the name of the god Siva,* Ḍittha, Ḍavittha, *and other proper names.*

* These four are the Categories of the Hindu *grammarian.*

Actions. *d.* "Actions" are habits of a thing *not settled, as qualities are—see* § 12. *b.*—but in course of accomplishment—such as "cooking"—*which is the habit of a thing whilst in progress towards being ready for eating* :—for, what is denoted by such a word as "cooking" is the collection of proceedings, from first to last, such as the putting on *the pot with the rice to boil* and ultimately taking it off *the fire* again.

e. For only in r spect of these *four*—§ 12.—distinguishing characters of all individual cases *that call for the employment of words* is a convention made, and not in regard to individual cases themselves—lest there should befal the fault of endlessness *in the fabrication of words*, or of vagueness, *inasmuch as—to use the illustration of the* Kávya Pradípa—*if, in assigning to such and such individuals the name of "cow," we made no convention as to the* generic *character of the individuals, then water-jars would lay claim to the name as fairly as any cows not specified individually.*

f. Now "Indication"—*the second power of a word—see* § 10—*is explained.*

TEXT.

Indication—what power of a word. 13. Where the principal meaning *of a word—see* § 11—is incompatible *with the rest of the sentence—see* § 6. *a.*—this power of Indication is communicated *to the word,* whereby another meaning *than the expressed one—yet* in connection therewith, becomes apprehended, either through Notoriety *of the employment of the word in some particular secondary sense* or through a Motive—*discernible in the connotation—for using the word rather than some other word which would have merely denoted the thing expressly.*

COMMENTARY.

a. The power by which, in such *an expression* as "The impetuous Kalinga," a word, such as "Kalinga," incompatible *with the epithet "impetuous"—if taken* in its own sense—such as that of a particular country *on the Coromandel coast,* causes one to think of, *not the country, for instance, that the word denotes, but* the men, for instance, connected therewith ;—and—*to give a second example—the power* by which, in such *an expression* as "A herd-station on the Ganges," a word, such as "the Ganges," incompatible with the matter in question—*here, viz., the actual site of the station of herdsmen*—inasmuch as the thing that it denotes is in the shape, for instance, of a mass of water, *on the surface of which the herdsmen could not have built the huts of which the herd-station consists*, causes one to think of something connected with itself by the relation of proximity or the like—such as the river's bank,—THIS power of a word—COMMUNICATED to it (§ 13)—other than the power which (—to use the language of some—) belongs to it naturally, or which is not (—to use the language of others—) that given to it by God—*this second power it is that* is called Indication.

Two sources of the power of Indication—Notoriety, and a Motive.

b. In the former *of the two examples under* § 13. *a.* the reason *why the word denoting the region of Kalinga has the power of indicating the inhabitants of that region* is "Notoriety"* *see* § 13.,—the fact, simply, of its being familiarly known *that the name of the region is employed to signify its inhabitants.* In the latter of the examples, the "Motive" —*see* § 13.—*for using the word "Ganges," when we really mean "bank of the Ganges,"* consists in this, that it causes one to think of the extreme of coolness and purity *pertaining to the Ganges itself*, which would not have been thought of from the exposition of *the same matter in the shape of the expression* "A herd-station on the bank of the Ganges."

Why the *sources* of the power of Indication require to be specified.

c. If a word were, without a reason, to indicate whatsoever has any relation *to that which the word denotes*, then there would be an excessive influx *of all sorts of associated ideas—everything in the world being related in some way or other to everything else*—, hence *in the text*—§ 13—it is stated that this *power of Indication* arises "either through Notoriety or through a Motive"—*the ordinary relations furnishing which latter, are specified under* § 17. *e.*

Alleged instances of Indication rejected.

d. But some—*among whom is the author of the Kávya Prakás'a*—instance the expression "Expert in business" as an example of *the power of Indication arising—see* § 13—*from* "Notoriety." What they mean to say is this—that the primary meaning *of the word kus'ala "expert"*—that, viz., of "a

* In the original, रूढि which might be more intelligibly rendered *usage.* P. M.

gatherer of sacrificial grass"—from the etymology *kus'am láti* "who gets sacrificial grass"—being incompatible with the matter in question —*viz.*, "*business,*" causes one to think of the sense of "expert" which is connected *with the primary sense of* "*the gatherer of sacrificial grass*" through the relation of a similarity of character in respect of the being a person of discrimination—*which the gatherer of sacrificial grass must be, else he could not tell one kind of grass from another*. Others do not accept this *view of the matter*, for, *according to the view which these prefer*, the primary meaning of the word *kus'ala* is simply that of "expert"—notwithstanding that the sense of "gatherer of sacrificial grass" might be gathered from the etymology:—for, the reason for the *technically recognised* etymology of words is one thing—*viz.*, *the convenience of the Grammarians, who must find an etymology, however far-fetched, for every word that is not a radical*—, and the reason for the employment *of a word* is another—*viz.*, *the fact of the word's having, by convention, such a denotation as the speaker happens to have occasion for.* If the primary meaning *of every word* were that which is to be gathered from the etymology, then in the example "The cow sleeps" also there would be "Indication"—because *when speaking of the animal* even at the time of its sleeping *and therefore lying still*, one makes use of the word 'go' (cow,) which word 'go' is formed by the affix 'do' put after the root gam "to move"—according to *the direction of Páṇini—viz.* "gamerḍoh" *i. e.*, "*let the affix* "*do*" *come after the root* "*gam*" *and the word* "*go*" '*a cow*' *will be the result.*"

Indication divided into inclusive and indicative.

e. He next states the distinctions of this *power of Indication.*

TEXT.

Indication inclusive defined.

14. The primary meaning's hinting something else *which is required, in addition,* for the establishment of a logical connection among the things, *and not a mere grammatical connection among the words* in the sentence—let this, when *the primary meaning* itself also is taken in, be called therefore 'Inclusive Indication' (*upádána-lakshaṇa*).

COMMENTARY.

a. Inclusive Indication, where *the source of the power—see* § 13. *b.—is* Notoriety *is exemplified in such sentences* as "The White gallops;"—and where *the source is* a Motive—in such as "The Lances enter." For, in these two cases, "white" and "lances," being things inanimate, cannot alone have a logical connection, as agents, with the actions "galloping" and "entering," and so, with a view to the establishing of this *logical connection among the things expressed in each sentence,* they hint "horses," and "men," which are connected with themselves *i. e., with "white" and "lances"—so that we understand "The white* HORSE *gallops," "The* MEN WITH *lances enter."* In the former *of the two cases exemplified,* as there was no Motive *for speaking, for instance, of the horse as* white—*which term hints nothing beyond the whiteness,—the source of the Indicatory power in the expression is* Notoriety—*the horse being necessarily well known as "the white" by the person to whom the remark was intelligibly addressed.* In the latter *of the two cases exemplified,* the Motive *for speaking, for instance, of "lances" instead of "men with lances"* was *to direct attention to,* for instance, the extreme denseness of the *phalanx of* lances. And in these cases the primary sense also § 13. is taken in—*for the whiteness accompanied the horse in its gallop, and the lances accompanied the men who entered with them.* But in *simply* Indicative Indication there is implication only of something else—*to the exclusion of that which indicates.* Such is the distinction between the two *kinds of Indication;* and it is this *first kind* that is spoken of as "the use of a word without abandonment of its sense."

Indication inclusive — twofold —according to its source.

TEXT.

Indication indicative defined.

15. The abandonment of self, with a view to the establishment of the logical connection of something else with something in the sentence—this, since it is the cause of an indication, *and of nothing more,* is 'Indicative Indication' *or Indication' simply—(lakshaṇa-lakshaṇá).*

COMMENTARY.

a. For instance—"The impetuous Kalinga," and "A herd-station on the Ganges"—*see* § 13. *a.—are examples of Indication simply—*for, in these two *examples,* the two words "Kalinga" and "Ganges" give themselves up—*sacrificing their own sense—of a region and a* *river*—for the purpose of establishing, in logical connection with the things in the sentence, "a man" and "a bank;" or *we may have Indicative Indication in such a case as the following—addressed to one who had injured the speaker—viz.*,

"Much benefit have you done:—how is it to be expressed? Benevolence alone has been exhibited by you, Sir. Acting thus ever, O friend, may you be happy therefore for a hundred years."

Here, in order to establish, in logical connection with the other matters in the sentence, "injuries," &c. *which are what are really meant to be spoken of*—, the words "benefit" and the like give themselves up *and stand, ironically, for injuries and not for benefits at all.* In this example, there is an incompatibility in the primary meaning *of the sentence*, since it ascribes benefit &c. to an injurer. The relation *between what is here indicatory and what it indicates* is that of CONTRARIETY—*the mode of Irony*—, and the result is *this that* the EXCESS of injury *is understood to be complained of and imprecated.* It is this *kind of Indication* that is spoken of as "the use of a word WITH abandonment of its sense."

TEXT.

Further subdivision of fourfold Indication into the Superimponent and the Introsusceptive.

16. These, further, are severally twofold, through Superimposition *(áropa)* and Introsusception *(adhyavasána)*.

COMMENTARY.

a. "These"—i. e., the aforesaid four kinds of Indication—*see* § 13, *b. and e.*

TEXT.

17. Let that *Indication* be Superimponent which makes one think of the identity with something else of an object not swallowed *by that with which it is identified, but expressed along with it.* That *Indication* is held to be Introsusceptive *which makes one think of the identity with something else* of an object swallowed—*not expressed, but recognised as it were inside of that with which it is identified.*

COMMENTARY.

a. Thus, then, first we may have Superimponent Inclusive Indication (§ 14) the source *of the power*—§ 14. *a.*—being Notoriety:—as *in the following example*—" The horse—the white—gallops." For here the horse, the possessor of the quality " white,"—in the shape *of the unsuppressed term " horse"—and hence* of something " not swallowed" (§ 17),—is thought of as identical with the colour " white" which inheres in it:—*that is to say*—" *the horse*" *and* " *the white*" *are understood to mean here just one and the same thing.*

b. Secondly, we may have Superimponent Inclusive Indication—§ 17. *a.*—the source *of the power*—§ 14. *a.*—being a Motive:—as *in the following example*—" These—the lances—enter." Since the pronoun denotes the men bearing lances—*who—see* § 14. *a.—are denoted also by the word* " *lances*"—there is here a case of the Superimponent.

c. Thirdly we may have Superimponent Indicative Indication, (§ 17. *a.*,) the source being Notoriety (§ 13. *b.*,) as *in the example* " The Kalinga—the man—fights." Here *it may be remarked that* the relation between the " man" and *the region of* " Kalinga" is that of location and located.

d. Fourthly, we may have Superimponent Indicative Indication the source (§ 14. *a*) being a Motive—as *in the example* " Longevity—butter." Here " butter," the cause of " longevity," is thought of as identical with the " longevity" related to it through the relation of cause and effect. The Motive *for speaking of butter as* " *longevity*" is the fact, *which it is desired to call attention to*, of its causing longevity differently from anything else—*no other article of Hindu diet* being so nutritious—, and invariably—*butter, as a prolonger of life, being reckoned infallible.*

e. Or *of this fourth case*—§ 17. *d.—to take other examples illustrating the most ordinary relations, besides that of cause and effect, by which this employment of language is prompted*—as—when a man belonging to the king is going—*one may say* " The king—this one—goes." Here the relation is that called the relation of owner and owned. Or as—when *there is meant* only the foremost portion *of the arm from the elbow—all of which, in Sanskrit, is called* " *the hand*;" —*one may say* " The hand—this—*from the* wrist *downwards*." Here the relation is that called the relation of whole and part. *Or* when it is even a Bráhmaṇ *that one is speaking of, one may say* " The carpenter—he"—*while, strictly speaking, it is impossible that a man of the Bráhman tribe, though working in wood, should be a man of the carpenter tribe.* Here the relation is that of the doing the work of so and so. *Or* when sacrificial posts *to which the victims are tied* for Indra *are spoken of—one may say* "These Indras." Here the relation is that of being for the sake of so and so. And so in other cases.

f. The Introsusceptive *Indication* which makes one apprehend the identity with something else of the "object swallowed" (§ 17), on the other hand,—*the examples from* § 17. *a. downwards having illustrated the case of objects* "not *swallowed*"—of this, in its four varieties, the preceding examples *may serve as exemplifications, if you expunge the term denoting the "object swallowed,"—thus reducing the examples to the following form—viz. "The White gallops"—"The Lances enter"—"The Kalinga fights"—and—*BUTTER *being meant by it—'Longevity"—as when we say "He eats longevity," meaning "He eats butter, which will make him long-lived."*

TEXT.

Further subdivision of eightfold Indication into the Pure and the Qualitative.

18. All these, when the relation is other than that of LIKENESS, are *called* Pure *(suddha)*; but when *they arise* from likeness, they are reckoned Qualitative *(Gauṇa)*. By this they are divided into sixteen.

COMMENTARY.

a. "These"—i. e., the aforesaid eight kinds of Indication. "Relations other than that of likeness" are the relation of cause and effect. &c. *see* (§ 17. *e.*)

b. Of the Pure *varieties* among these, the preceding examples *from* § 13. *a. to* 17. *b. inclusive are exemplifications.*

c. Superimponent Inclusive Indication Qualitative, when *the source of the power* (*see* § 17. *a.*)—*is* Notoriety, *is exhibited in such an example* as "These oils—pleasant in the cold weather, *when, rubbed on the body, they keep out the cold.*" Here the word "oil," taking along with it—(whence the Indication—see § 14—is "inclusive"—) its primary meaning, which is in the shape of the unctuous matter expressed from sesamum seeds (*—the Sanskrit name of this fluid—viz.,* taila*—being derived from the name of its most usual source—viz.,* tila *"the seeds of the sesamum," as the English word "oil" is derived from the Latin name of the olive tree,*) is applied *notoriously* to other unctuous fluids also, such as that expressed from mustard seed, *which fluids are like it. It may be remarked that the Indication in this example is termed Superimponent because of the presence of the pronoun "these:"—see* § 17. *b.*

d. This form of Indication—the Superimponent Inclusive Qualitative—when *the source of the power is* a Motive *is exemplified in such sentences* as "These—the princes—go"—*employed,—as such a sentence often is,* when princes and persons LIKE thereto, are going.

e. Introsusceptive Inclusive Indication Qualitative, when *the source of the power is* Notoriety, *may be exemplified by the example under* § 18. *c., omitting the pronoun*—thus—"Oils—pleasant in the cold season:" and when *the source of the power is* a Motive, *by the example under* § 18. *d., with the like omission*—thus—"The princes go."

f. Then again we have Superimponent INDICATIVE Indication Qualitative, when *the source of the power is* Notoriety:—as "The king clears away the paltry foe—the chief of Gauḍa,"—*where the word 'kanṭaka' which primarily means a thorn* is idiomatically, or according to common usage,† used in the sense of a small foe, from a likeness between the two objects:*—and when *the source of the power is* a Motive —*in such an example* as "That cow—the ploughman."

g. Further, we have Introsusceptive Indicative Indication Qualitative—when *the source of the power is* Notoriety:—as "The king clears away the paltry foe (kanṭaka);"—and when *the source of the power is* a Motive:—as "That cow talks"—*these two examples differing from those under* § 18. *f. in the suppression, or introsusception of a term.*

Misconceptions disposed of.

h. In this case—*that of "That cow—the ploughman"*—§ 18. *f.—instead of admitting, as they ought, that the man is indicated by the word "cow"*—some say "The qualities which belong to a cow, such as senselessness and sluggishness, are indicated; and these serve as causes why the word 'cow' denotes the thing *properly called* 'ploughman.'" This is not right—because the word "cow" cannot DENOTE the thing *properly called* "ploughman," in respect of which no convention was entered into (—it being only through CONVENTION—see § 11—that a word

* Which sense it entirely gives up, and hence this is a case of *Indicative* Indication. P. M.

† So it is an Indication under *Notoriety*, or *Usage*. P. M.

can primarily DENOTE anything); and because it *denotatively* makes one think only of the *dewlapped and long-tailed* thing meant by the word "cow," since the power of denotation is exhausted therein, and there is no resuscitation of that power thus exhausted—*or functus officio, in making one think of the genus* "*cow*"—*see* § 12. Others again, *partially correcting the statement above quoted, say,* "The THING *properly called* 'ploughman' is not DENOTED by the word 'cow,' but only the QUALITIES belonging to the 'ploughman' are INDICATED as being of the same kind as the qualities belonging to the thing which *the word* '*cow*' itself denotes." This *second view* also, others *and we ourselves* do not accept. To explain:—In this *expression under discussion,* is the sense of "ploughman," understood from the word "cow," or is it not? On the former *of these alternatives—is this sense understood* merely from the word "cow" *employed denotatively,* or, through the inseparableness *of qualities from that in which they inhere—is it, I ask, understood* from the qualities *of sluggishness, &c.* indicated *by the word* "*cow?*" Not the first, *of this subordinate pair of alternatives, can be accepted,* because this word "*cow*" is not assigned by convention to the thing *properly called* "ploughman;" nor the second, because there is no room for a sense gathered from inseparableness—*such, e. g., as that of a quality in respect of that whereof it is inseparably the quality*—when there is a concordance between the WORDS—*as we see there is in the example —the two words being in apposition—in the same case—as denoting the same thing,* for a WORD's expectancy—*when looking out for another to agree with it—see* § 6. *b.*—is fulfilled only by a WORD—*and not by a sense connoted in a word and such as, if expressly declared, would appear under the form of a word in a* DIFFERENT *case—e. g.*— "*a man* OF *bovine stupidity.*" Nor is the second *alternative, of the first pair, admissible*—for, if the sense of "ploughman," is NOT understood from the word "cow," then the agreement in case, of this and of the word "ploughman" *which the example exhibits,* would be improper—*it being only words signifying the same thing that agree in case.* Hence here the word "cow" having no logical connection in its PRIMARY character *i. e., as a denotative term—see* § 11—with the word "ploughman," INDICATES the thing *properly called* "ploughman" through the relation (*see* § 13. *c.*) of community of properties *between the cow and the man*—such as ignorance. The Motive (§ 13.,) *in which the power of Indication here takes its rise* is the causing one to think of the EXCESS of ignorance and the like in the ploughman.

Why the terms Pure and Qualitative are made use of.

i. And this *kind of Indication*—§ 18. *c. d. e. f. g.*—is called Qualitative because of the association of a quality—*the thing indicated being understood, in this case, to have the* QUALITIES *of that by the name of which it is metaphorically indicated;* but the former *kind of Indication*—§ 18. *b.*—is Pure, there being no admixture of METAPHOR in it. For Metaphor consists in the simply covering up the apprehension of the difference between two things absolutely distinct, by means of *a reference to* the greatness of the amount of their likeness:—as that of "fire," and "a boy" *so hot-tempered that we call him a perfect fire.* But in "white" and "cloth," there is no apprehension of difference at all—*that which is really "cloth" being that which at the same time is really "white" and is not merely metaphorically called "white"*—*whilst that which is really a "boy" is not really "fire," but only* LIKE *it, and hence metaphorically called it.* Hence in such cases *as that where "cloth" is called "white"* the Indication is quite pure—(§ 18).

Further subdivision of one eightfold branch of Indication according to the Abstruseness or the Obviousness of what is suggested.

TEXT.

19. Let Indication FOR A PURPOSE be twofold, in respect of the Abstruseness or the Obviousness of what is suggested.

COMMENTARY.

a. Where *the source of the power of Indication*—§ 13 *b. is* a Motive, Indication of eight sorts has been exhibited—(§ 18.) These, having become severally twofold in respect of the Abstruseness and the Obviousness of what, in the shape of the Motive, is suggested, are sixteen. Of these—*the abstruse and the obvious*—the "Abstruse" is that which is to be understood only by the force of an intellect matured by the study of the sense of Poetry—as *is exemplified in the passage given under* § 15. *a., viz.,* "Much benefit have you done, &c." The "Obvious" is that which, through its extreme clearness, is intelligible to every body—as *is the purport of the following—viz.,* "It is the intoxication of youth alone that teaches the blandishments of enamoured maidens." Here, by the word "teaches," the sense of "brings out into manifestation," is indicated; and the emphatic character of the manifestation—*i. e., how perfectly the intoxication does bring out the blandishments*—is apprehended as clearly as if the thing had been stated expressly, *instead of being indicated by the word "teaches."*

TEXT.

Further subdivision of the sixteenfold branch of Indication according to the site of what is suggested.

20. These also are twofold, through the fact that the fruit—*viz., the excessiveness suggested—see* § 14. *a.*, pertains to the thing *indicated*, or pertains to a quality *not inherent in the thing.*

COMMENTARY.

a. "These"—i. e., the sixteen kinds of Indication just mentioned —*under* § 19. *a.* These, having severally become doubled through the fruit's pertaining to the thing or to the quality, give thirty-two kinds. He exemplifies *the two kinds* in succession:—

"There are the clouds, in which the cranes disport, and with whose smooth dark loveliness the sky is overspread:—there are the dewy winds, and the melodious joyful screams of *peacocks*, friends of the clouds. Be all these as they list. I, very firmly stout of heart, am RA'MA. I endure all, *hard though it be to bear those vernal sights and sounds with patience, which enhance the joy of lovers when united.* But how will SHE be now—Videha's daughter? Alas—my goddess —O do thou be patient."

In this *speech of Ráma, from the Víra Charitra of Bhavabhúti,* Ráma being indicated *by the expression "I am Ráma," which is insignificant taken literally*, in the shape of a person extremely patient of affliction, and *this indicated Ráma* being the possessor of the quality *of patience—suggested, under the circumstances, by the emphatic and indicating employment of the proper name—which proper name otherwise, being simply denotative, would connote nothing,*—the fruit—the exceedingness *of the patience*—pertains to him *the thing indicated.*

b. Again in this *second example viz.*, "a herd-station on the Ganges"—*see* § 13. *a.*, where the BANK is indicated, the fruit, the EXCEEDINGNESS, pertains to the character consisting of coolness, purity,

&c., *and* NOT *to the* BANK—*the thing indicated—which—see* § 13. *b.* —*is not regarded as the locus of these qualities.*

TEXT.

21. Thus then are the varieties of Indication held by the intelligent to be forty.

COMMENTARY.

a. That is to say there are eight where *the source of the power is* Notoriety § 18, and thirty-two where *the source of the power is a Motive in the shape of some* fruit (§ 20. *a.*); hence the varieties of Indication—*so far as we have yet seen*—are forty. Moreover--

TEXT.

Final subdivision of fortyfold Indication accordingly as its instrument is a word or a sentence.

22. These also are severally twofold accordingly as it—*the power of Indication*—resides in a WORD or in a SENTENCE.

COMMENTARY.

a. "These"—i. e., these *kinds of Indication* just mentioned *under* § 21. Among these *we have an example of Indication distinguished* by the fact of its residing in a Word *in such a case* as "A herd-station on the Ganges—*(see* § 13. *a)*; and *of Indication distinguished by the fact of its residing in a Sentence—and not in any separate word thereof—in such a case* as "Much benefit have you done, &c."—*(see* § 15. *a.)*

b. Thus is Indication of eighty different kinds.

c. Now "Suggestion"—*the third power of a word—see* § 10—*is explained.*

TEXT.

Suggestion—what power of a word.

23. When Denotation &c., repose *after having done their duty*, that function, of a word or its sense &c., by which a further meaning is caused to be thought of, is what we call Suggestion *(vyanjaná)*,

COMMENTARY.

a. It is a maxim that when a Word, a Cognition or Idea,* and an Action cease *after a single exertion*, there is, *as far as that individual*

* For instance, the act of my Cognitive Faculty by which I have *this* moment the idea or perception of Fire is limited to, and ends in, that perception *only*; and the perception I continue to have through the succeeding moments is not *one and the same*—is not *indivisible* but the continuous result of distinct acts of the Cognitive Faculty, or (to speak more strictly and plainly) is a succession of

case is concerned, an annihilation of their agency. When, in accordance with this maxim, the three functions called Denotation (§ 11), Indication (§ 13) and Drift—*or purport of the sentence as a whole—which may be found treated of in the Kávya Prakás'a*—are exhausted, after having caused each its own appropriate thing to be thought of, that function of a word, or of a sense, or of a radical, or of an affix, &c., through which another meaning is caused to be thought of,—*that function* which takes the various names of "suggesting," "hinting," "conveying," "acquainting," and the like, is what we call *the power of* Suggestion.

b. In this *power of Suggestion, two varieties are comprised—for:*

TEXT.

Suggestion twofold, as founded on Denotation or on Indication.

24. Founded on its Denotation, or *founded on* its *power of* Indication, a word's *power of* Suggestion is twofold.

COMMENTARY.

a. He describes that which is founded on Denotation *as follows.*

TEXT.

Of Suggestion founded on Denotation.

25. That *power of* Suggestion which is the cause why something else is understood from a word which, though having *possibly* more meanings than one, has been restricted to a single meaning by conjunction or the like, is *that power of Suggestion which is spoken of—in* § 24—*as being* founded on Denotation.

COMMENTARY.

a. By the expression "or the like"—*in the phrase "restricted to a single meaning by Conjunction or the like*"—is meant Disjunction, &c.—for, *to expand the "&c.,"* it is said *by Bhartṛihari in his Vákyapadíya*—"Conjunction, and disjunction, companionship, hostility, a motive, the circumstances of the case, a characteristic, the juxtaposition of another word, power, congruity, place, time, gender, accent, &c., are causes of one's recollecting a special sense *of some word* when the sense of the word is not *of itself* definite." Thus—*to exemplify the defining power*

How the Denotation of ambiguous terms is restricted.

distinct cognitions. These nice thinkers had observed what Berkeley himself failed to do, viz. that the ideas which we are accustomed to call the same, are not really the *same* but *exactly similar*. See Mill's Logic, Vol. II. B. V. p. 450. P. M.

of each of these causes in their order—in the example "Hari with his conch-shell and discus," the word Hari denotes Vishṇu alone—*and not a "lion" or a "monkey" or any other of the meanings of the Sanscrit word hari*—because of the 'conjunction' of the conch-shell and the discus; and in the example "Hari without his conch-shell and discus," *it denotes* him alone, too—*seeing that the 'Disjunction' would be unmeaningly declared in respect of what—e. g., a lion—had never been conjoined with a characteristic conch-shell or the like.* In the example "Bhíma and Arjuna," the Arjuna is the son of Prithá—*he, and not the thousand-armed king of the same name slain by Paras'u-ráma—as told in the Mahábhárata—being the 'comrade' of Bhíma.* In the example "Karṇa and Arjuna," the Karṇa is the son of the Sun-god—*famed for his 'hostility' to Arjuna—and not any one else of the persons named Karṇa.* In the example "I salute Sthánu," the word *sthánu* means the god S'iva—*and not a "post"—as there is no 'motive' for saluting a post.* In the example "My lord knows all," the word "lord" means "you, Sir,"—*and not the Deity—the 'circumstances of the case' being understood to be these, that the words are addressed to a king or some other great man.* In the example "the angry one on whose banner is the alligator," the God of Love is meant—*and not the Ocean, which also has an alligator for a heraldic device, but of which anger is held to be no 'characteristic.'* In the example "The God, the foe of Pura," S'iva is meant—*as we gather from the 'juxtaposition' of the word "God"—for, otherwise, the term purári might have stood as well for the "foe of the city" as for the "foe of the demon Pura."* In the example "The cuckoo intoxicated with the Spring" the word *madhu, it is obvious*, means the "Spring" *—the Spring-time being the only thing, among those denoted by the word, that has 'power' to intoxicate the cuckoo—and not "nectar" or "distilled spirits" which it does not meddle with.* In the example "May the meeting with your beloved preserve you," the word "mukha" means "encountering" or "coming face to face"—*because there is no 'congruity' between the desired result and "a face" or any other sense of the word mukha.* In the example "The moon shines in the sky," *we are certified, by the 'place' that the word* 'chandra' *means the "moon" and not "gold" or "camphor," &c.* In the example "The fire at night," *we know, from the 'time,' that* the word 'chitrabhánu' here means a "fire" *and not the* "*sun.*" In the example "The wheel glows," *we know that* the word 'rathánga' means a "wheel" *and not a* "*ruddy goose,*" from its having the termination of the neuter 'gender.' As 'accent' modifies the sense in the Vedas only, and not in Poetry, no example of its occurrence is here given.

The rejection of Accent from among the restricters of Denotation justified against objectors.

b. And some, not able to endure this assertion,—*in* § 25. *a.—that Accent operates for the removal of ambiguities not in poetry, but only in the Veda—which assertion was made before me by the author of the Kávya Prakás'a,*—say "Accent also, in the shape of change of voice and the like, is really, in Poetry, the cause of the understanding in a particular sense *something that would otherwise be ambiguous*:—and again, according to the showing in the lectures of the holy sage *Bharata*, 'It,—*viz., accent* in the shape of the acute, &c., is really the cause of one's understanding, *to be intended,* some one particular Flavour—as, for example, the Erotic—*when, in the absence of accent, the Flavour intended might have been doubtful*'—hence, in the case of this also—*i. e., in the case of Accent, as well as the other defining agencies exemplified under* § 25. *a.*—some exemplification is proper;"—*but, to these objections, I reply,* this is not *right.* The accentuations, whether as changes of voice, &c., or as *the three varieties of accent called* the Acute, &c., cause one to understand one particular sense consisting in that only which is suggested; and not, assuredly, *does accentuation acquaint us with* any distinction in the shape of the restricting to a single sense some word with more senses than one—which—*see* § 25. *a.—and not anything respecting the matter suggested,* is the present subject of discussion.

Accent to be avoided in the case of "double entendre."

c. Moreover—if there were to be directed the restricting on every occasion, to a single sense, by the force of an appropriate accentuation, even of two meanings of ambiguous words left undetermined through the absence of fixation by the circumstances of the case or the like—*see* § 25 *a.*—then, in such a case, we should not find recognised *that Ornament, among those treated* of in *Ch.* 10th—*called Paronomasia*:—but it is not so,—*for we do find this ornament recognised by all the authorities, in cases where there would be no place for it, if the duplicity of meaning were banished by accentuation;* and therefore has it been said that "when the exhibition of paronomasia is the business in hand, then, in the paths of Poetry, accentuation is not esteemed *but is to be carefully avoided;*"—and this is a maxim *of common sense—seeing that the accentuation would defeat the end in view.* But enough of this *idly censorious* glancing—*on the part of these objectors—see* § 25. *b.*—at the declarations of the venerable *author of the Kávya Prakás'a, to whom—though constrained to find fault with him occasionally myself—I am indebted for so much of the materials of my work, that I may call him justly the* bestower of my livelihood.

d. By the "&c." *in the extract from Bhartṛihari given under* § 25. *a.*, *is meant,* in such a case as *that of one's saying* "A female with breasts just so big," *the making one aware* by gestures of the hand, &c.,—*the fingers being just so far opened as to mark the size intended*—that the breasts, or the like, resemble the unexpanded lotus; and so in other cases.

e. When *a word is* thus restricted, in respect of its Denotation, to a single meaning, that power which is the cause of one's thinking of another sense of the word, is *the power termed, in* § 25, Suggestion founded on Denotation. *This occurs,* for example, *in the following verses* of my father—*literally, of the feet of my father*—the great minister, the lover of the nymph *consisting* of the fourteen dialects, the chief of great poets, the venerable Chandra S'ekhara, minister of peace and war,—*the verses being these—viz.*,

"Whose body is embraced by Durgá, overwhelming by his radiance the god of Love, on whom, *as a crest-ornament,* has arisen a digit of the moon, venerable, surrounded everywhere by his snakes, whose eyes are made of the chief of stars, who has a solid affection for the most majestic of mountains—*the Himálaya,*—having mounted on a cow —*the emblem of the earth,*—with his body adorned with ashes,—resplendent is this beloved of Umá."

Here, from the "circumstances of the case"—*see* § 25. *a.*—*the minister intending to describe, not the god S'iva who reduced the god of Love to ashes by a glance of his eye, and who is decorated with cobra da capellos, but his own king who is lovelier than Cupid, and who is surrounded by his* ministers—*and so on through the weary string of puns*—the sense of the terms *in the expression* " beloved of Umá" being restricted, in respect of the Denotation, to that of the queen named Umá and her husband king Bhánudeva, *it follows that* the sense of the " beloved of the goddess Gaurí,"—*i. e. the god S'iva*—is understood—*to the glorification of king Bhánudeva by the comparison*—only through Suggestion. And so of other cases.

f. He *next* describes that *power of Suggestion* which is founded on Indication (§ 24.)

TEXT.

Suggestion founded on Indication.

26. But that Motive for the sake of which *the power of* Indication is resorted to, let that *power* whereby that *Motive* is caused to be thought of be *called* Suggestion founded on Indication.

COMMENTARY.

a. When, in such *an expression* as " A herd-station on the Ganges" —*see* § 13. *a.*—the power of Denotation has desisted—*see* § 23. *a.*— after causing one to think of such an object as a mass of water *which the word* " *Ganges*," *denotes*, and the *thereto subsequent* power of Indication has desisted after causing one to think of such an object as the bank,—*then* that *power* by which such a thing as the excess of coolness and purity—*the* '*Motive*' *for employing the particular form of expression*—*see* § 13. *b.*, is caused to be thought of, is *the power called* ' Suggestion founded on Indication.'

b. Having thus described—*in* § 25 *and* 26—Suggestion pertaining to WORDS—*see* § 23, he describes Suggestion pertaining to the THINGS *signified by the words.*

TEXT.

Suggestion founded on the Sense.

27. That arises from the SENSE *of words* which causes one to think of something else through the speciality of the Speaker, or the Addressed, or the Sentence, or the Proximity of another, or the Drift, or the Occasion, or the Place, or Time, or Emphasis, or Gesture, or the like.

COMMENTARY.

a. In saying "*That arises, &c.*" the word "Suggestion" is *to be supplied* in construction—*the text, without ellipsis, being* "*That (power of) Suggestion arises, &c.*"

b. Among these *various specialities, there may be an example* where there is some speciality in respect of the Speaker, the Sentence, the Occasion, the Place, and the Time—as *is the case in* my own *lines here following—viz.*,

"The season is the Spring-time—and he of the flowery bow, *the god of Love* now rages—: gently flow the breezes that bear away with them the languor of love;—this pleasure-garden too is beautiful with its arbours of the cane:—my husband is far away:—tell me—what is to be done to-day?"

Here some one hints to her confidante—*likely to guess the 'drift' of this 'Speaker'*—"let my unavowed lover be sent speedily to this place."

c. Where the speciality is in respect of the person addressed—§ 27—*we may have such an example* as *the following, viz.*,

"The border of thy breasts has lost the whole of the sandal-wood *with the cooling unguent of which they had been anointed*:—the colour of thy lip has been rubbed out:—thine eyes are quite devoid of collyrium:—this thy slender body has every hair erect:—O falsely speaking go-between!—heedless of the access of pain to *me* thy friend, thou wentest hence to bathe in the lake—not, *as I had sent thee*, to that wretch."

Here, by 'Indication of the contrary'—*see* § 15. *a.*—"Thou hast gone near him" is indicated; and, through the speciality of the messenger 'addressed'—*she being not a messenger simply, but one regarded as "falsely speaking"*—it is understood to be suggested—*on the ground of this sense—see* § 27—that "*Thou wentest* to dally with that *wretch*."

d. Where the speciality is in respect of the Proximity of another —§ 27—*we may have such an example* as *the following—viz.*

"That crane stands unmoved and undisturbed on the leaf of the lotus—like a conch-shell placed on a tray of pure emerald."

Here, from the immobility of the crane its security *is inferred*, and, from that, the fact that the place is devoid of people; and thus *i. e., by directing attention to the fact*, it is said *not expressly but suggestively* by some one to her unavowed lover by HER SIDE (—*for else, the remark on the solitariness of the spot, would not have given rise to the same suggestion,*)—" This—*where the wary crane stands fearing no intrusion* —is the place for an assignation." Here the Motive *for the remark —or, in other words, the thing sought to be suggested*—is that speciality—*of fitness, namely, for an assignation*—of a thing *antecedently* suggested—this *thing antecedently suggested* consisting in the fact that the place is devoid of people:—*so that here we have Suggestion founded on Suggestion.*

Emphasis—what.

e. " It is an *emotional* alteration of the sound in the throat that is called, by the learned, Emphasis (*káku.*)"* The varieties of Emphasis, which is of the just mentioned description, are to be learnt from the original works *on Poetry by Bharata, &c. To take an example* where the speciality consists in this, *we may have such a couplet* as *the following :—viz.*

" In submission to his preceptor, alas, he is prepared to depart to a far country. In the Spring-time, joyous with its bee-swarms and its cuckoos,—he WONT come back—eh, friend of mine ?"

Here *she says* " he wont come back"—but, by the *slily appropriate* Emphasis, it is suggested that " he assuredly WILL come back."

f. Where the speciality consists in Gesture (*cheshṭá*) *we may have such an example* as *the following—viz.*

" Perceiving that her lover had his mind *anxious* about the time of assignation, the quick-witted dame closed the lotus-flower with which she was playing—whilst her laughing eye conveyed to it the import."

Here, by the gesture of closing the lotus, &c., it is suggested by some woman that " The twilight—*when the lotus-flowers close their petals*—is the time of assignation."

g. In the same way *as in the cases above exemplified* the case is to be understood when there is a Speciality in respect of the Speaker and the rest, *enumerated in* § 27,—taken either separately or any way combined.

TEXT.

Division of Suggestion according to the threefold division of Meanings.

28.† Through the threefold division of Meanings, the *power of Suggestion* is held to be, in respect of each *of the above-mentioned varieties*—threefold.

* Röer mistakes this sentence for a text of the book. P. M.
† 29 in Röer's edition.

COMMENTARY.

a. By reason that Meanings have a threefold nature, through their being Expressed or Indicated or Suggested—*see* § 9,—all the just-mentioned powers of Suggestion are threefold. Among these—there is—*for instance,* the power of Suggestion belonging to an EXPRESSED meaning—as—*in the example under* § 27. *b.*—"The season is the Spring-time, &c.," *the words of which are all to be understood literally:—2ndly there is that* belonging to an INDICATED meaning—as *in the example under* § 27. *c.* "The border of thy breasts has lost the whole of the sandal-wood, &c."—*where the words indicate the reverse of what is said, and the Suggestion originates in this indicated meaning:—and 3rdly there is that* belonging to a SUGGESTED meaning—as *in the example under* § 27. *d.*—"That crane stands unmoved, &c.," *where the Suggestion of its being a suitable place of assignation arises out of the suggested secludedness of the spot.*

b. But Suggestiveness pertaining, (*see* § 23. *a.*,) to the RADICAL PART of a word or to an AFFIX will be treated at length *in the latter portion of chap. 4th.*

c. Some one might object that we were told, at § 3., *that Poetry is a Sentence, and further, at* § 6., *that a Sentence consists of Words; but, on the other hand, we are told, at* § 2. *r.*, *that Poetry consists in Suggestion, and further, at* § 23, *that Suggestion may come from the sense and not from the words—so that we are left in perplexity as to which does constitute Poetry—the words or the sense. To remove this perplexity the author declares, as follows:—*

TEXT.

The mutual relation of Words and Meanings in respect to the constituting of Poetry.

29.* The MEANING conveyed by a word suggests, and so also does a WORD applied in another sense—*than that which it then* suggests, *but might elsewhere* denote—*see the example under* § 25. *e.* When the one suggests, then the other is its coadjutor.

COMMENTARY.

a. Because a WORD, when it suggests, has an eye to another MEANING *without which it would fail of suggesting*; and so too a MEANING, *when it suggests, has an eye* to the word—*without which the meaning*

* 30 in Röer's edition.

would vanish :—hence, when the one suggests, the co-operation of the other must needs be admitted.

TEXT.

Division of a Word according to the accident of its function.

30.* Through the being distinguished by the three accidents of Denotation, &c. (§ 10.) a Word also is held—*as the Meaning thereof is*—to be of three kinds—Expressive, Indicative, and Suggestive.

COMMENTARY.

a. When it has the accident of *the power of* Denotation, the word is *simply* Expressive *(váchaka)* ;—when it has the accident of Indication, it is Indicative *(lakshaka)* : when it has the accident of Suggestion, it is Suggestive *(vyanjaka)*.

b. Moreover—*the senses conveyed by separate words, in virtue of their exerting one or other of these three functions, being supposed decided—a difference of opinion presents itself in regard to how words act in concert. On this the author proceeds to remark.*

TEXT.

Purport, a function of the sentence, according to the Naiyáyikas.

31.† Some say that there is function called Purport *(tátparyya) which function consists* in making one apprehend the connection among the meanings of the words ; the sense from the Purport being the 'drift,' and the Sentence, as a whole, being what conveys that drift *by the said function*.

COMMENTARY.

a. Because of the surcease of the power of Denotation—§ 23. *a.*—when the meanings of the several words have been conveyed, there is a function, called Purport, declaratory of the CONNECTION AMONG THE MEANINGS OF THE WORDS, in the shape of THE SENSE OF THE SENTENCE ; the sense coming from the Purport being called the Drift, and the sentence, as a whole, being the conveyer of that drift *through that function (see* § 267, *b.)*

b. So much for the 2nd chapter of the *Sáhitya Darpaṇa*, entitled the "Declaration of the nature of a Sentence."

* 31 in Röer's edition.
† 32 in Röer's edition.

CHAPTER III.

The Declaration of the 'Flavours,' the 'Moods,' &c.

Now what is this Flavour—*rasa*—*see* § 3. *b.*? To this it is replied:—

Text.

Flavour defined. 32.* Love or the like, brought out into manifestness, ***not by the direct mention thereof, but*** by an Excitant, an Ensuant or an Accessory, ***and being*** the permanent mood, *or main sentiment in* ***any composition—see*** § 203,—attains to the condition of a Flavour in the man of poetical sensibility.

Commentary.

a. ***What*** the "Excitants, &c." ***are***, will be mentioned *under* § 61—160—***and*** 166.

b. And the 'Spontaneous' ***indications of strong feeling—see*** § 164—are not mentioned separately ***in the text—although*** *some persons may imagine that they ought to have been*—because they really are Ensuants,—*and these are mentioned in the text.*

c. ***When*** *he speaks of the Flavour as something* "brought out into manifestness," *he means to say, that*, Flavour is this *something* made manifest in a different character to which it is changed—just as curd or the like *consists of milk or the like presented under a change of character;* but *he does* not *mean to say* that something previously completed *and previously so extant*, is, *in this case*, revealed, as a *previously extant* jar is *revealed, unchanged*, by a lamp. This is stated by the author of the 'Lochana,'—*the* "*Eye,*" *scilicet of criticism—when he says* "The expression 'The Flavours are perceived' is employed just as the expression 'He is cooking the boiled rice' is employed—*neither expression, however convenient, being strictly correct, inasmuch as the matter operated upon in the one case is not 'boiled rice' but only becomes such through being cooked; and the matter operated upon in the other case is not 'Flavour' but only becomes such through being perceived.*"

d. And in this *text* § 32, although merely through our taking the word, "Love, &c." the fact of its being a "permanent" mood is also *implied* there—"*love, &c.*"—*see* 203—*being just what constitute*

* 33 in Röer's edition.

these permanent moods, or main sentiments in a composition—yet the word "permanent" is taken in again, *not tautologically, but in reliance on the maxim "exceptio probat regulam,"** with a view to the declaring that these are not *necessarily* main or permanent conditions where there are other Flavours. And hence Laughter, Anger, &c. are only Accessories (§ 168,) when there is, *as the Flavour or Sentiment of the composition*, the Erotic, the Heroic, or the like:—as it is said "Only when in the position of the Flavour *of any given composition* does a 'mood' *(bháva)* attain to being a main or permanent one."

e. The manner of the fruition thereof, *i. e. of Flavour*, shall now be told—which will involve a declaration of its nature.

TEXT.

How Flavour is apprehended.

33.† This Flavour, *arising* from the exaltation of *that leading element, of the three, held to constitute Nature, that is termed* 'Purity,' indivisible, self-manifested, made up of joy and thought *in their identity*, free from the contact of aught else perceived, akin, *as a uterine brother*, to the *ecstatic* contemplator's perception of God, the life whereof is hyper-physical wonder, is enjoyed, by those competent, in inseparableness *of the Flavour from the fruition thereof*,—like the form of the Deity *which is—according to the Vedánta—itself the joy with which it is recognised by the liberated soul.*

COMMENTARY.

a. As it is said—" A mind untouched by Foulness and Darkness —*two out of the three that, according to the Sánkhya Philosophy, constitute Nature—see "Lecture on the Tattwa-samása," No.* 49, *and Prof. Wilson's Sánkhya Káriká, p.* 52—is here called Purity (*sattwa*):"—so a certain internal character, of this just-mentioned description, which leads one to a turning away of the face from extraneous things cognizable, is *what we speak of in the text as* 'Purity.' Its "exaltation," *spoken of in the text*, is its manifestation when it has risen above *the two other constituents of Nature, viz.*, Foulness and Darkness *as above-mentioned.* And the cause hereof—*i. e., of this mental character*—is the study of such like supermundane matters of Poetry *as may be mentioned here or elsewhere.*

* See Whately's Logic—B. ii. Ch. v. § 6.

† 34 in Röer's edition.

b. *By calling it* "indivisible" *he means to say that* this *Flavour —though consisting, in some sort,—see* § 52—*of a number of elements,* is one thing only —consisting of the wonder that arises from the display of the "Excitants, &c." *that give rise to Emotion—see* § 61, and of *the Emotions themselves—such as* Love, &c. The cause of this—*i. e., of its indivisibility* we shall tell—*further on—see* § 60.

c. It is "self-manifested," &c., *the text informs us—and this it is* in the way that we shall mention *at* § 60.

d. *In the epithet applied to Flavour—viz.*—'chinmaya,' the affix 'mayat'—*see Páṇini V.* 4. 21.—gives the sense of "consisting of"—*Flavour being made up of thought.*

e. "Wonder" is a kind of expanding of the mind. Another term with the same import is "Surprise." And the proof of this—*that the life of Flavour is 'Wonder'*—is the dictum of my great great grandfather, the most venerable in the assembly of the intelligent, the chief of learned poets, the illustrious Náráyaṇa. Dharmadatta mentions that *dictum of my great great grandfather's, when he says*:—"In Flavour, even in every case, Wonder is felt as its essence. Since Wonder is its essence, *it follows that* Flavour, even in every case, is *that Sentiment or Flavour, called* the 'Marvellous' (—see § 237,)—hence the learned Náráyaṇa has acknowledged only one Flavour, the Marvellous, *and no other.*"

The opinion that all poetic Flavour is reducible, to 'Wonder.'

f. *By* "those competent" *he here means* men with merits acquired in a former birth, *in respect of whom the statement of the text is true,* since it has been declared:—"The VIRTUOUS apprehend the expanse of Flavour, as the ecstatic contemplator *discerns God in beatific vision.*"

Indifference of object and operation in the Gustation of Flavour.

g. *We are told that* "The gustation *of Flavonr* is the arising of joy in the soul from the contact of matters of Poetry":—now, on this showing, it is *plainly* declared that Flavour is nothing distinct from the gustation thereof;—but still, *though admitting this,* we *find it convenient to* employ such expressions as "Flavour is tasted," either admitting, *for convenience,* a FICTITIOUS distinction *between the tasting and the flavour tasted,* or employing the verb reflectively—*see the Laghu Kaumudí, p.* 313. The same thing is stated *by another authority, who* *says*, "Since its essence consists in its being tasted,* Flavour is nothing other, *in respect of its body—if it can be said to have one*—than the body *consisting* of *its* manifestation." And so in similar places elsewhere such applications *of the term Flavour as indicate something distinct from its perception—see* § 51. *a.*—are to be understood tropically.

A supposed objection to this no objection.

h. "But then," *some one—fancying that he is giving utterance to an objection—may say*, "by all this you assert that Flavour—*in which Poetry consists—see* § 3. is not an OBJECT of knowledge *but a* MODE *of knowledge*; and since Suggestion is a mode of knowledge *the result of which—see* § 2. *r. and* 59—*is declared to be alone Poetry*—it turns out that these two are one. And yet *hear what the author of the Vyaktiviveka says—viz.*—'What we mean by a Suggester *or manifester—vyanjaka*—is a cause, through the knowledge due to itself, of the knowledge of some other extant thing,—as a lamp *is, in relation to a jar or the like.* And if it be otherwise—*i. e., if you do not grant that Suggestion is the manifester of Flavour already extant*, then what difference is there between this *manifester of something not previously extant* and a maker? *which all deny, it to be—Flavour not being a product—see* § 52. According to this showing, *as opposed to your view of the identity of the manifestation and the thing manifested*, there is really a distinction between the Suggested and the Suggester, as between a jar and a lamp,—and so how can Flavour, *which you identify with the act of manifestation or Suggestion*, be the thing Suggested?"—If, *O friendly objector, you say all this*, you say rightly. And therefore have they declared that this, the making *of Flavour* called Gustation, is a certain operation quite peculiar *and distinct* from the *ordinary* kinds of 'making' and 'manifesting;' and therefore *does the author of the Vyaktiviveka say* "Tasting, Relishing, and Wondering, are quite peculiar names." And therefore, by myself and others who take it to be established as the only *explanation of the phenomena in question*, that there is a function—*viz.*, '*Suggestion*'—*denied by the Grammarians and by the Naiyáyikas*—distinct from Denotation, &c., *therefore, I repeat, by myself*

* Compare Berkeley's expressions with respect to ideas—"the existence of an idea consists in its being perceived;"—and again with respect to things,—"their *esse* is *percipi*." Principles of Human Knowledge, Chs. 2 and 3.

and those who think with me it is stated that the Flavours, &c. consist of *what we choose, for convenience, to regard sometimes as an object of knowledge, and which we then call* the *meaning* 'Suggested' (*vyangya*).

i. But again—*adverting to the assertion of the text that Flavour is made up of joy—some one may object*—"*Then, since the* '*Pathetic*' (§ 228) and such like Flavours are made up of pain, they cannot be Flavours at all." To this it is replied *as follows.*

TEXT.

Things painful in reality are in poetry sources of pleasure only.

34.* Of the fact that, even in such a Flavour as the 'Pathetic,' &c., *in reality*, pleasure only is produced—the consciousness of the intelligent is the only proof.

COMMENTARY.

a. By the "&c," *he means such other Flavours as* the 'Disgustful,' the 'Terrible,' &c. *see* § 236 and 235.

b. Still—*though the authority cited in the text ought to suffice—yet*, in order to close the mouths of those that want poetical sensibility, the opposite side of the argument—*see Aphorisms of the Nyáya*, 39 *a.*—is mentioned, *and disposed of, as follows.*

TEXT.

35.* Moreover, if in these (§ 34) there were pain, then no one would turn a look towards them—*which, however, people do*—

COMMENTARY.

a. For no one, possessed of understanding, engages—*knowingly, and without some ulterior view*—in paining himself; and *yet* we see that every one enters with engrossing interest into the 'Pathetic,' &c.

b. As another illustration of the unfitness *of the objection*, he remarks *as follows.*

TEXT.

36. *If it were* so—*see* § 35—then such *compositions* as the Rámáyaṇa would be causes of pain—*instead of giving delight to every man of taste.*

COMMENTARY.

a. For since—*according to the supposed objection see* § 33. *i*, the 'Pathetic' is a cause of pain, we should find cause of pain even in

* 35 & 36 in Röer's edition.

such *heart-delighting compositions* as the Rámáyaṇa, the leading Sentiment of which is the 'Pathetic.'

b. But how then, *some one may ask*, can pleasure arise from causes of pain? To this he replies *as follows.*

TEXT.

37. Grant that mundane sorrow, joy, &c. be produced from what things, so far as they belong to the world, happen to be causes of sorrow, joy, &c.—yet what harm is there if we say that pleasure is produced even from all these, when, through their being consigned to *the transcendental world of* Poetry, they have attained to being hyper-physical EXCITANTS?

COMMENTARY.

a. For, what things indeed, such as *the banished* Ráma's dwelling in the forest, are called causes of pain in the world—*or in their actual occurrence,*—those very things, when consigned to Poetry and to dramatic representation, in consequence of their assuming the function of 'hyper-physical excitation,' (§ 44. *b.*,) having left off being denoted by the term CAUSES, possess the right to be denoted by the term hyper-physical EXCITANTS *(vibháva)*;—and from these, only pleasure is produced—as from bites *and scratches* and the like in toying. And hence it is only in the *actual* world that the rule holds that from worldly causes of sorrow, joy, &c., worldly sorrow, joy, &c. *respectively* arise; whilst in *the transcendental world of* Poetry, on the other hand, pleasure alone arises from all the exciting agencies, &c.—and, according to this determination of the state of the case, there is no fault *in the text under consideration.*

Tears no proof that in poetry anything but pleasure is produced.

b. But if the poetic representation of sufferings produces only pleasure, how then are tear-sheddings, &c. produced by the seeing or hearing, in a poem or in a dramatic performance, the *sad* adventures of Harischandra *in the Mahá-bhárata* and the like? To this it is replied *as follows.*

TEXT.

38. In like manner tear-sheddings, &c. (§ 37. *b.*) are held to come from the mind's being MELTED—*not pained.*

COMMENTARY.

Why poetry does not delight all alike.

a. How then does this perception of Flavour from Poetry not take place in the case of ALL? To this he replies *as follows.*

TEXT.

39. The Gustation thereof *i. e., of Flavour*, does not take place without the Imagination of Love, &c.—*i. e. without the capacity of conceiving whatever passion is intended to be depicted.*

COMMENTARY.

a. And Imagination, *or cultivated intellectual Susceptibility (vásaná)*, both now developed and not neutralized by past demerit—*literally "present" and "ancient"*—is the cause of the gustation of Flavour. If the former of these were not *necessary*, then this *power of relishing poetry* would belong even to Bráhmaṇs learned in the Vedas, and to students of the old Logic, &c.—*who, however, do not read poetry, and cannot therefore acquire a sensibility in regard to it—this sensibility requiring to be matured by cultivation—see* § 19. *a.*; and if the second were not *necessary*, then it would not happen—*as, however, it does happen*—that even some of the most eager *students of Poetry* are seen not to have a *right* perception of Flavour—*which is explicable, in the case of these commendable strugglers, only on the supposition that demerit incurred in some anterior state of existence frustrates their efforts.*

b. And it is said by Dharmmadatta—"Those present *at a dramatic representation* who have Imagination, may relish the Flavour *of the composition represented*; but those devoid of Imagination are, in the theatre, like the wood-work, the walls, and the stones."

Sympathy arises from the spectator's identifying himself with the hero.

c. But—from those causes which excite love, &c., in Ráma, &c.,—such as *his beloved* Sítá, &c., how is it that love, &c., is excited in the SPECTATOR? To this it is replied *as follows.*

TEXT.

40. The Excitants, &c, (§ 61) have an operation called the 'making common'—*through sympathy*, by force of which the person competent *to appreciate Poetry—see* § 39—makes himself out to be not a distinct person from him—*the hero*—whose jumping across the sea

—as Hanumán does in the Rámáyaṇa—&c. are the *matters represented.*

COMMENTARY.

a. But *some one may ask—objecting to the possibility of one's imagining himself the possesser of superhuman power*—how can a man imagine *himself to possess* the vigour to jump across the sea, &c.? To this it is replied *as follows.*

TEXT.

Sympathy not prevented by the superiority of the hero to the spectator.

41. The idea *arising in the mind* even of *mere* men, of *possessing* such valour, &c., as *is required* in jumping across the sea, &c., is not censurable *as an impossibility—such idea resulting* from the conceit of community *with the hero of the poem.*

COMMENTARY.

a. Love, &c., also*—as well as heroism*—are felt through this community *of the spectator with the hero*—hence he remarks *as follows.*

TEXT.

42. Through community *or sympathy*, in like manner, Love, &c., are felt.

COMMENTARY.

a. For if Love, &c., were recognised *by each spectator* as being located in one's self ONLY, then the spectators would ACTUALLY experience shame, tremor, &c., *which they do not,** or if *the feelings represented on the stage were recognised by them* as located in another ONLY*—e. g., in the hero regarded as quite distinct from themselves,* then there would be insipidity, *or an absence of all Flavour: so they are recognised as* COMMON *to both one's self and the hero.*

b. Moveover *not only are the emotions common to both, but* the Excitants, &c., *of emotion*, in the first place,*—the Flavour eventually resulting being, logically and analytically if not chronologically and really, subsequent to the exciting agencies*—are recognised as being common *to the hero with the spectator rightly recognising them*—on which he remarks *as follows.*

TEXT.

43. At *the time of* the gustation thereof *i. e., of Flavour,* there is no distribution of the Excitants, &c., *of emotion—such as could put*

* And if they *did*, they would derive no pleasure from the performance. P. M.

it into the head of a spectator to say "this is the other's ONLY *i. e. the hero's exclusively*—that is not the OTHER'S—this is MINE—that is not MINE;" *so that of the Excitants &c. too, there is felt a* COMMUNITY, *and not an* EXCLUSIVENESS to *the hero or the spectator's self.*

COMMENTARY.

a. But still—how have these Excitants, &c., a character thus extraordinary? To this it is replied *as follows.*

TEXT.

44. *In the eyes* of those who admit that the functions called Excitation, &c. are hyper-physical—*see* § 33,—their extraordinariness is their beauty not their blame.

COMMENTARY.

a. By the "&c." *he means* Accommodation (§ 44. *c.*) and Accessoriness (§ 44. *d.*)

b. Here (§ 44.) 'Excitation,' *or alterant action* (*vibhávana*) means the producing the requisite arrangement for the germination* *or springing up* of the gustation of some particular kind *of emotion* such—e. g.—as Love—*see* § 61. *a.*

c. 'Accommodation *of the plastic mind or body to this alterant agency* (*anubhávana*) means the perception of such Love, &c., *as is spoken of in the preceding paragraph*, in the shape of Flavour, &c.,—(*meaning by the* "*&c.*" *an* '*incomplete Flavour*' or a 'semblance of Flavour'—*see* § 3. *c.*,) immediately thereafter—*i. e. immediately after the arrangement specified in* § 44. *b.*

d. 'Accessoriness' (*sanchárana* means the promoting *and serving by concomitance to heighten* this *Flavour* that has become such *as just described in* § 44. *c.*

e. But then—*some one may ask*—if the Excitants, &c., in the order of their enumeration, are—*as they seem to have been just described to be, respectively, nothing other than* Causes, EFFECTS, and Concurrent causes—how are all the three *spoken of—at* § 32—*as if they were all* Causes of the apprehending of Flavour? To this it is replied *as follows, that such is simply the fact.*

TEXT.

45. For, though in the ordinary course of life the Excitants, &c., (§ 61) are in the shape of Causes, EFFECTS, and Concurrent causes, yet

* Compare Taylor's expression—"the undeveloped initiatives of good things to come:"—see 'Saturday Evening,' p. 6.

they are held to be Causes alone in respect of the apprehending of Flavour.

COMMENTARY.

a. But how then, in the gustation of Flavour, do these *three* seem to be ONE? To this it is replied *as follows.*

TEXT.

How Flavour is single, though spoken of as resulting from a composition of causes.

46. Each, as perceived at first separately, is spoken of as a cause; and then all this commingled—the Excitants and the rest—when relished by the man of taste, becomes Flavour, resembling the composite flavour of sherbet.

COMMENTARY.

a. As, from the commingling of sugar, pepper, &c., a certain unprecedented relish is produced in the shape of the flavour of the sherbet; so is it here also, from the commingling of the Excitants, &c.—such is the meaning *of the text* § 46.

b. But then *some one may ask*—if Flavour is produced only from Excitants, Ensuants, and Accessories COMMINGLED, how can it be found—*as you will not deny that it is*—where there exists but one *of the three*, or two? To this it is replied *as follows.*

TEXT.

What might seem wanting in the utterance of poetry is supplied by the Association of Ideas.

47. If there be present, out of *the three—viz.*, the Excitants and the others, two or *even* one, then there is no fault, for there is instantaneously a supplying of the others *by the Association of Ideas.*

COMMENTARY.

a. And this supplying—*of what is wanting may occur* in virtue of the *suggestive character of the* matter in hand, or of something else. For example—*take the following verses.*

"A face, long-eyed, fair as the autumnal moon; arms sloping at the shoulders; and a bosom compact, with close high breasts; sides—as if polished; span-measured waist; loins joined with handsome hips; feet with the toes upturned; and her whole person disposed just according to the wish of the Agitator of mind *(Káma).*"*

Here, whilst Agnimitra, in love with Málaviká, describes only Excitants *of the emotion of Love* in the shape of *the various beauties*

* Dr. B.'s rendering of this portion was—'just like the utter unconstraint of a blithe dancer's mind'—which is more poetical but not correct. P. M.

of Málaviká, there is, through the mere fitness of things, a *mental* supplying of 'Accessories' such as the longing *of the lover describing his mistress*, and of Ensuants,—such as the *rapturous* rolling of the eyes. And thus in regard to the supplying of others *of the three, when not all are conveyed in the poet's words*, an inference is to be made *by the intelligent reader, for himself—it being unnecessary to multiply examples.*

b. To those who—*not holding the correct view laid down in* § 43—say that the Flavour is located in the one represented—*i. e. in the hero,*—he says *as follows.*

TEXT.

The *locus* of the Flavour not the hero—and why.

48. The excitement of Love, &c. in the person represented,—*recognized by the spectator*—would not become Flavour—for this *Love, &c., so far forth as belonging entirely to him*, was limited *to the hero himself*, and was mundane—*whereas Flavour—see* § 33—*is hyperphysical,*—and it, *the Love, &c. of the Hero,* is separated by a long interval,—*the hero having possibly died a thousand years ago—whereas the spectator belongs to the time present —whatever that may be—and Flavour* (*see* § 54)—*is irrespective of Time.*

COMMENTARY.

a. For, the excitement, *or feeling*, of Love or the like, in Ráma or the like, produced by the sight of *his beloved* Síta or the like, was limited *to the single lover, and does not belong to a whole theatrical audience ;* and it pertained to the *every-day* world ; and it is separated by a long interval from the witnessing, &c., of the play or the poem *in which the incident is described.* Hence, how should IT attain (§ 32) to the state of being a Flavour—seeing that Flavour is characterized by its being devoid of this triad of characters—*being not limited to one—not mundane but hyperphysical—and not of the past but irrespective of Time ?*

b. He rejects also *the notion of* its being located in the representer *of the hero—i. e. of its being in the actor :—remarking as follows.*

TEXT.

Nor is the locus of the Flavour the histrionic repre-

49. It is not the player—*poor hungry wretch*— that is the taster of the Flavour—exhibiting *as he*

senter of the hero. *does* the appearance—*i. e. performing the part*—of Ráma, or the like, merely as he has been taught, or as he has learned by practice.

COMMENTARY.

a. Moreover—*to meet an obvious objection—he adds.*

TEXT.

The actor, so far'forth as he is a man of taste, ranks as a spectator.

50. By his realizing to himself—*if he does so*—the import of the poetry—*which he more probably repeats with indifference if not with weariness*—he too ranks as a spectator.

COMMENTARY.

a. *That is to say*—if, on the other hand, through his realizing the import of the poetry, he enacts the character of Ráma as if *he felt it to be* his own, then he—*the actor*—too is reckoned among the audience—*and whatever we may remark of them, applies so far to him.*

TEXT.

Flavour not an objective entity.

51. This *Flavour* is not something that may be made known—for the perception of it is inseparable from its very existence.

COMMENTARY.

a. For, 'what may be made known' *(jnápya,)* as a jar for instance—*by the light thrown upon it by a lamp or the like*,—that, even whilst existing, is sometimes not perceived; but not so this *Flavour*, for, apart from perception, it does not exist—(§ 33. *h.*).

TEXT.

Flavour not a product.

52. Since this *Flavour* has its essence, *or is not itself except*, in necessary connection with the aggregate of Excitants, &c , *on which it depends*, therefore it is not an effect *or product.*

COMMENTARY.

a. If Flavour were an effect—*or product—like ordinary mundane things*—then it would be one having for its cause—*inasmuch as it could have no other cause*—the knowledge, *i. e. the perception*, of the Excitants, &c.; and therefore, at the time of the perception of Flavour, the Excitants, &c., would not be perceived—for we do not see *that there occurs* simultaneously the perception of a cause and the perception of the effect of that *cause* :—for—*to give an illustration of our meaning*—the perception of the TOUCH of the sandalwood-unguent, and the perception of the PLEASURE produced thereby, cannot take place simultaneously, *however rapidly the one may succeed the other;* and, *on the other hand*, the perception of the Excitants, &c. is not—*in the mundane and ordinary sense of the word*—the cause of the perception of Flavour, since this *Flavour* exists, *as we have said*, in necessary connection with the aggregate of the Excitants, &c. *and is therefore perceived simultaneously with them;—and as these are therefore not to be spoken of as its cause, it is not to be called their effect;*—such is the purport *of the text.*

TEXT.

Flavour independent of Time past, present and future.

53. Nor is it eternal—as it does not reside in the perception previous *to that of the Excitants, &c.*, and—*as remarked at* § 51. *a.*, at the time when it is not perceived, it does not even exist.

COMMENTARY.

a. Verily it does not belong to a thing that is eternal to be incapable of existing at a time when it is not perceived.

TEXT.

54. Nor is it, *Flavour*, moreover, something that will be—*continuing perdurably, apart from the perception of it, after having once come into existence*—because it consists in *nothing else than* its own manifestation in the shape of positively apparent joy *felt then and there;—and yet* neither is it, moreover, of the present,—for it is of a nature distinct alike from an 'effect' (§ 52) and from 'what can be made known' (§ 51)*—*to one or other of which heads everything merely mundane and of time present can be referred—while—like the Deity—this 'Flavour' is irrespective of Time.* Since its object—*or what furnishes the occasion of its manifestation*—is the experiencing of the Excitants, &c. (§ 61,) and also since it is apprehended by the intelligent in the shape of pre-eminent delight, clearly its conveyer is not wished to be—*i. e. cannot be allowed to be*—'unconditioned' *(nirvikapaka)* knowledge—*the mere knowledge that 'this is* SOMETHING;' *and yet* in like manner neither it is perceived as 'conditioned' (*savikalpaka*), because of the absence of adaptability in it to *being described by* any combination of terms—*as will be explained in the commentary here following.*

* So much is incorporated by Röer with the preceding commentary. P. M.

COMMENTARY.

a. I say that the object apprehended, when 'Flavour' is apprehended, is not 'conditioned' knowledge, because whatever *cognitions* are received through 'conditioned'* knowledge are adaptable to some employment of language,—*i. e. an account can be given of them in separate and intelligible terms*—but not so is 'Flavour'—*which, being every way indivisible,—see* § 60—*cannot be analyzed and then defined in terms of the analysis.*

TEXT.

No. 55. And it, "*Flavour,*" is not something imperceptible, for it is something MANIFESTED (*see* § 30;) and *yet* its manifestation is not PER SE perceptible, because the possibility *of its being apprehended* is *dependent* on sound—*i. e. on the words that constitute the poetry.*

COMMENTARY.

a. "Do tell then"—*the reader will be ready to exclaim*—"what like is the real nature—*the tattwa, or 'quiddity'*—of this strangely characterised sort of thing such as was never seen or heard of before?" To this it is replied.

TEXT.

Flavour altogether hyperphysical.

No. 56. Therefore, *i. e. since 'Flavour' does not fall under any division in these exhaustive classifications of mundane knowledge*—truly it is to be regarded by the intelligent as hyperphysical *(alaukika).*

* The terms *nirvikalpaka* and *savikalpaka* are explained in the *Tarka Sangraha* as follow:—"That—*viz. Perception—pratyaksha*—is of two sorts—*nirvikalpaka* and *savikalpaka*. That knowledge which does not involve the *knowledge of the* species or sort, is *nirvikalpaka i. e. 'without an alternative'*—as *the knowledge that* 'This is something.' That knowledge which does include specification, *or the reference of the object to one of the categories*—see § 12—is *savikalpaka—i. e. 'with an alternative'—for the object might possibly be correctly referrible to a different subdivision of the category*—as *the knowledge that* 'This is *the man called* Dittha,' 'This is a bráhman,' 'This is black,' *not red, or yellow.*" [The *nirvikalpaka* and *savikalpaka pratyksha* of the Hindu philosophers exactly correspond to Hamilton's simple Perception and Thought proper. The following example given by him in illustration of this distinction may, I think, be usefully quoted here: "An object is presented, say a book; this object determines an impression, and I am even conscious of the impression, but without recognising to myself what the thing is; in that case, there is only a perception, and not properly a thought. But suppose I do recognise it for what it is, in other words, compare it with and reduce it under a certain concept, class, or complement of attributes, which I call *book*; in that case, there is more than a perception,—there is a thought." Lectures, Vol. III. p. 14. P. M.]

COMMENTARY.

a. Then again what is the evidence that this '*Flavour*' is an entity? To this he replies.

TEXT.

Proof that there is such a thing as Flavour at all.

No 57. The evidence of this—*i. e. of Flavour's being an entity*—is considered by the learned to be just the Gustation thereof—*which exists*—*see* § 33. *g.*—in inseparableness from *the* '*Flavour*' itself.

COMMENTARY.

a. 'Gustation' means tasting;—and that is of the kind described *by the author of the Dhwani* as follows:—" 'Tasting' is the arising of soul-joy from contact with the meaning of Poetry."

b. But then *some one may object*—if 'Flavour' is not a product—*as it is denied to be—here implicitly—and explicitly at* § 52—then how is it characterised, by the great saint *Bharata*, as follows—viz. —"The PRODUCTION of Flavour takes place from the union of the Excitants, the Ensuants, and the Accessories?" To this it is replied.

TEXT.

No. 58. By reason of the production of its Gustation—*which, in the sense to be explained in the Commentary,* MAY *be said to take place*—the production of this '*Flavour*'—*which*—*see* § 52—*is not a product*, is *spoken of* TROPICALLY.

COMMENTARY.

a. Although the Gustation *of* '*Flavour*' also is not *really* a product, seeing that it is nothing distinct from the Flavour *itself*—*which is no product*,—yet its being a product is spoken of tropically—for it is a product, in a SECONDARY sense of the word, in respect of its OCCASIONALNESS—*seeing that every man does not experience it, nor any man at all times.*

TEXT.

No. 59. Its not being the "Expressed, &c." *but only the Suggested*"—*see* § 2. *v.*—I shall declare in the exposition of 'Suggestion' *in chap. 5th.*

COMMENTARY.

a. "Its"—i. e. Flavour's. By the "&c." is meant its not being the 'Indicated, &c.' *see* § 9.

b. But then *some one may object*—if 'Flavour' consists of 'Love and the rest'—*meaning by* "*the rest*" *the appropriate concomitants of each emotion*—COMMINGLED—*as declared at* § 46—how *are we to understand* its self-manifestation (*see* § 33) and its indivisibility (§ 33)? To this it is replied.

TEXT.

Flavour, being knowledge, is self-manifested.

No. 60. Since 'Flavour' *exists* only from its being identical with the KNOWLEDGE of *the emotions and concomitants, such as* Love, &c.—hence is established its self-manifestation—*knowledge being itself light*,—and its indivisibleness.

COMMENTARY.

a. If 'Love, &c.' were something distinct from the body of light, *or knowledge*, then only could its self-manifestation not be established; but the case is not so,—for its identity therewith is admitted *by all the authorities*, as it is declared *by the author of the Dhwani*—thus—"Although, by reason of its being nothing other than the 'Flavour,' the 'Gustation' *of Flavour* is NOT a product (§ 52,) still being assumed to be a product in respect of its OCCASIONALNESS (§ 58. *a.*,) it is moreover treated as divisible into Love *and the various poetic emotions* &c., *these being supposed to subsist* in the shape of modifications—*as curd is a modification of milk*—of that increate Imagination which is identical therewith *i. e. with increate Flavour*:"—and '*Flavour*,' *I repeat, is held to be identical with Knowledge as he elsewhere declares* thus—"And on assenting to the identity of Joy, &c. *with* '*Gustation*' *and* '*Flavour*,' having reposed upon our couch of established doctrine, mayest thou enjoy the slumber of delight for a thousand years of the gods!"—and *as he again declares* thus—"It, *Flavour*, is undivided from its enjoyer, being made an object of cognition identical with the Love *or other emotion*, &c., of the possessor of Imagination."

b. On *the shoulders of* those who do not admit the fact that Knowledge IS self-manifesting—the rod must be let fall by the Vedántists *who more especially cherish the tenet disallowed by these*.

c. The 'indivisibleness' thereof *i. e. of Flavour*—*is to be inferred* just from its identity *with the knowledge of the emotions, &c.*—for Love *and the other emotions*, &c., in the first place being recognised severally, attain to being 'Flavour' only as they appear when having all become ONE. This is declared *by the author of the Dhwani* as follows—"The Excitants, the Ensuants, the Involuntary *indications of emotion*, and the Accessories, being recognised first dividedly, attain to indivisibility:"—and *again—as he remarks in prose*—"But in strict reality this *Flavour* is to be apprehended only as something indivisible, like the nature of the Deity as set forth in *the theological system of* the Vedánta."

d. Now what are those 'Excitants,' 'Ensuants' and 'Accessories' (§ 32)? With reference to this *question*, he tells us what is an 'Excitant,' *as follows*.

TEXT.

What is meant by an 'Excitant.

No. 61. What things in the *every-day* world awaken in one Love or any other *of the emotions*, are, *when represented* in Poetry and the Drama, called 'Excitants' *(vibháva)*.

COMMENTARY.

a. What things,—e. g. Sítá, *the beloved of Ráma*, &c. are, in the *actual* world, causes of the excitement of Love or Laughter or any other *emotion* in Ráma &c.—these same, when consigned to Poetry or the Drama, are called 'vibháva'—*the term being derived from the causal form of the verb bhú 'to become' preceded by the particle vi implying 'difference' or 'alteration'*—for, by these—*which we may call 'Excitants' or 'Alterants'*—the *mental or bodily* states *(bháva)*, such as Love or other *emotion*, of the spectators are altered *(vibhávyante)*, i. e. are made suitable for the manifestation (§ 32) of the first sprout of 'Gustation'—*see* § 44, *b.—which sprout requires, for its full development, the artistic treatment which will be detailed in due order*. This is declared by Bhartrihari *in the Vákyapadíya* as follows:—"He, *the intelligent reader or spectator*, thinks of *the tyrant* Kansa, and the like, *energising* as if they were presented to his senses, when these *personages* have become objects of his understanding in the shapes bestowed upon them by *the poet's* words."

b. He *next* mentions the two varieties thereof—*i. e. of the 'Excitants.'*

TEXT.

Division of the Excitants into the Substantial and the Enhancer.

No. 62. The two divisions thereof—*i. e. of the Excitants—see* § 61—are those called the substantial *or essential (álambana)* and the enhancer *(uddípana)*.

COMMENTARY.

a. *The meaning of the text is* plain. Among these *he proceeds to explain the former of the two varieties.*

TEXT.

The Substantials or indispensable ingredients of poetry.

No. 63. The substantial (§ 62) is *such a material and indispensable ingredient as* the hero, &c.—for thereupon is the arising of Flavour *altogether* dependent.

COMMENTARY.

a. By the "&c." *is meant* the heroine, the rival *of the hero*, &c.

b. The proper Excitant of each particular Flavour will be mentioned in the exposition of the nature of the latter.

c. Among these *Excitants, then*, there is the Hero—*whose generic description follows.*

TEXT.

Definition of the Hero.

No. 64. Liberal, learned, of good family, graceful, with the ardour of youth and beauty, clever, a general favourite, and possessed of spirit, wit, and virtue,—such is the leading character.

COMMENTARY.

a. 'Clever'—i. e. swift in act.—'Virtue'—i. e. good conduct.

b. The leading character possessed of qualities such as these is the Hero *(náyaka)*.

c. He now mentions the divisions thereof—*i. e. of the genus Hero.*

TEXT.

Fourfold division of the genus Hero.

No. 65. He—*i. e. the Hero*—is first declared to be of four kinds—viz. (1) 'high-spirited, but temperate and firm' *(dhírodátta)*; (2) 'firm and haughty' *(dhíroddhata)*; (3) 'gay and thoughtless, yet firm *(dhíralalita)*; and (4) 'firm and mild' *(dhírapras'ánta)*.*

COMMENTARY.

a. *All this is* plain.

b. Among these, the 'high-spirited, but temperate and firm' *hero is of the following description.*

* Firmness, though belonging to every kind of hero, is mentioned in the description because its presence or absence occasions a subdivision of the *heroines*—(see § 102),

TEXT.

The hero high-spirited but temperate and firm.

No. 66. Not given to boasting, placable, very profound, with great self-command, resolute, whose self-esteem is concealed, faithful to his engagements—*such is the hero who* is called 'high-spirited, but temperate and firm:' (§ 65.)

COMMENTARY.

a. 'Not given to boasting'—i. e. not a practiser of self-praise. 'With great self-command'—i. e. who is not of a nature to be overpowered by joy or sorrow, &c. 'Whose self-esteem is concealed'—i. e. whose *proper* pride is covered by decorum. 'Faithful to his engagements'—i. e. who carries out what he has undertaken.

b. *Such is the first class of heroes—heroes such* as Ráma, Yudhishṭhira, and the like.

c. Now the 'firm and haughty' *hero is of the following description.*

TEXT.

The hero firm and haughty.

No. 67. Given to deceiving, hot, unsteady, having much egotism and arrogance, fond of praising himself—*such is the hero who* by the learned is called the 'firm and haughty.'

COMMENTARY.

a. *Such is the second class of heroes—heroes such* as Bhímasena and the like.

b. Now the 'gay and thoughtless, yet firm' *hero is described.*

TEXT.

The hero gay and thoughtless yet firm.

No. 68. Free from care, ever gentle, devoted to the arts—let this be the hero 'gay and thoughtless, yet firm.'

COMMENTARY.

a. "Arts"—i. e. pantomimic action, &c.

b. *Such is the third class of heroes—heroes such* as the king of Vatsa in *the play called* the Ratnávali.*

c. Now the 'firm and mild' *hero is described.*

* Translated in Wilson's "Specimens of the Theatre of the Hindus."

TEXT.

The hero firm and mild.

No. 69. Possessing largely the generic good qualities *of a hero—see* § 64—a Bráhmaṇ or the like—let this be the *hero* 'firm and mild.'

COMMENTARY.

a. Such is the fourth class of heroes—heroes such as Mádhava in *the play of* 'Málatí and Mádhava,' &c.*

b. And he next states the subdivisions *of these four classes of heroes*—§ 65—according to their character as LOVERS.

TEXT.

Subdivision of the four classes of heroes into sixteen kinds.

No. 70. But *heroes are constituted* of sixteen kinds, by these *four divisions—see* § 65—which may have *severally* the character of (1) 'impartial,' (2) 'saucy' (3) 'faithful,' and (4) 'sly,' *in matters of love.*

COMMENTARY.

a. That is to say :—through the fact that these—viz. the 'high-spirited, but temperate and firm,' &c., may be severally 'impartial,' 'saucy,' 'faithful,' or 'sly,' *in the character of a lover—69. b.,*—a hero may be of sixteen descriptions.

TEXT.

The hero whose fondness is impartially distributed.

No. 71. But among these *various kinds of heroes mentioned in* § 70, that one is called the 'impartial' *in matters of love* who is equally attached to several women.

COMMENTARY.

a. That is to say the 'impartial' hero is he whose affection towards two, three, four, or more women, is equal :—as *is the case with the hero in the following example.*

"'The daughter of the king of Kuntala stands *awaiting you*, having bathed ; the turn is of the sister of the king of Anga ; but the night has been won by Kamalá with the dice ; and her Majesty, *the chief queen*, too, is to be conciliated to-night'—The king, having been informed respecting the fair ones of the harem, *in the foregoing terms*, by me, *the chief eunuch*, who had ascertained *these matters*, stood for two or three hours *of twenty-four minutes each*, with his mind perplexed by indecision."

* See Wilson's "Theatre of the Hindus."

TEXT.

The hero who is saucy in his loves.

No. 72. Though culpable, yet undismayed; when reproached, yet not ashamed; lying *bare-facedly* even when his offence was seen;—such is the one called—*as regards his amatory conduct—see* § 69. *b.*—the 'saucy' hero.

COMMENTARY.

a. Mine *are the following verses illustrative of this character.*

"Perceiving her countenance crimson with passion, I went near *intending* to kiss her. Then she spurned me with her foot; but I having nimbly caught hold of it whilst I burst out laughing,—O my friend, the anger of the fair-browed one, shedding tears, from her then being unable to do anything, prolongs, whenever thought of, the amusement of my mind."

The hero who is constant to one loved one.

TEXT.

No. 73. The 'faithful' is he who is devoted to one.

COMMENTARY.

a. *That is to say* the 'faithful' hero is he who is attached to only one heroine:—as *is the, case with the hero whose wife speaks of him in the following verses.*

"My garments, O friend, are not beautiful, the ornaments of my neck are not resplendent, my gait is not *coquettishly* curvilinear, my laugh is not loud, nor have I any *of the hoydenish blandishment called* pride;—yet other people say 'Her beloved, though beautiful, never throws a look on any else;'—therefore do I hold that; by thus much, all others are ill-off, *compared with me.*"

TEXT.

The hero who simulates affection.

No. 74. The 'sly' is he who, being attached to *only* one, acts, covertly, with unkindness towards another, *whilst* showing affection outwardly.

COMMENTARY.

a. *That is to say*—he, again, who, being attached to only one heroine, whilst exhibiting ostensibly an affection for two heroines, acts, underhand, unkindly towards the other heroine, is the 'sly' hero: as *is the hero of the following verses.*

"O sly one! where then shall I tell this, that, even whilst embracing, thou didst hastily relax the knot of thy arms on hearing the tinkle of the zone-gems of this other *wife of thine approaching? I need not tell it to* HER—*for*—my fair friend, giddy from the poison of thy many buttered and honeyed speeches, heeds me not at all."

TEXT.

Subdivision of heroes into 'best,' 'middling,' and 'lowest.'

No. 75. And the aforesaid divisions of heroes, through their being all threefold in respect of their being of the 'best,' the 'middling' or the 'lowest' description, are *further subdivided into* forty-eight.

COMMENTARY.

a. "All"—i. e. the aforesaid sixteen divisions—*see* § 70.

The various assistants of the hero.

b. Now he speaks of the assistants of these *heroes*, since this *topic* is connected *with the foregoing, so that this is its proper place.*

TEXT.

The comrade of the hero.

No. 76. But let that one be called his 'comrade' who, somewhat deficient in the qualifications of him —*i. e. of the hero,*—is his assistant in some wide-extending collateral business.

COMMENTARY.

a. That is to say—he is called 'comrade' *(píṭhamardda)*, who, coming somewhat short of the just mentioned generic qualities of the hero—*see* § 64,—is the assistant of him—i. e. of the hero—throughout the extensive transactions collaterally connected *with the main business that the latter is engaged in* :—as were Sugríva, *the monkey king of Kishkindhyá*, &c., *comrades* of Rámachandra, &c.

b. Now the assistants *of the hero—not in extensive and diversified transactions—see* § 76. *a.—but* in *affairs of* love, *are to be described.*

TEXT.

The hero's assistants in matters of love.

No. 77. Let the assistants in *affairs of* love be the 'humble friend' *(viṭa)*, the 'dependant' *(cheṭa)*, the 'buffoon' *(vidúshaka)*, &c.,—*and let these be* faithful, skilful in jests, removers of the pride of angry dames, pure.

COMMENTARY.

a. By the "&c." *are meant* makers of garlands, washermen, purveyors of the betel-nut, perfumers, &c.

b. Among these *described generically in* § 77—*he proceeds to describe specifically* the 'humble friend.'

TEXT.

The 'humble friend.' No. 78. But the 'humble friend' is one whose possessions fall short of *what would furnish the means of* enjoyment:—he is subtle, acquainted with some portion of the arts, ingenious in dress and address, eloquent, pleasing, much esteemed in company.

COMMENTARY.

a. What a 'dependant,' *or servant—see* § 77—is, is perfectly well known—*and therefore any account of him need not be given.*

TEXT.

The 'buffoon.' No. 79. Let the 'buffoon' be one with a *whimsical* name such as "Flower-spring," a causer of laughter by his actions, his person, and his speeches, &c., delighting in squabbles,—acquainted with his own business.

COMMENTARY.

a. "His own business"—i. e. eating, &c.

b. He next mentions the assistants *of the hero* in taking thought about affairs *of state.*

TEXT.

The assistants in affairs of state. No. 80. Let the 'minister' be *the assistant of the hero* in the taking thought about affairs *of state.*

COMMENTARY.

a. "Affairs *of state*" —i. e. —politics, diplomacy,* &c.

b. But as for what is set down by some one, as a definition, when the topic is the describing of 'assistants'—viz., "The minister, or *the king* himself, or both of them, are the agents in taking thought about affairs of state;"—this *I say* ought to have been reserved for a definition *in some work on Politics* where the topic was *expressly* the definition of a king's MEANS of taking thought about his state affairs, but not when the matter in question was the description of 'ASSISTANTS' *—meaning thereby persons so named and considered only in so far as they do for the hero what he is thereby released from the necessity of doing for himself unless he chooses. And the definition censured is chargeable*

* See the commentary on verse 89th of the 2d Canto of Mágha's poem the *S'is'upála-vadha* —[Röer erroneously incorporates this into the preceding text. P. M.]

with the irrelevancy animadverted upon—for if it were only said "The minister is the assistant of the hero in his—*i. e.* ***the hero's***—taking thought about state affairs," it would be inferred from the sense *of the sentence*, that the hero is *one of the agents in taking thought about state affairs.*—And as for *what* is said *by some one, in reference to the same topic of 'assistants'*—viz. "The thoughtless *king*—§ 68—has his kingly functions subordinated to his ministers; the others (§ 66, 67, *and* 69) have theirs in the charge of their ministers and themselves *jointly*;"—this also is a point the mention of which is mistimed, because, by the mere mention of his characteristic ***thoughtlessness***, it was settled that the "thoughtless hero" is one the taking thought about whose state affairs is entirely in the charge of his minister. And, in the taking thought about state affairs, his minister is not his ASSISTANT—*and the present topic, be it remembered*—§ 80—***is that of "assistants"***—but is himself the sole manager,—for he, ***the thoughtless hero***, takes no thought about affairs of state ***and cannot therefore have an assistant in doing it.***

The assistants belonging to the inner apartments.

c. Now the assistants belonging to the inner apartments *are described.*

TEXT.

No. 81. In like manner, in the harem,* *the following are assistants —viz.*—dwarfs, eunuchs, mountaineers *retained as guards*, barbarians, cow-herds, left-hand brothers-in-law, hump-backs, &c. Possessed of pride, folly, and vanity, one of low family, raised, *by the connection*, to power, the brother of an unmarried *concubine* and, *in so far*, brother-in-law of a king, is called a left-hand brother-in-law.

COMMENTARY.

a. By the "&c." are meant mutes and others.

b. Among these *enumerated in* § 81, the eunuchs, dwarfs, mountaineers, hump-backs, &c. *are to be found spoken of in such passages as the following one which occurs* in the *play called Ratnávali.*†

"The eunuchs—*alarmed at the approach of the monkey of the stable which had broken its chain* fled, having abandoned shame because of their not being reckoned among men; the dwarf, in terror,

* Röer wrongly reads this clause in the preceding commentary. P. M.

† Translated by Professor Wilson in his Specimens of the Theatre of the Hindus.

ensconces himself within the *loose and wide* trowsers of the chamberlain; the mountaineers, the guardians of the bounds, acted in a style accordant with their name *derived from kri 'to do'—i. e. they did valiantly, not running away from the monkey**—; while the humpbacks fearing that they may be seen *by the monkey*, cowering down, slink quietly off."

c. The "left-hand brother-in-law" *such as the cruel coxcomb Samsthánaka* in such *plays* as the *Mrichchhakatí*,† *or the "Toycart"* is well known. The others too *of the assistants not here exemplified in quotations* may be recognised as they present themselves.

d. Now the assistants in punishing, *or in the administration of criminal justice—are to be described.*

TEXT.

The assistants in matters of police.

No. 82. In regard to punishments, *the assistants of the king are* his friends, the princes *his sons*, foresters *employed as police*, lords lieutenant, soldiers, &c.

COMMENTARY.

a. "Punishment" means the chastisement of evil-doers;—*all this is* plain.—Now of the assistants in religious duties.

TEXT.

The assistants in things sacred.

No. 83. In his religious duties let these *i. e. his assistants* be chaplains and domestic priests, and so too ascetics, knowers of *Brahma*.

COMMENTARY.

a. "Knowers of *Brahma*"—i. e. knowers of the Veda, or knowers of the *divine* soul.

b. Amongst these *various classes of assistants there is not an equality in point of rank—for—*

TEXT.

Respective rank of the classes of assistants.

No. 84. The highest *in rank, among the various classes of assistants*, are 'comrades' (§ 76,) &c.

* Such is one explanation of the pun. Professor Wilson suggests another—"*Kiráta*, a mountaineer, being derived from the roots *krí* to scatter and *ata* to go, that is, they scattered or ran away." This is more in keeping with the conduct of the others—but the humour would perhaps be heightened by its lying on the ironical tribute to the valour of the guards who alone were not afraid—of a *monkey*. [*But the etymology upon which this explanation is founded is not admitted by the Grammarians.* P. M.]

† Specimens of the Theatre of the Hindus.

COMMENTARY.

a. By the "&c." are meant ministers (§ 80), priests (§ 83), &c.

TEXT.

No. 85. In the middle rank *among assistants* are the humble friend (§ 78) and the buffoon (§ 79) :—in like manner the left-hand brother-in-law (§ 81 *b.*) domestics, &c., are called the lowest in rank.

COMMENTARY.

a. By the "&c." are meant purveyors of betel-nut, perfumers, &c., (§ 77. *a.*)

b. Now, since this is the appropriate place for it, he gives, in respect of MESSENGERS, a definition which includes their division.

TEXT.

Messengers defined and divided.

No. 86. A messenger—some one sent on some affair—is of three kinds—(1) the discreet, (2) the cautious, and (3) the *mere* conveyer of a message; and *female* messengers also are of the like descriptions.

COMMENTARY.

a. In this passage—§ 86—the definition—*apart from the division which it involves—see* § 85. *b.*—is, *or consists of the words* "A messenger—some one sent on some affair."

TEXT.

No. 87. But the one called the 'discreet' *messenger*—§ 86—is he who, having formed his judgment as to the mind of both, speaks according to his own discretion, and executes his commission well and neatly.

COMMENTARY.

a. "Of both"—i. e. the one by whom he was sent, and the one to whom he was sent.

TEXT.

No. 88. The 'cautious' *messenger*—§ 86—is one of measured speech, who executes his commission *and no more.* The *mere* 'conveyer of a message' (§ 86) is he who conveys, *without perhaps understanding*, the message as it was spoken to him.

COMMENTARY.

a. Now the amiable qualities of a hero *are to be described.*

TEXT.

The eight amiable qualities of a hero.

No. 89. Brilliancy, vivacity, sweetness *of temper*, depth *of character*, steadfastness, keen sense of honour, gallantry, and magnanimity,—such are the eight manly qualities that originate in *the element** *of* goodness.

COMMENTARY.

a. Among these *eight amiable qualities, the first is defined as follows.*

TEXT.

Brilliancy in the character of a hero—what.

No. 90. They call that *quality*—§ 89—'brilliancy' *(s'obhá)*, from which—*as being the constituents of it*—there come herosim, dexterity, veracity, great perseverance, complaisance, tenderness towards inferiors, and the holding one's own with the great.

COMMENTARY.

Complaisance.

a. Among these—there is 'complaisance,' as *exemplified in the following passage.*

"Every one of his subjects thought *to himself* 'I myself am esteemed by this lord of the earth.' Disrespect was shown by him in no quarter, as *none is shown* by the ocean to a hundred streams—*every one of which alike it receives into its bosom.*"

b. And so *examples might be given, were it necessary,* in regard to the others *of the list in* § 90.

c. Now 'vivacity'—§ 89—*is described.*

TEXT.

Vivacity.

No. 91. In 'vivacity' there is a steady glance, a striking gait, and laughing voice.

COMMENTARY.

a. Of this we may have an example such as the following.

"His glance values at a straw the strength of the creatures of the three worlds;—his firm and haughty tread appears to bend the earth. What! Is this the spirit of Heroism *incarnate* even in a *mere* youth, yet having such weight as a mountain might have,—or is it Pride *personified?*"

* See Lecture on the Sánkhya—§ 50.

TEXT.

Placidity. No. 92. The not being discomposed even amid agitations, is what is called 'sweetness' *of temper*—§ 89.

COMMENTARY.

a. An example may be inferred *by the reader for himself.*

TEXT.

Equanimity. No. 93. The not being altered by fear, grief, anger, joy, &c., is *what we mean by* 'depth' *of character*—§ 89.

COMMENTARY.

a. Of this we may have such an example as *the following testimony to the equanimity of the hero Ráma.*

"Not the slightest discomposure in his aspect was observed by me—either when he was summoned to his inauguration or when he was banished to the forest."

TEXT.

Steadfastness. No. 94. The not departing from one's intent, even where the obstructions are great, is *what is meant—see* § 89—by 'steadfastness.'

COMMENTARY.

a. As—

"Even at the moment when he heard the song of the Sirens, S'iva continued intent upon his meditations;—for, of those who are masters of their own souls, no obstructions whatever have force enough to divert the attention."

TEXT.

Sensitiveness, Gallantry, and Magnanimity. No. 95. The not enduring, even at the expense of life, *in the recalcitration against it,*—of any imputation or disrespect, &c., cast upon one by another, is what is called a 'keen sense of honour'—§ 89.— 'Gallantry' (§ 89) implies elegance in language and dress, and likewise in amatory demeanour. 'Magnanimity' (§ 89) implies liberality, affability of address, and equality *of behaviour* towards friend and foe.

COMMENTARY.

a. Of these also, examples may be inferred *by the reader for himself.*

TEXT.

The Heroine defined, and divided into 'one's own,' 'another's,' and 'anybody's.'

No. 96. But now, the Heroine is of three kinds —(1) one's own, (2) another's *wife or daughter*, or (3) a common woman. She is a woman possessed of the generic qualities of the hero so far as this is possible.

COMMENTARY.

a. The heroine again is possessed of the generic qualities of the hero, liberality and the like—§ 64—, so far as these are compatible—"*mutatis mutandis*"—*considering the difference of sex.* And she is of three sorts—*inasmuch as she may be* one's own wife, or a female belonging to another, or a common woman, *i. e. a courtesan.*

b. Among these *three kinds of heroines*—§ 96—, 'one's own' wife *is the one defined as follows.*

TEXT.

No. 97. 'One's own'—§ 96—is she who is possessed of modesty, sincerity, &c., who is intent on the affairs of the house, and faithful to her husband.

COMMENTARY.

a. As—

"In the house of the fortunate are wives whose best ornament is modesty, who never long for *those who are* husbands of other *women*, who know not to behave improperly.

TEXT.

The Heroine—'one's own'—subdivided.

No. 98. She too—*i. e.* '*one's own*' (*see* § 97) is named of three sorts, (1) the youthful, (2) the adolescent, and (3) the mature.

COMMENTARY.

a. Among these—

TEXT.

The Youthful heroine.

No. 99. She is called the 'youthful'—*or* '*artless*' (§ 98)—who, on the arrival of *the period of* youth,—being altered by love *then first felt*, shrinks from caresses, is gentle amid her indignation, and extremely bashful.

COMMENTARY.

Youthfulness exemplified.

a. Among these *various characteristics we may exemplify each severally—and first then of the* '*youthful*' *damsel in respect of her being* 'at the first arrival of the period of youth'—as *in the following verses* of my father.

"The loins now take to themselves the bulkiness *which previously was the characteristic* of the waist; the belly takes possession of the depression *which previously was the characteristic* of the breasts; the line of hair on the body, *characteristic of the period,* runs after the straightness of the glances *which then fall into a sidelong habit.* Seeing Cupid newly inaugurated in the empire of her mind, the members of the fair-browed one, for the moment, as it were, mutually plunder one another, *as people are wont to do at the commencement of a new reign before the king can ascertain what properly belongs to each.*"

The first sensations of love.

b. Now of the '*youthful*' *damsel in respect of her being* 'altered by love then first taking possession *of her mind*'—as *in the following verses which occur* in my Prabhávatí-pariṇaya *or* "*Marriage of Prabhávatí.*"

"Lazily and languidly she sets her footsteps on the ground; she never goes out of the inner apartments; she no longer laughs unconstrainedly, but practises every moment some bashful restraint or other. Little she speaks, and that little always somewhat touched, *or tinged,* by a certain sort of deep covert significance; and she looks up with a frown at her female friend who entertains her with a discourse about her sweetheart."

Maiden Coyness exemplified.

c. Now of the '*youthful*' *damsel in respect of her being one* 'who shrinks from caresses'—as—

"When looked at, she casts down her eyes; she speaks not when spoken to; she stands turning away from the couch; when clasped perforce, she trembles; when her female friends *who have conducted her to the bridegroom's house* are about to retire, she too wishes to depart from the dwelling. By this very coyness my beloved bride has become now more than ever dear to me."

Gentleness.

d. Now of the '*youthful*' *damsel in respect of her being* 'gentle amid her indignation'—as—

"On the occasion of her husband's first offence, she does not know—in the absence of a female friend's advice—though every limb is trembling with agitation—how to convey a sarcasm. With her rolling lotus eyes the girl just merely weeps—with the pure tears dropping from the lower part of her pure cheek, while her ringlets dangle shaking among them."

Bashfulness. *e. Then the* '*youthful*' *damsel, in respect of her being* 'extremely bashful'—*may be exemplified*—as in the verses *already given under* § 99. *b.* viz., "Lazily and languidly she sets," &c.

f. Here—*i. e. in the enumeration of the characteristics of the* '*youthful*' *heroine*—§ 99,—the separate mention of the 'shrinking from caresses,' which *characteristic* is included also under the head of 'extreme bashfulness'—*so that the definition might seem chargeable with tautology*,—is made because this is a remarkable species *of the forms which bashfulness assumes.*

g. Now the 'adolescent' *heroine—literally the one* '*middlemost*' *between the* '*artless*' *young wife or maiden and the dame mature and* '*bold*'—§ 98—*is described.*

Text.

The Adolescent heroine. No. 100. By the 'adolescent' is meant one wonderful in caressings; who has become more impassioned while waxing in youth; somewhat bold in speech, and with a midding amount of modesty.

Commentary.

a. Among these '*various characteristics we may exemplify each severally,—and first then of the* '*adolescent*' *dame in respect of her being* 'wonderful in caressings'—as—

"Towards her lover, by the fawn-eyed one, when her fondness was excited, there was somehow shown such ingenuity in caresses, that several times the hundreds of pigeons belonging to the house set themselves as scholars to imitate her cooings."

b. The '*adolescent*' *dame in respect of her being* one 'become more impassioned,' is as *exhibited* in this same example *just given* —§ 100. *a.*

c. Now the '*adolescent*' *dame* 'that has waxed in youth'—is as *described in these verses* of mine.

"Her two eyes, *in vivacity of movement,* shame the wagtail; her two hands rival the lake-born *lotus;* her breasts attain a height that causes a doubt whether they be not the *gracefully swelling* temples of the elephant; her brilliancy is like that of gold or of the Michelia Champaka; her voice rivals nectar; the flash of her side glance is like a wreath of expanded nymphaeæ cæruleæ."

d. And so in respect of the others also—*of the characteristics enumerated in* § 100—*exemplifications might be given were it needful.*

e. Now the dame 'mature'—

TEXT.

The Mature heroine.

No. 101. Infatuated with love; of robust *and no longer tender* youth; learned in all kinds of caresses; lofty of demeanour; with no great amount of modesty, and ruling her lover.

COMMENTARY.

a. Now the 'mature' dame in respect of her being 'infatuated with love'—as—

"*Bravo!—or, literally,* fortunate art thou, who, when meeting with thy beloved, utterest, in the midst of caresses, hundreds of confiding and endearing phrases:—but—*as for me*—my friend,—when my lover puts his hand to the knot that binds my robe,—I'll swear if I recollect anything whatever."

b. Now the 'mature' dame, in respect of her being 'of robust *and no longer of tenderly budding but of full-blown* youth'—as—

"Her bosom hath very lofty breasts; her eyes are very long; curved are her eye-brows, and still more *curved or indirect* than these is her speech; her waist is very slender; not a little massive are her hips; and somewhat slow is the gait of this one whose youth is wondrous *in its full-blown gorgeousness.*"

c. Now the 'mature' dame, in respect of her being 'learned in all kinds of caresses'—as—

"This sheet—in one place marked with the *juice of the chewed* betel, stained in another place with the marks of the unguent made of fragrant wood, in another place giving out the lime *which is chewed along with the betel,* and in another place *trampled* by a foot *reddened* with lac-dye,—with its crumplings, its rents, and its disorder, together with the withered flowers fallen from her hair, tells of the woman's having been dallying in every fashion."

d. Now the 'mature' dame, in respect of her being 'lofty of demeanour'—as—

" By sweet discourse—yet mingled with frowns ;—by admonitory shakings of the finger; and by languidly moving bodily gestures, whose kindred, *as being closely related thereto—in the order of cause and effect*—are great passions *excited in the beholder of her blandishments*, many a time and oft does she, with her great staring side-glances, assist the possessor of the five arrows—*the god of love*—in the subjugation of the three worlds."

e. The 'mature' dame, in respect of her being one 'with very little modesty,' is as *exemplified* in *the verses under* § 101. *a.*, " Bravo! thou that utterest," &c.

f. Now the 'mature' dame, in respect of her being one 'ruling her lover'—as—

" 'Lord of mine, curl my ringlets ;—my dear, give my forehead its sectarial mark again ;—my soul's lord, do unite again my necklace which is broken on the border of my bosom :'—thus speaking, at the time of desisting from caresses, she, whose face is like the full moon, quivering when touched by him, sunk again in the ecstasy of love."

g. He now mentions other divisions of the heroines 'adolescent' and 'mature.'

TEXT.

Subdivision of heroines according as they can or cannot keep their temper.

No. 102. These two are (1) possessed of self-command, or (2) not possessed of self-command, or (3) partly possessing and partly not possessing self-command ;—hence of six sorts.

COMMENTARY.

a. "These two"—i. e. the 'adolescent' (§ 100) and the 'mature' (101).

b. Among these *are those described as follows.*

TEXT.

No. 103. *When moved* by anger, the 'adolescent' *heroine*, if possessed of self-command' (§ 102,) will burn her lover with derisive sarcasms ; if 'partly possessing and partly not possessing self-command,' *she will burn him* with her tears ; and if 'not possessed of self-command,' *she will assail him* with harsh speeches.

Commentary.

a. Among these *three varieties of angry dames—we may have* the 'adolescent' who is 'possessed of self-command'—as—

"In saying 'Thou art my beloved' thou sayest truly,—since thou hast come to my bower dressed in the gown belonging to thy sweetheart;—for, by being beheld by the loved one, the beauty of a lover's ornaments attains its end—*and thou hast come dressed, forgetfully, in the garments of my rival.*"

b. Now the 'adolescent' who partly 'possesses and partly does not possess self-command'—as—

"'My girl!'—'My lord?'—'Lay aside thine anger, indignant one.' —'What has my anger done?'—'It has vexed me.'—'Your honour never offends ME,—all the offences are on MY side.' 'Then why dost thou weep with sobbing voice?'—'Before whom am I weeping?' 'Why—is it not before ME?'—'What am I to thee?' 'My cherished one.'—'I am NOT, and therefore do I weep.'

c. Now this same one—*the 'adolescent'*—when 'not possessed of self-command'—as—

"O wretch! That loved one, with hundreds of desires, stands alone in thy mind—though attractive only through her artificial blandishments;—and there is no room for me,—therefore enough of the farce of *thy* falling at *my* feet *when thou lovest not me with thy heart.*"

Text.

No. 104. The 'mature' dame, *when indignant*, if she be 'possessed of self-command,' then, concealing the appearance of anger, takes no concern about fondnesses, whilst ostensibly showing all respect towards him.

Commentary.

a. 'Towards him'—i. e. towards her lover:—for example—

"She balked his sitting down beside her by advancing to meet him; and even a hasty embrace was prevented by the pretence of fetching the betel-nut *to present to him*, while he was yet at some distance; and no conversation with him was entered into by her, keeping her people employed near her:—thus, indirectly, did the sharp-witted dame cause her anger against her lover to attain its object."

TEXT.

No. 105. But she, '*the mature*' *dame*, who 'partly possesses and partly does not possess self-command,' will, *when indignant*, vex him with ironical speeches.

COMMENTARY.

a. "Him"--i. e the hero:—as *in the following verses* of mine—

"Since, even when unadorned, O beauteous youth, thou dost forcibly carry off my heart,--how much more now--adorned as thou art with the scratches of the nails of her, *my rival!*"

TEXT.

No. 106. The other will scold and beat him.

COMMENTARY.

a. "The other"—i. e. the '*mature*' *dame* 'NOT possessed of self-command'—as *the dame spoken of in the verses under* § 72. *a. viz.*, "Perceiving her countenance crimson with passion," &c.

b. And in all these *descriptions of behaviour*, (*from* § 103 to § 106 *inclusive*,) the expression '*when moved* by anger' is supplied *from* § 103.

TEXT.

Subdivision of heroines according to the rank they respectively hold in the affections of the Hero.

No. 107. These, moreover, are severally two-fold, through their being in the shape of the lower or the higher in the affections of the hero.

COMMENTARY.

a. "These"—i. e. the six kinds of heroines mentioned close by—*see* § 102:—as—

"Seeing his two dearest ones seated together on one seat, having approached behind, having politely closed the eyes of one, he made a pretence of engaging in play with her. *At the same time* gently turning his neck, quivering with pleasure, the wretch kisses the other one, the page of whose cheek shone with inward laughter, while her heart bounded with delight."

TEXT.

The heroine 'who is another's' divided.

No. 108. Hence—*see* § 107—twelve varieties of the 'adolescent' and 'mature' *heroines, together*, are spoken of; but the 'youthful' *heroine*—§ 99—is of but one kind—*so far as we have yet gone;* therefore let the divisions of 'one's own' —*see* § 97—be thirteen. The one 'belonging to another'—*the second in the list of heroines in* § 96—is spoken of as of two kinds—(1) 'another's wife,' and (2) a 'maiden.'

COMMENTARY.

a. Among these—

TEXT.

No. 109. *The heroine who is* 'another's wife' is one addicted to wandering, &c., who brings dishonour on her family, and whose modesty is lost.

COMMENTARY.

a. As—

"My husband, if I even breathe, calumniates me; my fellow-wives are ever smelling my mind, *or guessing at my thoughts*; my mother-in-law is the very goddess of gestures, *and exercises her sagacity in misinterpreting every gesture of mine*; my sisters-in-law lick the purposes of my two eyes, *finding, no doubt, a flavour of mischief in every glance.* Therefore, from a distance, do I, *in entreaty*, join my hands to thee—forbear from casting love-glances upon me NOW—O thou sweet of wit and voluptuous in dalliance, this labour of thine is vain at such a place as THIS."

b. For in this *passage*, that her affections find their object in a hero other *than her husband*, is understood through the force of the meaning SUGGESTED—*see* § 23—viz, "my husband, inasmuch as he gives me food and raiment, is my lord but not my love; but thou, being 'sweet of wit and voluptuous in dalliance,' art my beloved," &c.

TEXT.

No. 110. But the 'maiden' (§ 109) is one whose marriage has not taken place,—bashful, newly arrived at *the period of* youth.

COMMENTARY.

Why the maiden heroine is ranged with those that are 'another's.'

a. And her being reckoned as 'belonging to another,' is because of her being dependent on her father or some one else—as, for example, Málatí, in *the play of* Málatí and Mádhava*—and the like.

* Translated in Wilson's "Specimens of the Theatre of the Hindus."

TEXT.

Definition of the heroine who is 'anybody's.'

No. 111. Let the 'common' heroine (§ 96,) be a courtesan, possessed of self-command (*see* § 102)—skilled in arts (*see* § 68. *a.*)—She hates not the worthless, nor does she love the good. Only with an eye to gain will she exhibit fondness:—she will make her mother turn out of doors, even though he may be agreeably acceptable to her, the man whose money is expended,—with the wish that they may meet again *when he is better provided.* In general, the paramours of these women are thieves, persons diseased through excess, fools, and those who have come by money lightly,—pretended devotees, secret libertines, and the like. In some cases, however, when love obtains the mastery, she becomes honestly enamoured. Whether she be attached, or devoid of attachment, the possession of her is hard to obtain.

COMMENTARY.

a. A "person diseased through excess" is one with the gout or a disease from debauchery and the like. "Secret libertines" are those who pursue their pleasures clandestinely.

b. Among these '*common*' *women*, the one 'devoid of attachment' is such a one as Madanamanjarí in the *play called the* Naṭaka-melaka.

c. A '*common*' *woman—honestly* 'enamoured' is one such as Vasantasená in the Mrichchhakaṭiká* *or the* "*Toy-cart.*"

d. And again—

TEXT.

The sixteen kinds of heroines now obtained, further subdivided according to an eightfold diversity in their 'condition.'

No. 112. These *heroines* that have been separated into sixteen divisions—*viz. the sets of thirteen and two in* § 108, *and the one in* § 111—become *severally* eight, *thus giving one hundred and twenty-eight kinds,* through their CONDITIONS—*for each one may be* (1) 'one who has an obsequious lover;' and, in like manner, (2) who is 'ill-treated,' or (3) 'who goes after *her lover*,' or (4) 'who is separated by quarrel,' or (5) who is 'neglected,' or (6) 'whose husband is abroad,' or (7) who is 'prepared in her house,' or (8) who is 'longing in absence' *of a lover not intentionally neglectful.*

* Translated in Wilson's "Specimens of the Theatre of the Hindus."

COMMENTARY.

a. Among these—

TEXT.

The heroine sincerely loved.

No. 113. Whose lover, attracted by her amiable qualities, leaves not her side; who has surprising charms, and is fondly attached,—let such a one be the one 'who has an obsequious lover.'

COMMENTARY.

a. As is *exemplified in the verses under* § 73. *a.*—" My garments, O friend," &c.

TEXT.

The heroine sinned against.

No. 114. Whose lover goes near her bearing the marks of his having been toying with another,—this one, red with jealousy, is called, by the learned, the 'ill-treated' one.

COMMENTARY.

a. As *is the lady in the verses under* § 103. *a.*—" Thou hast said truly," &c.

TEXT.

The heroine making advances.

No. 115. She who, acknowledging the power of Love, sends to seek her lover, or goes herself to seek him,—this one is called, by the learned, the one 'who goes after *her lover.*'

COMMENTARY.

a. *These two cases are here exemplified* in their order—as—

" 'Having understood his feelings thoroughly, speak to him in such a manner that he may not discern my levity *in sending to lure him back after having capriciously repelled him*, and that he may act tenderly towards me:'—thus did a certain one instruct her female messenger."*

" 'I have laid aside this my pair of bracelets; I have fastened my girdle tight; with much pains I have produced dumbness in my chattering anklets;—and, O my dear friend, just when I had begun to be eagerly impatient to set out on Love's errand, this wretch of a Moon throws aside the protecting mantle of the dark!' "

TEXT.

How heroines of different descriptions go out on assignations.

No. 116. If one of good family goes in search *of her lover*, she goes crouching—*literally—melted or absorbed into her own limbs—making herself as*

* *Mágha*—Canto, ix. v. 56.

small as possible,—with all her *tinkling* ornaments silenced, and veiled in her wrappers. But a courtesan, if she goes in search *of her lover,* will have a dress of wondrous splendour, her anklets tinkling as they move, and a face all smiles of joy. A female servant, if she goes in search *of her lover,* while she gets along with great strides, will have her speech stammering through delight and her eyes staring wide open in her flurry.

COMMENTARY.

a. In the case of the first of these *we have an example in such verses as those under* § 115. *a.—viz.* "I have laid aside," &c.

b. Among these the 'female servant that goes in search' *of her lover, is one such as the damsel described in the verses following*—viz.

"Here the servant girl, repeatedly exhibiting her betel-stained teeth, laughing without a reason and with an affected tone of voice resembling the neigh of a mare, flauntingly setting her staggering footsteps here, there, and everywhere, with her hips dancing high, stays wriggling about in front of the young men."*

c. Examples of the others are to be inferred *by the reader for himself.*

d. As being connected with this topic, the PLACES of going on an assignation are next mentioned.

TEXT.

Localities adapted for assignations. No. 117. A field, a garden, a ruined temple, the house of a female messenger, a grove, a caravansera, and a cemetery,—so too the bank of a river, &c.—thus there are eight places for the satisfaction of those who, following after men, set out on an assignation;—and moreover there is a resource anywhere in places screened by darkness.

The heroine repenting her own caprice. But she who, in anger, having repulsed her soul's lord even when wooing, afterwards experiences remorse, is *the heroine called* the one 'separated by quarrel.'

COMMENTARY.

a. As *in these verses* of my father's,

"I did not listen to his fond speeches, nor was the necklace *which he presented* near me regarded by my sight; the admonitions too of

* The portion marked *b* is evidently an interpolation, being incompatible with the dual number in अन्ययोः (others) in § *c.* My MS. has it not. P. M.

my female friend, to the effect that I should show kindness to my lover, were rejected. When he fell at my feet, alas, at that moment why was not he, when departing, retained by me—fool that I am—with my two arms, and clasped eagerly to my neck?"

TEXT.

The heroine outraged by neglect.

No. 118. But she—most disrespectfully treated—to whom her lover does not come, after having made an assignation, is to be known as 'the neglected.'

COMMENTARY.

a. As—

"Arise, my messenger—let us go. A watch *of three hours* has gone, and he is not come. He has gone elsewhere;—long life to him—may he be the life's lord of her *to whom I resign him.*"*

TEXT.

The heroine pining in absence.

No. 119. Let her, whose lord, by constraint of various affairs, has gone to a far country, afflicted by the pains of affection, be the one 'whose husband is abroad.'

COMMENTARY.

a. As—

"You may recognise her, of measured discourse, my second life, in the absence of me her companion, like a solitary duck.† I can fancy the girl, grievously pining whilst these heavy days go by, altered in appearance like a lotus pinched by the cold."‡

TEXT.

The heroine expectant.

No. 120. But let her who is arranging herself—being all ready in her house, expecting the arrival of her lover—be the one 'prepared in her house.'

COMMENTARY.

a. As in *the following passage which occurs in* a drama of Rághavánanda—

* The translation of this portion, though not altogether incompatible with the *reading* of the text, is so with the *writing* adopted in Röer's edition as also in my own MS. According to this the following is the correct rendering: Let him be the life's lord of HER who should LIVE after this *sad disappointment* (—i. e. neither shall I survive nor will he be my life's lord.) P. M.

† The *chakraváka*, or Brahmany duck, is supposed to lie under the necessity that the male and female shall pass the night on opposite banks of the river.

‡ See the "Cloud-messenger"—Stanza 82.

"Remove my armlets ;—enough—*nay too much*—with these strings of jewels on my two wrists ;—what need of this necklace ?—it weighs on my neck like *the heavy and clinging branches of* a creeper !—O do thou put upon me *nothing besides* one single new pearl-necklace. Unsuitable is a superfluity of *bodily* DECORATIONS when one is concerned with the festival of him—*viz. the god of love*—who has not *even*—a BODY—*his body having been reduced to ashes by the fiery glance of S'iva when the god of love rashly shot him.*"*

TEXT.

The heroine disappointed through misadventure.

No. 121. But she whose lover, though he intended to come, through accident did not come,—she, afflicted with the grief of his not coming, is the one 'longing in absence' *of a lover not intentionally neglectful.*

COMMENTARY.

a. As—

"'What—has he been stopped by some *other* mistress ?—or has he been vexed at my female friend—*who carried my message and may not have delivered it properly*—?—or has there been some matter of moment, that my lover has not come to-day ?' Thus reflecting, the fawn-eyed one, leaning her lotus-face upon her hand, sighed deeply —and long she wept, and the garlands of flowers she flung away from her."

TEXT.

The hundred and twenty-eight kinds of heroines subdivided into three-hundred & eighty-four.

No. 122. Let the one hundred and twenty-eight *kinds of heroines*—*see* § 112—inasmuch as they may be of the first-rate, the medium, or the lowest, description, be eighty and four added to three hundred.

COMMENTARY.

a. And on this point—*viz. the subdivision of all heroines alike according to the eight 'conditions' specified under* § 112, some one says—"Those two *kinds of* women who 'belong to another'—*see* § 108—, viz. the maiden and the married woman *whose affections are set elsewhere than on her husband*, are not subdivisible according to all those 'conditions'—but only according to some of them :—*for example*, before an assignation *has been made with them by any lover*, they may, *no doubt*, be 'longing in absence'—*see* § 121. Then again after *an*

* See the *Kumára-sambhava*, 3d Canto, stanza 72.

assignation has been fixed, setting forth, along with the buffoon (§ 79) or some one else, they may become 'goers after' *see* § 115 ;—and if, for some reason, the hero have not come to the appointed place, they may be 'neglected'—*see* § 118 ;—such alone *out of the eight* are the three 'conditions' applicable to these two, because the other conditions —*such, for instance, as the being separated by quarrel*—§ 117—are incompatible with these two whilst they have no lover devoted to them."

TEXT.

Heroines of composite character.

No. 123. In some examples a mutual commingling of *the various characters of* these *various kinds of heroines—see* § 122—is seen.

COMMENTARY.

a. AS—

"'Not WE, indeed, are worthy of the gift of this *branch with its new shoots that you offer us, to be worn as an ornament behind in our ear.* Go, give this branch—*etymologically the cherisher of its* '*shoots*' —*viṭa*—to her who in secret drinks *the lips of,* and cherishes thee—*viṭa—or* '*rogue*'—*as thou art.* Let the two—*alike entitled to the name of viṭapa*—be joined, since the junction of like things has been long *the rule.* Wretch! what should WE do with thy needlessly deposited earfuls of the shoots and flowers of plants? Have not BOTH my ears been long filled full with your honour's unkind words—well-known to everybody?'—Thus speaking, the other dame struck her lover simultaneously with the dark lotus and with her eye—the lovely eyelashes of the one expanding wide like the filaments of the other—*and vice versâ,*—and each being confined by her ear*—*the ear being the boundary of her beautifully long eye—and the lotus with which she strikes him having been previously worn behind her ear as an ornament.*"

b. For this one—*the heroine of the foregoing verses,*— (1) by her sarcasms, (2) by her harsh language, and (3) by her striking him with the flower *which had served as the ornament* of her ear, is compounded of the character of (1) the 'adolescent heroine who possesses self-command' (*see* § 103,) (2) of the 'adolescent heroine who does not possess self-command' (*see* § 103,) and (3) of the 'mature heroine who does

* *Mágha,* Canto 7th, verses 53, 54, and 56.

not possess self-command' (*see* § 106). In like manner in other cases the reader can judge for himself *out of what elements the character of any given heroine is compounded.*

TEXT.

The further subdivision of heroines given up as endless.

No. 124. There are others also, *besides the three hundred and eighty-four mentioned in* § 122, *with the varieties suggested in* § 123, beyond number; but these are not specified for fear of prolixity.

COMMENTARY.

a. "These"—i. e. heroines.

b. Now the GRACES of these *heroines are to be described.*

TEXT.

The twenty-eight graces of the heroine.

No. 125. In youth these *heroines* have—*divided amongst them*—twenty-eight ornaments, *or graces,* arising from the quality of 'purity'—*sattwa*—the *source—see Tattwa-samása, p.* 25—*of all that is best and brightest in the phenomenal world.* Among these *twenty-eight,* three, viz. (1) 'the slight personal indication of natural emotion' (*bháva*), (2) 'its stronger expression' (*háva*), and (3) 'the decided manifestation of feeling' (*helá*), are produced by bodily movement;—(4) 'brilliancy' (*s'obhá*), and (5) 'loveliness' (*kánti*), and (6) 'radiancy' (*dípti*), and (7) 'sweetness' (*mádhurya*), (8) 'boldness' (*pragalbhatá*), (9) 'meekness' (*audárya*), (10) 'constancy' (*dhairya*),—let these be the seven (*from* 3 *to* 10) that arise *naturally* without effort;—eighteen in number are the following —viz. (11) 'fun' (*lílá*), (12) 'flutter of delight' (*vilása*), (13) 'simplicity in dress' (*vichchhitti*), (14) 'affectation of indifference' (*vivvoka*), (15) 'hysterical delight' (*kilakinchita*), (16) 'the mute involuntary expression of affection' (*moṭṭáyita*), (17) 'the affected repulse of a lover's endearments' (*kuṭṭamita*), (18) 'fluster' (*vibhrama*), (19) 'voluptuous gracefulness' (*lalita*), (20) 'arrogance' (*mada*), (21) 'the suppression of the sentiments of the heart through bashfulness' (*vikrita*), (22) 'pining' (*tapana*), (23) 'simplicity verging on silliness' (*maugdhya*), and (24) 'distractedness' (*vikshepa*), (25) 'impetuous curiosity' (*kutúhala*), (26) 'giggling' (*hasita*), (27) 'trepidation' (*chakita*), and (28) 'sportiveness' (*keli*).

And the *first* ten natural *graces*, beginning with 'the slight personal indication of natural emotion' *(bháva)*, belong to those of the male sex also.

COMMENTARY.

Some of these graces may belong to the male sex, but have not the interest that they have in the female.

a. The first ten, beginning with 'the slight per sonal indication of emotion' *(bháva)*, and ending with 'constancy' *(dhairya)*, may belong also to heroes, but all these produce a special admiration only when lodged in heroines,—*for—what reader cares about the hero's first tremours, &c., compared with those of the heroine?*

b. Of these *twenty-eight*, the 'slight personal indication of natural emotion' *(bháva)*, *is defined as follows.*

TEXT.

No. 126. 'Bháva' is the first alteration in a mind previously unaltered.

COMMENTARY.

The grace called *bháva*—what.

a. That is to say—'bháva' (§ 125) means a change, barely awaking, in a mind *previously tranquil and* unaltered from the time of birth forward,—as *is noted in the heroine of the following lines.*

"'Again there is the same spring time, and the same *aromatic* breeze from Malaya, and this is the very same maiden,—yet her mind is, as it were, altered.'"

b. Now of 'háva,' (§ 125)—

TEXT.

The grace called *háva*—what.

No. 127. But bháva (§ 126,) where the alteration is slightly modified—so as to show, by alterations of the eyebrows or eyes, &c., the desire for mutual enjoyment,—is called 'háva.'

COMMENTARY.

a. As *is exemplified in the following description of Párvatí, from the* Kumára Sambhava, *canto, III. v.* 68.

"With limbs like the young flowers of the Nauclea Kadamba *in which each filament stands on end*, the daughter of the mountain betraying the 'change' *in her heart now warmed with love for S'iva*, stood, with her lovely face turned aside, while her eyes glanced hither and thither."

b. Now of 'helá' (§ 125) :—

TEXT.

The grace called *helá*—what. No. 128. And let 'helá' mean the same when the change is perceived to be very great.

COMMENTARY.

a. "The same"—i. e, 'bháva'—*see* § 126. For example :—

"Such is the behaviour of the woman, agitated in every limb, that the mind of her female friends is in doubt whether she be any longer one of the 'artless' *heroines mentioned in* § 99, *and not promoted into the next class mentioned under* § 100."

Brilliancy. *b.* Now of 'brilliancy' *(s'obhá—*§ 125*)*.

TEXT.

No. 129. What is called 'Brilliancy' is that grace of limb which is derived from beauty, youth, high spirits, and high feeding.

COMMENTARY.

a. Of these *varieties* we may have the brilliancy due to YOUTH—as *in the following from the Kumára Sambhava, canto I. v.* 31.

"She now entered upon the age beyond that of childhood, *that period of adolescence* which is an ornament, of the straight person, not supplied *ab extra, as dresses and jewels require to be,* a cause of intoxication yet not having the name of wine, a weapon of Cupid other than the flowers *which serve as his arrows.*"

b. And so too in the case of the others—*derived from high spirits, &c.* Now of 'Loveliness' (*kánti*—§ 125).

TEXT.

Loveliness. No. 130. This same 'Brilliancy,' when increased by love *which adds greatly to the attractions of the woman loving,* becomes 'Loveliness.'

COMMENTARY.

a. That is to say—'brilliancy' (§ 129) when much increased by the arising of love, takes the name of 'loveliness :'—as *is exemplified in the verses under No.* 100—*beginning* "Her two eyes shame the wagtail," &c.

b. Now of 'Radiancy' *(dípti*—§ 125*)*.

TEXT.

Radiancy. No. 131. Loveliness, when expanded exceedingly, is called 'Radiancy.'

COMMENTARY.

a. As *is exhibited in* the description of Chandrakalá, in my play of the same name:—e. g.

"She is the ecstasy of youthfulness—the laugh of the abundance of excessive beauty,—the ornament of the face of the earth,—the subjugation of the minds of the young men."*

b. Now of 'Sweetness' (*mádhurya*—§ 125).

TEXT.

Sweetness. No. 132. 'Sweetness' is pleasingness in all kinds of states—*whether sick, naked, in exile, &c. &c.*

COMMENTARY.

a. For example—*take the following passage from the drama of S'akuntalá:*—

"The lotus is beautiful even when clogged with confervæ,—even the dark spots of the *gentle* Moon enhance her beauty. This slender maid, though clad in bark, is most charming,—for of gentle forms pray, what is NOT the ornament?"

b. Now of 'Boldness' (*pragalbhatá*—§ 125).

TEXT.

Boldness. No. 133. 'Boldness' is the being devoid of fear.

COMMENTARY.

a. For example:—

"These women make their lover their slave, by hugging when hugged, by kisses in return when kissed, and by bites when bitten."

b. Now of 'Meekness' (*audárya*—§ 125).

TEXT.

Meekness. No. 134. 'Meekness' is mildness at all times.

COMMENTARY.

a. "She utters no harsh word—though my offence is proved,—she makes no frown, she throws not on the ground, *in testy rage*, the ornament of her ear:—*but* towards the face of her female friend, contemplating her from without through the lattice, she only turns her two eyes suffused with tears."

b. Now of 'Constancy' (*dhairya*—§ 125).

* The preference of abstract to concrete terms, in this as in other comparatively recent specimens of composition, is noticeable.

TEXT.

Constancy. No. 135. By 'constancy' is here meant the state of mind called steadfastness, unattended with self-praise.

a. For example *take Málatí, Act ii., preferring death to marriage with any other then her beloved.*

"Let the full moon, *agonizing to separated lovers*, blaze in the sky; let Love scorch me,—what can he do beyond death? My father is beloved and honoured, my mother of unblemished descent, and so too my family;—But *I* am nothing,—I no longer exist,—*nor will I consent to exist if, honourably descended as I am, I am forced to wed with other than the man I love.*

b. Now of 'Fun' (*lílá*—§ 125).

TEXT.

Fun. No. 136. The mimicking of a lover in respect of the manners, dress, ornaments, and loving speeches, which his fondness had moved him to employ, they call 'Fun.'

COMMENTARY.

a. For example *we find Párvati reminded of her making fun of S'iva in the following invocation.*

"May Párvatí protect the world,—playfully mimicking S'iva,—having as a snake-bracelet the creeping root of a lotus *instead of the cobra da capello,* and having made the cluster of her locks into a wild top-knot *such as is cultivated by S'iva and other ascetics.*"

b. Next of the 'Flutter of delight' (*vilása*—§ 125).

TEXT.

Flutter of delight. No. 137. But let that peculiarity in movement, in the way of standing, or sitting, or in the action of the mouth or eyes, &c., which is caused by the sight, for instance, of the desired one, be called the 'Flutter of delight.'

COMMENTARY.

a. As an example *take Mádhava's account of Málatí's manner on recognizing him,—Act I. sc.* 2.

"Meanwhile there was manifested a certain triumphant specimen of Love's teaching, the wondrousness of which transcends the power of speech, raising an agitation in the long-eyed maid, and scattering to the winds my self-command,—so richly was this *specimen of Love's teaching* diversified with all that is exquisite."

b. Next of 'Simplicity in dress' (*vichchhitti*—§ 125).

TEXT.

Simplicity in dress.

No. 138. 'Simplicity in dress,' which adds to loveliness,* consists in the employment of little ornament.

COMMENTARY.

a. As an illustration *see the instructions in the following lines of Mágha, canto VIII. v.* 70.

"The body cleansed by ablution with pure water, the lip adorned by the lustre of the chewed betel, a thin white robe,—let thus much constitute the decoration of fluttering dames,—provided he be not fancy-free,—*in which case a more elaborate toilet may have to be put in requisition to produce an impression.*"

b. Next of the 'Affectation of indifference' (*vivvoka*—§ 125).

TEXT.

Affectation of indifference.

No. 139. But 'Affectation of indifference' is *the showing of* disrespect even towards a desired object, through exceeding haughtiness.

COMMENTARY.

a. For example:—

"Who, while they do find good qualities, make great allegations of fault,—who would rather yield their lives than look their lover full in the face,—whose very affirmation even in regard to what they exceedingly desire is negative,—may those women—of a nature strangely different from the three worlds—be auspicious to thee!"

b. Next of 'Hysterical delight' (*kilakinchita*—§ 125).

TEXT.

Hysterical delight.

No. 140. The commingling of smiles, and of weeping with unwet eyes, laughter, alarm, anger, fatigue, &c, from the delight produced, for instance, by meeting with the best beloved, is what we call 'Hysterical delight.'

COMMENTARY.

a. As an example *take the following from the poem of Mágha, canto X. v.* 69.

* The 'simplex munditiis' of classical quoters.

"Even in her joy, the taper-limbed girl repulsed her lover's hand—not wishing to repulse it,—chid him amid the sweetest smiles, and wept ravishingly without a tear."

b. Next of the 'Mute involuntary expression of affection' (*moṭṭáyita.*)

TEXT.

Mute involuntary expression of affection. No. 141. Her mind being taken up by the thought of him,—when her lover is, for instance, talked of,—her scratching her ear, or the like, they call a 'Mute involuntary expression of affection.'

a. As an example *take the gestures of the woman from which the speaker of the following lines infers her love for his friend.*

"O fortunate man! when they begin to speak about thee, that woman has an inclination to scratch her ear, a yawn comes to her lotus mouth, and she stretches all her limbs."

b. Next of the 'Affected repulse of a lover's endearments' (*kuṭṭamita*—§ 125).

TEXT.

Affected repulse of a lover's endearments. No. 142. When he takes her hair, her bosom, or her lip, &c.,—*the prohibition* "*Don't*"—*whether conveyed by the* shaking of the head or the hand,—through agitation, even when she is delighted, is what they call the 'Affected repulse of a lover's endearments.'

COMMENTARY.

a. For example *the prohibition may be expressed by the hand as in the following instance.*

"When her lover bit her cherry-lip, friend *to the hand*, being both equally comparable to the tender leaf,—an expression of *sympathetic* pain was as it were uttered by that limb of the girl as the bracelet rattled shrilly upon it."

b. Next of 'Fluster' (*vibhrama*—§ 125).

TEXT.

Fluster. No. 143. The application of ornaments, &c. to the wrong places, through hurry arising from delight or eagerness, on such occasions as the arrival of the beloved one, is what we mean by 'Fluster.'

COMMENTARY.

a. *For example:—*

"Having heard her beloved approaching outside, she—not having yet completed her toilet—applied to her forehead the black antimony *intended for her eyes*, to her eyes the lac-dye *intended for her lips*, and to her cheek the patch *which should have decorated the centre of the forehead.*"

b. Next of 'Voluptuous gracefulness,' (*lalita*—§ 125).

TEXT.

Voluptuous gracefulness. No. 144. Let the disposition of the limbs with elegant delicacy be called 'Voluptuous gracefulness.'

COMMENTARY.

a. As *is exemplified in the demeanour of the heroine of the following verses from the poem of Mágha, canto VII. v.* 18.

"She walked with a step languid through love, with her anklets sounding with a graver music *than when in brisker movement*, with her lotus-like left foot gracefully dancing, while planting the other one not so coquettishly."

b. Next of 'Arrogance' (*mada*—§ 125).

TEXT.

Arrogance. No. 145. 'Arrogance' is a change produced by the pride of prosperity, youth, &c.

COMMENTARY.

a. For example *we have Arrogance* rebuked in the following verses.*

"Exalt not thy conceit, though on thy cheek there shines, drawn by thy lover's hand, a flower-bud *designed as an ornament.* Is no one else, thinkest thou, the recipient of such decorations?—were it not that the trembling *of the lover's hand* is an unfriendly obstacle,—*while thy lover is so cool and collected that his hand never trembles even when sketching a flower-bud on thy cheek!*"

b. Next of 'Bashfulness' (*vikrita*—§ 125).

* Arrogance may seem an odd *ornament* of the heroine, yet it is a topic which can supply the poet with the means of embellishing a picture. The same remark applies to some others of the so-called 'ornaments.' Besides, unreasoning hoydens are to be regarded with a degree of indulgence, and Bacon has remarked that Pride, which is laughable in a man, is graceful in a horse.

TEXT.

Bashfulness. No. 146. Through modesty, not to speak even when one ought to speak, is what we mean by 'Bashfulness.'

COMMENTARY.

a. For example :—

" Being asked after her health, by me who had come from afar, she answered nothing ; but her two eyes bathed in tears told all *that she had suffered in my absence and now felt at my return.*"

b. Next of 'Pining' (*tapana*—§ 125).

TEXT.

Pining. No. 147. 'Pining' is the conduct arising from a possession with love in separation from the beloved one.

COMMENTARY.

a. For example *take these verses* of mine.

" She pours forth sighs, and rolls upon the ground ; she looks out upon your road, and long she weeps ; she flings hither and thither her weak tendrils of arms ;—moreover, O dear to her as life !—longing to be re-united with you even in her dreams, she yearns for sleep, but her hapless fate bestows it not."

b. Next of 'Silliness' (*maugdhya*—§ 125).

TEXT.

Silliness. No. 148. The asking, as if from ignorance, even of what she perfectly well knows, in the presence of her lover,—this is called 'Silliness' by those who know things rightly.

COMMENTARY.

a. For example,—*in the following verses, the heroine knowing very well that pearls are obtained from the sea, asks, with touching simplicity*—

" My lord, what trees are they, and in what village, and by whom planted, of which the seed-pearls of my bracelet are the fruit ?"

b. Next of Distractedness' (*vikshepa*—§ 125).

TEXT.

Distractedness. No. 149. The half arranging one's ornaments, the wildly gazing in every direction, and a partial blabbing of secrets, constitute 'Distractedness,' *arising from some cause or other*, when near a husband or a lover.

COMMENTARY.

a. For example:—

"Her hair is half loosened, and in like manner she but partly forms the ornamental mark on her forehead;—something of a secret she gives utterance to, and startledly the slender dame gazes in every direction."

b. Next of 'Impetuous curiosity' (*kutúhala*—§ 125).

TEXT.

Impetuous curiosity. No. 150. Let the lively desire to behold a pleasant object be called 'Impetuous curiosity.'

COMMENTARY.

a. For example, *impetuous curiosity appears in the lively desire of the ladies to get a sight of the king entering the city with his bride,—as described in canto VII. of the Raghuvans'a, the 7th verse of which here follows.*

"One lady, withdrawing the foremost foot, which was supported by the female decorator *employed in tingeing it with lac-dye*, dripping as it was with the pigment, neglecting all gracefulness of gait, traced a path stained by the lac-dye up to the window *which she hurried to look out at.*"

b. Next of 'Giggling' (*hasita*—§ 125).

TEXT.

Giggling. No. 151. But 'Giggling' is aimless laughter resulting from the outbursting of youth.

COMMENTARY.

a. For example:—

"Since the slender-limbed one has again laughed without a reason, surely he of the flower-tipped arrows is establishing his rule within her."

b. Next of 'Trepidation' (*chakita*—§ 125).

TEXT.

Trepidation. No. 152. 'Trepidation,' is agitation from fear, before a lover, from whatever cause.

COMMENTARY.

a. As an example *take a verse, canto VIII. v. 24., from the passage in the poem of Mágha descriptive of the sports of the bathers.*

"Trembling, when struck on the thigh by the passing fish, the fair-limbed one fell into excess of agitation. The ladies are nervous—O exceedingly—even without a cause, in sports;—how much more, then, when there is a cause—*such as this bumping of a fish against one!*"

b. Next of 'Sportiveness' (*keli*—§ 125).

TEXT.

Sportiveness. No. 153. Playing when walking about with one's lover is called 'Sportiveness.'

COMMENTARY.

a. For example:—

"Her lover, unsuccessful in removing from her eye, with his breath, the pollen of the flower *which had got into it*, the bold and high-plump-breasted damsel pushed away with a knock of her bosom upon his."

b. Now, as regards the amatory demeanour of the artless and the unmarried *of the fair sex, we have to remark as follows.*

TEXT.

The demeanour of an enamoured artless girl. No. 154. When looked at, she exhibits bashfulness, and never returns the look to his face: she looks at her beloved either furtively or when he is walking about, or after he has passed. Even after having been many times asked, she usually answers her lover something in a stammering tone, slowly, and with face down-looking. She ever attentively hearkens to a conversation about him carried on by others,—turning her eyes elsewhere;—thus acts a girl when enamoured of her lord.

COMMENTARY.

a. Now, as regards the amatory demeanour of all heroines *we have to remark as follows.*

TEXT.

The demeanour of enamoured heroines in general. No. 155. She wishes her beloved to remain long near her; she goes not within the range of his vision unadorned. On one occasion, under the pretence of covering or fastening her hair, she will display plainly her armpit, her breasts, or her lotus navel. She gratifies the attendants of her beloved by words and other things;—she places confidence in his friends and treats them with great respect. In the midst of her female friends she recites his praises; she bestows upon him all her wealth; she sleeps when he sleeps, grieves in his grief and rejoices in his joy. Standing in the line of his sight, from a distance she ever gazes on her beloved. She speaks to his attendants in his presence. On beholding any symptom of fondness in him, she laughs with delight. In like manner, she scratches her ear, loosens and ties up her hair, yawns, and stretches her limbs, or catches up a child and kisses it. She begins making the ornamental mark on the forehead of her female friend;—she writes on the ground with the point of her toe, and looks up with a sidelong glance. She bites her lip, and looks on the ground when she speaks to her beloved, and quits not the spot where her lover is to be seen. She goes to his house on any sort of pretence of business. Anything given to her by her lover, having placed on her person. she long gazes at. She ever rejoices in his society, and in his absence she is miserable, and thin. Greatly does she admire his disposition, and she loves whatever is dear to him. She asks from him, *as keepsakes*, things of little value; and when sleeping she turns not her back on him. In his presence, she gives way to the blameless moods *of trembling, stammering, &c., mentioned under* § 166. Kindly and blandly does the fond dame converse with him. Among these *points of demeanour here enumerated*, the more bashful gestures belong to the young wife, those of which the modesty is of a medium description to the middle class of heroines—*see* § 98,—and those where modesty has waned to heroines who are the wives of others, and dames maturely bold, and courtesans.

COMMENTARY.

a. As a mere hint of what is meant, take my *verses here following.* "Even when I draw near her, this one seeing, yet pretending not to see me, displays her armpit adorned by fresh nail-scratches."

b. And so—

TEXT.

Means available to a lady for revealing her affection.

No. 156. By sending of letters, by soft looks and gentle words, and by sending female messengers, it is agreed *by the learned* that a woman may reveal her sentiments.

COMMENTARY.

a. Next, then, of female messengers.

TEXT.

What females may serve as messengers

No. 157. Female messengers may be a friend, an actress, a slave-girl, a foster-sister, a neighbour, a girl, a wandering ascetic, a workwoman, a female artist, &c.; and likewise one's self.

COMMENTARY.

a. By a 'workwoman' is meant a washer-woman, or the like. By a 'female artist' is meant a woman who makes pictures, or the like. By the '&c.' are meant female purveyors of betel-nut, perfumers, and the like. Among these, the 'friend,' *acting as a messenger, may be recognised in the narrator of the heroine's sad case in the verses, quoted under* § 147, *beginning* as follows:—

"She pours forth sighs," &c.

b. One acting as messenger for one's self may be recognised in the following lines of mine.

"O traveller,—thou seemest thirsty;—why, then, goest thou elsewhere? There is none here to present the slightest obstacle—do drink water in this house, *or, as I secretly mean, quaff the sweets of amorous enjoyment.*"

c. And these (§ 157) serve the hero also as messengers to the heroine.

d. The author next mentions the qualifications of a female messenger.

TEXT.

The qualifications of a female messenger.

No. 158. Her qualifications are skill in the *lighter* arts, perseverance, fidelity, penetration, a good memory, sweetness, readiness to understand a joke, and fluency of speech. These women too—*as well as the heroines mentioned under* § 75—are, in their own line, either of the first class, of the lowest, or of the intermediate order *of merit*.

COMMENTARY.

a. 'These,'—that is to say these female messengers.

b. Now, as for the 'rival' *mentioned under* § 63 *as one of the 'substantial ingredients' in poetry*:—

TEXT.

No. 159. The 'rival,' *or opponent of the hero*, is a firm, haughty, dissipated, sinful person.

Commentary.

As is Rávaṇa in respect of Ráma.

a. Now, *having fully explained the 'substantial' division of the Excitants of poetic Flavour, we have to remark upon the second division of the two mentioned under* § 62—*viz.* the Excitants which ENHANCE *the Flavour which is more essentially dependent on the others.*

Text.

No. 160. The 'Enhancing Excitants' *(uddípana-vibháva)* are those which enhance the Flavour.

Commentary.

a. And these '*enhancing excitants*' *are as follows :—*

The Excitants specified which enhance the Flavour.

No. 161. The gestures, &c. of any principal character (§ 63,) and in like manner places and times, &c.

Commentary.

a. By the '&c.' after 'gestures,' are meant beauty, decorations, and the like. By the '&c.' after 'times,' are meant, the moon, sandal-wood ointment, the voice of the Cuculus Indicus, the hum of bees, and the like. Of these the moon *as enhancing the sentiment of the scene, may be exemplified* as in these lines of mine. "Resting his rays—*as if they were a hand—which the word kara also means in Sanskrit*—on the swelling bosom of the eastern hill from which the mantle of the covering of darkness had fallen off, the moon kisses the face of the eastern horizon which opened its eyes—viz. the lilies *that expand when the moon rises.*

b. Of what Flavour each of these (§ 160) is the appropriately enhancing excitant, will be mentioned when describing each *Flavour :— see* § 209, &c.

c. Now, *having given an account of the Excitants mentioned at* § 32, *we have next to speak of* the 'Ensuants' *which also give rise to Flavour.*

Text.

An Ensuant defined.

No. 162. That which, displaying an external condition occasioned by its appropriate causes, in ordinary life ranks as an EFFECT, is *reckoned,* in Poetry and the Drama, an ENSUANT *(anubháva).*

Commentary.

a. That *gesture or the like* which, manifesting externally the love, &c. excited in the mind of Ráma, or the like, by the appropriate causes,—by Sítá, for example, as the principal cause, and the moonlight, for instance, as an enhancer of the sentiment,—is called, in ordinary life, an EFFECT *of love, or the like,*—this, in poetry and the drama, is, on the other hand, called an ENSUANT—*because here it is of no importance what things are causes and effects as regards each other objectively,—the only consideration of importance being—what things, whether causes or effects among themselves, serve as causes in respect of Flavour. See* § *44. e. and 45.*

b. What, then, is this '*Ensuant*'—*which you thus define?* To this he replies as follows:—

Text.

The Ensuants enumerated.

No. 163. In the shape thereof are those feminine graces mentioned *in the enumeration under* § 125 which result from bodily movement, and those graces which result without bodily effort, and the involuntary *indications of strong feeling* —§ 32. *b.*, as well as other gestures *than the involuntary,—so far as these are effects which serve in poetry as causes, and are therefore termed ensuants to distinguish them from effects simply.*

Commentary.

a. 'In the shape thereof,'—i. e. in the shape of Ensuants. And in regard to these,—what Ensuant is conducive to each sentiment shall be stated when describing these *sentiments:—see* § 209, *&c.*

b. Among these *Ensuants* the involuntary *(sáttwika) indications of strong feeling* are defined as follows.

Text.

Involuntary evidences of feeling.

No 164. Those changes *in a human being* are called involuntary—*or honest and spontaneous*— which arise from sincerity *(sattwa).*

Commentary.

a. Sincerity—*as we may here render the term which, in Indian philosophy, stands for the cause of all that is best and brightest in the phenomenal world*—is a certain inward disposition which *spontane-*

ously reveals the repose of one's soul *where it does not interfere to modify the indication.*

TEXT.

No. 165. These *involuntary evidences of feeling* differ from the Ensuants in general (§ 163) only in their taking their rise in honest sincerity.

COMMENTARY.

a. As a stout bull *differs* from an ordinary specimen of the cow-kind,—such is the remainder *which requires to be supplied in order to complete the sense of the text.*

b. Now, which are these? To this he replies.

Text.

These specified. No. 166. Stupefaction *(stambha)*, perspiration *(sweda)*, and horripilation *(románcha)*, disturbance of speech *(swara-bhanga)*, trembling *(vepathu)*, change of colour *(vaivarnya)*, tears *(ás'ru)*, and fainting *(pralaya)*,—these eight are what are called the involuntary *evidences of strong emotion.*

COMMENTARY.

a. Among these—

TEXT.

And explained. No. 167. By Stupefaction is meant a prevention of motion, by fear, or joy, or pain, &c. Perspiration is an exudation from the body, caused by love, or warmth, or toil, &c. Horripilation is a change in regard to the hair of the body, caused by joy, or surprise, or fear, &c. What they call disturbance of speech, is stammering, occasioned by intoxication, or joy, or pain, &c. Trembling, means a shaking of the body, arising from desire, aversion, fatigue, &c. Change of colour is an alteration in the colour caused by sorrow, or intoxication, or anger, &c. Tears are water flowing from the eye, originating in anger, or in grief, or in great joy. Fainting is the cessation, through joy or grief, of motion and also—*which distinguishes it from mere stupefaction*—of consciousness.

COMMENTARY.

a. *These—or some of these—may be exemplified* as in the following verses of mine.

"At the touch of her person—Ah—my eyes half close;—my whole body becomes petrified, while every hair stands on end; my cheeks are wet with perspiration; my mind, altogether withdrawn from all other objects, attains to great joy—even to absolute deity."

b. So of the others—*enumerated in* (§ 166).

c. Now of the 'Accessories' (§ 32).

TEXT.

The Accessories in the production of Flavour.

No. 168. The 'Accessories'—*(vyabhichári)* are those that more especially—*which is the force of the vi*—co-operatingly—*which is here the force of the abhi*—go along with,—whether immersed in or distinguishable from,—the permanent agency; and thirty-three are kinds thereof.

COMMENTARY.

a. For, in regard to Love, or the like, while it remains the main sentiment, Self-disparagement *(nirvveda)*, and other such things, are called 'Accessories,' inasmuch as they tend in the same direction, whether obviously or covertly.

b. Well—which are these? To this he replies.

TEXT.

The Accessories specified.

No. 169. Self-disparagement, Flurry, Depression, Weariness, Intoxication, Stupefaction, Sternness, Distraction, Awaking, Dreaming, Dementedness, Arrogance, Death, Indolence, Impatience of opposition, Drowsiness, Dissembling, Longing, Derangement, Apprehension, Recollection, Resolve, Sickness, Alarm, Shame, Joy, Envy, Despondency, Equanimity, Unsteadiness, Debility, Painful Reflection, and Debate.

COMMENTARY.

a. Among these, 'Self-disparagement' *(nirvveda*—§ 169*)*.

TEXT.

No. 170. Self-disparagement consists in a dis-esteeming of oneself in consequence of arriving at the knowledge of the Truth—*that the world is an illusion and God alone is the real existence*, or in consequence of calamity, or of bitter jealousy,—this leading to depression (§ 172), painful reflection (§ 201), tears, sighs of expiration, changes of colour, and sighs of inspiration.

COMMENTARY.

a. Among these *varieties of self-disparagement*, the self-disparagement resulting from a knowledge of the truth, *or rather from that state preparatory thereto, called vairágya, which may be translated 'heavenly-mindedness,' may be illustrated* as follows:—

"Alas! I have pounded down a conch-shell with convolutions from left to right,* wishing to mend a chink left in an earthen jar by a grain of sand, *for I have devoted and sacrificed my divine nature of Man to the illusive enjoyments of the world.*"

TEXT.

Flurry. No. 171. 'Flurry' (*âvega*—§ 169—) means disturbance. When it is occasioned by rain, it is *shown in the shape of* distress in the limbs; when occasioned by some portentous phenomenon, *it shows itself* as petrifaction of the limbs; when occasioned by fire, as perplexity about smoke, &c.; when occasioned by the invasion, &c. of a *hostile* king, *flurry is manifested in* the getting ready one's weapons and elephants, &c.; when occasioned by *wild or excited* elephants or the like, *it is shown in* paralysis, trembling, &c.; when occasioned by the wind, *it appears as* perplexity about dust, &c.; when occasioned by something desirable, *it appears as* rejoicings; and when occasioned by something undesirable, as grievings;—and so its other modifications are to be understood according to circumstances.

COMMENTARY.

a. Among these, *there may be Flurry* occasioned by an enemy;—as for example *in the Raghuvans'a, canto* 11, *v.* 69.

"He, not regarding the king, who was calling out 'Hail! hail!' kept fixed in the direction of Bharata s elder brother his glance which flashed flames of wrath against the Kshattras, whilst the eye-balls fiercely projected."

b. Examples of the others may be inferred according to this *sample of illustration, which may therefore suffice.*

c. Next of 'Depression' (*dainya*—§ 169).

TEXT.

Depression. No. 172. Depression, arising from misfortune, &c., is a lacklustreness which shows itself in squalor, &c.

COMMENTARY.

a. For example:—

"The husband, old and blind, reclines on the bedstead; of the house only the posts remain; the rainy season is at hand, and there is no good news of the son. The jar containing the carefully collected

* Such a conch-shell is believed to ensure prosperity to the house in which it remains.

oil-drops is broken ;—so, looking sorrowfully at her daughter-in-law weak through pregnancy, the mother-in-law takes a good long cry."

b. Next of 'weariness' (*s'rama*—§ 169).

TEXT.

Weariness. No. 173. Weariness is fatigue, arising from indulgence, travel, &c., and occasioning sighing, drowsiness, &c.

COMMENTARY.

a. For example :—

"Tender as the Acacia Sirísa, straightway, when yet close to the city, having gone hastily but three or four steps, Sítá caused the first tears to fall from the eyes of Ráma—*unmoved by any thought of his own hard fate*—by exclaiming many a time, "Oh—how far is it that we have to go?"

b. Next of 'Intoxication'(*mada*—§ 169).

TEXT.

Intoxication, and its effects on different characters. No. 174. 'Intoxication' is a combination of confusion and delight occasioned by the employment of wine. By this, the best kind of man is put to sleep; while your middling description of man laughs and sings, and he that is of the baser sort talks rudely and blubbers.

COMMENTARY.

a. For example—*take a verse from Mágha, canto* 10, *v.* 12.

"The joke was a-foot, entertaining through the invention of indirect *witty* speeches, ludicrously revealing profound secrets, on the part of dames brilliantly elevated by triple draughts* of wine."

b. Next of 'Stupefaction' (*jaḍatá*—§ 169).

TEXT.

Stupefaction. No. 175. Let 'Stupefaction' signify incapacity for action, occasioned, *for example*, by seeing, or hearing, anything *extremely* agreeable or disagreeable. In this case there is a gazing with unwinking eyes, silence, &c.

COMMENTARY.

a. For example, in the following verses from my Prákrit poem the 'Adventures of Kuvalayás'wa.'

"Then the youthful pair, separated, only stood for a moment with

* Here, for त्रिसरकेण, Röer reads त्रिरसकेन P. M.

their eyes, dull with weeping, mutually fixed on one another, as if they were figures in a painting."

b. Next of 'Sternness' (*ugratá*—§ 169).

TEXT.

Sternness. No. 176. Let 'Sternness' be the harshness which arises from *rude* valour, or from *another's* offences, &c. In this case we have perspiration, shaking of the head, reviling, striking, &c.

COMMENTARY.

a. For example—*see the sternness of Mádhava,—Act V.,—addressing Aghoraghanṭa who was going to immolate Málatí.*

"On the head of thee who hast raised the sword, for destruction, against that body which shrinks even from the blows of a soft 'sirísha'-flower, where the sentiment associated with the blows is no other than the sportive humour of an affectionate female friend, may this my arm fall like the mace of Yama *the god of death*, untimely *to take thee to the infernal regions.*

b. Next of 'Distraction' (*moha*—§ 169).

TEXT.

Distraction. No. 177. By 'Distraction' is meant perplexity, arising from fear, or grief, or impetuosity, or painful recollection,—causing giddiness, falls, staggerings, failure of sight, &c.

COMMENTARY.

a. For example—*see the Kumára-sambhava, canto* 3, *v.* 73.

"The goddess of love was for a moment as it were benefited by the distraction arising from this sharp affliction, which paralysed the action of her faculties,—she being thus, *for the moment,* unconscious of her husband's fate."

b. Next of 'Awaking' (*vibodha*—§ 169).

TEXT.

Awaking. No. 178. 'Awaking' means the return of consciousness, from causes that remove sleep, and occasioning yawns, stretching of limbs, twinkling of the eyes, and the reviewing of one's limbs—*a process the more strictly consequential if the person awaking be a Vedántí who believes that his limbs cease to exist when he ceases to think of them.*

COMMENTARY.

a. For example:—

"These women, keeping their bodies unmoved *in order not to awake their husbands*, having been, though the last to fall asleep, yet the first to awake, do not even unclasp the circling embrace of the listless arms of their lovers enjoying repose after the lassitude consequent on long indulgence."

b. Next of 'Dreaming' (*swapna*—§ 169).

TEXT.

Dreaming. No. 179. But 'Dreaming' is a sleeping person's, notion of objects, which is a cause of anger, or of agitation, or fear, or debility, or joy, or grief, &c.

COMMENTARY.

a. For example—*Megha-dúta, v.* 106.

"Frequently indeed do the tear-drops of the deities of the spot fall, large as pearls, on the buds of the trees, as they behold me with arms outstretched in empty space for the sake of stringently embracing thee *whom I fondly imagine myself to have* obtained somehow or other in the visions of a dream!"

b. Next of 'Dementedness' (*apasmára*—§ 169).

TEXT.

Dementedness. No. 180. But by 'Dementedness' is meant a disturbance of mind occasioned by such a thing as the influence of one of the planets;—this leading to falls, tremblings, perspiration, foamings at the mouth, slavering, &c.

COMMENTARY.

a. For example: *look at the ocean as described by Mágha, canto* 3, *v.* 72.

"He doubted whether the Lord of the Rivers *i. e. the Ocean*, clinging to the earth, foaming, and roaring, *and tossing high* his huge waves like wanton arms, were not one possessed."

b. Next of 'Arrogance' (*garvva*—§ 169).

TEXT.

Arrogance. No. 181. 'Arrogance' is pride arising from valour, or beauty, or learning, or greatness of family, &c., and leading to acts of disrespect, coquettish displays of the person, immodesty, &c.

COMMENTARY.

a. For example—*Mahábhárata*—

"Whilst *I* bear arms, what need of other weapons? What is not achieved by my weapon, by whom will it be achieved?"

b. Next of 'Death' (*maraṇa*—§ 169).

TEXT.

Death. No. 182. 'Death' is the quitting of life, this being occasioned by weapons or otherwise, and leading to the falling down of the body, &c.

COMMENTARY.

a. For example, *Raghuvans'a, canto* 11. *v.* 20.

"Wounded in the heart by the irresistible arrow of that Cupid Ráma, the female fiend departed to the dwelling of Life's lord—*viz. the god of death*—being sprinkled with her *ill* smelling blood as *a woman going to the dwelling of her life's lord or lover, is sprinkled with sweetly smelling* sandalwood unguent."

b. Next of 'Indolence' (*álasya*—§ 169).

TEXT.

Indolence. No. 183. 'Indolence' is an aversion to movement, this being occasioned by fatigue, or pregnancy, &c., and being a cause of yawning, continuing seated, &c.

COMMENTARY.

a. For example:—

"She no longer adorns her person, nor does she converse with her female friend, but, indolent, through the load of pregnancy, the girl, long seated, yawns."

b. Next of 'Impatience of opposition' (*amarsha*—§ 169).

TEXT.

Impatience of opposition. No. 184. 'Impatience of opposition' is a determination of purpose occasioned by censure, abuse, disrespect, &c., and leading to redness of the eyes, shaking of the head, knitting of the brows, violent abuse, &c.

COMMENTARY.

a. For example, (Víra Charita, Act III):—

"I will perform penance for having acted otherwise than I ought towards you—worthy of all honour as you are;—but still I will not belie my great vow of taking arms *in tamely suffering the insult offered to me by Ráma, breaking, as he did, the bow of my divine preceptor.*

b. Next of 'Drowsiness' (*nidrá*—§ 169).

TEXT.

Drowsiness. No. 185. 'Drowsiness' is a contraction of the mental faculties, occasioned by fatigue, exhaustion, intoxication, &c., and causing yawning, closing of the eyes, deep inspirations, relaxation, of the muscles, &c.

COMMENTARY.

a. For example:—

"She is as it were pictured in my heart, with her eyes half closed through drowsiness, as she uttered words partly with sense and partly unmeaning, in which the syllables were languidly articulated."

b. Next of 'Dissembling' (*avahitthá*—§ 169).

TEXT.

Dissembling. No. 186. 'Dissembling' is the hiding of appearances of joy, &c., this being caused by fear, or dignified importance, or modesty, &c., and leading to employment in some other matter, or to language or looks, &c., directed otherwise *than to that in regard to which concealment of sentiment is aimed at.*

COMMENTARY.

a. For example—*Kumára-sambhava, canto* 6, *v.* 84.

"Whilst thus the divine sage spoke, Párvatí, at her father's side, holding down her head, counted the leaves of the lotus with which she played."

b. Next of 'Longing' (*autsukya*—§ 169).

TEXT.

Longing. No. 187. 'Longing' is impatience of the lapse of time, occasioned by the non-attainment of a desired object, and causing mental fever, hastiness, perspiration, long sighs, &c.

COMMENTARY.

a. For example:—

"There is that very husband who gained me as a girl, and those same April nights, and the bold breezes *wafting perfume* from the Naucleas, and fragrant with the odours of the full-blown jasmine—and I too am the same:—but still my heart longs for the sportive doings, in the shape of toyings, under the ratan-trees on the banks of the Revá."

b. What the author of the Kávya-prakás'a says in regard to this passage—*already remarked upon under* § 2. *p.* 7 that the main thing in it is the Flavour,—this is to be regarded as superfluous, because an 'Accessory,' *such as is exemplified in the present instance*, is entitled (*see* § 47) to be called a 'Flavour,' since it is associated with the property of flavouring,—*and therefore there was no occasion, tautologically, to make the assertion—true though it be.*

c. Next of 'Derangement' (*unmáda*—§ 169).

TEXT.

Derangement. No. 188. 'Derangement' is a confusion of thought, arising from love, or grief, or fear, &c., and giving rise to inappropriate laughter, or weeping, or singing, or absurd talking, &c.

COMMENTARY.

a. For example:—take these verses of mine:—

"Brother bee! whilst wandering everywhere, hast thou seen her who is dearer to me than my life?" (Having attended to the humming of the bee, which sounds like the Sanskrit word *om* 'yes'—the speaker continues joyfully—) "What!—dost thou say 'yes'? Then quickly tell me, friend, what is she doing, and where is she, and how?"

b. Next of 'Apprehension' (*s'anká*—§ 169).

TEXT.

Apprehension. No. 189. 'Apprehension' is the anticipation of evil from the cruelty of another, or from one's own misconduct, &c., this leading to changes of colour, trembling, side-looks, and dryness of the mouth.

COMMENTARY.

a. For example:—take these verses of mine:—

"Apprehensive *of discovery*, at dawn, she long applies the sandalwood unguent to her limbs scratched by her lover; she applies again and again the red dye to her lip wounded by his teeth,—the tender-limbed one all the while startledly casting her eyes around."

b. Next of 'Recollection' (*smriti*—§ 169).

TEXT.

Recollection. No. 190. What is called 'Recollection' is knowledge having as its object something previously cognized, this being excited by such causes as our perceiving or thinking of something similar, and leading to a raising of the brows, &c.

COMMENTARY.

a. For example:—take these verses of mine:—

"O how well I recollect that ever-smiling face of the lotus-eyed one, bashfully held down on seeing her female friend smiling, when I, artfully directing my eyes somewhat in some direction, in some measure caught her eye, *which would not consent to meet my direct glance,—that eye of hers* the pupil of which was dilated in a sidelong fashion, *as she stole what she fancied an unobserved look at me!*"

b. Next of 'Resolve' (*mati*—§ 169).

TEXT.

Resolve. No. 191. 'Resolve' consists in making up one's mind upon a point by attention to the rules of morality, &c., whence there arise smiles, confidence and delight, and self-satisfiedness.

COMMENTARY.

a. For example—(*S'akuntalá, Act I.*)

"Undoubtedly she is fit to be married by a Kshattriya, because my virtuous mind is enamoured of her. For in all doubtful points the dictates of the conscience are the guide of the virtuous."

b. Next of 'Sickness' (*vyádhi*—§ 169).

TEXT.

Sickness. No. 192. 'Sickness' means a fever, for example, arising from humours, &c., and causing a wish to lie on the ground, or causing trembling, &c.

COMMENTARY.

a. When this consists of inflammation, *as in fever*, then there is a wish to lie on the *cold* earth, &c. When it consists of cold, *as in agues*, then there are tremblings, &c. Examples of this are evident *and need not be here cited.*

b. Next of 'Alarm' (*trása*—§ 169).

TEXT.

Alarm. No. 193. 'Alarm,' occasioned by thunder, lightning, meteors, &c., causes tremblings, &c.

COMMENTARY.

a. For example, *Kirátárjuníya, canto* 8. *v.* 45.

"When touched gently on the thighs by the fishes that were gliding about, the nymphs, with their eyes rolling in alarm, and with their hands like the tender leaf quivering, attracted the look even of their female companions.

b. Next of 'Shame' (*vríḍá*—§ 169).

TEXT.

Shame. No. 194. 'Shame' is the absence of boldness, causing the face to hang down, &c., in consequence of misconduct.

COMMENTARY.

a. For example:—

"O how well I recollect" *&c.* (*see* § 190. *a.*)

b. Next of 'Joy' (*harsha*—§ 169).

TEXT.

Joy. No. 195. But 'Joy' is mental complacency, on the attainment of a desired object, which occasions tears and sobbings, &c.

COMMENTARY.

a. For example:—

"Having long gazed on the countenance of his son, as a poor man gazes on that of a treasure-jar, the father, through the joy of his soul, could scarcely be contained in his body, like the ocean swelling up *in full tide* on the rise of the moon, *which the ocean regards with a parental feeling,—the moon having, it is said, been produced by the churning of the ocean.*"

b. Next of 'Envy' (*asúyá*—§ 169).

TEXT.

Envy. No. 196. 'Envy' is impatience of another's merits and prosperity, arising from pride, and leading to the inveighing against faults, frowns, disrespect, signs of anger, &c.

COMMENTARY.

a. For example—*Mágha, canto* 15. *v.* 1.

"Well, the lord of Chedi (*S'is'upála*) could not endure the honour shown in that assembly by the son of Páṇḍu (*Yuddhishṭhira*) to the enemy of Madhu, (*Krishṇa,*) for the mind of the arrogant is intolerant of another's advancement."

b. Next of 'Despondency' (*visháda*—§ 169).

TEXT.

Despondency. No. 197. But 'Despondency' is a loss of vigour

—arising from the absence of expedients *to meet impending calamity*, causing panting and sighing, and distress, and a seeking for aid, &c.

COMMENTARY.

a. For example—my verses:—

"This thy top-knot, formed of a close twisted bunch of hair, while, like an iron rod, it breaks my heart, like a black snake too, bites it."

b. Next of 'Equanimity' (*dhṛiti*—§ 169).

TEXT.

Equanimity. No 198. But 'Equanimity' is complete contentment, arising from true knowledge, or from the arrival of a desired object, &c.; conducing to the production of amiable discourse, to cheerful liveliness, &c.

COMMENTARY.

a. For example, my *picture of a reformed reprobate*:—

"After having long oppressed the poor, and waged a war of altercation with my own people, and given no regard to the heavy punishments of another life—now, forsooth, this same body, for which I had collected stores of wealth, has its wants satisfied by a handful of wild rice."

b. Next of 'Unsteadiness' (*chapalatá*—§ 169).

TEXT.

Unsteadiness. No. 199. But 'Unsteadiness' is an instability arising from envy, aversion, desire, &c., and causing abuse, harsh language, and self-willedness, &c.

COMMENTARY.

a. For example—*a lady reproves, in the following address to a bee, the unsteadiness of her own fickle lover in going after a younger mistress.*

"O bee! amuse your wanton mind with other flower-stalks that can bear your handling. Why dost thou prematurely and unprofitably render useless the young juiceless bud of the unblown jasmine?"

b. Next of 'Debility' (*gláni*—§ 169).

TEXT.

Debility. No. 200. 'Debility' is an unliveliness resulting from enjoyment, or fatigue, or sorrow, hunger, thirst, &c, and causing tremblings, emaciation, inactivity, &c.

COMMENTARY.

a. For example—*Uttara-ráma-charita* :—

"Long and bitter sorrow, withering her heart's flower like a tender young shoot severed from the stem, debilitates her pale and delicate frame as the autumnal heat the inner leaves of the 'ketakí.'

b. Next of 'Painful reflection' (*chintá*—§ 169).

TEXT.

Painful reflection.

No. 201. 'Painful reflection' is meditation arising from the non-possession of a beloved object, producing desolateness, sighs, and feverishness.

COMMENTARY.

a. For example—my verses:—

"Leaning thy cheek upon thy hand, and thus, *in appearance,* joining with the expanded lotus its enemy the moon, what dost thou mournfully revolve, fair one, in thine inmost heart?"

b. Next of 'Debate' (*vitarka*—§ 169).

TEXT.

Debate.

No. 202. 'Debate' is discussion, originating in doubt, and causing one to shake the brows, the head, or the finger.

COMMENTARY.

a. For example:—

"What,—has he been stopped by some lover?" &c. (*see* § 121. *a.*)

Others than these come under the definition of an Accessory.

b. And as for the statement—*see* § 168—that these thirty-three are kinds of 'Accessory,'—this was intended to include also things analogous; the author therefore proceeds to remark as follows:—

TEXT.

No. 203. 'Love,' also (§ 206,) &c., in reference to several of the Flavours, may be 'Accessories' (§ 202. *b*).

COMMENTARY.

a. To explain:—when the flavour is, for example, the 'Erotic' (§ 210,) 'love' alone—*of all the permanent conditions*—§ 206—is denoted by the term 'permanent,' because this must remain—being indispensable; while 'mirth'—*another of the permanent conditions*—§ 206,—on the other hand, when it occurs *in the course of an erotic composition,* is merely an 'Accessory,' because the definition of an 'Accessory' (*see*

§ 202. *b.)*—applies to it,—*the comic element, where not the principal one, serving, in 'Romeo and Juliet' for example, to enhance the effect of the erotic.*

b. This has been declared—*by the Dhwanikára*—*(as already remarked under* § 32. *c.)* as follows:—"Only when *inseparably* permanent in the Flavour *of any given composition*, does a 'condition' *(bháva)* take rank as the PERMANENT one" (—§ 205).

c. Then in respect of what Flavour may what 'conditions' permanent, *when principal*, serve as 'Accessories?' To this he replies:—

TEXT.

Which Flavours may serve as Accessories to which.

No. 204. In the 'Erotic' and the 'Heroic' (§ 209,) 'Mirth' (§ 206)—*is an appropriate Accessory*, and so in the 'Heroic' is 'Resentment' held to be:—then, again, in the 'Quietistic'—§ 209, 'Disgust' (§ 206) is declared to be an Accessory. The rest, besides this, may be inferred, for themselves, by those who can weigh their thoughts.

COMMENTARY.

a. Now of the 'permanent conditions' (*sthàyi-bháva*).

TEXT.

A permanent condition defined.

No. 205. That condition which neither those akin to it nor those opposed to it can overpower,—the root of the sprout of Gustation (§ 44 *b.*), this is held to be the 'permanent condition,' *or main sentiment of the composition.*

COMMENTARY.

a. As is declared *by the Dhwanikára*—"This permanent condition, running through the other conditions like the thread of a garland, is not overpowered by them but only reinforced."

b. He enumerates the divisions thereof.

TEXT.

The permanent conditions enumerated.

No. 206. 'Love' *or 'Desire' (rati)*, 'Mirth' *(hása)*, 'Sorrow' *(s'oka)*, 'Resentment' *(krodha)*, 'Magnanimity' *(utsáha)*, 'Terror' *(bhaya)*, 'Disgust' *(jugupsá)*, and 'Surprise' *(vismaya)*,—thus there are eight *permanent conditions* and there is also 'Quietism' *(s'ama)*.

COMMENTARY.

a. Among these—

TEXT.

No. 207. 'Love' is a tendency of the mind towards a thing that is conformable to the mind; by 'Mirth' is intended an expansion of the mind excited by absurdity of expression, &c.; what is designated by the word 'Sorrow' is a commotion of the mind occasioned by the loss of a beloved object, &c.; by 'Resentment' is meant a feeling of sharpness towards opponents; what is called 'Magnanimity' is a steady audacity where any action has been entered upon; but 'Terror,' occasioning disturbance of mind, is what is produced by the power of what is terrific; 'Disgust' is aversion, arising in respect of any object, from seeing or otherwise perceiving in it what is offensive; but what is meant by 'Surprise' is an agitation of mind in regard to strange things that transcend the limits of the mundane; 'Quietism' is the happiness arising from the repose of the soul in a state of indifference *to the transitory concerns of time.*"

COMMENTARY.

a. For example,—in *the play of* 'Málati and Mádhava,' *the permanent condition is* 'Love;' in the 'Naṭaka-melaka,' 'Mirth;' in the 'Rámáyana,' 'Sorrow;' in the 'Mahábhárata,' 'Quietism.' And so of the others.

Why these conditions are called permanent.

b. And these conditions are called permanent, because these are ascertained, by the direct cognizance of men of taste, to be not destroyed, but on the contrary just reinforced, by other conditions, among these *above enumerated,* occurring, whether these be akin to or opposed to *that one which happens to be the main* sentiment.

c. Moreover—

TEXT.

No. 208. These,—the 'permanent' (§ 206), the 'accessory' (§ 168), and the 'involuntary' (§ 166),—are therefore called 'bháva' *(which we have rendered 'condition')*—because they GIVE OCCASION FOR THE EXISTENCE OF *(bhávayanti)* the 'Flavours' which depend upon the various gestures *or other indications of passion on the part of the actors.*

COMMENTARY.

a. As is declared as follows *by the Dhwanikára*—" A 'condition' *(bháva)* consists in, *or takes the name it does, in virtue of* the causing of this *Flavour* to take place, through joy or sorrow or other things."

b. Now he states the divisions of 'Flavour.'

TEXT.

The Flavours enumerated.

No. 209. The 'Erotic' *(s'ṛingára)*, the 'Comic' *(hásya)*, the 'Pathetic' *(karuṇa)*, the 'Furious' *(raudra)*, the 'Heroic' *(víra)*, the 'Terrible' *(bhayánaka)*, the 'Disgustful' *(bíbhatsa)*, and the Marvellous *(adbhuta)* : these eight are 'Flavours'; and so is the 'Quietistic' *(s'ánta)* held to be *by some.*

COMMENTARY.

a. Of these, the 'Erotic' *is first to be discussed.*

TEXT.

The Erotic described.

No. 210. By *s'ṛinga—literally a 'horn'—which sprouts from the head of a bull as a plant does from the earth*—is meant the budding of lŏve ; and by the word *s'ṛingára —from 's'ṛingam ṛichchhati,' it has the horn for its cause*—is meant that 'Flavour,' generally most manifest in the noblest natures, which has for its condition the coming on or existence thereof—*for one devoid of that sentiment cannot enjoy it.* In this case let the substantial ingredients(§ 63) be the heroines,—excluding another's wife, and a courtezan if not *honestly* enamoured, (§ 111), and the heroes, the 'impartial' &c. (§ 70.) The moon, sandalwood ointment, the hum of bees, &c., are held to be 'enhancers' (§ 160.) Motions of the eyebrows, and side-glances, &c., are found as its symptoms ; and its 'accessories' may be any (§ 169) except 'Sternness,' 'Death,' 'Indolence,' and 'Disgust.' Here the 'permanent' condition (§ 206) is 'Love ;'—and—*according to the fancy of the mythologists* it is black-coloured, and its deity is Vishṇu—*who in his incarnation as the amorous Krishṇa was remarkable for the darkness of his colour.*

COMMENTARY.

a. For an example—*we have a case of the 'Erotic' in the verses quoted under* § 3. *b., beginning—*

"Perceiving that the house was empty," &c.

b. Here a husband of the just-mentioned description, and a girl of the just-mentioned description, are the two 'substantial excitants' (§ 63 ;) the empty house is an enhancing 'excitant,' (§ 160) ; the kissing is an 'ensuant' (§ 32 ;) the bashfulness and the mirth are 'accessories' (§ 194 *and* 203 ;)—the condition of love, developed by all these in a man of taste, assumes the nature of *what we call* the 'Erotic' *Flavour*.

c. He mentions the divisions of this '*Erotic*' *flavour*.

TEXT.

The Erotic subdivided.

No. 211. Now, it is held to be of two kinds, viz., 'separation' and 'union.'

COMMENTARY.

a. Of these two—*he describes the former.*

TEXT.

Love in separation.

No. 212. But where excessive love does not attain the beloved object, this is 'separation.'

COMMENTARY.

a. 'The beloved object'—i. e. the hero or the heroine.

TEXT.

This subdivided.

No. 213. And let this *love in separation* be of four kinds,—consisting of (1) 'affection arising before the parties meet' *(púrva-rága)*, (2) 'indignation' *(mána)*, (3) 'the being abroad' *(pravása)*, and (4) the 'sorrow' *(karuṇá) of one who has no hope of a re-union which yet is destined to take place.*

COMMENTARY.

a. Among these *four*—

TEXT.

Love between persons yet strangers to each other.

No. 214. What is called 'affection arising before the parties meet'—*i. e. while the parties are strangers to one another,*—is the peculiar condition which belongs, before they have attained their wishes, to two persons mutually enamoured through having heard of or seen one another. And here the hearing may be from the mouth of a messenger, or a bard, or a female friend; and the seeing may be by magic—*as when Cornelius Agrippa, with his mirror, showed to Surrey the lady Geraldine,*—or in a picture, or face to face, or in a dream. In such a case the following ten are the conditions of love, viz. longing, thoughtfulness, reminiscence, the mentioning the qualities *of the loved one,* anxiety, and discourse where the person addressed is not, confusion of mind, sickness, stupefaction, and death. By 'longing' we mean wishing; 'thoughtfulness' means the thinking about the means of attainment, &c.; and 'confusion of mind' means the not distinguishing even between intelligent beings and things unintelligent. Let 'discourse where the person addressed is not' mean ravings, resulting from extreme confusion of mind. But 'sickness' mea long sighs, paleness, emaciation, &c. 'Stupefaction' means an incapability of action whether bodily or mental.

COMMENTARY.

The effects of love, under such circumstances, exemplified.

a. The rest is plain. Now for examples in their order.

"May those naturally sweet, loving, and affectionate ways of the fair-eyed one be all mine own, from which, in our interviews, great love has arisen,—on the very imagining of which for a moment as possible, my heart dissolves in a flood of joy, so that the action of my external organs is stopped short."

Here we see the 'longing' of Mádhava—*Act V.*—who has become enamoured through seeing Málatí face to face.

b. "'How shall I see the fawn-eyed maid, the god of love's very treasure?' Thus disturbed by thoughtfulness, the lover all night long goes not to sleep."

Here we have the 'thoughtfulness' of a lover who has become enamoured through seeing a certain heroine by means of magic.—The distich is mine.

c. In the verses, beginning, "O how well I recollect that ever-smiling face!" (§ 190 *a.*), we have a lover's 'reminiscence.'

d. In the example (§ 100. *c.*) beginning "Her two eyes shaming the wagtail,"—we have the 'mentioning of the qualities' *of the loved one.*

e. In the passage (§ 147. *a.*) beginning "She utters sighs," 'anxiety' is exemplified.

f. "When a third part of the night remained, having for a moment closed her eyes, she used suddenly to wake up. Exclaiming aimlessly 'Where art thou going, S'iva?'—she clasped her arms around no real neck."

Here—*Kumára Sambhava, canto V. v.* 57—we have 'discourse where the person addressed is not.'

g. In the example (§ 188. *a.*) beginning "Brother bee!"—we have 'confusion of mind' ***such that the speaker addresses an unintelligent creature.***

h. "Thy face pale and thin; thy heart impassioned and thy body weak,—all this, my friend, markedly indicates an incurable disorder in thy heart."

Here we see the 'sickness' of lovers.

i. "Her every limb is motionless—stretched on the couch of lotus-leaves; the number of her long deep sighs alone proves that she yet lives."

Here we have 'stupefaction.' The example is my own.

TEXT.

Death—under what circumstances an improper or a proper subject of description.

No. 215. 'Death' *which, as mentioned at* § 214, *is a condition to which one may be brought by love,* is not described *in poetry and the drama, where the other conditions, such as 'anxiety' &c., are constantly described*, because it—*instead of enhancing*—causes the destruction of 'Flavour.' But it may be spoken of (1) as having nearly taken place, or (2) as being mentally wished for; and it is *with propriety* described (3) if there is to be, at no distant date, a restoration to life.

COMMENTARY.

a. The first of these cases may be exemplified as follows:—

"With difficulty was that slender sufferer able to retain the vital spirit when she beheld *at midnight* the expanded Nyctanthes, *the harbinger of spring*, but now when she hears the crowing of the cocks, *awaking her from the visions of the night to the consciousness of desolation*,—I know not what will become of her."

b. Then the second case, for example:—

"The bees may fill every quarter with the sound of their hummings; and the breeze rising where there are the groves of sandalwood, may gently approach; the playful tame cuckoos on the mango-top may make their musical note—*the fifth, or dominant, according to musical authorities*—but may my vital spirit, hard as adamant, quickly go from me,—let it begone."

These two examples are my own.

c. There is an example of the third case, in the story of Mahás'wetá, and Puṇḍaríka, in the 'Kádambarí;' and this variety, as we shall mention *under* § 224. *a.* is a case of pathetic separation.

d. But some, *not accepting the list given under* § 214, say that the ten conditions of love are *in the following ascending series* (1) in the first place fondness on exchanging glances, (2) union of minds,

(3) then thoughtfulness, (4) sleeplessness, (5) growing thin, (6) neglect of all objects, (7) abandonment of shame, (8) distraction, (9) insensibility, and (10) death.

e. And here *i. e. in the case of there being an affection arising between parties yet strangers to one another,—the following is to be attended to.*

TEXT.

Theory that the advances come best on the part of the lady.

No. 216. Let the passion of the lady be first mentioned, and that of the gentleman as resulting from her proceedings.

COMMENTARY.

a. The proceedings *of women in love* have been mentioned (§ 155). *The rule laid down in the text is to be followed,* as in the Ratnávalí *the passion* of Ságariká and the king of Vatsa *is described;—the lady being there the first smitten.* Although the gentleman MAY be the first to fall in love, yet the delectability is greater, when the thing is arranged thus *as directed in the text.*

TEXT.

No. 217. And 'affection arising before the parties meet,' is of three kinds, *named fancifully after,* (1) the indigo, (2) the safflower, and (3) the madder. That fondness which makes no great show, and which yet, when it has come into the mind, does not depart, they call the INDIGO love—*the indigo being a colour that will well stand washing;*—such was the love of Ráma and Sítá. They call that the SAFFLOWER love which shines but departs—*like the dye of safflower which fades in the washing.* They call that the MADDER love which does not depart, and which does shine.

COMMENTARY.

a. Next of 'indignation' (*mána,*—the second of the conditions of the separation of lovers,—§ 213).

TEXT.

Lovers' quarrels.

No. 218. 'Indignation' means anger. But this is of two kinds, (1) arising from fondness, or (2) from jealousy. Let that anger be 'indignation from fondness,' which, without any cause, through the capricious waywardness of affection, takes place in the case of two, even when there is very great love between them.

COMMENTARY.

Arising from the mere wantonness of affection.

a. 'Of two,'—i. e. of the hero and of the heroine. Of each of these is the 'indignation arising from fondness' to be described. There is, for example, that of the hero *affecting to be asleep, and addressed upon the point as follows.*

"O my lord, that affectest to be asleep, with thine eyes firmly closed, yet with thy body quivering as I kiss thy cheek,—do give me room,—I wont delay again."

b. On the part of the heroine—as, in the *Kumára Sambhava, canto VIII.*, on the occasion of the description of evening.

c. And this affected indignation may be on BOTH sides, for example.

"Of the two indignant ones, fondly angry, and pretending to be both asleep, kept apart by indignation, and listening with checked and suppressed breathing, which is the stronger *and will hold out the longest?*"

d. Or, for example.

"Of the spouses, on one and the same couch, silently longing *for each other*, but with averted faces *doggedly* keeping up their dignity, though reconcilement was in the heart of each severally,—when gently by the moving of the corners of the eyes their eyes had met,—the contest of indignation was broken up, and with laughter was there quickly a close embracing of necks."*

An exceptional case, where zest is thus only added to love in union.

e. But when this *distance of behaviour through indignation* cannot be kept up *by the lady* until conciliation, then the case is one, not of a species of SEPARATION (§ 212 *and* 213,) but of a condition called jealousy which may be an accessory *and enhancer* of love in UNION. For example:

"Even when I get up a frown, my eyes look *at him* the more longingly; and when I check my voice, this confounded face of mine gets a smile on it; when my mind is bent on severity, my body falls into a thrill of delight;—how can I keep up my indignation, when I see this person *whom it is in vain to be angry with, ill as he may behave himself?*"

* This example which is superfluous seems to be an interpolation; it is not given in my MS. of the text, nor referred to in the commentary. P. M.

TEXT.

Where there is ground for jealousy.

No. 219. When the husband's attachment to some other loved one is seen, or inferred, or heard of, let the lady's indignation be that of jealousy (§ 218). But, among these *three* cases, inference—*for the cases of ocular demonstration and testimony require no subdivision*—is of three kinds, inasmuch as it may result from (1) behaviour on starting out of sleep, or (2) signs of dalliance, or (3) blurting out the name *of the loved one in the hearing of the jealous one.*

COMMENTARY.

Indignation at open favour shown to a rival.

a. Among these *cases enumerated in* § 219, where it—*the fondness shown a rival* is SEEN; for example *take the following from Mágha, canto VII. v.* 57.

"When the fond one, with the breath of his mouth, removed the pollen of the flower from the eye of the fair-eyed dame, both eyes of the young rival wife were exceedingly filled with the dust of indignation."

b. Then again there is the case where it—*the fondness shown to a rival*—§ 219—is inferred from signs of toying:—for example *in the Amaru-s'ataka*—

"Thou hidest with thy garment thy limbs newly marked by her nails; thou coverest also with thy hand the lip bitten by her tooth; but by what means can be concealed the odour of the fresh perfume that creeps out in every direction *from thy perspiring person* proclaiming that thou hast been toying with another woman?"

c. So in regard to other cases *referred to in* § 219, *which do not call for separate illustration.*

TEXT.

Means of removing indignation.

No. 220. Conciliation, division, presents, submission, disregard, change of humour,—such are the six expedients which the husband should employ in succession for the removal thereof—*i. e. of the lady's indignation.* Among these *six expedients,* what we mean by 'conciliation' is affectionate language; 'division' is the gaining over of her female friend *to the offender's side;* 'presents' should be of ornaments or the like, on some pretext; 'submission' means falling at her feet. But when 'conciliation' and these others have failed, then let there be 'disregard'—i. e. neglect. By a 'change of humour' we mean the indignation's being put to flight by some sudden terror or joy, &c.

COMMENTARY.

a. For example—

"I did not hearken to his fond speeches," &c.—*see* § 117. *a.*

In this example the five, beginning with 'conciliation,' are suggested, *the matter ending in the gentleman's walking off with an affectation of disregard.* The 'change of humour' *when sudden terror, for instance, causes the lady to forget her indignation, does not require illustration, and* may be imagined *by the intelligent reader.*

b. Now of 'being abroad' § 213.

TEXT.

The separation of lovers in different countries.

No. 221. 'Being abroad' means being in a different country, in consequence of business, or a curse *launched by some deity*, or a confusion *in the midst of which one of the lovers is separated from the other.* In this case what takes place is filthiness of person and clothing, a head with a single braid *into which all the locks are gathered as a sign of mourning*, sighs, sobs, weepings, fallings on the ground, &c.

COMMENTARY.

a. Moreover—

TEXT.

No. 222. There may be squalor of the person, fever, paleness, emaciation, distaste for everything, languor, desolateness, the being absorbed in *the thought of* her, frenzy, insensibility, and death;—such, in their order, are to be understood to be the ten conditions of love in this case *of separation*—§ 221. 'Squalor' is the being beset with filth; but 'Fever' is the sickness of separation; 'Distaste for everything' is indifference towards things; 'Languor' is disinclination for everything; and what is called 'Desolateness' is the vacancy of the mind; 'The being absorbed in her'—i. e. she appears everywhere, both without and within,—*in the heart of the lover, in the beauty of the flower, in the brightness of the moon, &c.*

COMMENTARY.

a. The rest is plain. *These conditions are* partly *exemplified in the following verses*, for example, of my father.

"Her mind is paralysed by anxiety, her cheek rests on her hand, her face is pale as the morning moon, her lip is wearied with mere sighing, her fever is not alleviated by the fresh leaves of the lotus or the spray of the water,—who is her beloved, hard to be come at, who suffers to continue such a wretched state?"

TEXT.

Separation may be viewed as future, present, or past.

No. 223. Among these *three kinds of exile*—(§ 221)—let that which is 'in consequence of business' be of three kinds, viz. future, present, and past.

COMMENTARY.

a. This threefold character belongs to that which is 'in consequence of business,' because this is preceded by an understanding *that the exile is to take place,—whereas in the case of a curse or of one's being unexpectedly snatched away, there is no room for contemplating the separation as something future.* Among these there is the 'future' *or contemplated separation,* as in my verses:—

"'Fair one, I depart.'—'Depart, O traveller.'—'Dear one, sorrow not in vain.'—'Why should I sorrow at thy departure?'—'Nay why then dost thou weep?'—'Because thou departest not quickly'—'Why this thy haste to have me gone?'—'Because great is the eagerness of this my spirit along with thee to take its flight.'"

b. 'Present' *separation, at the moment of its taking place, may be exemplified* as follows:—

"My bracelets have departed—*thrown off as my husband takes his departure;* my tears, which are friends of yours—*O my vital spirit—as being destined to be near you, while you remain on earth,*—depart *from my eyes* incessantly; my composure rests not for a moment *from taking its departure;*—my intellect has resolved to go off even before him;—thus all have set out together, since it was the resolution of my best beloved to depart,—and as it is time to be gone, why, O my vital spirit, dost thou forsake the company of these thy dear friends *and omit to depart at the same time?*

c. 'Past' *separation—i. e. completed and continuing,—may be exemplified* as follows:—

"Her mind is paralysed by anxiety," &c. (§ 222. *a.*)

d. Next we may exemplify separation resulting from a 'curse' (§ 221,) for example:—

"Thou mayest recognise her," &c.—§ 119. *d.—Megha-dúta, v.* 82.

e. 'A confusion' *which, in* § 221, *is specified as one of the sources of the separation of lovers,* may arise from divine or human agency, whirlwinds, earthquakes, or other portents. Take as an example the separation of Urvas'í and Purúravas, in the *Vikramorvas'í, Act 4th.*

f. Though the 'longing,' &c., which are mentioned *under* § 214 as the conditions of 'affection arising before the parties meet,' and personal 'squalor,' &c, also, which are mentioned as belonging to these *cases of separation just treated of*—§ 221 *and* 222—might each serve for either case *with equal propriety,* they have been distinctively set forth here in conformity with ancient usage.

g. Next of the 'sorrow'—§ 213—*of one who has no hope of a reunion which yet is destined to take place.*

Text.

Of lovers separated by death, and yet to meet again.

No. 224. Either of two young lovers being dead, and being yet to be regained *through some supernatural interposition,* when the one *left behind* is sorrowful, then let it be called the 'separation of tender sadness.'

Commentary.

a. As, for example, in the Kádambarí, in the story of Puṇḍaríka and Mahás'wetá.

b. But if *the lost one be* not regainable, or regainable *only after transmigration* in another body, the flavour is called the 'Pathetic simply'—*there being, in this case, no room for any admixture of the 'Erotic'*;—but in the case just mentioned—*of Puṇḍaríka and Mahás'wetá,* immediately on Saraswatí's declaration from the sky *that the lovers should be reunited,* there is the 'Erotic' *in its form of 'separation of tender sadness,'*—for desire arises on the expectation of reunion, but PREVIOUSLY *to Saraswatí's promise* there was the 'Pathetic';—such is the opinion of the competent authorities.

c. And as for what some say in regard to the case *of Puṇḍaríka and Mahás'wetá,* that, "moreover AFTER the expectation of reunion —*excited by Saraswatí's promise to that effect,*—there is merely your honour's variety of 'love in absence' (§ 222) the one which you call 'being abroad' (§ 221,)"—others hold it to be distinct, because of the presence of that distinction, DEATH—*which is something else than merely being abroad.*

d. Next of 'love in union' (§ 211).

TEXT.

Love in union. No. 225. There is said to be 'love in union' where two lovers, mutually enamoured, are engaged in looking on one another, touching one another, &c.

COMMENTARY.

a. By the '&c.' is meant the mutual drinking *the nectar* of each others lips, kissing, &c. For instance—"Perceiving that the house was empty," &c.—*see* § 3. *b.*

TEXT.

No. 226. This 'love in union' is, by the learned, asserted to be one only, because, in consequence of its many varieties of kissing, embracing, &c. it would be impossible that they should be *separately* reckoned. *As accessories* in regard to this, let there be the six seasons *with their several persuasives to loving fondness*, the moon and the sun, and so too their settings, gambols in the water, rambles in groves, the morning, draughts of nectar, the night, &c., anointments and adornments, &c., and whatever else is pure and fair.

COMMENTARY.

a. And to the same effect, Bharata declares—"whatever in the world is pure, and fair, and bright and sightly, all such suits with the Erotic," i. e. befits it.

b. Moroever—

TEXT.

No. 227. But this *love in union* is said to be of four kinds from its coming after 'love antecedent' *to personal acquaintance*, &c. —(*see* § 213.)

COMMENTARY.

a. As has been declared—"Not without *previous* separation does the union *of lovers* prosper; for it is after clothes or the like have been soaped that their colour increases the more."

b. Among these,—there is union after becoming previously enamoured, in the case, for example, of Párvatí and S'iva in the *Kumára-Sambhava;* and union after *separation* by being abroad, as in the following verses of my father's.

"Is it well with thee,—thou with the deep-fringed eyes?"—"My welfare is slender, though my person be so plump."*—"Wherefore is there such slenderness *in thy welfare?*"†—"Because thy person is so stout."—"Why am *I* stout, darling?"—"From the embraces of thy beloved."—"I have none, save THEE my fair-browed one."—"If this be so, why dost thou ask after my welfare?—*thy own wretchedness in absence,—didst thou but love as I do,—would have told thee mine.*"

And so examples of the other cases may be inferred *from this illustration.*

c. Next of the 'Comic' (*hásya* § 209).

TEXT.

The 'Comic,' described.

No 228. The 'Comic,' in which the 'permanent condition' (§ 206) is 'Mirth,' and which, *according to the fancy of the mythologists*, is white-coloured, and has the attendants of S'iva as its presiding deities,—may arise from the fun of distorted shapes, words, dresses, gestures, &c. Whatever a person laughs at, when he beholds it distorted in respect of form, speech, or gesture, this they call the 'substantial' *element of the Comic,'—see* § 63,—and the gestures thereunto pertaining are held to be the 'enhancers' (§ 62). Among its 'ensuants' are closings of the eyes, smilings of the countenance, &c., and the 'accessories' (§ 169) may be Drowsiness, Indolence, Dissembling, &c. *When under the influence of the 'Comic,'* the best kind of persons slightly smile or else smile; the middling sort laugh, or laugh aloud; the baser sort roar with laughter, or are convulsed with laughter; such are the six kinds *of mirthful expression.* Let a 'slight smile' *(smita)* have the eyes a little opened and the lip quivering;—by the learned, among these *varieties of mirthful expression*, that is called a 'smile' *(hasita)* where the teeth are somewhat shown; a 'laugh' *(vihasita)* is attended by a soft sound; loud 'laughter' *(avahasita)* is that which is attended by shakings of the head and shoulders; a 'roar of laughter' *(apahasita)* has the eyes filled with tears; a 'convulsion of laughter' *(atihasita)* is that where the limbs lose all controul.

How men of different characters show their sense of the ridiculous.

* The scholiast explains this sentence thus:—"That my body is so much emaciated, this is my welfare." P. M.

† "—Thinness in thy body," according to the commentator. P. M.

COMMENTARY.

a. For an example *of the 'Comic'—take* my verses—

"Having for five days studied the words of the teacher *Brihaspati or Prabhákara*, and for three *whole* days the Vedánta system, and having sniffed a smell of the disquisitions of Logic, this Dr. Cock has arrived *in full feather*."

b. The full devolopment of this—*i. e. of the 'Comic'*—is to be seen in the *Naṭaka-melaka*, &c.

c. And in regard to this, *the following is to be remarked.*

TEXT.

The representation of the subject of the 'Comic' or other sentiment not indispensable.

No. 229. And even if the *person* to whom, *as its subject*, belongs *the sentiment of* laughter is not directly exhibited anywhere, still he is discerned through the force of the excitants, &c. *which cannot indeed bi realized in their completeness, unless we suppose a* HERO, *under the influence of the sentiment, exhibiting his sense of the ludicrous by external marks, in Poetry called Ensuants.* These Excitants, &c. are apprehended by reason of there being through Sympathy (§ 40), an identification *of the spectator with the actor ;* and thence is this flavour, the 'Comic,' experienced by the spectators.

COMMENTARY.

a. The same is to be understood in regard to the other flavours also.

b. Next of the 'Pathetic' *(karuṇa* § 209).

TEXT.

The 'Pathetic' described.

No. 230. Let that flavour be called the 'Pathetic' which arises from the advent of what is unplesant, or from the loss of what is loved. By the learned it is *mythologically* spoken of as dove-coloured, while its presiding deity is the god of death. Let sorrow be here the permanent mood (§ 206);—what is held to be the Essential Excitant (§ 63) is the object sorrowed for. Let the 'enhancers' (§ 62) be such things as when this—*the dead body of the loved one*—is being burnt. Its 'Ensuants' are the cursing one's destiny, falling on the ground, wailing &c., changes of colour, sighs, and sobs, stupefaction, and raving. Its 'accessaries' are indifference *to all worldly objects*, fainting, epilepsy, sickness, debility, reminiscences, weariness, distress, insensibility, madness, anxiety, &c.

COMMENTARY.

a. The 'object sorrowed for' is a deceased relative, or the like. For example—in my Rághava-vilása—

"How unsuited are this thy lovely form and the cultivation of matted locks in the forest! Is not fate's coupling the two *as inappropriate as* a cutting of the Acacia-flower with a sword?"

For here we have Das'aratha blaming destiny, he being pained with the sorrow produced by Ráma's having to dwell in the woods—*when he was so much better qualified to adorn a palace.*

b. In like manner examples might be adduced where there is separation from relatives, loss of wealth, &c. But the full development *of the 'Pathetic'* is to be seen in the Mahábhárata, in *the section entitled* the Strí-parvvan.

c. He now states the difference *of this—i. e. of the real 'Pathetic'*—from 'separation of tender sadness' (§ 224).

TEXT.

No. 231. This flavour, *the 'Pathetic,'* differs from the 'separation' *of those who are destined to be reunited,* through its having Sorrow as its 'permanent mood.' In the 'separation,' *spoken of under* § 224, 'the permanent mood,' *or groundwork of the sentiment,* is Desire,—this being occasioned by *the hope of* enjoying reunion.

COMMENTARY.

a. Next of the 'Furious' (*raudra* § 209).

TEXT.

The 'Furious' described.

No. 232. The 'Furious,' in which Anger is the 'permanent mood' (§ 206) is—*according to the mythologists,* red-coloured, and has Rudra as its presiding deity. Its 'essential excitant' (§ 63) is an enemy; and his behaviour is regarded as its 'enhancer' (§ 62). Its liveliness may be enhanced by strikings with the fist, fallings, rudeness, cuttings and tearings, fights and confusions. Its 'Ensuants' are knitting of the brows, biting of the lips, swelling of the arms, threatening gestures, telling of one's achievements, and brandishing of weapons; so also reviling, and angry looks, &c. Let sternness, flurry, horripilation, perspiration, trembling, intoxication, delirium, impatience, &c., be its 'accessory' moods.

COMMENTARY.

a. For example—*hear As'watthâman in the Veni-sanhára.*

"By whichsoever unmannerly beasts of men among you, armed as you are, this heavy sin *of Drona's murder* was perpetrated or approved or witnessed, I shall make a sacrifice to all the quarters of heaven with the blood, fat, and flesh of them, though they include Bhíma and Arjuna with *Krishna*, the foe of Maraka."

b. He states the difference of this from the martial 'Heroic.'

TEXT.

No. 233. And it is the redness of the face and eyes that differences this, *the 'Furious,'* from the martial 'Heroic'—*which is to be next described.*

COMMENTARY.

a. Next of the 'Heroic' *(víra* § 209).

TEXT.

The 'Heroic' described.

No. 234. The 'Heroic,' which belongs to the noblest men, has energy as its 'permanent mood' (§ 206). It is stated *by the mythologists* to be yellow-coloured, and to have the great Indra as its presiding deity. But its 'Essential Excitants' (§ 63) are held to be persons that are to be conquered, &c. Its 'enhancers' are the behaviour, &c., of the persons to be conquered, &c. But let its 'Ensuants' be the seeking for allies, &c. But its 'accessories' are firmness, resolution, pride, reminiscences, reasonings, and horripilation. And it may be of four kinds, as being conversant about liberality, or duty, or war, or benevolence.

COMMENTARY.

The 'Heroic' divided.

a. 'And it'—i. e. the 'Heroic.' It is of four kinds. (1) The 'Heroic of liberality,' (2) the 'Heroic of duty,' (3) the 'Heroic of war,' and (4) the 'Heroic of benevolence.'

b. Among these the 'Heroic of liberality'—for example Paras'uráma, *whose liberality is spoken of as follows.*

The 'Heroic' of liberality.

"His liberality extended to the giving away, without any affectation, of the earth girdled by the seven seas."

Here the 'permanent mood,' Paras'uráma's energy in dispensing, attains to being the 'Heroic of liberality,' it—*the Flavour in question*—being excited by the 'Essential Excitants' (§ 63) the brahmanical recipients, and by such 'enhancing excitants' (§ 62) as the goodness and determination of *the benefactor;* and exhibiting as 'ensuant' on it the relinquishment of one's whole possessions, &c.; and being brought to its highest development by such 'accessories' as cheerfulness *in the parting with all one's possessions,* firmness, &c.

c. The 'Heroic of duty'—for example—Yudhishṭhira—*who speaks as follows.*

The 'Heroic' of duty.

"My kingdom, and my wealth, and my body, and those who are my wife, my brothers, and my children, and whatever in this world I am possessed of, all this is ever ready *to be sacrificed* to my duty."

d. The 'Heroic of war'—for example—the illustrious Rámchandra —*whose ambassdor, Angada the son of Báli, thus speaks.*

The 'Heroic' of war.

"O *Rávana* lord of Ceylon, let *Sítá* the daughter of Janaka be restored. Ráma himself begs this. What confusion of thy wits is this? Bethink thee of p̣ropriety. Even up to to-day nothing is lost* to thee *in Ceylon,—but count not on further forbearance.* If thou wilt not do thus, this arrow of mine,—already stained with the neck-blood of *thy friends* Khara, and Dúshaṇa, and Tris'iras,—once let it make friends with the bow-string that joins it, will forbear no further."

e. The 'Heroic of benevolence'—for example—Jímútaváhana—*who —outshining Prometheus—thus addresses a hungry vulture which has stopped eating him.*

The 'Heroic' of benevolence.

"The blood is still circulated by the valves of my veins, and there is still flesh on my body;—I do not see that thou art yet satiated;—why then, O bird, hast thou desisted from devouring?"

f. In the case of these also (§ 234. *c. d. e.)*, the *appropriate* 'conditions,' &c. may be inferred *by the reader for himself,* as in the previous example—(§ 234 *b.)—where they are stated with sufficient fulness.*

g. Next of the 'Terrible' *(bhayánaka* § 209).

TEXT.

The 'Terrible' described.

No. 235. The 'Terrible' has fear for its 'permanent mood' (§ 206,) and Time for its presiding deity. It belongs to women and mean persons, and is regarded *under a*

* Here the edition of 1828 reads गतं and the translation is according to this reading instead of छलं, that in Röer's edition. P. M.

mystical or mythological aspect by the learned as being black-coloured. In this case THAT is regarded as the 'Essential excitant' (§ 63) by which the fear is produced. Again, let the 'enhancers' be its fierce gestures. The 'ensuants,' in this case, are changes of colour and speaking with a stammering tone, faintings, perspiration, horripilation, trembling, looking in every direction, &c. Its 'accessories' are aversion, agitation, bewilderment, terror, debility, prostration, doubt, epilepsy, confusion, death, &c.

COMMENTARY.

a. For example—

"The eunuchs fled, having abandoned shame, because of their not being reckoned among men; the dwarf, in terror, ensconces himself within the *loose and wide* trowsers of the chamberlain; the mountaineers, the guardians of the bounds, acted in a style accordant with their name—*see* § 81. *b.*; while the hump-backs, fearing that they may be seen *by the monkey who has occasioned all this alarm*, cowering down, slink quietly off."

b. Next of the 'Disgustful' (*bíbhatsa* § 209).

TEXT.

The 'Disgustful' described. No. 236. But that Flavour is called the 'Disgustful' where the 'permanent mood' (§ 206) is Aversion. It is alleged *by the mythologists* to be blue-coloured and to have Mahákála (an awful form of S'iva) as its presiding deity. Stinking flesh and fibre and fat, are regarded as its 'Substantial excitant' (§ 63). In the same, the presence of worms &c. are instanced as the 'enhancers.' Spitting, averting of the face, closing of the eyes, &c., are regarded as 'ensuants' in this case; and, in like manner, let the 'accessories' be bewilderment, epilepsy, agitation, sickness, death, &c.

COMMENTARY.

a. For example—*Málatí Mádhava Act V.*—

"Having first torn and stripped off the skin, then having devoured the swollen and violently stinking lumps of flesh that were readily to be got from such parts of the mass as the shoulders, buttocks, and back,—casting his eyes within *the skeleton*, and with his teeth displayed, the beggarly ghost is eating at his ease, from the skeleton placed in his lap, what flesh remains upon the bones or is to be found at the joints."

b. Next of the 'Marvellous' (*adbhuta* § 209).

TEXT.

The 'Marvellous' described.

No. 237. The 'Marvellous' has wonder *or surprise* (§ 206)—as its 'permanent mood' (§ 63), and a Gandharva as its presiding deity. It is alleged *by the mythologists* to be gold-coloured. Its 'essential excitant' (§ 63) is held to be any supernatural thing. Then again let the greatness of the qualities of that *supernatural thing* be the 'enhancers' *of the sentiment.* Stupefaction, perspiration, horripilation, stammering speech, agitation, and so too wide opening of the eyes, and the like, are said to be its 'ensuants.' Its 'accessories' are 'debate' (§ 202), flurry, confusion, joy, &c.

COMMENTARY.

a. For example—*listen to Lakshmaṇa in the Víracharita of Bhavabhúti, Act I.*

"The sound of the clang raised by the breaking of the bow-staff of the Moon-crested *S'iva*, which (bow) had got into his (Ráma's) arms —*or literally arm-staffs,*—as a drum for proclaiming the boy-play of my elder brother--reverberating with its force condensed in the belly of the receptacle of Brahmá's egg—OUR *universe*—the halves of which, violently shaken, have collapsed as a box *so that the sound can't get out,* —ha!—how!—does it not even YET subside?"

b. Next of the 'Quietistic' (*s'ánta,* § 219).

TEXT.

The 'Quietistic' described.

No. 238. The 'Quietistic' has quietism (§ 207) as its 'permanent mood' (§ 206), and is esteemed the mood of the very best *of men.* Its beauty is fair as jessamine and as the moon, and the adorable Náráyaṇa is its presiding deity. Its 'essential excitant' (§ 63) is the emptiness or vanity of all things by reason of their not being lasting,—or else it is the form of the Supreme Spirit,—*i. e. God —the only entity in the opinion of the quietist.* Its 'enhancers' (§ 161) consist of holy hermitages, sacred places, places of pilgrimage, pleasant groves, and the like,—the society of great men, &c. And let its 'ensuants' be horripilation, &c.; and in like manner let its 'accessories' be self-disparagement, joy, remembrance, resolve (§ 169), kindness towards *all* beings, &c.

COMMENTARY.

a. This is an example :—

When will the crow fearlessly carry away the food placed as alms in my joined hands, as I move along the high way, wearing rags of a worn-out patched garment, looked at by the citizens in the road with fear, with curiosity, and with pity, sleeping in the unfeigned bliss of relishing the nectar of spirituality?

b. The fulness *of this flavour* is to be seen in the Mahábhárata, &c.

TEXT.

The Quietistic not identical with the 'Heroic-in-mercy,' &c.

No. 239. The 'Heroic-in-mercy,' or the like,* is not the same with this *flavour*, as the latter is of a nature without egotism.

COMMENTARY.

a. In the Heroic-in-mercy and the like, such, for example, as Jímúta-váhana, we do not find an extinction of egotism, inasmuch as in the middle of the drama *Nágánanda, whereof he is the hero*, his love for Malayavatí and, in the end, his acquiring the sole monarchy of the Vidyádharas are observed. The Quietistic, however, consisting only in the extinction of egotism in every way, is not to be included therein (viz. in the Heroic-in-mercy, &c.) Hence, in the Nágánanda the Quietistic's being the principal sentiment is confuted.

b. But, then, (some one may ask)—

An objection stated against the Quietistic's being a Flavour.

["That in which there is neither pain, nor pleasure, nor thought, nor hatred, nor affection, nor any desire—is called by the chief sages the Quietistic Flavour, which has, among all the sentiments, Quietism for its principal mood."] How can the Quietistic being of the nature *described in the preceding couplet*, arising only in the state of Emancipation (*which is* defined to be the attainment of the *real* nature of the Soul) and wherein there is an absence of the Accessories, &c. be a flavour? To this it is replied *as follows* :—

TEXT.

The Quietistic a Flavour, while the Soul is only *about* to be emancipated.

No. 240. As that quietism only, which exists in the state wherein the mind is joined to and disjoined from the Soul (or, in other words, when the human Soul is not completely absorbed in the Divine) attains to

* The 'Heroic-in-religion,' devotional love, &c. (See § 233, a—e, where the terms are somewhat differently rendered.)

the nature of flavour, the presence in it of Accessories also is not hindered.

COMMENTARY.

a. As for the declaration of the absence, therein, even of pleasure, it refers only to worldly pleasure, and consequently there is no contradiction. For it is asserted—

The bliss of quietism supreme over heavenly as well as earthly pleasures.

'The earthly pleasures of sense and the great pleasure in heaven: these are not worth the sixteenth part of the bliss springing from the quelling of all desires.'

TEXT.

When the Heroic-in-mercy becomes the Quietistic.

*The 'Heroic-in-mercy,' &c. are entitled to be included herein (i. e. in the Quietistic Flavour) if they attain to a state devoid of egotism in every way.

COMMENTARY.

a. By the '&c.' are meant the 'Heroic-in-religion,' the 'Heroic-in-generosity,' 'love having a deity for its object' and others. Amongst them, love having a deity for its object is *exhibited*, for example, *in the following lines*:—

Devotional love illustrated.

"When shall I pass *my* days as a moment, dwelling in Váránasí here on the bank of the Divine River (Gangá), wearing a waist-cloth,† holding my hands joined on my head, and crying out—"O Lord of Gaurí, Destroyer of Tripura, Three-eyed Sámbhu,‡ be propitious!"

b. Now the flavour of 'parental affection' acknowledged by the chief of the sages (Bharata) *shall be defined.*

TEXT.

The Flavour of 'Parental Affection' described,

No. 241. From its evident charmingness they consider Parental Affection also as a Flavour. Its Permanent Condition is parental affection, and a son, &c. are considered its Essential Excitants. The Enhancing

* The numbering of this Text has been omitted in conformity with the edition of the original by Dr. Roer, who erringly considers it as a portion of the preceding commentary

† In the original, कौपीन or a small bit of cloth worn over the privities.

‡ One of the names of S'iva, as the Author of good, or the Deity in his Supreme blessedness when he has withdrawn His energy manifest as the universe.

Excitants are their actions, learning, heroism, benevolence, &c. Embraces, touching their body, kissing their head, gazing at them, erection of the hair of the body, tears of joy and others, are declared to be the Ensuants. Apprehension of evil, delight, pride, &c. are considered the Accessories. Its (the Flavour's) colour is shining like the interior of a lotus and the Mothers of the World are its deity.

a. The following is an example :—

and illustrated.

"That child heightened the joy of the father as it uttered what its nurse first spoke, *as it* walked clinging to her finger, and as it stooped being taught to bow down."

b. Now, he states the incongruity among the Flavours :—

TEXT.

Which Flavours are incongruous with which.

No. 242. The First is opposed to the Pathetic, the Disgustful, the Furious, the Heroic and the Fearful; the Comic, to the Fearful and the Pathetic. The Pathetic is inconsistent with the Comic and the Erotic; the Furious, with the Comic, the Erotic and the Fearful; the Heroic, with the Fearful and the Quietistic; the Fearful, with the Erotic, the Heroic, the Furious, the Comic and the Quietistic; the Quietistic, with the Heroic, the Erotic, the Furious, the Comic and the Fearful; and the Disgustful is incongruous with the Erotic. Thus has the inconsistency been stated.

COMMENTARY.

a. By 'the First' *is meant* the Erotic.

b. The ways of introducing these *Flavours* shall be mentioned afterwards (See Text 601 & Com.)

TEXT.

Madness, &c. not 'permanent conditions' though sometimes apparent as such.

No. 243. Madness and the like,* though from some cause attaining to *an apparent* permanency somewhere, are not 'Permanent Conditions,' as they do not become permanent in the Hero *of a drama or a poem, (or, in other words, as the Hero does not act principally in those conditions).*

* I. e. the other Accessories (see Text No. 169) which are only concomitants of some one main sentiment, such as Love for instance, and this alone is consequently spoken of as a 'Permanent condition.'

s 2

COMMENTARY.

a. As, for example, the madness of Purúravas in the fourth Act of Vikramorvasí.

TEXT.

All poetical sentiments, being relishable, are flavours tropically.

No. 244. Flavour and Incomplete Flavour, their 'semblances,' the 'quelling' and the 'excitement' of a sentiment* and the 'conjunction' and 'commixture' of *sentiments*—even all these *may be considered as* Flavours from their being tasted.

COMMENTARY.

a. From their possessing the quality of being tasted, even the Incomplete Flavour, &c. are Flavours, metaphorically. This is the purport.

b. The Incomplete Flavour, &c. are defined as follows:

TEXT.

An Incomplete Flavour what.

No. 245. The principal Accessories, Love a Deity, &c. being its object, and a 'Permanent condition' merely awakened *(and immediately quelled)* are denominated 'Incomplete Flavours' *(or sentiments simply.)*

COMMENTARY.

a. "There is no Flavour without a sentiment, nor a sentiment devoid of Flavour: a Flavour and a sentiment are completed by each other." Now from a full consideration in the way suggested above, such Accessories as,—though they are always concomitants of Flavour in which they finally end—are, for the time, principally developed, like a servant followed by his king in his marriage procession; Love having a deity, a sage, a spiritual guide, a king or the like for its object; and such 'permanent conditions' as are merely awakened, or, *in other words* have not attained the nature of a Flavour from their not being fully developed by the Excitants, &c.—are denoted by the word 'sentiment' or 'mood' (Bháva).

* More properly, condition or state of being, for the original word bháva comprehends in its sense feelings and mental states, together with conditions of the body.

An Accessory attaining to the rank of an Incomplete Flavour illustrated.

b. Among these an 'Accessory, *prominently developed*' is exemplified in—"Whilst thus the divine sage spoke, Párvati, at her father's side, holding down her head, counted the leaves of the lotus, with which she played."* Here, 'Dissembling' (Avahitthá) is the Accessory.

c. Love—a Deity being its object—as in this stanza of the Kunda Málá:—

Love for a Divinity, an Incomplete Flavour, exemplified.

"I am willing to dwell in heaven, or on earth, or in hell, O, Destroyer of Naraka!† May I only meditate even in death on thy feet that scorn the red lotus of Autumn!"

d. Love having a saint for its object, e. g.—

Love for a sage, the same, exemplified.

Through the sin-destroying sight alone of thee I have obtained my end, still do I feel a wish to hear thy weighty words, for who is ever satiated with Supreme felicity?

e. Love having a king for its object as *in the following:*

Love for a king, the same, illustrated.

"S'iva, afraid of the immense weight, bears not the Ganges on his head, muddy as it is with the heaps of dust raised by the multitude of thy horses."

f. So of others (i. e. love having other objects).

g. A 'permanent condition,' merely, awakened—as—

An undeveloped 'permanent condition,' the same, exemplified.

"But S'iva, like the ocean at the time when the moon is about to rise, with his tranquillity slightly disturbed busied his three eyes on Umá's face with lips like the Vimba‡ fruit." Here is exhibited the love of the Holy One for Párvati—*merely awakened.*

The possibility of an Accessory's being principally developed in a Flavour questioned.

h. But, (*—as some one may object—*) it has been declared that 'the ONE *or simple* perception of the excitants, &c. is Flavour,'§—how then can an accessory, which has no severalty therein, be principally developed? To this it is replied—

* Kumára Sambhava, C. 6, v. 86.

† Vishnu who destroyed a Demon of this name.

‡ The gourd of the Momordica Monadelpha.—*Wilson's Dic.*

§ See § 60. c.

TEXT.

The singleness of flavour not militated against by an Accessory's being principally developed in it.

No. 246. As in the sherbet which is a union of pepper, &c. there is sometimes an excess of some one *of the ingredients*, so there is an excess of an Accessory in a Flavour.

COMMENTARY.

a. Now on the 'semblance of Flavour,' and the 'semblance of Incomplete Flavour.'

TEXT.

The 'semblance of flavour' and the 'semblance of Incomplete flavour' generically defined.

No. 247. When a Flavour and an Incomplete Flavour are brought about with impropriety, they are called the semblances thereof.

COMMENTARY.

a. 'Here, the 'impropriety' is to be understood to mean the defectiveness of the Flavours as defined by Bharata, &c., when there is a lack of entireness in them *as regards their ingredients*.

b. This *impropriety*, is partially elucidated, for the instruction of the unlearned, as follows:

TEXT.

How Flavours are reduced to mere semblances.

No. 248. There is an impropriety in the Erotic, when Love is resident in a Secondary hero and when it is fixed on the wife of a sage or a spiritual guide, when it has many heroes for its objects and when it does not exist in both *the parties*, when it exists in a rival-hero, as also when it is in a low person, in the inferior animals, &c.

There is an impropriety in the Furious, if a spiritual guide or the like be the object of Anger; in the Quietistic dwelling in a vile person; in the Comic having a spiritual guide, &c. for its objects; in the Heroic when the bravery is shown in killing a Bráhmaṇa, &c. or when it abides in a low person; in the Fearful when the emotion *of fear* is excited in a noble personage, and similarly in the other Flavours.

COMMENTARY.

a. Among these 'the semblance of a Flavour' resulting from Love having a secondary hero for its object is displayed, for example, in these verses of mine :—

Love for a secondary hero a semblance —illustrated.

"'Simple enough is my husband, thick is this wood, and I am a solitary girl here, and the overspreading darkness, black like the Tamála tree, mantles over the earth,—make way for me, therefore, O lovely one, O Krishna, immediately'—may Hari preserve you, as he, hearing these words of the milk-maid embraces her and is engaged in the endearments of love."

b. Love having many heroes for its objects—as—

Love for a number of heroes, the same, exemplified.

"O thou of fair form, they only, I believe, are lovers in the three worlds, for whose sake this thy cheek is pale."

c. Love not existing in both the parties is, for instance, the love of Nandana for Málatí in *Bhavabhúti's drama* the 'Málatí and Mádhavá.'

Love, until it is mutual, a semblance of Flavour.

d. "Love existing, first, in one is a 'semblance of Flavour' though it be mutual, afterwards."

This is the dictum of the venerable author of the Lochana. There is an example of it in Ratnávalí *(a drama by king Harsha)* wherein Ságariká loves Vatsa-rája, before they see each other.

Love in a rival hero, the same.

e. Love in a rival hero—as, for example, in the description of Hayagríva's sports in the water, in the Hayagríva badha.

f. Love in a low man—as in the following :

Love in a low man, the same, exemplified.

"A female Bheel with a string of leaves tied round her waist, having picked some mountain Jasmine and sitting upon the hill before her husband, made him comb her hair."

g. Love in an inferior animal—as—

Love in an inferior animal, the same.

"The female bee, with notes melodiously fluctuating like those of the warbling* lyre, betook herself to singing, as she called her lover within a creeper,—*roving* in the midst of the woods delightful with Jasmine flowers."

* Lit. Vibrating.

h. By the '&c.' *after* '*animals*,' (see the Text) are meant ascetics and others.

i. The semblance of the Furious is exemplified in—

The semblance of the Furious exemplified.

" Yonder, enters Arjuna to slay Yudhishṭhira —leaving Karṇa (his enemy)—fiercely striking on his shoulders, holding his bow and arrows, fearless (*even* while Krishna beholds him) burning at the harsh words *of Yudhishṭhira* and extolling the valour of his own arms, while his large rolling eyes sparkle red and his body trembles, *through anger*, again and again !"

j. The semblance of the Fearful—as—

The semblance of the Fearful illustrated.

Indra, unable, with his eyes perplexed, to bear the sight of him, as of the Thousand-rayed *Sun*, —having entered into a cave-house of Himálaya, passed his days affrighted." *Herein there is the semblance of the Fearful*, for the *real* nature of the Flavour is Fear residing in a woman or a low man.

k. Thus with the other *Flavours*.

TEXT.

The semblance of Incomplete Flavour defined.

No. 248. The semblance of Incomplete Flavour exists, for instance, in 'shame' residing in a courtezan.

COMMENTARY.

a. The Text is clear.

TEXT.

The 'quelling,' the 'excitement,' the 'conjunction' and the 'commixture' of sentiments defined.

No. 249. By the 'quelling,' the 'excitement,' the 'conjunction' and the 'commixture' of sentiments (see Text 244,) are meant, respectively the cessation, the coming forth, the co-existence and the confusion of sentiments.

COMMENTARY.

a. These are exemplified in the following four extracts, respectively :—

The quelling of a sentiment.

" 'Fair-formed one ! forego thy anger, see me fallen at thy feet ; O ! never was thy anger such before'—as thus her lord spake she shed not a few tear drops but spoke not a word, as she partly opened her eyes to look down."

b. Here *is exhibited* the quelling of the concomitant feeling named 'jealousy'* through the shedding of tears.

The 'excitement' of a sentiment.

"Heaving a deep sigh, she with her hand placed upon her bosom fixed upon her female friends her sight obstructed by tears in her eyes, as her lover was going away, desisting from propitiating her through her rejection of his falling at her feet, and ruffled with anger at being called by her a disguised cheat."

c. Here is the excitement of 'Despondency.'

The 'conjunction' of sentiments.

"O! this form, ecstatic to my eyes but hard to obtain even through imagination,—O! the one with drunken eyes gladdens my heart yet torments it."

d. Here is the conjunction of 'Joy' and 'Despondency.'

The 'commixture' of sentiments.

"O, a bad action, and the offspring of the moon!—*how inconsistent!*—May she be seen again!—I have my sacred knowledge for the removal of my faults;—oh! how lovely her face even in anger!—What will wise men say—they whose sins are purged off? O! she is hard to obtain even in a dream;—my mind! be thou tranquil;—O what fortunate youth will suck her underlip."

e. Herein, *is exhibited* the commixture of Debate, Longing, Resolve, Recollection, Apprehension, Depression, Equanimity and Painful Reflection.

f. So much for the "Declaration of Flavour, Incomplete Flavour, &c."—the third chapter of the "Mirror of Composition."

CHAPTER IV.

The Declaration of the Divisions of Poetry.

He now states the divisions of Poetry.

TEXT.

Division of Poetry into (1) 'Suggestive' and (2) 'That wherein the suggested meaning is subordinate to the expressed.'

No. 250. Poetry is held to be of two sorts, viz. (1) 'Suggestive' and (2) 'That wherein the Suggested (§9) is subordinate to the Expressed *meaning*.'

COMMENTARY.

Of these—

* Jealousy is one of the accessories of the Erotic Flavour.

TEXT.

Suggestive Poetry, the highest Poetry, defined.

No. 251. 'Suggestive Poetry' is that in which the Suggested prevails over the Expressed, and this is held to be the Highest Poetry.

COMMENTARY.

a. The Highest Poetry denominated 'Suggestive' is that wherein the suggested meaning is more striking *or surprising* than the expressed, *the Sanskrit word for suggestive poetry, viz., 'Dhwani,'—derived from the root 'dhwan' (to sound)*—signifying that wherein *some secret, distinct meaning* sounds *as it were.*

TEXT.

Two-fold sub-division of Suggestive Poetry, as founded on Indication and Denotation.

No. 252. Of 'Suggestive Poetry' also are mentioned two distinctions—originating in 'Indication' and 'Denotation, *respectively—which are* (1) That wherein the expressed *meaning* is NOT desired to be conveyed and (2) That wherein the expressed *meaning*—implying, *or tending to,* another (i. e. a suggestion)—IS desired to be conveyed.

COMMENTARY.

a. Of these *two distinctions,* the 'Suggestive Poetry' named 'That wherein the expressed meaning is not desired to be conveyed' has for its source 'Indication.' And it is from its originating in Indication that in it the expressed meaning is not desired to be conveyed or is made nugatory.

b. But, 'That wherein the expressed meaning—tending to another—IS desired to be conveyed' has for its source 'Denotation,' and hence it is that wherein the expressed meaning is desired to be conveyed.

c. 'Tending to another' (see the Text) *means* ending in a suggested *sense.*

d. In this *second distinction* the expressed meaning manifesting indeed its own self is the manifester of the 'suggested,' just as a lamp is of a jar.

e. The sort of Suggestive Poetry that originates in Denotation, requiring much detail, is mentioned after.

f. He states the two divisions of 'That wherein the expressed meaning is not desired to be conveyed' as follows :—

TEXT.

Two-fold further sub-division of the Suggestive Poetry founded on Indication.

No. 253. The Suggestive Poetry wherein the expressed meaning is not desired to be conveyed, also, becomes of two sorts, accordingly as the expressed meaning passes over into another sense, or as it is made to disappear absolutely.

COMMENTARY.

a. The Suggestive Poetry named 'That wherein the expressed meaning is not desired to be conveyed' is two-fold, viz. (1) 'That wherein the expressed meaning is made to pass over into another meaning' and (2) 'That wherein the expressed meaning is made to disappear absolutely.'

b. That (i. e. the first sort of Suggestive Poetry) in which the principal sense, not being itself appropriate, is changed into another in the form of its own species—is called 'That wherein the expressed meaning passes over into another meaning,' from the passage of the principal sense into a specific signification, *or, in other words, from the thing denoted by a word, for instance, being recognized in a particular manner*. The following is an example :—

"The plantain is *but* the plantain, the lower side of the hand is but the lower side of the hand, and the trunk of Airávata* is but the trunk of Airávata—these thighs of the deer-eyed one bear not a likeness to anything, even, in the three worlds."

c. Here, (—to take, for example's sake, one of the three expressions repeated) the second 'plantain,' being hindered, through the fear of tautology, from conveying its principal meaning, viz. a plantain tree, simply *recognized as such*, conveys the sense of the tree, *particularly considered as* characterized by the qualities of frigidity, &c.; and the EXCESS of frigidity, &c. *of the plantain and its consequent utter unfitness to be compared to the thighs of the lady are suggested.*

d. The *Suggestive Poetry*—in which an expression, entirely giving up its own *(i. e. literal)* sense, is changed into a different signification, —is called 'That wherein the expressed meaning is made to disappear absolutely,'—from the principal sense being made to disappear in every way. The following is an example of this sort :—

"The moon, like the mirror blind with the breath,† shines not."

* Indra's Elephant, the chief of all the Elephants.

† Or the vapour of the mouth.

e. Here, the word 'blind,' having its primary meaning cancelled, conveys the sense of 'dim,' and the excess of dimness is suggested.

f. This verse is not an instance of 'That in which the expressed meaning passes into another one,' blindness and dimness not being in the predicament of genus and species, *or, in other words, dimness not being a species of blindness. Whilst in the preceding couplet, the second 'plantain,' for instance, though really conveying the same sense as the first, is poetically strained to mean the tree, with particular reference to its qualities of frigidity, &c. and, hence, may be considered to be used in a specific sense.*

g. He guards against a misconception that is likely to arise with regard to the distinction between the two first divisions of Suggestive Poetry founded, respectively, on Indication and Denotation. (See Text., 252).

"Stroll, securely, O devotee! that dog was killed to-day by a fierce lion dwelling in the grove on the bank of the Godávarí river."

h. Because, from the 'stroll, O devotee!' the direction for strolling, not being suited to the circumstances of the case, ends in the prohibition of walking—it is not to be supposed that there is in this couplet the 'Indication of the contrary,' for there only is an occasion of it where an 'injunction' and a 'prohibition' end in a 'prohibition' and an 'injunction' respectively, AS SOON AS they spring up *as ideas in our mind.* Whilst that is an instance of suggestion simply *(as the above couplet)* in which a prohibition and an injunction are understood from an injunction and a prohibition, *respectively,* ON THE CONSIDERATION OF THE CIRCUMSTANCES OF THE CASE. To this effect has it been declared:—

"Somewhere the *very* EXPRESSION is *made* nugatorily, *as to its literal sense;* somewhere the *thing* EXPRESSED is nullified: let there be Indication in the former, and Denotation in the latter *instance.*"

i. The first passage *(commencing with 'The plantain is but the plantain')* contains an instance of the passage OR THE ENTRANCE OF THE PRIMARY MEANING INTO A DIFFERENT SENSE, not of its ABSOLUTE DISAPPEARANCE. Hence it is that here is the 'Indication WITHOUT abandonment of its sense.'* Whilst in the second *passage* there is the 'Indication WITH abandonment of its sense,'† from the primary meaning *of the word 'blind'* being made to disappear entirely.

* See Text 14 & Com. † See Text 15 with Com.

TEXT.

Two-fold subdivision of the Suggestive Poetry founded on Denotation.

No. 254. 'That,' also, 'where the expressed meaning IS desired to be conveyed' is considered first as two-fold, accordingly as the Suggested sense therein (1) has its process NOT perceptible and (2) HAS its process perceptible.

COMMENTARY.

a. The Suggestive Poetry named 'That wherein the expressed meaning—tending to another—IS desired to be conveyed' is also of two sorts being (1) 'That in which the Suggested is of imperceptible process and (2) 'That in which the Suggested is of perceptible process.'

TEXT.

The Suggestive Poetry in which the Suggested is of imperceptible process—reckoned as of one sort.

No. 255. Of these the first *(viz. the Suggested of imperceptible process)* consisting of Flavour, Incomplete Flavour, &c. is generically reckoned here as one only, since not even one division *thereof* can be definitely described because of the infinity *of its varieties.*

COMMENTARY.

Flavour, &c. are what are suggested, as it were, imperceptibly.

a. Flavour, Incomplete Flavour, &c., being of the nature already described, are the 'Suggested of imperceptible process.'* Now, the perception of the Suggested, caused as it is by, and hence succeeding, the perception of the Accessories, &c., HAS necessarily a process, but from its quickness it is not perceived, like *the process of* the *apparently simultaneous* piercing through of a hundred lotus leaves *placed one upon another.*

b. Of these—Flavour, &c.—even one distinction does not admit of an enumeration *of all its subdivisions* from *their* infinity; hence the Poetry named 'Suggestive Poetry wherein the Suggested is of imperceptible process,' is declared to be of one form only. For,—not to speak of all the Flavours—the varieties of even the single division of the Erotic *Flavour*, viz. 'Love in enjoyment' are not capable of being

* The reader must bear in mind, that Hindu writers on Taste, curiously enough, speak of Poetical Relish together with the sentiments excited by Poetry as being SUGGESTED by it.

enumerated, inasmuch as they are endless in the shape of mutual embracing, sipping the lips and kissing, &c. in each of which, again, there are peculiarities of the Accessories, &c.

TEXT.

The 'Suggestive Poetry of perceptible process,' three-fold, the Suggested being founded on the power of a word, of the sense, or of both.

No. 256. The 'Suggestive Poetry wherein the Suggested is of perceptible process' is declared by the learned to be three-fold, for the Suggested sense—comparable to an echo—may arise from the power of a word, of a meaning, or of both.

COMMENTARY.

a. That Suggested sense, which is like the resonance *of the expressed* from the perceptibility of its succession *to it*, being three-fold, from its originating in the power of a word, from its originating in the power of a sense, and from its originating in the power of both a word and a sense *together*,—the Suggestive Poetry named 'That wherein the Suggested is of perceptible process' is also three-fold.

b. Of these *three divisions*—

TEXT.

The Suggested sense founded on the power of a word, two-fold, viz.

No. 257. The Suggested sense arising from the power of a word is two-fold, from its being either a *simple* matter or an ornament.

COMMENTARY.

a. From the separate mention of 'ornament' *in the Text*, a simple matter without an ornament is meant by *the word* 'matter' in the same.

(1) a simple matter,

b. Of these *two divisions* the 'Suggested sense arising from the power of a word' being in the form of a *simple* matter, is exemplified *in the following couplet* :—

"O traveller, there is not even a little bedding in this village—a place of stones, but seeing the clouds* risen, if thou dwellest, do dwell."

Here by the power of the words 'bedding,' &c. is suggested the matter, viz. 'If you are able to enjoy, then remain.'

* In the original, पयोधर which signifies breast also.

(2) an ornament. *c.* The Suggested sense arising from the power of a word, being in the form of an embellishment, is shown in these verses.

"Who, by his fort, is insurmountable in battle, who dazzles Cupid himself by his radiance, attended upon by an assembly of mighty princes, venerable, surrounded on all sides by men of affluence, who *out of contempt* looks not at the Kshattriya chiefs, who has a deep devotion to *S'iva*—Lord of the mountain *Kailása*, who holds the whole earth in possession, whose form is adorned with majesty—resplendent is this beloved of Umá."*

Here Bhánudeva and the Lord (—*S'iva*—) are supposed to be with respect to each other in the predicament of the compared and what is compared to, lest the description of the husband of Párvatí—who is not in question—hinted by the second sense of the *verses*, turn out unconnected with the description of king Bhánudeva the husband of the queen named Umá who is in question. Hence here is suggested the ornament of simile, viz. 'the husband of Umá, *the queen*, is like the husband of Uma *the goddess*."

d. Or take another example—

"O lord, thou art a source of joy to us, immense as thou art with the glories acquired in war, and, associated with good fame, thou art an enemy of the wicked."

Here from the absence of the particle अपि ('though') after the words अमित ('immense,') &c. the semblance of the ornament named 'contradiction'† (विरोध) is SUGGESTED.‡

* The second sense of this stanza, as rendered by Dr. Ballantyne, (see § 25 c.) is with some little emendation, the following:—

"Whose body is never left by Durgá, overwhelming by his radiance the god of love, on whom *as a crest-ornament* has risen a digit of the moon, venerable, surrounded everywhere by his snakes, whose *left* eye is made of the lord of the stars *(the moon)*, who has a solid affection for the most majestic of mountains *(—the Himálaya—)*, having mounted on a bull—*the emblem of justice*—with his body adorned with ashes,—resplendent is this beloved of Umá."

† See Chap. X. Text 718.

‡ To explain the passage:—'Amitah' followed in the original by 'samitah' and 'ahitah' by 'sahitah'—which are opposite words in their 2nd meanings—SUGGEST the semblance of contradiction (i. e. a contradiction in words, not in sense) which they would have EXPRESSED, if the particle 'api' ('though' or 'yet') expressive of opposition, had been put between each of the above two pairs of contradictory words.

e. The Suggested meaning, through strictly what is ornamented,* is figuratively spoken of here as the ornament, with reference to its being an ornament in another condition,† just as we use the word 'Bráhman-mendicant' (ब्राह्मणश्रमण) *which, though it etymologically means an absurdity viz. a mendicant, or one not a Bráhman, who is a Bráhman, tropically signifies one who* WAS *a Bráhman.*

TEXT.

The Suggested sense founded on the power of a sense, twelve-fold.

No. 258. A sense is two-fold, being either a matter, or an ornament and *each of these two* being either self-possible, established by the poet's bold assertion, or established by that of one figured by him—a sense is six-fold; hence the Suggested arising from the power of a sense becomes twelve-fold, each of its two forms, viz. a matter and an ornament being suggested by each of the above six.

COMMENTARY.

a. 'Self-possible' i. e. possible even in the external world, from its (*i. e.* the thing's) fitness.

b. Established by 'bold assertion,' i. e. not through fitness, *or not according to the laws of nature.*

c. These *twelve sorts* are exemplified in order, as follows:

(1) THE SELF-POSSIBLE SENSE.

(*a*) *Matter Suggested by matter.*

"O neighbour, will you cast your eyes for a moment on our house also?—the father of this child will scarcely drink the tasteless water of a well: though alone, I am quickly going hence to the river with its bank covered with Tamála trees,—let the densely swarming knots of the reeds with their hard projections scratch my body."

By this self-possible simple matter, *viz. the knots scratching the body*, is suggested the simple matter, viz. the speaker's concealing the nail-scratches, &c. to be caused by her dallying with another man.

* For the Suggested sense, being the most striking in Poetry, is its body or principal part, and hence is that which is ornamented and not the extraneous or unessential thing—its ornament.

† I. e. when it is expressly used, and not hinted through the suggestive power of words as in the foregoing two stanzas.

(*b*) *Ornament suggested by matter.*

"The splendour even of the sun decreases on the southern side, and on that very side the Pándyas could not endure the prowess of Raghu."

By this self-possible matter is suggested the ornament of 'Contrast' (व्यतिरेक) or that the prowess of Ṛaghu is superior to the splendour of the sun.

(*c*) *Matter suggested by Ornament.*

"Balaráma, with his valour collected, marked him coming at a distance, as a lion *beholds* an elephant *his prey*."

Here by the self-possible suggestive sense in the form of the ornament of simile (उपमा) is suggested the 'matter,' that Baladeva will effect the destruction of the Demon Veṇudárin even in a moment.

(*d*) *Ornament suggested by Ornament.*

"Who, biting in battle his under-lip with rage, freed the coral lips of the wives of his enemies from the calamity of being pained by the deep wounds caused by the teeth of their lords."

Here by the self-possible ornament of 'Contradiction'* (विरोध) is suggested the ornament of 'Conjunction'† (samuchchaya) or that the under-lip was bitten and the enemies were killed.

(2.) The sense established by the poet's bold assertion.

(*a*) *Matter suggested by Matter.*

"The season of sweet scents (Spring) prepares, but delivers not yet, the arrows of the Incorporeal one (Cupid,) well fitted for their marks—the young women—*arrows* such as the new-blown, fragrant, mango plants, feathered with the tender leaves."

Here, Spring *represented* as the arrow-maker, Cupid, as the archer, the young women, as the marks, the flowers, as the arrows—all this *collective* matter, established by the bold assertion of the poet, displaying itself‡ suggests the matter, viz. the first excitement of Love.

(*b*) *Ornament suggested by Matter.*

"O hero, the expanse of thy fame whitens perpetually the whole round of the earth, lighted only by night by the beams of the pure-rayed *moon*."

Here by the matter, established by the poet's bold assertion, (*viz. the whitening of the world by the hero's fame*), is suggested the

* See Chap. X. Text 718. † See Chap. X. Text 739.

‡ I. e. being first understood *literally* from the words or through their power of Denotation (§9.).

ornament of 'Contrast'* (vyatireka) consisting in the wide-spread fame's being an illuminator through a greater duration than the moon-beams are.

(*c*) *Matter suggested by Ornament.*

"Tear-drops of the Fortune of the Demons fell to the earth, disguised as gems, from the crests of the Ten-headed *Rávaṇa*."

Here by the ornament of 'Concealment' (apahnuti),† established by the poet's bold assertion, is suggested the matter of the future destruction of the fortune of the Demons.

(*d*) *Ornament suggested by Ornament.*

"Ornament‡ of the land of Trikaliṅga! thy heap of fame, though one, has attained to being the various decorations on the bodies of the beautiful-browed ones of Indra's city—'the bunch of new jasmine on their locks, the white lotus in their hands, the pearl necklace on their necks, and the thick Sandal unguent on their breasts."

Here, by the ornament of Metaphor (rúpaka,§) established by the poet's bold assertion, is suggested the ornament of 'Peculiar Causation' (vibhávaná‖) that 'though on earth, thou doest good to those in heaven.'

(3.) THE SENSE ESTABLISHED BY THE BOLD ASSERTION OF ONE FIGURED BY THE POET.

(*a*) *Matter suggested by Matter.*

"On what mountain, how long and what kind of austerities did that little parrot practise, by which, O fair-faced one! it bites the vimba fruit of thy under-lip's redness."

Here by this matter, *(viz. the parrot's biting the vimba fruit through its previous austerities,)* established by the bold language of a lover figured by the poet, is suggested the matter that 'thy under lip is to be obtained by an excess of good deeds.'

(*b*) *Ornament suggested by Matter.*

"Fair one! in Spring the arrows of the maddening god having attained the number of ten millions left the state of quintuplicity¶—quintuplicity (death) alas! befell the separated lovers."

* See Chap. X. §700. † Chap. X. §683 & 684.

‡ Literally the ornamenting mark on the forehead (tilaka).

§ §669. ‖ §716.

¶ Káma the Hindu Cupid is represented with a flowery bow and *five* arrows of the same material.

Here, by the matter, established by the bold declaration of a speaker figured by the poet, viz. the death of all the absent lovers from Cupid's arrows attaining to the number of ten millions—is suggested the ornament of 'Uncommon Supposition,' viz. the quintuplicity of the arrows having quitted them took possession of the separated lovers.

(c) *Matter suggested by Ornament.*

"Wrathful one, the humming bee on the jasmine bud beautifully looks as if blowing the conch in the ***victorious*** march of him with the five arrows (Cupid)."

Here, by the ornament of 'Uncommon Supposition,' (utprekshá—see § 686—692) established by the bold word of a speaker figured by the poet, is suggested the matter, viz. 'this, the maddening time of Cupid is arrived, why then dost thou not give up thy anger, indignant one!"

(d) *Ornament suggested by Ornament.*

"O fortunate youth, she, not obtaining a place in thy heart filled with a thousand fair women, emaciates her frame, slender as it is, making that her only business."

Here, by the 'not obtaining a place'—the ornament of 'Poetical Reason' (kávya-linga*) established by the bold language of a speaker figured by the poet is suggested the ornament of 'Peculiar Allegation,' (vis'eshokti,†) viz. 'In spite of her emaciating her body she ***gets*** no ***room*** to dwell in thy heart.'

d. The poet indeed is not possessed by passion, &c. like one figured by the poet, hence the bold assertion of the speaker figured by the poet, being more striking to the man of sensibility, is separately described.

e. But, where the suggestion is as to an ornament, there it necessarily respects the matter ornamented—why then recognize ornament distinctively? Because, among these *(i. e. the above examples)* in the instances of suggestion as to an ornament, it is the FIGURES of Metaphor, Uncommon Supposition, Contrast, &c. that are perceived as striking by the man of taste, and not WHAT ARE FIGURED severally under these embellishments and hence the prominence belongs to the ornament *or the figurative expression and not to the matter figured.*

* §710. † §717.

TEXT.

Suggestion based on the power of a word and of a sense, single.

No. 259. When the suggestion arises from the power of a word and a meaning, *Suggestive Poetry is* one (§256).

COMMENTARY.

a. When the suggested sense is founded on the power of both *together*, there is *only* one sort of Suggestive Poetry, as—

"Mádhava (i. e. Krishṇa or Spring) *ornamented* with the lotus,* and beautiful like (or with) the moon free from mists, who gladdened the Twice-born (the Bráhmans or the birds,) who generated Love (the deity or the passion), and who cheered the gods (or purified wine†)—long was he the great delight of the beautiful women."

Here we have the ornament of Simile, viz. 'Mádhava or Krishṇa is like Mádhava, the Spring,' suggested *by the power of the mere words 'dwija' (a Brahman or a bird,) 'Mádhava,'‡ &c. and of the senses of the words 'janita-mínaketana' (who generated Love,) &c.*

b. Thus, the divisions of Suggestive Poetry are founded on the divisions of the Suggested Sense.

TEXT.

No. 260. So Suggestive Poetry is eighteen-fold.

COMMENTARY.

The eighteen main sub-divisions of Suggestive Poetry, summed up.

a. 'That in which the expressed sense is not desired to be conveyed' is two fold, viz. (1) 'That in which the expressed sense passes over into another' and (2) 'That in which the expressed sense is made to disappear entirely.' 'That in which the expressed sense—tending to another—is desired to be conveyed' is single, when it is 'That in which the Suggested is of imperceptible process'—and is fifteen-fold, when it is 'That wherein the Suggested is of perceptible process' founded on the power of a word, a sense and of both.

Thus there are eighteen varieties of Suggestive Poetry.

b. And of these—

* Or as qualifying 'Krishna,'—'associated with Lakshmi.'

† Wine is buried in Áshádha (June, July) and is dug out greatly improved in the Spring.

‡ These cannot be exchanged for their synonyms, without an alteration in the sense of the passage, whilst 'janita-mínaketana, &c. can: so the Double Entendre is founded partly on words and partly on sense.

TEXT.

No. 261. The Poetry of Suggestion founded on the power of word and of meaning dwells in a sentence *only;* the others *reside* in a word and a sentence.

COMMENTARY.

a. Among these *latter*, 'Suggestive Poetry wherein the expressed sense passes over into another' existing in a word—as—

"Blessed is that youth alone and his eyes are eyes indeed, in whose presence will be this fair-faced one—this enchantment of young men."

The second 'eye' here implies an eye characterized by the qualities of being fortunate, &c.

b. The same residing in a sentence is exemplified in—

"I tell you (twám asmi vachmi)—here stays an assembly of the learned, so make your stay here, having collected your wits."

Here, from the very presence of the addressee before *the addresser*, the fact of his being the person addressed is understood, yet the word twám 'you' is used here to indicate the sense of 'you' qualified by the exclusion of others *(or more briefly, to signify you exclusively.)* Similarly, from the simple word 'vachmi' (dico) the agent is understood, yet the expression 'asmi' (I) indicates the sense of 'I' qualified by the exclusion of others. Likewise, as by simply saying 'An assembly of the learned, &c.' the speech of the addresser might be fulfilled, the expression 'vachmi' *('I tell,' which taken in its literal or Expressed sense is superfluous)* conveys by its power of Indication the sense of 'I advise' implying a particular form of telling. These *things* being indicated, suggest their 'exceedingness' *or are forcibly understood:* so the purport of the whole sentence is this—'my word is extremely friendly to you, you must therefore *do it.*' Thus it is *an instance* of 'Suggestive Poetry in which the Expressed passes over into another meaning'—residing in a sentence.

c. 'That wherein the Expressed sense disappears entirely'—dwelling in a word—, as—

"Like a mirror, blind with the breath, the moon shines not" (§253, *c*).

d. The same, in a sentence—for example—"Much benefit have you done &c." (§15. *a.*)

e. The others *(viz. the varieties of the Poetry of Suggestion in which the Expressed—tending to another—is desired to be conveyed)* as residing in a sentence, have already been exemplified, (§257, 258 and 259).

f. As residing in a word, they are exemplified as follows :—

THE SUGGESTION OF IMPERCEPTIBLE PROCESS.

A Flavour suggested.

" That beauty, that loveliness, that form, that address were then full of nectar, but alas ! now *(in absence)* they are a fierce fever *to me.**

Here, the prominence belongs to the pronominal words 'tat' &c. only *(—which all correspond to 'that'—)* being suggestive of the beauty &c. as they were then perceived and as passing description. The other words being only subsidiary to them, the claim of the above stanza to the title of Suggestive Poetry is founded on them only. To this effect, has it been declared by the author of the 'Dhwani' :

" Like a beautiful woman with a single member ornamented, a sentence of a good poet shines with Suggestion displayed by a single word."

Similarly is it to be understood with respect to Incomplete Flavour &c. *how they are principally suggested by a word.*

SUGGESTION OF PERCEPTIBLE PROCESS—FOUNDED ON THE POWER OF A WORD.

A matter suggested.

" In whom does not the good scripture (or the arrival of a good man) produce a flow of joy—causing, as it does, temporal as well as spiritual happiness,† and leading to retirement."

Here the word 'Sadágama' [sat,—good + ágama, scripture or arrival] expressing to the secondary hero (*i. e.* her lover) staying near *the female speaker* the sense of 'good scripture', suggests the matter viz. the arrival of a good man.

But—*as some one might object*—why should it not be held as an instance of the suggestion of a Simile, viz. 'good scripture is like the arrival of a good man ?' *To this we reply : Not so*, because the two significations of the word 'Sadágama' are not desired to be spoken of as being in the predicament of the compared and what is compared to, for the employment of the equivocal word is only for the conceal-

* The sub-division of the Erotic Flavour, technically called 'Love in separation' (§212,) is what is suggested in this stanza.

† In respect of the arrival of the 'good man,' the word in the original for temporal and spiritual happiness viz. 'bhukti and 'mukti' mean respectively enjoyment and freedom from domestic business.

ment of the secret *of her love for the so-called good man*, and because the incongruity here of speaking of the good scripture is evident from the consideration of the circumstances of the case, &c.

An ornament suggested.

"With wisdom unrivalled, and protecting the whole earth, indescribably shines in the world that monarch—that best of persons."

Here is the suggestion of a Simile viz. the best of personages (purushottama) is like the Supreme of persons or Vishnu.

In these two examples are exhibited the two distinctions of the Suggestion of perceptible process arising from the power of a word.

SUGGESTION OF PERCEPTIBLE PROCESS, ARISING FROM THE POWER OF A SENSE. THE SELF-POSSIBLE SENSE.

Matter suggested by Matter.

"In the evening thou hast had recourse to bathing and anointed thy body with sandal; the Ethereal Gem (the Sun) has reached the crest of the Western Mountain (the mountain of setting—Astáchala), and thou hast securely come here. O! wonderful is the delicacy about thee, through which thou art exhausted NOW! and thy eyes cannot remain, without being constantly closed."

Here by a self-possible matter is suggested the matter, viz. 'Thou hast bathed having had intercourse with a lover.' The word 'now' intimating, as it does, that 'thou art now exhausted, but never before was such an exhaustion of thine seen' is more prominent than the other words, inasmuch as this intimation sets off the significancy of the other words.

Ornament suggested by matter.

"Another milk-maid, confined, obtained Emancipation (or final salvation), meditating upon the Origin of the Universe (Krishṇa) whose true form is the Supreme Spirit—her endless sins having been dissolved by her mighty pang in not obtaining him, and the store of her good deeds having been wasted away by her exuberant joy in reflecting on him."

Here, by the force of the words 'endless' and 'store' the pang of separation from the Holy One and the joy of meditating on him are recognized as identical with the immensity of the fruits of merit and demerit to be experienced for many thousands of years: so our recognition of the two Hyperboles (atis'ayokti) is occasioned by the words 'endless' and 'store'. The Suggestive matter here (viz. the Emancipation of the milk-maid in the manner described), being possible independently of a 'bold assertion' *or not merely in the Poet's imagination**), is self-possible.'

THE SENSE ESTABLISHED BY THE POET'S BOLD ASSERTION.

Ornament suggested by Ornament.

"O Sire, Gangá who flows through three ways *only (or Heaven, Earth and Pátála)*, conceals herself, through shame, on Mahádeva's head, as she beholds the river, *formed* of the waters *poured* in thy donations, streaming through innumerable passages."

The *couplet* is mine. Here, the expression 'as she beholds &c.' which is an instance of the figure of Poetical Reason (Kávya-linga, §710) established by the poet's bold language, and *particularly* the word 'innumerable' suggests the ornament of Contrast (vyatireka), viz. 'there are no other donors equal to thee,' or '*thy liberality is mighty—that of others, insignificant.*'

Thus may it be exemplified with respect to the other divisions also of the Suggestion of perceptible process arising from the power of a sense.

The said eighteen kinds of Suggestive Poetry, with one exception, being further sub-divided according as they abide in a sentence or a word, there result thirty-five varieties.

g. So, among the said eighteen descriptions of Suggestive Poetry, that founded on the power of a word and a meaning is one, being possible only in a sentence, whilst the other seventeen being possible both in a sentence and a word become thirty-four: thus we have thirty-five divisions of the Poetry of Suggestion.

TEXT.

Suggestive Poetry founded on the power of a sense, possible also in a Great Sentence.

No. 262. The Suggestive Poetry founded on the power of a sense is considered by the learned to be possible, also in an entire composition.

COMMENTARY.

a. 'Entire composition'—in a Great Sentence.

b. '*Suggestive Poetry* founded on the power of a sense' *i. e.* the kind whereof the twelve divisions have been mentioned.

c. The *following* dialogue between a vulture and a jackal in the Mahábhárata (S'ánti parvan, sl. 5675—5800) is an example :—

Vulture—"You need not stay longer in this horrible cemetery crowded with vultures and jackals, abounding with skeletons, and

* Seeing that the All-merciful God could give them salvation so easily.

fearful to all that breathe: nor has any one subjugated by Death, revived here, whether beloved or hated: such is the condition of animals."

It was the wish of the vulture that the men staying with the dead child might leave it there in the day-time, and depart.

Jackal—"Fools! the sun is yet up, be tender for the present moment: this time *of evening* has many obstacles, and the poor boy may revive when it is over. How should you, O ignorant men, from the vulture's word, leave unsuspectingly that boy shining like gold, who has not yet attained to youth.

To the jackal who was active at night, the quitting of the boy during the day was not desirable. These two facts are suggested by the collective sentence *formed of a number of such alternate discourses of the two carnivorous philosophers.* The suggestive matter here is self-possible.

d. Similarly might the other eleven distinctions be exemplified.

e. Thus has *the Suggestive Poetry founded on the power of a sense* been exemplified *in all its twelve main distinctions* (§258), *and some of its sub-divisions,* when the expressed meaning is the suggester.

f. When the Indicated meaning is the Suggester we may take for

Suggestion from an Indicated sense.

an example—"The border of thy breasts has lost the whole of the sandal wood &c." (§27. *c*).

Suggestion from a Suggested sense.

g. When the Suggested meaning is the Suggester—for example—"The crane stands unmoved &c." (§27. *d*).

In these two *examples* the respective indicated and suggested meanings are 'self-possible' suggesters.

h. Similarly, might the other eleven divisions (§258) be exemplified in the case of an indicated or a suggested sense being the suggester.

TEXT.

Suggestion of Imperceptible process may come from parts of a word, letters, style, and an entire composition.

No. 263. *Suggestion* whereof the process is not clear or 'Suggestive Poetry wherein the Suggested is of imperceptible process' is possible in the *several* parts of an inflected word (pada), in the letters, in style, and in an entire composition.

COMMENTARY.

Of these, that residing in the parts of a word—

a.—is manifold, from the distinctions of the radical part, the affix, the prefix, a particle, &c.; as may be exemplified in the following stanzas:—

"Thou touchest frequently those trembling eyes with quivering corners; hovering near her ear thou hummest softly as if to speak some secret; thou sippest that under lip—Love's whole property, as she waves her hand *in confusion*—blessed art thou indeed, O honey-maker! whilst we are killed by our scrupulous search after the truth *as to whether she is really fit to be married by a Kshattriya.*"

Here (*in this speech of Dushyanta in respect of Sakuntalá, in Kálidása's drama*) since the expression हताः *(we are killed)* is used rather than दुःखं प्राप्तवन्तः *(we are distressed)*, the suggestion of the king's 'love in separation' *particularly* comes from the radical part हन् *of the word* हताः

"The face of her with long-lashed eyes, turned to the shoulder, with lips repeatedly covered by her fingers, *doubly* charming, as she in the confusion of coyness uttered the syllables of forbidding—was with difficulty raised by me, but oh! not kissed."

Here, the suggestion of *the king's* regret *at not having kissed his love Sakuntalá* originates *(chiefly)* in the particle तु (but).

"For this indeed is an utter contempt of me that there are foes &c." (§2. *f*). In this stanza the following are suggestive:—the plural number in अरयः (foes); the singular number in तापसः (anchoret); the pronoun अत्र (here—in this place); the verbal inflection तिङ् (present, 3rd sing.) in निहन्ति (slaughters) and जीवति (does live); the indeclinable अहो (O wonder!); the *diminutive* nominal affix (taddhita) क *used in contempt in the word* ग्रामटिका (poor villages); the prefix वि (implying particularity) *of the word* विलुण्ठन (plundering, 'carrying off the spoils'), and the plural number in भुजैः (from these arms).

"Thou hast a distaste for food (आहारे विरतिः), and an utter indifference to the whole set of objects, thy sight is fixed at the end of thy nose, and there is this further that thy mind is abstracted in meditation, and there is this silence with thee, and this world now absolutely appears empty to thee; so say, friend—ho! art thou indeed an ascetic?—or rather a separated lover *art thou?*"

Here the locative case, in the sense of 'object,' of the word आहारे* (in food);—the two epithets समस्त (whole) and परा (utter);—the pronoun इदम् in मौनञ्चेदम् (and this silence) that refers to a thing under actual perception *and consequently marks a peculiarity in the lady's silence;*—the prefix आ in आभाति (absolutely appears);—the word सखि (friend) that reminds her of *worldly* love *which is foreign to the character of an ascetic;*—the jocular expression असि भोः (art thou, ho!); the particle वा (or rather) in किंवा that hints the strength *or probability* of the latter supposition viz. *Thou art a separated lover;*—the present tense inflection of असि (thou art)—to each of these belongs a suggestion peculiar to it and to be perceived *only* by the man of poetical sensibility.

b. *Suggestive Poetry* in Letters and that in Style (§263) shall be exemplified *in chap. 8th and 9th respectively.*

c. Suggestion in an entire composition is such, for example, as the Quictistic in the Mahábhárata, the Pathetic in the Rámáyaṇa, the Erotic in the Málatí Mádhava *of Bhavabhúti,* the Ratnávalí of S'rí Harsha &c.:† so in the others.

TEXT.

5355 subdivisions of Suggestive Poetry, finally obtained.

No. 264. Thus then of Suggestion we have fifty-one divisions: these from the threefold Commixture (see §757) and the uniform Conjunction (see §756) make up the number *marked inversely by the quadruple* Veda, the *empty* Ether, the *triple* Fire *as kept by the Bráhmans,* and the *five* Arrows *of Cupid, i. e.* 5304,‡ *which* together with the pure

* The expression आहारे विरतिः (distaste for food) is used here rather than आहाराद् विरतिः (cessation from taking food). It therefore suggests 'Thou hast given up eating, simply from mental distress, unlike a hermitess (योगिनी) who purposely desists, but not altogether, from taking food, simply because too much eating is an obstruction to her wished-for emancipation from 'this mortal coil.'

† These being the main sentiments of the poems and dramas respectively are held to be what are suggested by them; the other passions or feelings acting as ancillary to these principal ones.

‡ As each of the fifty-one sorts admits of being combined, in four different ways, with a similar kind as well as with the fifty other sorts,—the sum, which in Algebra is one of Combination when two and two are taken together, may thus be explained:—

$$(51 \times 4) + \left(\frac{51 \cdot 50}{2}\right) 4 = 5304.$$

ones attain to the number signified inversely by Arrow, Arrow, Fire and Arrow, or 5355.

COMMENTARY.

a. 'Together with the pure ones'—*i. e.* with the addition of the fifty-one pure divisions.

b. *A part of the compound sorts* (see the Text) is exemplified *in the following stanzas* :—

The Commixture of Suggestions, as 'abiding intimately together.'

"With breasts extremely raised and with eyes large and tremulous, she, standing at the door to hail his (her husband's) arrival, holds the auspicious omens of the full jar and the collection of garlands on the gate arch, brought about without effort."

Here the breasts *of the lady being hinted at as being* the full jars and her looks as the garlands of fresh lotuses—*which are auspicious omens displayed at the gate to one returning home from a distance,* we have a Commixture of the Suggestion of Metaphor and that of Flavour (viz. Love in enjoyment) as 'abiding intimately together' (see §757. *c.*) *or as implied in the same expressions.*

The Conjunction of Suggestions.

"These spring days cheer *the heart*—when bees increase their hums for joy—but alas! when the heart of the distant lover* shudders—when the winds are proud of their intimacy with the fragrance of the lotus faces of those with countenances like the moon without drowsiness."

Here we have the Conjunction (§ 264) of Suggestions founded on Indication (§26, 27. c) viz. those in the expressions 'without drowsiness,' 'intimacy,' &c.

c. Now of the Poetry named 'That wherein the Suggested is subordinate'† (see §250).

TEXT.

The inferior sort of Poetry, that of Subordinate Suggestion.

No. 265. Whilst the Poetry of Subordinate Suggestion is the inferior sort, in which the Suggested is not more striking than the Expressed.

COMMENTARY.

a. 'The inferior sort'—*i. e.* the inferior sort of Poetry.

* Lit. Traveller.

† 'Poetry of Subordinate Suggestion' would be a more manageable term, though less literal in rendering.

b. The *circumstance of the Suggested meaning's* being not more striking is possible, both when it is inferior and equal to the Expressed.

TEXT.

Eight-fold division of this, according to the ways in which the Suggested is Subordinate.

No. 266. In this *second rate Poetry*, the Suggested may be 'ancillary to another,' 'hinted by the tone,' 'subservient to the completion of the Expressed,' 'of doubtful prominence,' 'of equal prominence,' 'obscure,' 'unconcealed,' or 'not beautiful:' thus there are reckoned eight divisions of it.

COMMENTARY.

a. 'Ancillary to another'—*i. e.* to another Flavour, or the like.

b. When the Suggested in the shape of a Flavour or the like is Ancillary to some other Flavour or the like, we have the following examples:—

The widow of Bhúris'raváh laments her husband killed in battle, thus:—

The Suggested, 'ancillary to another,' exemplified.

"This is that hand which drew my girdle; which pressed my plump breasts; which touched my navel, thigh and hip; and which loosened the end of my waist-cloth."

Here the Suggested Erotic is 'ancillary' to the Pathetic.

Another example.

"Alas! how do the lovers fare in the series of the palaces of thy enemy's capital, when their ears are tormented with the *sudden* tumult of the ocean of thy army, as they are seeking to propitiate their beloved ones elevated with pride."

Here, the Pathetic heightened with the Conjunction (see §249) of Longing and Alarm is 'ancillary' to 'Love having a king for its object' (§245).

"I have wandered in the abodes of men (जनस्थाने,—or in the part called जनस्थान of the Daṇḍaka forest), with my mind filled with the mirage of gold (or with the desire of the golden deer); at every step have I, with tears, cried 'O give!' (or O Sítá!) I have *fawningly* interwoven *my words* with the texture of those of bad masters (or have fastened arrows to the series of the heads of Lanká's lord); oh I have become Ráma, but not obtained an affluent fortune (or have not obtained her—*Sitá*—whose sons were Kusá and Lava)."

Here even without the expression 'I have become Ráma,' the speaker's *verbal* identity with him might be understood by the power merely of the *other* words *as arranged in the stanza.* But the express declaration, manifesting, as it does, the speaker's identification of himself with Ráma founded on his *verbal* resemblance *to him*, removes the concealment of the resemblance ; hence the almost EXPRESSED resemblance (—though meant to be SUGGESTED—) being made to show the logical connection in the sense of the sentence* is reduced to being subservient *to the Expressed sense.*†

c. *The Suggested sense*, 'hinted by the tone'—as—

The Suggested, 'hinted by the tone.'

"I am not destroying, with wrath, the hundred Kauravas in war, I am not sucking the blood of Dus'sásana from *his* breast, I am not pounding with my club the thighs of Duryodhana—let your king make peace with *them* on the condition *of receiving the five poor villages.*"

Here the Suggested viz. 'I AM to destroy' remains in intimate connection with the Expressed denial, *or in other words, is conveyed simultaneously with it.*

The Suggested, 'ancillary to the completion of the Expressed.'

d. "O king of kings, this thy power, the forest flame of the enemy's family (वंश), burns in every direction, illuminating the space between heaven and earth."

Here the Suggested, viz. the ascribing the nature of a bamboo to the family *of the enemy* (through the equivocal वंश which means a bamboo also) is 'ancillary' *or subservient* to the ascribing of the character of the forest flame to the power of the king.

The Suggested 'of doubtful prominence.'

e. The Suggested 'of doubtful prominence'—as for example in the verses beginning 'But Siva, like the ocean' (§245. *g*), where we have a doubt as to which of the two notions, whether the *Expressed* busying of the eyes, or the *Suggested* desire of kissing is prominent.

The Suggested 'of equal prominence.'

f. "It will be to your own prosperity, if you avoid insulting a Bráhman—else Paras'u Ráma your friend becomes displeased."‡

* For the connection between the sense of the clause 'I have become Ráma' and the first sense of the main stanza is only seen when we observe that a resemblance is suggested by a play upon the words: thus the Suggested sense is ancillary to the Expressed.

† The stanza is evidently an example of the third sort (see the Text) strangely introduced here, though another instance of the same occurs at the proper place. The Commentator does not even notice the incongruity. Is it merely from the author's oversight?

‡ This is a minister's advice to Rávaṇa, dissuading him from his dangerous

Here the Suggested, viz. Paras'u Ráma will destroy the Giant race, and the expressed signification of the sentence are of equal prominence, *inasmuch as they both* EQUALLY *tend to the advice—'You ought not to be hostile to Paras'u Ráma.'*

The Suggested, 'obscure.'

g. "In peace there is the seizure of *my* whole property; in war, the destruction of *my* life—there can be neither peace nor war with king Anwápadína."*

Here the Suggested sense viz. 'There is no means of pacifying the king named Anwápadína, except conciliation, presents, or the like, is not quickly perceived even by the erudite.

The Suggested, 'unconcealed.'

h. "By this Instructor of mankind, the Expounder of the duties of the good, I a virtuous female have freely been—what need is there of saying more."

Here S'ákya Muni's ravishing the female of an inferior animal, though suggested, fares from its extreme clearness like an expressed *idea.* Hence it is an instance of the 'unconcealed' *Suggestion.*

The Suggested, 'not beautiful.'

i. "The members of the young woman, engaged in domestic business, languish as she hears the noise of the birds that had flown up from the bower *near her house.*"

Here, the Expressed sense in 'the members languish, *(i. e. through the eagerness of love)*' is perceived by the man of taste to be more striking than the Suggested one, viz. 'some one *previously* appointed entered the bower:' so it is *an example of* the *Suggestion designated* 'not beautiful.'†

A circumstantial Suggestion, but a subordinate Suggestion.

j. Now, an ornament such as the simile, suggested, for instance, in the Figure Dípaka or the Tulyayogitá (see Chap. X. Texts 695 and 696)

attempt to overcome the terrible destroyer of Kshattriyas, who was yet a friend to him.

* According to some, the name is Allápadína, being that of a Muhammadan king.

† Let the reader be here cautioned against supposing, as he naturally would do, that all these examples are intended to be *distinctive* instances of what they are cited to illustrate. The present distich, for example, might, under one view, be considered as an instance of the first rate or Suggestive Poetry, inasmuch as the strikingness of the expression 'the members languish' rests on the 'Love in separation,' a division of the Erotic Flavour (§212), that it *suggests.* Moreover, it is impossible to believe that the more than 5000 divisions of Suggestive Poetry can all, or any considerable portion of them, be distinctively illustrated. The object in making the divisions seems therefore, to mark, not distinct *classes,* but distinct *properties* or *circumstances.*

is no other than a subordinate suggestion, inasmuch as a piece of Poetry with one of such embellishments strikes us simply through that, *and not as suggestive of the Simile or the like that is only incidentally implied.*

To this effect has it been said by the author of the 'Dhwani'—

"A piece of poetry is not held to be suggestive, even if an ornament besides *an expressed one* is recognized therein—in case the piece does not expressly tend to it."

Suggestion, laid open, becomes subordinate.

k. That also is an instance of a subordinate suggestion where the beauty of concealment, *or covert, implicative speech,* is destroyed by a word or the like. For example—

"'O Kesa'va! my sight stolen by the dust *raised* by the cows (or by my love for a cowherd—गोपराग—) I saw not aught, and thence, lord, I have fallen down: wherefore dost thou not hold me up—thou art the sole refuge of all the weak with minds troubled by hardships (or the fair ones troubled by him of the five arrows*)'—thus spoken to equivocally by the milk-maid, may Hari in the herd-station ever preserve you."

Here, the suggested significations viz. 'love for a cowherd' &c. of the words गोपराग &c. appear manifest *(or with their poetical cover opened)* by the word 'equivocally:' leave out the word and it is Suggestive Poetry.

Poetry of subordinate Suggestion becomes Suggestive Poetry, when with a principal Flavour besides.

l. A passage, however, which has its suggested meaning in the shape of a matter, an ornament or a Flavour or the like in a subordinate condition, but which has a principal Flavour besides, is considered Poetry in respect of this latter Flavour. This has been declared by the same author *that is quoted above,* thus—

"This description of Poetry, again, viz. that of a subordinate suggestion assumes the nature of Suggestive Poetry from the consideration of its tendency, *(if any,)* to develope a Flavour or the like."

A circumstantial suggestion of Flavour, the true constituent of the inferior Poetry.

m. But as one might object—what is the use of recognizing this second division of Poetry, when it may finally rank as Suggestive Poetry on account of the Flavour principally Suggested?—the author points out as its subject such pieces as have no flavour in them principally

* Lit. He that bears an odd number of arrows, or Kámadeva.

suggested, and are yet held as Poetry in respect of one subordinately or incidentally suggested. The following is an example—

"Where the red gem (ruby), producing, with its heaven-licking* rays, the delusion of evening in the love-intoxicated fair ones, employs them even untimely in making the toilet of Cupid, (i. e. the dress most fitted to charm their lovers)."

Such sentences as this, where a Flavour or the like is ancillary to a simple matter in the shape of circumstances attending a city, or of the like, are reckoned Poetry on account only of that *Flavour or the like*, subordinate though it be, as being not the principal *or direct* object of description *in such cases*. To this effect has it been said by our blood-relation, the chief of poets and scholars, the venerable Chaṇḍidása—

Relish alone, the essence of Poetry.

'At the moment of relishing a poetical sentiment when we are absorbed in it, we cannot perceive of it—apprehensible as it is by an undivided imagination—whether it is in a subordinate or a principal condition; but afterwards (*i. e.* when we come to criticise the piece) on our reflecting on the circumstances of the case, though it should be discovered *that the sentiment is but collaterally suggested*, this circumstance cannot destroy the claim of the sentiment to the title of Poetry, for that depends on relish alone.'

A third kind of Poetry, the Fanciful, recognized by some —no Poetry.

n. Some (*Mammaṭácharya, the author of the Kávya-prakás'a*) would have a third species of Poetry, viz. the Fanciful (chitra); hence he says —"That Poetry which is without Suggestion is reckoned as the lowest sort—being either 'Fanciful in sound' (s'abdachittra) or 'Fanciful in sense' (váchyachittra)." *But we say*—it is not so, for if by the expression 'without Suggestion' is meant 'totally wanting suggestion,' then, as we have already declared, such a sentence is not Poetry at all; if *by the expression is meant* 'a little, *or slightly* Suggestive,' I ask—what do you mean by poetry being a little suggestive? *Do you mean by it* poetry that has a Suggested sense relishable, or poetry that has a suggested sense not relishable? If *you mean* the former, then it falls within the two divisions made before; if, the latter, it is not Poetry. Besides, *taking the former for your meaning*, if the Suggestion is relishable, it cannot be little *or slight*, for if it is so, it cannot be relishable. This has been said by the author of the

* Lit. Cloud-licking.

, Dhwani :'—' Thus there are settled two species of Poetry, from the suggested either being in a principal or a subordinate condition : what is other than these, is styled the Fanciful.'

o. So much for the Declaration of the divisions of Poetry, styled 'Suggestive' and 'That of a Subordinate Suggestion'—the fourth chapter of the Mirror of Composition.

CHAPTER V.*

The establishment of the function of Suggestion.

Now, what is this new power, named Suggestion, *from which originates the essence of poetry—viz. what is Suggested?*

To this *question* he proceeds to reply—

TEXT.

What power conveys Flavour.

No. 267. There must be acknowledged a fourth function, exerted in causing the perception of Flavour and the like, after the cessation of the functions named Denotation, Purport, and Indication (§11, 13 and 31).

COMMENTARY.

Denotation, not it.

a. Denotation has not the power to give us the perception of a matter, an ornament, or a Flavour or the like, suggested—ceasing, as it does, after conveying the conventional (i. e. the literal) meaning only; for Flavour &c. are not matters of convention. Nor is the denoting *or representation* of the Excitants, &c. a denotation of Flavour, for we do not acknowledge its identity with them. Moreover, on the contrary, to signify it by its own name is a fault, as we shall see *afterwards*, (Chap. VII. §577).

Flavour, not perceived by a mere mention thereof.

Sometimes even when it IS signified by its own name, we do not perceive it—for it is of the nature of self-manifest joy.

* The substance of a considerable part of this Chapter may be given thus :— Ideas or Notions are what are conveyed by words, severally, through their power of Denotation. These, put together into a sentence, convey a complete Thought, through the supposed power of the sentence, styled Purport. Now, consistently enough, another power in the words must be resorted to, to account for the pleasurable sentiments, collectively spoken of as Flavour, consequent upon, and therefore distinct from, the simple thought.

Suggestion, not conveyed by the 'Purport' of the Naiyáyikas.

b. That Function entitled 'Purport' (tátparyá) which is acknowledged by those *Naiyáyikas** who hold that the *logical* connection among the notions *belonging to the several words in a sentence* is apprehended after they are *severally* conveyed—that Function even, being exhausted in simply making us apprehend the connection, does not convey the Suggested sense.

c. As for the assertion of some—'Such is the more and more extensive function of Denotation, like that of an arrow *first piercing the armour, then the body, and then perhaps a tree*;'—and also as for the declaration of Dhanika, viz., 'The Suggestive power of a word being no other than Purport, it is not to be *distinctively* called Suggestion, for Purport which extends to all the functions is not *to be supposed to be* measured by the balance *(or confined to the single business of making us understand the connection in the meanings).*' On these two objectors let those let fall the rod *of refutation* who hold that Word, Perception, and Action have an annihilation of their business *or operation, (as far as that individual case is concerned)*, when they have ceased after producing their respective single effects. Moreover, on the supposition *of the former of these two writers*, what need is there of having recourse even to Indication, since the sense, conveyed by that *power, also* might be understood through the more, and more extending function of Denotation? Why *do* not *you as well say* that joy and sorrow, for instance, are conveyed through Denotation *to the addressee* by such a sentence as this—'A son is born to thee, O Bráhman, and thy unmarried daughter is pregnant.'

* They are called Abhihitánwaya-vádins in contradistinction to the Anwitábhidhána-vadins, the followers of the Mímáṇsá school of Philosophy who (the latter) held that no meaning in severalty is conveyed by any word, or no notion exists but in connection with another; so that then only do words really mean anything when they are joined into a sentence. The men of this school deny the necessity of supposing a Function, distinct from Denotation, viz. the Purport, as belonging to the whole sentence. For, in their opinion, all notions (or, meanings of separate words) being, of necessity, connected,—such a Nominative with such a verb only brings to our mind such a particular Thought. This opinion would, at first sight, appear absurd, but, in truth, it is founded on a strict analysis of the manner of our conceiving ideas. This will be evident if we only try to form the notion of an action (the meaning of a verb) without connecting it, at the same time, with that of an agent, and vice versâ. In fact, this theory looks somewhat similar to Berkeley's denial of abstract ideas.

d. As for the assertion—'All sentences, whether human or divine,* tend to some purpose. Not tending to one, they are not acceptable *or useless,* and consequently are like those *uttered* by a mad man Hence, as there is no other motive to be found, than the relish of exquisite joy, actuating the hearer and the chanter *of poetry* towards their respective occupations, it is the relish of exquisite joy that is held to be the purpose of the sentences of poetry, according to the rule—what a word tends to is its purpose. Here it is to be asked—What do you mean by the expression—'A sentence tends to a purpose?' Do you mean by it, (*a*) 'a sentence has a thing for its purpose,' or (*b*) 'a sentence causes the notion of the thing by the function called Purport?'—If, the former (*a*), there is no dispute between us, for a thing, though suggested by, may yet be the purpose of, a sentence. If, the latter (*b*), I ask what is this function entitled Purport? Is it what is admitted by those (see §267. *b.* and note) who hold the 'connection of the expressed' (abhihitánwaya)—or any other power? If it is the former, we have already replied; if, the latter, the dispute is simply upon a name, for according to this opinion also there is a fourth function established.

e. But if you say—'well, let the perception of the connection among the Excitants, &c. and that of Flavour or the like be simultaneously caused by the power of Purport'—*that is* not *possible,* for they are held to be in the predicament of cause and effect—as says the sage—'The production of Flavour takes place from the association of the Excitants, the Ensuants, and the Accessories.' And, how can they be related to each other as cause and effect, if the two perceptions should spring up together like the right and left horns of a beast, when there is an absence of priority and subsequence *necessary to a cause and its effect respectively.*

Indication, no source of Suggestion.

f. Nor can that power of words, styled Indication, be supposed to convey the suggested sense; for in such a sentence, for example, as 'The herd-station on the Ganges' how can Indication convey the suggestion of coolness and purifying power, whilst it ceases *from any further operation,* after conveying such a sense, merely, as the bank?

* Human Sentences—works by man, such as the Laws of Manu. Divine Sentences—the Word of God, *i. e.* the Vedas.

g. Hence, it is not to be disputed that a fourth Function must be had recourse to.

h. Moreover—

TEXT.

The Suggested, distinct from the Expressed in many ways.

No. 268. The Suggested sense is distinct from the Expressed, by reason of the difference of its perceiver, nature, number, occasion, effect, perception, time, location, addressee, &c. *from those of the Expressed.*

COMMENTARY.

It is distinct as to the Perceiver.

a. There is a distinction between the perceiver of the Expressed sense and that of the Suggested, as the former is perceivable EVEN by Grammarians expert merely in the knowledge of words and their meanings, whilst the latter, ONLY by the man of sensibility.

It is different as to its Form.

b. The Suggested is sometimes in the form of a prohibition when the Expressed is in the shape of an injunction, as, for example, in—'Stroll securely, O devotee, &c.' (§253. *g.*) ; sometimes it is in the form of an affirmation whilst the latter is in that of a denial, as in—'The border of thy breasts has lost the whole sandal-wood &c.' (see §27. *c.*) : hence there is a distinction as to their natures.

It is distinct as to the Number.

c. In such a sentence as—'The sun is set'—one only expressed sense is perceived, whilst the suggested sense is not one, being—according to the various descriptions of the perceiver (*i. e.* the addressee) thereof—sometimes thus—'Resort to your lover,' or—'Let the cows be bound,' or—'This is the time of thy lover's arrival,' or thus—'There is no heat now:' hence there is a distinction as to the number.

The Suggested, apprehensible only by a refined intellect: not so the Expressed.

d. The Expressed sense is to be understood on the mere utterance of the words, whilst this—*Suggested sense* is perceivable through that peculiar refinement of the intellect and the like: thus is there a difference as to the occasion *or means* of their apprehension.

The Suggested, different as to its effect.

e. *The Suggested sense* brings surprise, *whilst the Expressed,* a mere cognition: so they are distinct as to the effect.

The perception of the Suggested, mingled with surprise.

f. They are different as to the apprehension, the Suggested being surprising *in apprehension*, and the other being of a simple nature.

The Suggested, apprehended after the Expressed.

g. There is a distinction in respect of time, the Expressed being perceived first, and the Suggested, afterwards.

The Suggested, distinct as to its Locality.

h. There is a difference in location, the former residing in a word only; the latter, in a word, its parts, and its sense, in letters and in style.

The Suggested, different as to the Addressee.

i. "Who would not be angry, to see the lip of his beloved with a wound? Endure now the reproaches of thy lover, perverse as thou wert in smelling the lotus containing a bee—though prohibited *by me.*"

In this *example (where a female friend speaks to a woman with her lip bitten by a secondary hero, when her jealous husband chides her for it)*—the expressed sense is addressed to the friend, and the suggested to her husband: So there is a difference as to the addressee.

Text.

No. 269. Indication and Denotation are not the causers of the perception of Flavour or the like; since it has no existence *before being felt, or in other words, it is a subjective entity, and its existence consists in being felt* (§51). Moreover, Indication *(cannot produce the perception thereof)* when there is no cancelling of the primary *or the Expressed* sense (see §13).

Commentary.

a. 'Cannot produce the perception thereof'—*supply this in the Text after 'Moreover, Indication,' to make the sense complete.*

Flavour, not to be Indicated or Denoted, being no objective entity.

b. There is certainly no object established by proof, signifiable by the words Flavour &c., other than the act of relishing—that should be conveyed by these *powers of* Indication and Denotation. Moreover, Indication comes in, *or is brought into operation*, there only where the connection among the meanings of the words employed, no sooner takes place than it is destroyed, from its unfitness or absurdity, as in *the expression*—'A herd-station on the Ganges' or the like: as is said by Udayanácharya in his Kusumánjali, *a work* on the Nyáya—

Indication, exerted only where the literal sense is incongruous.

"A sentence does not seek another sense *than the literal*, when it is satisfactory (lit. without desire), by reason of the fitness of the connection among the literal meanings *of its component words;* but the connection among the significations of the words failing, it is made up by a *meaning tropically* hinted by any of the words."

Now, there is no cancelling of the primary meaning, for instance, in the sentence commencing—"Perceiving that the house was empty" (see §3. *b*), *and, therefore, Indication has no business herein, and yet the Erotic Flavour is developed by it.*

How what is spoken of as Suggested can not be Indicated.

c. If, again, you say that in such a sentence as 'A herd-station on the Ganges' the motive, *viz. the coolness, purifying power, &c.* (see Chap. II. §13. *b.*) is not Suggested, but Indicated, then 'bank' would become the primary meaning* of Ganges and consequently be cancelled,† and there must be acknowledged another motive,‡ as indicated, for the indication of this *first motive*, and a third motive, again, to this *second indication*, and so on ad infinitum.

Two notions, not to be simultaneously conveyed or by the same function.

d. Nor is Indication *exerted here* towards *the conveyance of the sense of* the 'bank' AS QUALIFIED by *coolness, &c.* the motive; for a simultaneous understanding of the object and the motive is impossible. *To take an analogous instance*, it is after the perception of the blue that the property *or speciality* of 'being known' (jṉátatá—*according to the technicality of the Grammarians)* can arise *in the blue;* or, *(as the Naiyáyikas say)* the consciousness (anuvyavasáya) of it can take place *in us.*§

TEXT.

No. 270. Nor is Inference able to cause the perception of Flavour, &c. suggested; the *reasons assigned as the basis of the inference* being fallacious: nor is the perception of Flavour, &c. a Recollection.

* For the 'motive' and the sense of 'bank' cannot both be Indicated.

† Since, there can be no Indication without the primary meaning's being cancelled.

‡ For there can be no indication without a motive which you suppose to be Indicated.

§ Our perception of the blue, occasioning, as it does, the consciousness thereof, must have preceded it. Similarly the understanding of the bank must be antecedent to that of its coolness, &c. for the knowledge of the coolness, &c. is occasioned by our knowledge that the place is contiguous to the sacred river.

COMMENTARY.

a. As for the declaration of the author of the Vyakti-viveka (Discussion of Suggestion), viz.

The notion of some that the perception of Flavour is an Inference.

"The perception of Flavour and the like which arise from the Excitants, &c. is also to be referred to the head of Inference. For, the cognition of the Excitants, &c. is held to be the instrument *or the occasion* of the perception of Flavour and the like, and they being respectively the causes, the effects, and the concomitants of the sentiments of Love, &c. (see Chap. III.) produce Flavour or the like by making us infer those sentiments, since it is these, apprehended by inference and having attained to the condition of being relishable, that are spoken of as Flavours. Hence there must necessarily be a process in the perception thereof, though it is not discerned through its quickness. And indeed such a process *or succession* is *admitted* even in the Suggestion *of the Flavours by those who hold that distinct function.*"

This refuted.

I would ask—Do you consider as Flavour the mere cognition of the affection, &c. residing in Ráma, &c. inferred through the apprehension of the Excitants, &c. represented in words (i. e. a Poem), or in action (i. e. the Drama:)—*or do you mean by Flavour* the self-manifest joy felt, through the conception of the affection, &c., by men of poetical imagination? If you mean the former, there is no dispute, but the only difference is, that we do not use the term Flavour in the sense of the mere cognition of the affection, &c. residing in Ráma, &c. But the latter, *i. e. Flavour in the sense of joy*, is not proved to be inferrible, as the reason, *mentioned by you as warranting this inference*, is fallacious, for it is not universal, *inasmuch as an old Mímánsaka, though he also has the perception of the Excitants, &c., has not the fruition of the self-manifest joy.*

b. As for the assertion made by him again, viz:—

Another argument of the opponent.

"The 'universal attendance' and the 'existence in the subject,'* *necessary to a logical conclusion*, are evident *with respect to the inference or logical conclusion of*

* These two logical technicalities may be illustrated as follows. All men are mortal, Socrates is a man, ∴ Socrates is mortal. Now the Naiyáyika would say—mortality *pervades* or universally attends humanity, and humanity exists in the 'subject' (viz. Socrates who is to be proved to be mortal); therefore we infer or conclude that mortality attends Socrates. For a full explanation see Dr. B.'s 'Lectures on the Nyáya Philosophy embracing the Text of the Tarka Sangraha.'

Flavour thus:—In whatsoever person the Excitants, the Ensuants, the Involuntary indications of strong feeling (see §164), and the Accessories—represented by words or action—*come in contact with a cultivated imagination giving scope to their operation*—in that person the Erotic Flavour &c., are excited;—*I am one of these persons: therefore I infer the Erotic Flavour &c. are excited in me.*"

And—

"The occasions, which you consider as essential in suggesting a different meaning, are held by us as reasons for the inference thereof—*us* who take the side of *those who consider that a suggestion is no other than* an inference."

The logical inference of one's being an apprehender of Flavour, not identical with the actual relish thereof.

To these again we reply—this is not opposed to our opinion, but such a notion is not considered by us as relishable, but the fulness of joy exquisite, felt only in its own manifestation, so that the reason *in your supposed inference* is a mere semblance leading, as it does, to the conclusion of a thing (viz. *I have the fruition of Flavour*), different from what you wished to conclude (viz. the fruition itself of Flavour).

c. As for the further assertion of the same writer—

Another objection.

"The Suggested matter in such a sentence as 'Stroll securely, O devotee, &c.' (see §253. *g.*); as also the Ornament of Metaphor, for instance, in the following are simply inferred—

"'May Krishṇa preserve the world—curious *to see the alternate* separation and union of the youthful couple of Bráhmaṇy ducks (Chakravāka), as, in his sports in the water, he *playfully* removes his quick hands from Rádhá's face, and covers it again:'

"To explain: Inference is the knowledge of the Signified, through the Sign qualified by its existence in the subject, its existence in similar instances, and its exclusion from opposite instances.* Now no unconnected sense *in the shape of the Suggested* can be understood from the Expressed, otherwise suggestion would be indefinite (*or a sentence would suggest anything*); so that there must be a connection

* As, (supposing a smoky hill to be the subject in which the existence of fire is to be inferred), we conclude in the subject the existence of fire the Signified, by the Sign smoke which we see existing in it as well as in 'similar instances,' such as the culinary hearth, where there is no doubt as to the existence of fire, and which we see absent from the 'opposite instances,' *i. e.* such places in which the absence of fire is certain. See Dr. B.'s Tarka Sangraha, §54.

between the sense (*i. e.* the Expressed), which causes the understanding of a different sense, and that (*i. e.* the Suggested), which is caused to be understood by it. Hence, the sense which causes, is the 'Sign,' and that which is caused to be understood, is the Signified. Now the former's 'existence in the subject' is expressed, and its 'existence in similar instances' and 'exclusion from opposite instances,' though not expressed, are to be made out through the *peculiar* tendency *of the sentence*, so that the Suggested sense as the Signified being understood from the Expressed sense as the Sign, the case ends simply in an inference."

The Suggested sense not inferable, the reason alleged being fallacious.

To this we reply—It is not so. Let us see. In such a sentence as—'Stroll securely, O devotee &c.' you would say that the *apparent* direction for strolling, resting on the circumstance of the dog being killed, leads us *finally* to infer the prohibition of strolling, by reason of the discovery of a lion on the bank of the Godávarí. Now, here the alleged reason in the inference, *(or the major Premise of your Syllogism)* is not universal, for it is possible that even a coward might resort to the *lion-infested* place at the command of a spiritual guide, or a master, or from affection for a beloved woman. The reason is also inconclusive on the score of its being doubtful as to whether the words of an amorous woman *(with respect to a lion's being found on the Godávari)* are to be believed or not.

d. As to *the stanza*—"May Krishṉa &c." it is not to be asserted that it is by inference that we understand here the Suggested sense in such a manner as the following—'What by its appearance and disappearance causes the separation and union of the Bráhmany ducks must be the moon.'* For your argument fails in the case of a frightening thing, *which might as well by its appearance and disappearance cause the separation and union of the ducks.*

Another false reasoning, repelled.

e. 'Such a sense intimates such another sense, because of its *(the former's)* being of the nature of such a sense, since whatever is not the intimater of such another sense is not such a sense.'† In such an inference, *also*, as the above, the reason is, to all intents and purposes, a mere semblance, for *from*

* See note, p. 78.

† This is but an apparent instance of Inference founded on the Kevala Vyatireki Linga (Sign that is only absent). See Dr. B.'s Tarka Sangraha, §53.

the reason assigned by you, viz. 'the sense being as it is,' there might as well be inferred such another sense—*be it what it may*—as was never wished *to be intimated by the sense.*

f. As to the stanza commencing, 'O neighbour, will you cast your eyes' (see §258. *c*), you would say—here the reed-knot's scratching the woman's body, and her going alone to the river are the Sign of her enjoying another lover, which is the Signified. But those *(viz. her going alone to the river &c. alleged by you as the Sign or Reason in your inference)* might, as well, be from her love for her husband as is declared in the very stanza; so that, your reason is not invariable or, in other words, dallying with a gallant is not universally predicable of a woman going alone to a river, or the like.

g. As to the stanza commencing—'The border of thy breasts has lost the whole sandal wood' (§27. *c*)—I ask—Is the dalliance of the female messenger with her *(the speaker's)* lover, *as hinted here,* inferred by the addressed viz. the female messenger, or by those others present there at the time, or by men of taste considering the sense of this piece of poetry? In the case of the two former *inferring the hinted sense,* there is no dispute, but in the case of the last *(viz. the readers of poetry) there can be no inference, as the reason assigned in the inference,* fails where such a sense is not intended *to be hinted.* It must not be alleged that the reason is qualified by being associated with the condition *or circumstance* of the speaker &c., since, *not being mentioned, we cannot arrive at a knowledge of it, and so* we want a general proposition *to base our inference upon.* Moreover, as it is not necessary that such poems, originating merely in the imagination of the poets, should have any authority at all, our reason *(in the inference of any other meaning than the Expressed)* must be imperfect *(or inconclusive)* from its doubtfulness. It has been asserted by the author of 'Vyakti' that the meanings of the words, *in the stanza above alluded to,* suggest the other sense only through the aid of the word 'wretch' (अधम); but *when there is reason for doubting* whether the lover, *referred to in the verses,* was really a wretch or not, how can there be an inference?

Logical inference has nothing to do with works of imagination.

The 'conclusion from the effect' also being an Inference, rejected from poetry.

h. All that *we have said before,* also precludes the notion of the Suggested meaning's being perceivable by *(what is called by the Mímánsakas)* the 'Conclusion from the effect,' for the 'conclusion from the effect' too must always depend upon an induction, *or general proposition,* previously established. As, *when we conclude* '*Chaittra resides some where else*' *from the* '*effect*' *of the proposition*—'Chaittra, who is not in this cow-herd-station, lives,' *our inference depends on the previously established induction, viz.* 'whoever lives must reside somewhere.'

Suggestion, not founded on convention.

i. Nor is the Suggested sense apprehended through an understanding of signs, in some such manner as the number 'ten' or the like is apprehended by us, for instance, at the time of buying cloth *from the dealer's raising his forefinger in signification of the price—suppose* 10 *Rs., of a certain piece.* Because, the understanding of a sign, being dependent on the common authority of convention &c., is also reckoned as a sort of inference.

The perception of Flavour, not a recollection.

j. As to the assertion of some that the apprehension of Flavour &c. being *founded on, or* derived from previous impression is simply a Recollection —it is not right, for their reason is only a semblance, in as much as it fails in the case of a Recognition which is also derived from previous *impression, and yet is not only a Recollection but a Perception also.*

k. Lastly, as to the allegation of Mahima Bhatta with respect to such a stanza as the one commencing 'Who, by his fort, is insurmountable in battle' (see §257. *c*)—that there exists no second sense in it, it is verily an elephantine wink *(or heedlessness of the palpable)* on his part to deny what is established by *actual* perception.

A fourth function settled.

l. So—*to recapitulate the reasons*—it is proved that a fourth function must be resorted to in a sentence, inasmuch as the sense in the shape of Flavour &c. established by the *universal* perception *of men of taste,* cannot be denied, as it appears and disappears with the *particular* words, *sense* &c.* by which it is conveyed, as it is not cognizable by such sources of knowledge as Inference &c., and as it is not to be conveyed by the three functions commencing with the Denotation. Further, this function comes into operation independently of any reference *on our part* to any *previous* induction or the like. All this is *now* clear.

* Scil. The words, the literal sense, the various parts of a word &c., which suggest another meaning or a particular sentiment. See Chap. IV.

m. The question then arising—How is this function designated? —it is replied—

TEXT.

This, named Suggestion or Gustation.

No. 271. This function is, by the learned, styled 'Suggestion' (vyanjaná). Some again call it Rasaná (Gustation) as suggestive of Flavour.

COMMENTARY.

a. This has been discriminately dwelt upon on the occasion of the decision of Flavour (see §33. *g.* and *h.*), and so it is all lucid.

So much for the 'establishment of the function of Suggesting'—the fifth chapter of the Mirror of Composition.

CHAPTER VI.

The Declaration of 'a Poem to be seen and heard' and 'a Poem only to be heard.'

Division of Poetry into the 'Visible' and the 'Audible.'

Thus having stated the two divisions of Poetry as (1) 'Suggestive' and (2) 'of a subordinate Suggestion,' he declares its two divisions again into the 'Visible' and the 'Audible.'

TEXT.

Visible Poetry defined.

No. 272. Poetry is considered again to be of two sorts, from the distinctions of Poetry to be seen *and heard*, and Poetry *only* to be heard. Of these the 'visible Poetry' is that which can be represented, and this—*(see the next Text)*—

COMMENTARY.

a. He states the reason for its appellation of 'Rúpaka' *(Poem of forms)*.

TEXT.

Why called 'Rúpaka.'

No. 273.—is *called* Rúpaka from the artificial assumption of forms *by the actors.*

COMMENTARY.

a. 'This'—'visible Poetry'—is styled Rúpaka by reason of the actors artificially assuming the forms of *(i. e. personating)* Ráma &c.

b. *Now,* what is this acting *or representation* (abhinaya)?—he replies—

TEXT.

Representation, fourfold.

No. 274. Acting is the imitation of conditions; it is of four kinds, viz. (1) Gestural (ángika), (2) Vocal (váchika), (3) Extraneous, *or pertaining to dress, ornament, &c.* (áhárya), and (4) Internal *or pertaining to the soul or internal feelings* (sáttwika).

COMMENTARY.

a. Acting is the imitation *or representation* of the conditions of Ráma, Yudhishthira, &c. by means of gesture,* *speech*, &c.

b. He declares the divisions of the Rúpaka.

TEXT.

The ten Rúpakas.

No. 275. The Nátaka, the Prakaraṇa, the Bháṇa, the Vyáyoyga, the Samavakára, the Ḍima, the Ɪhámṛiga, the Anka, the Víthí and the Prahasana: these are the ten Rúpakas.

COMMENTARY.

a. And—

TEXT.

The eighteen minor Rúpakas.

No. 276. The Náṭiká, the Troṭaka, the Goshṭhí, the Saṭṭaka, the Náṭyarásaka, the Prasthána, the Ullápya, the Kávya, the Preṇkhana, the Rásaka, the Saṇlápaka, the S'rígadita, the S'ilpaka, the Vilásiká, the Durmalliká, the Prakaraṇí, the Hallís'a, the Bháṇiká; these eighteen the learned call Uparúpakas (minor Rúpakas). All these in their general character are held to resemble the Náṭaka.

COMMENTARY.

a. 'All'—i. e. the Rúpakas beginning with the Prakaraṇa, and the Uparúpakas commencing with the Náṭiká.

b. Of these—

TEXT.

The Náṭaka described.

No. 277. The Náṭaka should have a celebrated story *for its plot;* be possessed of the five Junctures (see §332); have the qualities of 'Vivacity' (see §91), prosperity, &c. described; contain *or represent* personages *(or characters)* contributing to the various prosperities *of the Hero;* be abounding with the sentiments of pleasure and pain, as also with a variety of flavours. It is declared that the Náṭaka should consist of from five to ten Acts. The hero should be of the sort characterised 'high-

* Lit. By the corporeal members.

spirited, but temperate and firm' (§ 66), powerful and virtuous, being either a royal sage of renowned family, or a god, or a demigod; the principal Flavour must be one only, being either the Erotic or the Heroic, all other flavours should be subordinate, and the Marvellous *exhibited* in the fulfilment of the end, *or in the last Juncture, viz. the 'Conclusion.'* There must be four or five important personages engaged in the business of the hero, and the Náṭaka must be so composed as to end like a cow's tail.

Commentary.

a. 'Celebrated'—such as the famous story of the Rámáyaṇa, for instance, *that forms the plot of the drama* Rámacharita, &c.

b. The junctures shall be declared afterwards (see § 332).

c. 'Contain personages contributing to the various prosperities *of the hero*'—i. e. the Náṭaka should have mighty Assistants *for the hero.*

d. 'The sentiments of pleasure and pain'—as are clearly exhibited in the stories of Ráma, Yudhishṭhira, &c.

e. 'A royal sage'—such as Dushyanta and others.

f. 'A god'—i. e. such as the holy Krishṇa or the like.

g. 'A demigod'—i. e. one who, though a god, thinks himself a man, such as the divine Rámachandra.

h. 'So composed as to end like a cow's tail'—Some explain it to mean that each of the acts is to be gradually made shorter than the one preceding; while others say that as in a cow's tail some hairs are short and some long, so in the Náṭaka some *important* incidents are to be completed in the first or opening Juncture (Mukhasandhi), some in the juncture Pratimukha, and similarly the other incidents are to be distributed among the other junctures, without trying to make them equal, in number, in every Juncture.

Text.

The Act described. No. 278. The Act is declared to be of the following description. It represents visibly the actions of the hero; it is to be brilliant with Flavour and Incomplete flavour; its style must be clear; it should contain short prose sentences (chúrṇaka); it forms a division in the action *of the drama;* it may slightly touch the Vindu (see §319); it should not contain an abundance of incidents, nor should it represent the Víja (Germ), or the Catastrophe (saṉhriti);

it should contain various appropriate actions ;* it should not have too many verses in it ; it must not be composed so as to clash against the performance of the necessary duties, nor should it contain events of more than one day ;† it should always have the hero under immediate relation ; it should contain three or four personages ; it should be devoid of the following actions—calling at a distance, killing, battle, national calamity, marriage, eating, cursing, excretion, death, amorous dalliance, scratching with the teeth or nails, and others that excite shame ; as also sleeping, sipping the lip, besieging a city or the like, bathing and anointing the body ; it should not be too lengthy ; it visibly represents interesting deeds, pertaining, for example, to a queen and her attendants, to a minister and merchants, such as excite feeling and flavour—the characters all making their exit at the end.

COMMENTARY.

a. The Vindu &c. shall be mentioned afterwards.—'Necessary *duties*'—*i. e.* the morning and evening prayers, &c.

b. He describes the Interlude (Garbhánka) being in place after the declaration of the principal Act :—

TEXT.

The Interlude, described.

No. 279. A secondary Act contained within a principal one, having a Rangadwára, an Ámukha &c. of its own, and so also containing a Germ and an End, is styled Interlude.‡

COMMENTARY.

a. As, for example, in the Bála Rámáyaṇa—

"Eunuch. (—addressing Rávana—) This festival of Sítá's own choice *(i. e. of a husband)*, fit as it is to be drunk in by many an ear, and viewed by many a large eye, is, as it were, a drama composed for your majesty."§

Thus commences the Interlude named 'Sítá's own choice.'

* I. E. Tending to the main business of the drama.

† It will be observed here that Prof. Wilson was mistaken in saying—'The Sáhitya Darpana extends it (the duration of the Act) to a few days or even to one year.' Hindu Theatre, Vol. I. p. 9.

‡ For convenience sake I have used this word, though generally employed in a somewhat different sense.

§ We have another example in the Uttara Ráma Charita at the commencement of the 7th Act. So is the well known 'mouse trap to catch the conscience of the king,' in Hamlet.

TEXT.

Preliminary performances of the Drama.

No. 280. The first thing to be done in it is the Púrva Ranga, then Reverence to the assembly, then the mention of the name of the poet &c. as also of the drama, and then the Induction (Ámukha—see §283 and 287).

COMMENTARY.

a. 'In it'—*i. e.* in the Drama.

TEXT.

The Púrva-ranga.

No. 281. What the Actors perform before the commencement of the matter to be represented *or the main drama*, for the removal of the obstacles *likely to* happen to the stage in the course of it—is called Púrva Ranga, (Preliminary Performance). It consists of a variety of elements, such as the Pratyáhára &c., among which however the Benediction (Nándí) must be used as a *special* means of removing the obstacles.

COMMENTARY.

a. He states its *(the Nándí's)* nature :—

TEXT.

The Nándí or Benediction.

No. 282. What is recited in the praise of a Deity, a Bráhman, a king, or the like, combined with a benediction, is designated Nándí. It should suggest such auspicious things as the Vilwa (*Ægle Marmelos*), the Conch shell, the moon, the lotus, the Bráhmany duck, the lily ; and consist either of twelve inflected words or eight lines.

COMMENTARY.

a. The Nándí of eight lines is such, for example, as that in the Anargha Rághava commencing निष्प्रत्यूहम्* That of twelve words—as the following in the 'Pushpa-málá' (Flower-garland) of my venerable Father—

"The daughter of the Royal Mountain (*Párvatí*) with her moon face shining *at first* red *with resentment* towards Káma's enemy

* The first of the couple of stanzas here alluded to, is translated as follows : "I adore, for the removal of obstacles, the eyes of the Holy One, marked by the divine mace, (Vishnu)—glorious eyes, able one to gladden the Keka, the other to feast the Chakora ; which have made the white lotus-bud in the *Great God's* navel-pond equal to the Ethereal Conch in His hand, as, *struck by their respective solar and lunar rays*, half it wakes, and half it sleeps, sweet in charming beauty."

(S'iva) holding, as he does, on his head the River-Goddess *(Gangá)*—then, as her lord falls down at her feet, charming with a smile—may she bestow on you prosperity!"

b. Thus *might the Benediction be illustrated* in other instances.

The Nándí, properly, no part of the Púrva Ranga, the Rangadwára being the commencement.

c. The performance, *however, spoken of in Text* 281, I have designated Nándí according to the opinion of some, but others say—'it is in reality the part of the Púrva Ranga named Rangadwára (the Door or Opening of the Theatre), to which effect it has been said—

"Since acting is first *of all* introduced into this, it is known as the Rangadwára, consisting of vocal and gestural performance."

Now the Benediction (*or Nándí properly so called*), such as is described in the present text, being performed BEFORE the Rangadwára by the mere actors, is not mentioned by the great sage (Bharata). Moreover, the *above* definition of Nándí does not hold good, for instance, with respect to the following *stanza, prefacing the drama Vikramorvas'í* of that great poet—Kálidása:—

"May* He who is declared in the Upanishads to be the sole Person, pervading the heaven and the earth, in whom exclusively does the word Lord (I's'wara) attain to its true signification, who is sought within by the desirers of salvation with breath and organs controlled—may that S'iva, easy to be obtained by steady faith and devotion, be for your felicity!"

d. Further, it has been said—'the poet should compose beginning with the Rangadwára:' hence it is that in the old manuscripts the stanza beginning 'May He who is declared' is found written after *the words*—'Enter Manager (Sútradhára) at the end of the Benediction.' Where, however, this expression occurs after the stanza, there it is intended to intimate the poet's meaning—'the Manager shall read this after the Benediction: here commence I the drama.'

TEXT.

The drama, how to be introduced.

No. 283. The Manager, having just acted the Púrva Ranga, desists, and the Establisher (Sthápaka), equal to him, then entering, establishes *or introduces* the

* A commentator of the Sakuntalá reconciles the similar stanza, therein, with the above definition of Nándí, on the authority of Abhinava gupta A'chárya, the Expositor of the Bharata Sútras, who explains 'pada' to mean a clause as well as a line and an inflected word.

drama; he must hint the matter *or action*, if divine, or human, in the corresponding form, and if mixed, in either of the two forms; or he may hint the Víja (Germ), the Mukha (*Face*, *Opening*), or the hero.

COMMENTARY.

a. 'Establisher'—so called from *his office* of establishing *or bringing in* the action of the poem.

b. 'Like him'—*i. e.* with qualities and appearance like those of the Manager.

c. In these days from the absence of a complete performance of the Púrva Ranga, the custom is that the Manager alone does all.

d. The Sthápaka must hint a divine matter as a deity, a human matter as a human being, and a mixed matter in any of these characters.—'Matter' *i. e.* the Action *or the plot:* For example—

Intimation of the plot.

"Receiving the command of his Father as a garland on his head, Ráma resorts to the forest; Bharata, in devotion to him, abandons his whole kingdom together with his mother; those his *faithful* followers—Sugríva and Vibhíshaṇa—are raised to high prosperity; and his pride-elevated enemies, the Ten-headed demon and others, are all annihilated."

e. The Germ (víja) hinted—as in the Ratnávalí—

Intimation of the Germ.

"Favourable Fortune brings us speedily our wished-for object even from another continent, even from the bosom of the ocean, aye, even from the farthest quarter of the globe!"

Here, the admission of Ratnávalí, favoured by kind Fortune, into the king of Vatsa's house is the germ *or first means*, beginning to operate with Yaugandharayaṇa's exertions, of the king's obtaining the lady (Ratnávalí) who had been plunged by shipwreck into the midst of the sea, but afterwards saved.

Intimation of the opening action.

f. The Mukha is a sort of speech indicating, by means of an equivoque or the like, the incident to be presently represented; as the following—

"Smiling with the clear, silvery moon, and lustrous with the stars, Autumn has arrived—like the fair Ráma, radiant with his glittering sword unsheathed; like the hero he has destroyed the season of the rains, dark and dreadful like the ten-headed monster; and he has reloaded the Bandhujíva with flowers, still imitating that *gracious* prince who brought back life to his *slaughtered* friends."*

g. The Hero hinted, as in the Sakuntalá—

Introduction of the Hero.

"Suddenly was I carried away by the ravishing strains of thy song as is this king Dushyanta by the flying deer."

TEXT.

No. 284. Having propitiated the theatric spectators with sweet verses hinting the purport of the drama, he mentions the names of the drama and the poet, as well as his lineage &c., and generally describes some season with the action called Bhárati.

COMMENTARY.

a. 'He' *i. e.* the Establisher.—

b. 'Generally'—because sometimes there is no description made of the season, as in the Ratnávalí.

c. The action Bhárati *is now explained*—

TEXT.

The action Bhárati, defined.

No. 285. The Bhárati is a vocal action by an actor speaking mostly Sanskrit.

COMMENTARY.

a. The Bhárati is a performance chiefly consisting in a discourse being for the most part in Sanskrit.

TEXT.

Its elements.

No. 286. The Prarochaná (Propitiation), the Víthí, as also the Prahasana, and the Ámukha (Induction) are its component parts. Among these the Prarochaná is the excitement of the attention by means of eulogium.

COMMENTARY.

The Prarochaná, or Commendation.

a. The Prarochaná is the attraction of the attention of the Audience, by a commendation of the drama &c. to the actions *or representations* about to be performed. For example, in the Ratnávalí—

"The poet S'ríharsha is a perfect master *of his art*, and this assembly can well appreciate merit; the actions of Vatsa's king are charming to the people, and we are skilled in acting—each of these circum-

* This comparison is not perhaps wholly intended in the original—the actions of Ráma being meant simply to be hinted along with the description of the season by means of an equivocal collocation of words.

stances would singly lead to the attainment of the wished-for fruit: how much more then would all this assemblage of excellences, combined as they are from the excess of our good fortune?"

b. The Víthí and the Prahasana shall be *hereafter* described, (see §520 and 533).

c. *He now states the A'mukha:*

TEXT.

The A'mukha or Induction described.

No. 287. When the Actress, or the Vidúshaka (the Jester or Buffoon), or the Páripars'wika (Associate), discourses with the Manager in interesting speeches issuing out of their own business* and hinting *or bringing in* the subject in hand *(i. e. the matter to be represented)*—it is designated A'mukha (Prelude) or Prastávaná (Introduction).

COMMENTARY.

a. The Establisher (Sthápaka) also is called Manager being like him. The Páripárs'wika is his *(the Sthápaka's)* attendant. An Actor is a little inferior to the latter.

TEXT.

Its five varieties.

No. 288. There are five varieties of the Prelude, viz. the Udghátyaka, the Kathodgháta, the Prayogátis'aya, the Pravartaka, and the Avalagita.

COMMENTARY.

a. Among these—

TEXT.

The Udghátyaka.

No. 289. When having heard some words, and not understood their sense, they add some others *of their own* to make a meaning out of them—it is called Udghátyaka (striking up).

COMMENTARY.

a. For example, in the Mudrá Rákshasa (The Signet of the Minister)—

"Manager.—That malignant planet,† Ketu, wishes violently to overpower the Moon (Chandra) now in full circle"‡—*(Behind the scene, or lit. in the dressing-room—interrupting)* "*Cháṇakya.*—Ah!

* In the original स्वकार्य्यात्थैः, which the commentator explains—"suited to their purpose,—the entrance of one of the dramatis personæ."

† Krúra-graha, which equivocally means also 'of evil intention.'

‡ Sampúrṇamandala—'in a full circle of sovereignty.'

who is this that, whilst I live, wishes violently to overpower Chandragupta ?"

Here enters a personage *(Cháṇakya)* construing the words *of the Manager* into a different sense from what they import—owing to his having been engrossed by his own thoughts.

TEXT.

The Kathodgháta. No. 290. If a personage makes his entrance, catching up the words of the Manager, or their meaning—it is called Kathodgháta (Striking up of an event).

COMMENTARY.

This based (1) on the words. *a.* 'Catching up the words'—as in the Ratnávalí—'Favourable Fortune brings, &c.' (§ 283. *e.*) having been recited by the Manager, *a personage* repeats behind the scene, *the couplet* thus—'So it is, no doubt—Favourable Fortune, &c.'—and Yaugandharáyaṇa makes his entrance.

And (2) on the sense. *b. The entrance of a character* catching up the sense—as in the Veṇí-sanhára :—

"Manager—May the sons of Pándu rejoice with Mádhava, the fire of their antagonism extinguished from the enemies seeking peace ; and may the sons of king Dhritaráshtra with their protégés obtain tranquillity, having desisted from all fighting, and subdued the people's heart by their *protective* affection."*

Catching up the sense of the sentence spoken by the Manager, *some one cries out* behind the scene—"Ah wretch, thou vain chanter of peace *to my enemies*, how can the sons of Dhritaráshtra obtain tranquillity so long as I live ?" The Manager then goes out, and Bhímasena enters.

TEXT.

The Prayogátis'aya, or Supersession of a Part. No. 291. If a part or performance is superseded by another so that a personage enters, it is called Prayogatis'aya (*Supersession of a part*).

COMMENTARY.

a. For example, in the Kundamálá—"[Behind the Scene.] Madam, alight this side—this side—please.

* The second sense of the stanza is the following :—"May the sons of Pándu rejoice with Mádhava, the fire of their antagonism extinguished from the extinction of their foes ; and may *the departed souls of* king Dhritaráshtra's sons and of their protégés be in peace, having graced the Earth with the blood of their bodies wounded *in battle.*"

"Manager—Who is this verily that renders me assistance by calling my lady? [Looking closely—] O misery! It is most pitiful—Alas! it is Lakshmaṇa drawing Sítá to the woods—Sítá who though oppressed with the weight of pregnancy, has been banished the country by Ráma perplexed with the fear of his people's censure, as she had remained so long in the habitation of the king of Lanká."

Here the Manager, wishing his wife to be called for the purpose of dancing, goes out hinting the entrance of Sítá and Lakshmaṇa with *the exclamation*—"this is Lakshmaṇa leading Sítá to the woods"—and thus performs a part superseding that *which he had apparently intended* for his own, *viz. dancing. Hence the name Prayogátis'aya.*

TEXT.

The Pravartaka. No. 292. When the Manager makes a description taking the season current for the subject, and a personage enters thereupon—it is called Pravartaka (Introduction).

COMMENTARY.

a. As, for example, the stanza commencing 'Smiling with the clear silvery moon' (§283. *f.*) having been recited, Ráma enters as therein described.

TEXT.

The Avalagita. No. 293. When in a performance another business (*viz. the hinting of the entrance of the hero or the like*) is performed in unison with it—it is designated by the learned—Avalagita.

COMMENTARY.

a. For example in the S'akuntalá—"Manager—Suddenly was I carried away, &c., (see § 283. *g.*)"*—Then enters the king.

TEXT.

No. 294. Herein may also be admitted any of the other elements of the Víthí, according to the occasion.

COMMENTARY.

a. 'Herein'—*i. e.* in the Ámukha.

b. 'The other elements'—*i. e.* those besides the Udghátyaka and the Avalagita, to be described hereafter (see §521.)

c. Nakhakutta, however, declares—

* This is cited as an instance of the Prayogátisaya by Dhanika in his exposition of the Das'a-rúpa, see that work, chap. 3, s'l. 10.

Another variety of the Induction, according to some.

"In the Nátaka and the like, the Induction (Ámukha) may also be founded on words, heard to be spoken, either behind the scene, or in the air."

TEXT.

No. 295. The Manager should employ any of these varieties (*including those intimated last*), and thereby hinting either the matter or a personage, go out at the end and then represent the action.

COMMENTARY.

a. 'Action'—*i. e.* the series of incidents *that form the subject of the drama.*

TEXT.

Action two-fold. (1) The Principal.

No. 296. This Action again is held by the learned to be two-fold; the one is the Principal (Ádhikárika), and the other Incidental (Prásangika). Property (Adhikára) is the ownership *or possession* of the result; the holder of that ownership is the Principal person—*the Hero* (lit. Owner, Adhikárin), hence the story pertaining to him is designated by the poets Ádhikárika (*of the Principal personage*).

COMMENTARY.

a. 'Of the result'—*i. e.* of the principal fruit, (*such as Ráma's recovery of Sítá through the destruction of Rávana.*)

b. The story of Ráma, *or the main action,* in the *drama* Bála Rámáyaṇa, is an example *of the first of these divisions.*

TEXT.

(2.) The Incidental.

No. 297. Incidental, *or Episodical* is that which is subservient to it.

COMMENTARY.

a. That story *or plot* which is intended to be subservient 'to it' *i. e.* to the Principal action, is the Incidental: for example the actions of Sugríva or the like.

TEXT.

The Patáká-sthánaka, an important element in the action.

No. 298. The Patáká-sthánaka (Telling or Striking Point) is to be admitted here into the action with good judgment.

COMMENTARY.

a. 'Here *into the action*'—*i. e.* into the dramatic *action.*

TEXT.

This defined. No. 299. That is *called* the Patáká Sthánaka when instead of the thing thought of, or *expected*, another of the same character is brought in by some strange *or unexpected* circumstance.

COMMENTARY.

a. He states the divisions hereof:—

TEXT.

The first Patáká Sthánaka. No. 300. When an object is unexpectedly, and in an excellent manner, gained under a peculiarly favourable circumstance—it is declared to be the first Patáká Sthánaka.

COMMENTARY.

a. As, for example, in the Ratnávalí, when the king, thinking that it was Vásavadattá, *his wife, about to commit suicide from his falling in love with Ságariká,* unties the noose from her neck and then recognizing by her voice *the lady disguised as his wife* to be Ságariká exclaims—'How, is it, Ságariká, my love! O forbear from this desperate rashness.' Here we have an attainment of the principal object, viz., the company of Ságariká, excellent, that is to say happier, under the excessively favourable juncture, than the expected one *of Vásavadattá.*

TEXT.

The Second. No. 301. A speech extremely equivocal and containing a variety of epithets is declared to be the Second Patáká Sthánaka.

COMMENTARY.

a. For example, in the Vení Sanhára—

"Manager—May the sons of king Dhritaráshtra with their protégés obtain tranquillity, having desisted from all fighting (vigraha), and subdued the people's heart by their *protective* affection (rakta)."

As this sentence suggests the Germ* and the End† by means of an equivoque based on the words 'rakta,' 'vigraha,' &c, bearing the second significations of 'blood,' 'body,' &c., respectively,‡—happiness

* Viz., Yudhishthira's energy, roused by the indignation of Bhíma, which latter is first manifested at the Manager's recitation of the above lines.

† Scil. The binding of Draupadí's tresses through the destruction of Duryodhana and his brothers—the foes of the hero.

‡ See note—§ 290. *b.*

to the hero comes *unexpectedly* to be understood *from the lines, instead of blessing to the enemies which they, at first, seem to indicate: so the general definition of the Patáká Sthánaka (see § 299) holds good here.*

TEXT.

The Third. No. 302. What hints the Deed *(Kárya—see § 323)*, obscurely, and under a certainty as to some particular,—containing equivocal replies—is spoken of as the third Patáká Sthánaka.

COMMENTARY.

a. 'Obscurely'—*i. e.* under a sense not clearly expressed.

b. 'Containing equivocal replies'—*i. e.* containing replies fitly connected with the matter *in hand,* but used under a different import.

c. 'Under a certainty as to some particular'—*i. e.* under the attainment of certainty as to some particular matter.

d. What is characterized *by the above qualities* is the third Patáká Sthánaka: as, in the Veṇí Sanhára, Act II—

"*Eunuch.*—Broken, Sire, Broken—

King.—By whom?

Eunuch.—By the Fierce *(Bhímena)*—

King.—Whose?

Eu.—Your Majesty's.

King.—Ah! What dost thou babble?

Eu.—[Terrified.] Nay, my king, I say—Broken by the Fierce [wind], your Majesty's.

King.—Fie! thou wretched old man, whence is this hallucination in thee, just now?

Eu.—My king, it is no hallucination, it is indeed a reality.

Broken by the fierce wind, your Majesty's chariot-flag has been thrown down upon the ground—making, as it fell, a cry of lamentation with the sound of its tinkling string of bells."

Here is *exhibited* an intimation that ends in hinting the matter in hand, viz., the fracture of Duryodhana's thigh *by Bhímasena, which forms the catastrophe of the drama.*

TEXT.

The Fourth. No. 303. An equivocal arrangement of words *(or a double entendre)* well connected and fit for poetry—such as has an eye to a third sense, viz., the End, is the next *and last* Patáká Sthánaka.

COMMENTARY.

a. For example, in the Ratnávalí:

"I shall certainly make the countenance of the queen red with anger to-day—by looking—as on another woman inflamed with love—at this garden creeper entwining the Madana tree, powerfully blooming in blossoms white (pale with powerful anxieties—), about to be fully blown (yawning through langour—), and every moment shaking itself through the frequent puffs of the wind (—increasing her own pain by the frequent heaving of sighs)."*

Here is hinted the future event of the king's falling in love with Ságariká, *terminating in his union with the lady by marriage—which is the End of the business.*

The Patáká Sthánakas may be used any where throughout the play.

b. These four Patáká Sthánakas are employed in all the junctures (Sandhis—see § 332) sometimes for the purpose of intimating some blessing, sometimes a misfortune too; they may be multiplied according to the taste of the poet. As to what has been asserted by some, viz., 'They are to be employed respectively in the four junctures commencing with the Mukha (*Opening Juncture—see* § 333)'—in this others do not agree, for it is proper that all these, extremely acceptable as they are, should be used every where without restriction.

TEXT.

An improper incident in the hero's life to be omitted or altered in the plot.

No. 304. A matter *or incident* which is improper with respect to the hero, or opposed to relish, is to be altogether omitted, or shaped otherwise.

COMMENTARY.

a. An 'improper' event is, for instance, the killing of Válin by Ráma by an artifice. It is entirely omitted in the Udátta Rághava, and is altered in the Víra Charita, where Válin himself comes forward to slay Ráma in fight, and is killed by him.

* The qualifications enclosed within brackets, of course, apply to 'another woman inflamed with love.'—The difference between this and the second Patáká Sthánaka (§ 301), says the scholiast, lies in the latter (the 2nd) being entirely based upon a double entendre, whilst the former has an expressed comparison besides.

TEXT.

What incidents to be hinted in the Arthopakshepaka or Introductory Scene.

No. 305. Incidents which are not to be shown *or represented* in the Acts and are yet considered necessary to be told, as also such as extend through, from two days to a year (§ 278), and others too extensive, are to be hinted by the learned by means of the Arthopakshepakas* (Introductory Scenes).

COMMENTARY.

a. 'Incidents *or events* not to be shown in the Acts'—such as events of battle, &c.

TEXT.

No. 306. A business extending beyond a year should be comprised within a year.

COMMENTARY.

a. As has been said by the sage—

Its duration, not to be more than a year.

"All that was done in a month, or even in a year, should be performed in a separate *Introductory* Scene (Ankachheda), but never what extends beyond a year." So the destruction of Virádha, &c., parts of the story of Ráma's dwelling in the forest, though it extended over fourteen years, may be hinted, without opposition *to the above dictum*, to have occupied a year or any portion of it, such as a couple of days, &c.

TEXT.

A whole day's event also to be told by the Arthopakshepaka.

No. 307. What was done in a day, but in a whole day, is to be intimated by means of the Introductory Scenes apart from the main Act.

COMMENTARY.

a. The question arising—what are these Introductory Scenes?—he says—

TEXT.

Its divisions.

No. 308. The Introductory Scenes are five viz., the Vishkambhaka, the Praves'aka, the Chúliká, the Ankávatára, as also the Ankamukha (Protasis).

The Vishkambhaka pure, and mixed.

The Vishkambhaka is represented in the beginning of an act, being brief and exhibitive *or suggestive* of parts of the action both past and future. When acted

* Lit. Intimators of Matter.

by one or two middling personages, it is pure, but it is *spoken of* as mixed, if performed by a low and a middling character.

COMMENTARY.

a. Of these two divisions of the Vishkambhaka, the pure is, for instance, acted by Kapálakundalá in the cemetery, in the drama Málatí Mádhava *of Bhavabhûti;* the mixed, by Kshapaṇaka and Kápálika, in the Rámábhinanda.

TEXT.

The Praves'aka. No. 309. The Praves'aka (*Introducer*) is performed between two *consecutive* acts by one or two low characters, in an unelevated discourse; it is like the Vishkambhaka in other respects.

COMMENTARY.

a. 'Between two acts'—so it is forbidden *to be employed* in the first act.

b. An example of this is the part played by the couple of Demons in the Act—' As'watthámánka' (or Act of As'watthámàn) in the Veṇí Saṉhára.

c. Now of the Chúliká:—

The Chúliká. No 310. The hinting of a matter *or event* by those behind the curtain is the Chúliká:

COMMENTARY.

a. For example, in the Víra Charita, in the beginning of the fourth Act:—"(Behind the Scene—) Up! up! *Deities*, Riders in aëreal cars, up with theatrical festivities! &c."

Thus is hinted, by the persons behind the scene, the event of Paras'u Ráma's defeat by Ráma.

b. Now of the Ankávatára.

TEXT.

The Ankávatára. No. 311. When an Act, hinted by persons at the end of the preceding Act, is brought in continuity with the latter —this is called Ankávatára (Descent of an Act).

COMMENTARY.

a. As in the S'akuntalá, the 6th Act, having been hinted by persons, at the end of the 5th, is introduced as a portion, *or continuation*, as it were, of this Act.

b. Now of the Ankamukha (Protasis).

TEXT.

The Ankamukha, or Protasis.

No. 312. That part of an Act, wherein the subject of all the Acts is intimated, is styled Ankamukha (*Face or Opening of the Act*) which suggests the Germ (Víja) as well as the End (Artha).

a. For example, in the Málatí Mádhava, at the commencement of the first Act, Kámandakí and Avalokitá hint the parts to be played by Bhúrivasu and others, and collaterally the arrangement of the plot, in brief.

TEXT.

Another kind of Ankamukha.

No. 313. Or the Ankamukha may be, when persons, at the end of an act, hint the opening point of another Act, divided, or not continued, from it.

COMMENTARY.

a. 'Persons at the end of an Act'—*i. e.* persons entering at the end of an Act.

b. As, in the Víra Charita, at the conclusion of the second Act—

" *Sumantra*—(Entering—) The holy Vas'ishṭha and Vis'wámittra are calling you together with Bhárgava.

Others—Where are the holy sages?

Sumantra—With the great king Das'aratha.

Others—Let us then go there."

Here ends the Act. Now this is called Ankamukha (Face of an Act), as the Minister Sumantra, entering just at the conclusion of the Act—which suspends the action of Janaka and S'atánanda—hints *or introduces* the face *or opening* of the succeeding Act, viz. 'Enter Vasishtha, Vis'wámittra, and Paras'u Ráma seated.'

c. I have said this according to the opinion of Dhanika. Others, however, assert that this sort of Ankamukha is in fact the same with the Ankávatára.*

* The definitions of these two kinds of the Introductory Scene—nay the whole of this chapter, mostly without even the least alteration—are borrowed from the Das'a Rúpa the expositor whereof is Dhanika. Now the definitions mark a difference between them not less than that between other divisions. The example indeed, cited here to illustrate the Ankávatára, which is different from that of Dhanika, confounds the two divisions. Vide Das'a Rúpa—S'l. 55—56.

TEXT.

The Vishkambhaka when to succeed the A'mukha.

No. 314. When a good deal of the insipid matter, *forming the commencement of the story upon which a drama* is founded, is left out, and the remainder, required *to give us the clue to the story*, is to be exhibited, then the Vishkambhaka in the drama must be performed immediately after the Induction (A'mukha)—the characters of the former having been hinted in the latter:

COMMENTARY.

a. For example, in the Ratnávalí, the Vishkambhaka performed by Yogandharáyaṇa.

TEXT.

The Act when to succeed the A'mukha.

No. 315. But when relishable matter commences at the very opening of the story, then the Act must commence at the very beginning—introduced by the Induction:

COMMENTARY.

a. As, in the S'akuntalá.

TEXT.

The hero's death not even to be hinted. Passions and incidents to harmonize.

No. 316. The death (lit. killing) of the principal personage or hero (Adhikárin) is not to be declared even by means of the Vishkambhaka, &c.; nor should any of the two—Flavour (*Sentiments*) and matter (*Incidents*), cover over or out-balance the other.

COMMENTARY.

a. Flavour—*i. e.* the Erotic, &c. To this effect it has been said by Dhanika—

"The dramatist should neither disperse far the matter (*i. e. the incidents of his play*) by a superabundance of Flavour *or passionate descriptions*, nor should he cover over the Flavour by an excess of matter and embellishment."

TEXT.

The five Sources of the End.

No. 317. The Víja (Germ), the Vindu (Secondary Germ), the Pataká (Collateral action), the Prakarí (Episode), and the Kárya (Deed) are the five Sources of the End or the Grand Object—which are to be known and employed according to the rule.

COMMENTARY.

a. 'The Sources of the End'—*i. e.* the causes *or means* of the accomplishment of the *principal* object.

b. Of these the Germ *is defined as follows*—

TEXT.

The Germ (Víja) defined.

No. 318. That which is the first cause of gaining the end, is but slightly intimated, and expands itself in various ways, is denominated Víja.

COMMENTARY.

a. For example, in the Ratnávalí, the source of the monarch of Vatsa's obtaining Ratnávalí is the exertion of Yogandharáyaṇa, favoured by kind Fortune. Or, in the Veṇí Sanhára, the cause of the binding of Draupadí's tresses is the energy of Yudhishthira enhanced by the rage of Bhímasena.

TEXT.

The Vindu, defined.

No. 319. When the course of the business *of the drama* seems to be interrupted, the cause of its being developed again is called Vindu.*

COMMENTARY.

a. For example, in the Ratnávalí, the business, at the completion of the worship of Káma, being suspended, Ságariká, hearing these words of the bard—'They (the assembled princes) expect to see the feet of Udayana as the beams of the rising moon'—exclaims in joy —'How, is he the king Udayana!' This excites the succeeding part of the business†.

TEXT.

The Patáká or Collateral Action.

No. 320. A Collateral Story, pervading, *or stretching through*, the drama is styled Patáká.

COMMENTARY.

a. For example, in the Ráma Charita the story of Sugríva, &c.; in the Veṇí Sanhára, that of Bhíma, &c.; and in S'akuntalá that of the Vidúshaka.

* Lit. Drop, as a drop of oil on water quickly diffuses itself.

† Lit. 'This is the Spring or Germ of an intermediate object'—that which follows, viz. Ságariká's falling in love with the king. Thus the Vindu is distinguished from the Víja (Germ) as being the source of an intermediate object, whilst the latter is that of the principal one, and consequently being possibly more than one, whilst the latter can not but be one.

TEXT.

The hero's minor object, not the Patáká proper.

No. 321. An object of the hero other *than the principal* is not the Patáká, for that may be accomplished either in the Juncture Garbha or Vimarsha.

COMMENTARY.

a. For example, the attainment of the kingdom *of Bálin* by Sugríva, *which is a minor object of the hero Ráma fulfilled before the consummation of his principal object, the destruction of Rávaṇa.*

The object of the hero of the Patáká, also indicated by Bharata by Patáká.

b. As to what the sage has said viz.—'The Patáká is concluded either at the end of the Garbha or of the Vimarsha'—this the venerable Abhinava Gupta has thus explained: '*The word* Patáká here *denotes tropically* the object of the hero of the Patáká, for the Patáká, *properly so called,* is found to continue even to the Nirvahaṇa *or Conclusion.*

TEXT.

The Prakarí or Episode.

No. 322. A Collateral action of limited duration is what is meant by Prakarí.

COMMENTARY.

a. For example, in the act named Kulapati, the dialogue between Jatáyu and Rávaṇa.

TEXT.

The Deed (Kárya), defined.

No. 323. An object of the hero other than the principal is not the Prakarí.

That is called the Deed or Object (Kárya), through which is to be accomplished the sought for *End,* which is the motive of the business, and for the consummation of which the incidental *actions are performed.*

COMMENTARY.

a. As the killing of Rávaṇa for the recovery of Sítá in the Ráma Charita.

TEXT.

Five Stages of the Deed.

No 324. There are five conditions *or stages* of the Deed, undertaken by those that seek an End—viz., Commencement (árambha), Effort (yatna), Hope of Attainment (práptyás'á), Certainty of Attainment (niyatápti), and Attainment of the Fruit (phalágama).

COMMENTARY.

a. Of these—

TEXT.

The 'Commencement' defined.

No. 325. 'Commencement' is the anxiety that is *felt* for the accomplishment of the principal object.

COMMENTARY.

a. For example, in the Ratnávalí, the anxiety of Yaugandharáyaṇa to admit *the lady* Ratnávalí into the inner apartment or harem of the king.

b. So also may *the anxiety* of the hero, the heroine, &c. be observed in the originals (lit. mines) *or the dramatic works themselves whereupon these rules are based, and from which these illustrations are taken.*

TEXT.

The 'Effort' defined.

No. 326. 'Effort' is exertion combined with great celerity, in order to the attainment of the end.

COMMENTARY.

a. As, in the Ratnávalí—

"—Yet, as there is no other means of seeing him, let me paint any how a likeness of him, and do as I wish."

Here is intimated Ratnávalí's drawing a picture of the king of Vatsa—which is a means of her obtaining him.

b. So is the bridging of the sea in the Ráma Charita.

TEXT.

The 'Hope of Attainment' defined.

No. 327. The 'Hope of Attainment' is the mere possibility of obtaining the End from the existence of means and the apprehension of impediments.

COMMENTARY.

a. For example, in the Ratnávalí, Act III. we have Ratnávalí's Hope of Attainment in the absence of absolute certainty as to the obtaining of her object, viz. the company of the king of Vatsa,—under the means of attaining him, *secured* in the change of her dress and resort to the appointed spot &c., and under the apprehension of the obstacle in the shape of Vásavadattá, *the queen.* So in the other *dramas.*

TEXT.

The 'Certainty of Attainment' defined.

No. 328. The 'Certainty of Attainment' is the security of gaining the End, from the absence of obstacles.

COMMENTARY.

a. 'Certainty of Attainment' is the absolute confidence of obtaining the object from there being no obstacle or impediment.

b. For example, in the Ratnávalí—

"*King.* Excepting the propitiation of the queen I see no way to this."

Here is hinted the certain attainment of the object through the conciliation of the queen who is therein the impediment.

TEXT.

The 'Attainment of the Fruit' defined.

No. 329. That stage in which the fruit, *or ultimate object*, is completely gained, is called the 'Attainment of the Fruit.'

COMMENTARY.

a. For example, in the Ratnávalí, the obtaining of Ratnávalí *in marriage*, together with another fruit in the shape of an empire. So in the other *dramas*.

TEXT.

Five divisions of the plot, named Junctures, answering to the five stages of the deed.

No. 330. In accordance with these five stages respectively, there become as many divisions in the business *or plot*, called the five Junctures.

COMMENTARY.

a. He defines *the Juncture* :—

TEXT.

The Juncture generically defined.

No. 331. The Juncture is the connection with an intervening object *of the several portions of the business*, which all are connected with, *or tend to*, one *principal* object.

COMMENTARY.

a. Juncture is the connection that severally exists between minor objects and portions of the fable, which, however, are all linked to one *grand* end.

b. He declares their divisions—

TEXT.

The Junctures specified. No. 332. The Mukha (Protasis), the Pratimukha (Epitasis), the Garbha (Catastasis), the Vimarsha (Peripateia), and the Upasanhriti (Catastrophe): these five are its divisions the definitions whereof are stated in order, as follows:

COMMENTARY.

a. He states the definitions according to the order of *their* mention:

TEXT.

The Mukha. No. 333. That *Juncture* is designated Mukha (Protasis or Opening Juncture) wherein is the origination of the Germ (see §318), giving rise to a variety of matters and flavour, and containing the 'Commencement' (Árambha—see §325).

COMMENTARY.

a. As is exhibited in the first act of the Ratnávalí.

TEXT.

The Pratimukha. No. 334. The Pratimukha (Epitasis) is that in which the first cause or Germ (see §318) of the Fruit *(i. e. the End or Ultimate Object)*, laid in the Juncture Mukha, has sprouted but not in a very perceptible manner.

COMMENTARY.

a. For example in the second act of the Ratnávalí, we have the sprouting or discovery of the Germ of affection, the primary cause of the union of Vatsa-rája and Ságariká—which was intimated in the first act—since here it is somewhat marked on account of its being known by Susangatá and the Vidúshaka, and guessed by Vásavadattá through the circumstance of Ságariká's drawing the picture *of the king.*

TEXT.

The Garbha. No. 335. The Garbha (Catastasis) is that wherein the first cause or Germ of the Fruit, that has previously sprouted, is developed, but is attended with frequent hindrance *in its growth*, and search *for the object wished for.*

COMMENTARY.

a. This Juncture is called 'Garbha' (womb) from its being pregnant with the Fruit: As in the 2nd act of the Ratnávalí—

"*Susangatá.* Indeed, friend, thou art unkind now, as thou quittest not thy anger, though thus held by the hand by thy lord &c."

Here we have the development of the Germ *viz. Ságariká's love for the king of Vatsa, which has now become mutual and manifest.* Again we have a hindrance of it on the entrance of Vásavadattá. In the third act we have the 'search' *(for the beloved object)* in these words of the king—'How is it that Vasantaka, gone to seek intelligence of her, is delaying?' We have its (the Germ's) re-manifestation in the following—

"*Vidúshaka.* Ha! ha! the joy of my dear friend even on gaining the kingdom of Kaus'ámbí was not such as will be *felt by him* on hearing from me the news of his love."

There is again the obstruction in the recognition of Vásavadattá *by the king who had mistaken her for Ságariká disguised as the queen*; again the 'search' in Ságariká's resorting to the appointed place; and again the development in Ságariká's putting the noose of a creeper round her neck to kill herself.

b. Now of the Vimarsha—

TEXT.

The Vimarsha. No. 336. Where the means of gaining the End is developed more than in the Garbha, but is impeded by a curse or the like—that is known as the Vimarsha.

COMMENTARY.

a. For example, in the beginning of the fourth act of Sákuntalá—

"*Anasúyá.* Priyamvadá, complete as is the happiness of our beloved friend S'akuntalá through her marriage of love* (gándharva viváha), my heart is particularly satisfied that she has been united to a worthy husband."

The whole of the matter, commencing with this and extending up to the recognition of S'akuntalá represented in the seventh act, is embraced by the impediment in the shape of the king's forgetting S'akuntalá.

b. Now of the Nirvahaṇa.

TEXT.

The Nirvahaṇa. No. 337. The Nirvahaṇa (Catastrophe or Conclusion) is that in which the matters sprung and gradually developed from the Germ, that have occurred in their proper places in the Mukha &c., are caused to end in the consummation of one object.

COMMENTARY.

a. For example, in the Veṇí Saṇhára:—

"*Eunuch.* (Approaching with joy.) Triumphant is your Majesty,

* Or secret marriage by mutual consent.

great king: Here comes Bhímasena with his whole body reddened with Duryodhana's blood—hard to be recognized &c."

Here the various incidents, scattered in their proper places, of the Mukha and other Junctures,—that had originally sprung from the Germ, converge to one object, viz. the binding up of Draupadí's tresses.

Or, for example, in the seventh act of S'akuntalá, the whole body of the matter after the recognition of S'akuntalá.

b. He mentions the members or elements of each of these *Junctures*:—

TEXT.

The members of the Mukha. No. 338. Upakshepa, Parikara, Parinyása, Vilobhana, Yukṭi, Prápti, Samádháṇa, Vidhána, Paribhávaná, Udbheda, Karaṇa, Bheda: these are the elements in the Mukha.

COMMENTARY.

a. He defines these according to the order of their enumeration.

TEXT.

Upakshepa. No. 339. The springing up of the dramatic matter is designated Upakshepa (Hint).

COMMENTARY.

a. 'Dramatic matter'—*i. e.* the thing to be represented, viz. the action.

b. For example in the Veṇí Saṇhára—

"*Bhíma.* Shall the sons of Dhritaráshṭra be in peace, whilst I live —having struck at our lives and siezed our property, by setting fire to the resin-covered house *we had been treacherously sent to live in*, by giving us poisoned food, and by obliging us to enter the gambling assembly; and having laid violent hands on the garment and hair of the wife of the Pándavas?"

TEXT.

Parikara. No. 340. By the Parikara (Expansion) is meant the expansion of the matter *thus* sprung up.

COMMENTARY.

a. For example, in the same—

"Of that enmity that grew up between me and the Kurus while I was yet a boy, neither our revered brother (Yudhishṭhira) was the cause, nor Kirítí (Arjuna), nor were you two. Do you make peace—Bhíma, in wrath, breaks it asunder again like the broad breast of Jarasandha."

TEXT.

Parinyása. No. 341. The Parinyása (Establishment) is the settlement thereof (*i. e.* of the matter sprung up, §339) :

COMMENTARY

a. As, *again* in the same *drama*—

" I—Bhíma will adorn thy hair, O princess, with my hand red with the thick and abundantly gushing blood of Duryodhana when his thighs are smashed by the powerful blows of the club revolved by my whirling hand."

Now, the Upakshepa (Hint) is the mere intimation, in brief, of the object matter of the *dramatic* poem, *i. e.* of the plot. The Parikara is the exposition of the same. The Parinyása, implying a still greater determination than what is suggested in the Parikara, is, as it were, the fixing of the object about the heart. Such is the distinction among them. These elements must come in the order indicated. The other members *to be presently described* may occur otherwise, *or differently from their order*.

TEXT.

Vilobhana. No. 342. The Vilobhana (Allurement) is the declaration of excellence.

COMMENTARY.

a. For example, in the same—

" *Draupadí.*—My lord, what is hard for you to do, if excited with wrath ?"

Or, for instance, in my ' Chandrakalá' in the description of Chandrakalá, beginning—" Here is she, that Lustre of youth."

b. As to the description of the excellence of the deer, for instance, in the stanza of S'akuntalá, commencing " Charming with this turning of the neck" (ग्रीवाभङ्गाभिरामम्)—it is not a part of the Juncture, since it has no connection with the Germ and *through it*, the End. So is it to be understood with respect to the other members—*that they are members, only when connected with the Germ and the End.*

TEXT.

Yukti. No. 343. The Yukti (Resolution) is the determination of purpose.

COMMENTARY.

a. As in the Veṇí Sanhára—

" *Sahadeva.* (To Bhíma.) Have you, Sir, taken these words of His Majesty without reflecting *on their scope.*"

Commencing with this down to the speech of Bhíma—

" Wrathfully to destroy the family of the enemies shames you indeed before the people, but your partner's hair, siezed in the midst of the assembly, calls not up your blush."

TEXT.

Prápti. No. 344. The Prápti (Gain) is the access of delight.

COMMENTARY.

a For instance, in the same—

" I am not destroying, with wrath, the hundred Kauravas in war, &c." (see §266. *c.*)

Hearing this, Draupadí *exclaims* with joy—" My lord, such a heart-delighting speech was indeed never heard by me before.—O, utter it again and again."

TEXT.

Samádhána. No. 345. The Germ's *actually* coming *to be such*, is termed Samádhána (Deposition).

COMMENTARY.

a. As in the same—

" [Behind the scene.] Hear, ho, Viráṭa, Drupada, and others! That flame of wrath at Duryodhana's seizing the hair and garment of the princess (Draupadí); which was smothered by him all this time with care—his conscience shrinking from the breach of his vow of truth; nay, which was desired to be forgotten by the pacific king wishing peace to the house—that powerful Yudhishṭhirean flame, struck by the flint* of gambling, bursts forth now upon the forces of the Kurus."

The Germ exhibited in the stanza beginning—' Shall the sons of Dhritaráshṭra be in peace, whilst I live,'—is here, as it were, properly deposited, being agreed upon by the principal personage, the hero; hence the name Samádhána.

TEXT.

Vidhána. No. 346. A passage, containing sentiments of pleasure and pain together, is termed Vidhána.

* In the original—wood to produce fire from.

COMMENTARY.

a. For example, in the Bálacharita—

" *Bhárgava*—(To Ráma) My mind is at once possessed with joy and grief, as I see the excess of thy energy, dear child, as also thy tender age—*joy to have to cope with a worthy rival, and grief to have to kill a boy.*"

Or, as in my Prabhávatí, *the stanza* beginning—" O! this form, ecstatic to my eyes," (§249.)

TEXT.

Paribhávaná. No. 347. Words implying curiosity are called Paribhávaná.

COMMENTARY.

a. For example, in the Veṇísanhára, Draupadí, doubting whether the war would take place or not, enquires after the drum has sounded —' Why, my lord, is this martial drum, that roars like clouds in the universal dissolution, being struck now every moment?'

TEXT.

Udbheda. No. 348. The Udbheda (Sprouting) is the shooting forth of the Germ (víja).

COMMENTARY.

a. As in the same—

" *Draupadí.*—My lord, you will come and console me again.

" *Bhíma*—You will not see Bhíma again, with his face down-cast* through shame to have endured the enemy's insults—see me again without having destroyed to a man the descendants of Kuru."

TEXT.

Káraṇa. No. 349. The Káraṇa is the proper commencement of the main business.

COMMENTARY.

a. As in the same—

" We are now going, princess, for the destruction of the Kuru family."

TEXT.

Bheda. No. 350. Bheda (division) is the breach of a union.

COMMENTARY.

a. As in the same—" Hence is it that from this day I separate myself from you, Sirs."

* Or, according to another reading, 'cheerless' or 'sad.'

b. But some* say that Bheda is an urging or excitement.

c. Now of the members of the Pratimukha.

TEXT.

The Members of the Pratimukha. No. 351. Vilása, Parisarpa, Vidhúta, Tápana, Narma, Narmadyuti, Pragamana, Virodha, Paryupásana, Pushpa, Vajra, Upanyása, and Varṇasanhára belong to the Pratimukha.

COMMENTARY.

a. Of these—

TEXT.

Vilása. No. 352. Desire for the object of love is termed Vilása (Amorousness).

COMMENTARY.

a. Vilása is the desire for a woman or man who is the exciting cause or object of the sentiment of Love, as in S'akuntala:—

"My beloved is indeed not easy to obtain, yet my heart solaces itself in having seen her amorous gestures; and thus, though Cupid has not yet done his duty *in uniting us in marriage*, our mutual longing produces a delight almost equal to that enjoyed in actual embrace."

TEXT.

Parisarpa. No. 353. The pursuit *or seeking* after one seen once, but afterwards lost, is called Parisarpa (Going about).

COMMENTARY.

a. As in S'akuntalá—

"*King.*—She must be here; for here on the door-way to this *ratan bower*, bright with sands, I see fresh foot-prints, raised in the front but depressed behind from the weight of the loins."

TEXT.

Vidhúta. No. 354. Vidhúta (shaking off) is the non-acceptance, at first, of a courtesy or a wooing speech.

COMMENTARY.

a. For instance, in the same drama, *as is quoted above, S'akuntalá affects not to admit Dushyanta's professions of love thus*—"You need not longer detain the royal sage, anxious as he is in being separated from his harem."

* The author of the Das'arúpa is principally meant here.

b. According to some, however, Vidhúta is indifference *or a shaking off of love.*

TEXT.

Tápana. No. 355. The not finding of a means is named Tápana (Torment).

COMMENTARY.

a. As in the Ratnávalí—

" *Ságariká*—Difficult is that person to be obtained for whom longs my heart and my shame is great ; myself am dependent upon another and love is invincible—death, then, my dear friend, death is the only refuge *for me.*"

TEXT.

Narma. No. 356. Narma (Pleasantry or jest) is a jocular speech.

COMMENTARY.

a. As in the Ratnávalí :—

" *Susangatá*—Here, my friend, before thee stands he for whom thou hast come here.

" *Ságariká*—(With *seeming* anger.) For whom have I come ?

" *Susan.*—Nay for the picture, lady—suspect me not of meaning any thing else."

TEXT.

Narma-dyuti. No. 357. Whilst Narma-dyuti (Brilliancy of jest) is joy produced by joke.

COMMENTARY.

a. As in the same :—

" *Susangatá*—Thou art cruel now, friend, as thou quittest not thy anger, though thus held by the hand by thy lord.

" *Ságariká*—(With a frown and a smile.) Wilt thou not yet cease to jest, Susangatá ?"

Some, however, assert—'a joke covering over a fault is Narma-dyuti.'

TEXT.

Pragamana. No 358. The Pragamana is a speech containing an excellent answer.

COMMENTARY.

a. As in the Vikramorvas'í—

" *Urvas'í*—Victorious be thou, great king, be thou victorious !

" *King*—Victorious, indeed, have I become to whom victory has been proclaimed by thee, *fair lady* &c."

TEXT.

Virodha. No. 359. The Virodha (Adversity) is falling into danger.

COMMENTARY.

a. As in the Chaṇḍa Kaus'ika—

" Acting imprudently, I have, indeed, like a blind man, trodden under my feet, a fire with blazing flames."

TEXT.

Paryupásana. No. 360. Asking pardon for *a fault* done is Paryupásana.

COMMENTARY.

a. For example, in the Ratnávalí—

" *Vidushaka*—Pray, be not angry: it has flown into the plantain bower &c."

TEXT.

Pushpa. No. 361. A declaration of excellence is called the Pushpa.

COMMENTARY.

a. As in the same—

" (The king holds Ságariká by the hand.)

" *Vidúshaka*—This, my friend, is an extraordinary Beauty you have obtained.

" *King*—Indeed, friend, she is Beauty herself, and her hand is a sprout of the Párijata (Heavenly tree), otherwise how comes to ooze from it this nectarine liquid, disguised as heat-drops ?"

TEXT.

Vajra. No. 362. The Vajra is a speech directly cruel.

COMMENTARY.

a. For example in the same :—

" *King*—How could you know me here ?

" *Susangatá*—Not only you but the picture too, so I go to inform the queen of it."

TEXT.

Upanyása. No. 363. The Upanyása is a propitiation or gratifying.

COMMENTARY.

a. As in the same :—

" *Susangatá*—Let not my master suspect me. I have indeed played with these through the favour of my mistress. It would be a greater favour to me, should your majesty propitiate my dear friend Ságariká who is angry that I have drawn her likeness here."

b. Some, however, say—' an assertion made with a reason is termed Upanyása,' and cite, from the Ratnávalí, as an example—" This born-slave is extremely impertinent"—*where the assertion of impertinence, in respect of the female attendant Susangatá, is accompanied with the reason of her being a slave by birth.*

TEXT.

Varṇa-saṇhára. No. 364. A meeting of men of the four castes is called the Varṇa-saṇhára (Assemblage of the classes).

COMMENTARY.

a. For example in the 3rd act of the Víracharita :—

" This assembly of saints ; the hero Yudhájit ; the aged king Lomapáda together with his ministers ; as also this ancient lord of the Janakas, the perpetual performer of sacrifices and the teacher of Divine knowledge—solicit of thee a friendly conduct."

Here we have a meeting of men of different castes such as the Bráhman saints and the Kshattriyas.

Another interpretation of the Varṇa-saṇhára. *b.* The venerable writer Abhinava Gupta, however, asserts that the word ' varṇa' indicates personages *of the drama* and ' saṇhára' means a drawing together. He refers, as an example, to the passage in the second act of the Ratnávalí—

" This would be a greater favour to me * * * * * *
* * * * * * * * * * * * * * * * *
Hold her by the hand and then propitiate her. * * * * *
* * * * * * * * * * * * * * * * *

" *King*—Where is she [Vásavadattá (?)], where is she ?"

c. Now of the elements of the Garbha :—

TEXT.

The Members of the Garbha. No. 365. Abhútáharṇa, Márga, Rúpa, Udáharaṇa, Krama, Sangraha, Anumána, Prárthaná, Kshipti, Troṭaka, Adhibala, Udvega, and Vidrava are *the members* belonging to the Garbha.

Abhútáharaṇa. Of these the Abhútáharaṇa (Utterance of an unreality) is a speech founded on fraud.

COMMENTARY.

a. For example in As'wathåman's Act *of the Veṇísaṇhára* :—

"The son of Prithá (Yudhishṭhira) having clearly spoken—'As'wathåman is killed,' afterwards uttered—truthful indeed as he is—'the elephant,' indistinctly."

TEXT.

Márga. No. 366. Márga is the declaration of the truth.

COMMENTARY.

a. For example in the *drama* 'Chaṇḍa Kaus'ika' (Vis'wámittra Wroth).

"*King*—Holy saint! accept this that I have earned by selling my wife and children; for the rest *of the donation I have promised to you*, I will *sell* myself even to a Cháṇḍála."

TEXT.

Rúpa. No. 367. A speech implying reflection is Rúpa.

COMMENTARY.

a. As in the Ratnávalí :—

"*King*. How did Cupid pierce my mind with all his arrows together? restless as it is by nature and never to be perceived *(or aimed at)*."

TEXT.

Udáharaṇa. No. 368. An extolling or lofty speech is called the Udáharaṇa (Extolling).

COMMENTARY.

a. As in the As'watthámánka, *or the third act named after As'watthåman, of the Vení Saṇhára* :—

"Whoever holds a weapon in the troops of the Paṇḍavas; whoever belongs to the family of Pánchála, be he a grown up man, a boy, or even lying in the womb; whoever has witnessed *or connived at* that deed; and whoever opposes me whilst I walk in the field of battle—of every one of these I myself am the destroyer, mad with wrath,—though he be the destroyer of the worlds *or Death himself*."

TEXT.

Krama. No. 369. The discovery of the reality of one's love is termed the Krama.

COMMENTARY.

a. For example in the S'akuntalá :—

"Fit it is that my eyes looking at my love have forgotten to wink; since, the countenance of my angel,—with one of the eye-brows raised up, as she composes verses of love,—bespeaks, with quivering cheeks, her affection for me."

TEXT.

Sangraha. No. 370. The Sangraha again is the accomplishment of an object by means of sweet words and a gift.

COMMENTARY.

a. For example in the Ratnávalí.

"*King*—Bravo! my friend, this is your reward, (gives his golden bracelet.)"

TEXT.

Anumána. No. 371. The Anumána (Inference) is a conclusion from a *characteristic* sign.

COMMENTARY.

a. As in the drama Jánaki Rághava:

"*Ráma*—Causing the earth to waver even with his careless steps, and making the heads of all to bow down merely with his looks, he with a body radiant like gold, leads us to infer his solar descent as well as his irresistible prowess."

TEXT.

Prárthaná. No. 372. The Prárthaná (Request) is a wishing or calling for enjoyment, rejoicing, or festivity.

COMMENTARY.

a. For example, in the Ratnávalí :—

"*King*—Beloved Ságariká, thy face is the cool-beamed *moon*, thy eyes are a couple of blue lotuses, thy hands imitate the red lotus, that pair of thighs of thine shines like the plantain trunk, and thy arms may be compared to the lotus-stalk *in coolness*—come, O come, my love, who thus gladdenest with every one of thy members, embrace me at once without fear, and cool my members tormented with the fire of love."

The Prárthaná only a conditional element of the Garbha. *b.* This element—the Prárthaná—has been *but conditionally* admitted here upon the opinion of such as deny that there is any such element as the Pras'asti (see §405.) in the Conclusion or last division of the plot

(Nirvahaṇa—see §337) inasmuch as it has a place here *under the form of this Prárthaná.* Otherwise *than on this condition,* the elements would amount to 65, *whilst they are held to be 64 only.*

TEXT.

Kshipti. No. 373. The development of a concealed matter is *termed* the Kshipti (Hint).*

COMMENTARY.

a. As in As'watthâman's Act or the 3rd *in the Veṇí Sanhára :—*

"Dreadful has been the effect on the world of that single seizure of hair *(viz. of Draupadí's)*—surely mankind will all be annihilated on this second seizure *(i. e. of Droṇa's).*"

TEXT.

Troṭaka. No. 374. The Troṭaka again is a wrathful speech.

COMMENTARY.

a. For example, in the Chaṇda Kaus'ika :—

"*Kaus'ika*—Ah! How—are the donations of gold *thou hast promised to me* not yet ready?"

TEXT.

Adhibala. No. 375. The Adhibala (Overreaching) is an inquiry or examination by an artifice.

COMMENTARY.

a. For example, in the Ratnávalí Act III.

"*Kánchana-mála*—This, my lady, is the picture-gallery—let me beckon to Vasantaka &c."

TEXT.

Udvega. No. 376. Fear caused by a king or the like is termed the Udvega (Anxiety).

COMMENTARY.

a. For example in the Veṇí Sanhára, Act V.

"They have arrived, mounted in one car, inquiring for you here and there—that foe of Karṇa (Arjuna), and that fierce Vrikodara (Bhíma) of wolfish deeds."

* This is a deviation from the definition of the Das'a Rúpa and, as is the usual consequence in such cases, it is very obscure, being scarcely reconcilable with the example.

TEXT.

Vidrava. No. 377. By the Vidrava (Confusion) is meant the hurry occasioned by apprehension, fear, or terror.

COMMENTARY.

a. For example :

"There was an indescribable hurry produced in the army of the monkeys at the sight of the wrath-excited Ravaṇa with faces dreadful like black Death's."

b. Now of the Members of the Vimarsha :

TEXT.

The Members of the Vimarsha. No. 378. Apaváda, Sampheṭa, Vyavasáya, Drava, Dyuti, S'akti, Prasanga, Kheda, Pratishedha, Virodhana, Prarochaná, Ádána, Chhádana : these belong to the Vimarsha (§336).

Apaváda. Apaváda (Censure) is the declaration of fault.

COMMENTARY.

a. For example in the Veṇí Saṇhára, Act VI.

"*Yudhishṭhira.* Pánchálaka, have you discovered any where the traces of that wretch ?

"*Pánchálaka.* Not only his traces but the wretch himself has been found, the chief cause of that sin of touching the queen's tresses."

TEXT.

Sampheṭa. No. 379. The Sampheṭa is an angry interlocution.

COMMENTARY.

a. As in the same, Act V.

"*King.*—O thou son of Váyu, dost thou extol, before the old king, thy deeds, though detested ? Hear thou—Thy wife, or thine, O beast, or that prince's, or the twin brothers'—*the common wife of you all*—my slave won in gambling, was seized by the hair, before the princes, by my command, the lord of the earth. In that perverse enmity *between me and you*, say what harm did the princes do whom thou hast killed ?—and dost thou brag, even without having vanquished me fiercely proud of the cumbrous property of the might of these *brawny* arms ?

"*Bhíma.* (Angrily) Oh wretch !

"*King.* Oh villain ! &c."

TEXT.

Vyavasáya. No. 380. By Vyavasáya (Resolution) is to be understood a vow combined with a reason.

COMMENTARY.

a. For example in the same, Act V.:—

"*Bhíma.* He who has destroyed, one and all, the descendants of Kuru, who, intoxicated as he is with Dus's'ásana's blood, shall break the thighs of Duryodhana—here is Bhíma bowing down his head *to you, venerable old uncle.*"*

TEXT.

Drava. No. 381. Drava is rudeness shown to a superior from the agitation of grief or the like.

COMMENTARY.

a. For instance in the same, Act VI.:—

"*Yudhishṭhira.* Worthy elder brother of Krishṇa! brother of Subhadrá! You brought not to mind the affection you owe to your kindred, nor did you heed a Kshattriya's duty, nor the strong friendship that exists between your younger brother and Arjuna; well, however, might affection's chain tie your honour with equal strength to both your disciples—what, alas, is the conduct you have adopted, that you are altogether averse to my unhappy self?"

TEXT.

Dyuti. No. 382. The Dyuti is declared to consist in reviling and vexing.

COMMENTARY.

a. For example in the same, Act VI., the prince Bhíma thus speaks, *in bitter language*, to Duryodhana:

"Thou declarest thyself to be born in the spotless race of the moon; thou holdest yet thy club; me thou countest an enemy, drunk though I am with the wine of Dus's'ásana's warm blood; blind with pride, thou dealest haughtily even with Krishṇa, the destroyer of Madhu and Kaitabha; and now, thou beast of a man, having, through fear of me, quitted the field, shrinkest in the mud."

* That he is Bhíma (fierce) by his very name, and intoxicated with draughts of his enemy's blood is the reason in his vowing to destroy Duryodhana, his 'dearest enemy.'

TEXT.

S'akti. No. 383. S'akti is the quelling of opposition *or conflict.*

COMMENTARY.

a. For instance in the same:—

" Whether or not they reduce to ashes the heaps of the bodies *of warriors* killed by kindred in the midst of battle—let these *surviving* kinsmen, any how give *funeral* water, mixed with tears, to their *dead* relations; let them seek the bodies of their kindred, amidst this dense heap of corpses, dissevered by vultures and herons—behold, the sun is set together with the foes—back let the troops be called."

TEXT.

Prasañga. No. 384 Prasanga is a mentioning of one's sires.

COMMENTARY

a. As in the Mṛichchhakatiká or the Toy Cart, Act X. :—

" *Cháṇḍálaka.* This is Chárudatta, son of Ságaradatta, and grandson of the venerable Vinayadatta—being led, to be slain, to the place of execution, for he has murdered the courtezan Vasantasená, from avarice of gold.

" *Chárudatta.* That family of mine, purified by a hundred sacrifices, and formerly extolled in assembly by chanters of the Veda crowding the house,—is *now* proclaimed in *impure* defamation by unworthy wretches, as I stand in the condition of *a criminal* to be killed."

Here we have an instance of the Prasanga in the naming of Chárudatta's sires which suits the present occasion of his being taken to be executed.

TEXT.

Kheda. No. 385. Languor, produced (1) *simply* in the mind, or (2) by bodily exertion is called Kheda (Lassitude).

COMMENTARY

a. Languor, *or rather distress,* produced in the mind—as in the Málatí Mádhava (Málatí and Mádhava), Act IX. :—

" My heart bursts in deep anguish, but oh it breaks not into two; my frame distracted faints away, yet it loses not its consciousness absolutely; the internal flames burn my body, yet they reduce it not to ashes—Fate scourges me, cutting to the very quick, but alas! cuts not my life through."

b. So, the languor produced by exertion.

TEXT.

Pratishedha. No. 386. The obstruction of a wished-for object is called the Pratishedha (Prevention).

COMMENTARY.

a. For example in my Prabhávatí:—

"*Pradyumna.* (To the Vidúshaka) How is it, friend, that you are alone here—where is my most beloved Prabhávatí and her dear friends *the ladies*, that attend her?

"*Vidúshaka.* She has been called away somewhere by the lord of the Demons.

"*Pradyumna.* (Heaving a deep sigh) O! where art thou gone having abandoned me, thou, with face like the full moon, with eyes like the wanton Chakora (partridge), and with a body gently inclined—quickly do thou go now, my life; let Fortune, bent upon tormenting me, have her wishes fulfilled."

TEXT.

Virodhana. No. 387. The apprehension of failure in the purpose is called Virodhana (Obstruction).

COMMENTARY.

a. For example in the *beginning of Act VI. of the* Veṇí Saṇhára:—

"*Yudhishṭhira.* When the mighty ocean of Bhíshma has somehow been crossed, when the fire of Droṇa has been extinguished, when the poisonous serpent of Karṇa has been destroyed, and when S'alya has gone to heaven,—when our victory has almost been complete, we all have been at once put in danger of our lives by the rash Bhíma with his words."

TEXT.

Prarochaná. No. 388. The Prarochaná (Persuasion) is to be known as that which represents the End *as all but accomplished.**

COMMENTARY.

a. For example in the Veṇí Saṇhára, Act VI.:—

"*Pánchálaka.* I *have been sent to your Majesty* by the Divine Krishṇa. * * * * * * * * * * * * * * * * * * *

* The italicized part is from the Das'a Rúpa—p. 44.

Do away with all doubts. Let the gemmed jars be filled with water for your royal bathing;* let Krishṇá hold festivity in the business—so long neglected—of binding up the braid of her hair;—when Paras'u Ráma, eradicator of the Kshattra trees, with his hand glistening with his whetted battle-axe, and Bhímasena, blind with rage, move violently upon the field of battle—what doubt is there *of your victory?*"

TEXT.

Ádána. No. 389. The Ádána (Taking in) is the summing up of the main business.

COMMENTARY.

a. For instance in the Veṇí Saṇhára, Act VI.:—

"What ho! you who move on the Samanta-panchaka! I am neither a demon, nor a goblin; I am a passionate Kshattriya, who have crossed the impassable ocean of a dread vow, whose body has been cooled with the water of enemies' blood;—hear, Ye Kshattriya warriors, left by the devouring flames of the fire of war, forego this your terror that impels you thus shrinkingly to lie concealed among those carcases of elephants and horses."

Here we have the Ádána *exhibited* in the main business—the slaughter of all the enemies being summed up.

TEXT.

Chhádana. No. 390. An enduring of insult or the like for the fulfilment of the Deed is what they call the Chhádana.

COMMENTARY.

a. For example in the same, Act V.:—

"*Arjuna.* Worthy sir, let him use us ill—he is powerful in word, not in deed; what pain can come from the words of this miserable man who has lost his hundred brothers in battle?"

b. Now of the members of the Nirvahaṇa:—

TEXT.

The Members of the Nirvahaṇa. No. 391. Sandhi, Vibodha, Grathana, Nirṇaya, Paribháshaṇa, Kriti, Prasáda, Ánanda, Samaya, Upagúhana, Bháshaṇa, Púrvavákya, Kávyasaṇhára, and Pras'asti: thus are the members of the Saṇhára or Nirvahaṇa (Conclusion—see §337) *severally* designated.

* Bathing with the water of various sacred streams is one of the principal rites in the inauguration of a king.

COMMENTARY.

a. Of these:

TEXT.

Sandhi. No. 392. The Sandhi is the noticing of the Germ (Víja).

COMMENTARY.

a. For example in the Veṇí Saṇhára, Act VI. :—

" *Bhíma.* Lady born of the sacrificial altar, do you remember what I said that day—' I—Bhíma will adorn thy hair, O princess &c. ?' " (see § 341, *a.*)

Here the Germ, intimated in the Mukha, is recalled *to the mind*, and so it is *an instance of* the Sandhi.

TEXT.

Vibodha. No. 393. The Vibodha is the seeking after the End *or the consummation of the ultimate object.*

COMMENTARY.

a. As in the same, Act VI. :—

" *Bhíma.* Give me, sir, a moment's leave.

" *Yudhishṭhira.* What more is remaining ?

" *Bhíma.* A good deal is remaining. Let me bind up the tresses of Draupadí, that were pulled down by Dus's'ásana,—with these hands wet with Duryodhana's blood.

" *Yudhishṭhira.* Go, let the poor woman enjoy the pleasure of having her hair-braid bound up."

Here, the End, viz. the binding of the hair, being *actually* sought after, it is *an example of* the Vibodha.

TEXT.

Grathana. No. 394. Grathana is the intimation of the End.

COMMENTARY.

a. For instance in the same, Act VI. :—

" *Bhíma.* Do not, Draupadí, whilst I live, bind, with your own hands, thy tresses dishevelled by Dus's'ásana—stay, I myself am binding them."

TEXT.

Nirṇaya. No. 395. Nirṇaya (Certainty) again is the declaration of a fact personally known.

COMMENTARY.

a. As, in the same, Act VI. :—

" *Bhíma.* Sire, Ajátas'atru,* where still is that accursed Duryodhana ?—I have cast the body of that wretch upon the earth. With the blood, as with sandal, I have anointed my body. His fortune I have brought over to thee together with the earth bounded by the waters of the four oceans. His protégés, friends, warriors—the whole Kuru family I have burnt in the fire of war—that name only, which thou utterest, Preserver of the earth, is now the remnant of the son of Dhritaráshṭra."

TEXT.

Paribháshaṇa. No. 396. A speech implying censure is what they call Paribháshaṇa.†

COMMENTARY.

a. As in S'akuntalá, Act VII. :—

" *King.* Pray, madam, what is the name of the royal saint whose consort is this lady ?

" *Hermitess.* Who will take the name of that deserter of a lawful wife ?"

TEXT.

Kriti. No. 397. The consolation *or confirmation* of the object gained is the Kriti.

COMMENTARY.

a. For example in the Veṇí Saṇhára, Act VI. :—

" *Krishṇa.* The holy sages—Vyása, Válmíki, and others, wait holding the water for your royal bathing."

Here we have the Kriti exemplified in the confirmation, by the auspicious ceremonies of bathing &c., of the kingdom obtained *by Yudhishṭhira.*

TEXT.

Prasáda. No. 398. The Prasáda (Gratification) is a waiting upon or the like.

COMMENTARY.

a. For example in Act VI. of the same, the binding of Draupadí's hair by Bhíma.

* Etymologically—one who has not an enemy born—another name of Yudhishṭhira.

† In the Das'arúpa, this is explained simply to mean a mutual conversation.

TEXT.

Ánanda. No. 399. Ánanda (Joy) is the attainment of what was wished for *or the End.*

COMMENTARY.

a. For instance in the same, Act VI. :—

" *Draupadí. Long forsaken and therefore* forgotten, I shall again learn this business *of binding up my tresses,* through your favour, my lord."

TEXT.

Samaya. No. 400. Samaya (the Hour *of happiness*) is the removal of misery.

COMMENTARY.

a. As in the Ratnávalí :—

" *Vásavadattá.* (Embracing Ratnávalí) Sister, be thou consoled, be thou consoled!"

TEXT.

Upagúhana. No. 401. The arrival *or appearance* of a wonder is the Upagúhana.

COMMENTARY.

a. For instance, in my Prabhávatí Pariṇaya *or the Marriage of Prabhávatí,* the appearance of Nárada at which Pradyumna looking up says :—

" What is this *I behold!* Is it the *white* mountain Kailása falling from the heavens, whitening all space with beams of light bright like the dewy moon, and inwreathed, as with the lightning's streaks, with a garland of flowers wooed with songs by humming bees roving round for their sweet scent?"

TEXT.

Bháshaṇa. No. 402. The Bháshaṇa is conciliation, donation, or the like.

COMMENTARY.

a. For example, in the Chaṇḍa Kaus'ika :—

" *Dharma.** Come, then, inhabit the world of Dharma.

* Yama, the god of justice and ruler of the southern quarter,—here, as indicated by the milder appellation of Dharma, acting particularly in his character of the Rewarder of the virtuous, contradistinguished from that of the Punisher of the wicked, marked by his more common but dreaded name of Yama—Controller or Discipliner.

TEXT.

Púrva-vákya. No. 403. By Púrva-vákya (Previous Speech) is to be understood a reference to a thing as spoken before.

COMMENTARY.

a. As in the Veṇí Sañhára, Act VI.:—

" *Bhíma.*—Well, Buddhimatiká, where is our Bhánumatí?* let her now insult the wife of the Páṇḍavas."

Here Bhíma vindictively sneers at the taunt used by Bhánumatí towards Draupadí, in the beginning of the drama.

TEXT.

Kávya-sañhára. No. 404. The occasion of giving a boon is termed the Kávya-sañhára (Conclusion of the drama).

COMMENTARY.

a. As in all the dramas: " What may I do to please you further?"

TEXT.

Pras'asti. No. 405. The *declaration* of peace to the dominion of a king, &c. is designated Pras'asti (Benediction).

COMMENTARY.

a. For instance in the Prabhávatí:—

" May kings henceforth ever view their subjects exactly in the light of a son; may the good live long—they who appreciate merit, and readily discriminate good from evil; may the earth prosper with an increasing abundance of corn and wealth; and may the triple world have an unflagging faith in Náráyaṇa, *the Supreme Spirit!*"

b. Among these *members of the Nirvahaṇa,* the Upasañhára or Kávya-sañhára, and the Pras'asti occur only in the end, in one order, *or that exhibited in the text.*

Which of the Members chief in the several Junctures. *c.* " These two are the principal here *in the Juncture Nirvahaṇa;* the Upakshepa, Parikara, Parinyása, Yukti, Udbheda, and Samádhána, in the Mukha; the Parisarpa, Pragamana, Vajra, Upanyása, and Pushpa, in the Pratimukha; the Abhútáharaṇa, Márga, Troṭaka, and Kshipti, in the Garbha; and the Apaváda, S'akti, Vyavasáya, Prarochaná, and Ádána *are the most prominent* in the Vimarsha. The others too occur when there is occasion for them." Such is the opinion of some.

* Duryodhana's wife.

TEXT.

Junctural Members altogether 64—may be promiscuously introduced.

No. 406. These are the sixty-four kinds of members declared by the learned. They may be admitted into the Junctures even irregularly or promiscuously, taking care that they harmonize with the Flavour *of the play;* for Flavour alone is essential in Poetry.

COMMENTARY.

a. For instance in the third act of the Veṇí Sañhára the lengthy dialogue in Yukti or the Determination of Purpose (§343) between Karṇa and Duryodhana *is introduced irregularly.* So in other cases.

b. As to the declaration of Rudraṭa and others that it is a rule *to introduce the members into their proper Junctures,* it is opposed to *the dramas themselves* which are always kept in view *as guides in the formation of the dramatic rules.*

TEXT.

Use of the Members sixfold.

No. 407. The use of the Members is sixfold, viz. (1) composition of the intended matter, (2) excitement of surprise, (3) expansion of the plot, (4) increase of the interest of the performance, (5) the concealment of what is to be concealed, and (6) representation of what is to be represented. As a man without his limbs is never fit for work, so a drama without its members is not suitable for representation.

The Hero and the Rival Hero should represent the members of the Junctures; if they do not perform these, *they should represent* the Patáká and the two others (viz. Prakarí and Kárya—§317); and if not these latter, *they should represent* the Germ.

COMMENTARY.

a. The members of the Junctures are generally represented by the principal personage, but it is always best if the *first* three *members of the Juncture Mukha, i. e.* the Upakshepa, &c. (§338) are not represented by the hero, as the Germ is only slightly hinted in them.

TEXT.

The Members to be introduced only in consonance with Flavour.

No 408. These members are to be admitted only with the view to the development of Flavour, and not simply from a desire of following up the rules.

COMMENTARY.

a. For instance, Duryodhana's 'separation'* (vipralambha—see §212) from Bhánumatí, described in *the 2nd act* of the Veṇí Sañhára, is on that occasion, extremely improper.

TEXT.

A Superfluous matter also, to be omitted or altered.

No. 409. An incident, though not opposed to Flavour, yet not necessary to the development of it, is also (see §304) to be altered by the wise, or not mentioned at all.

COMMENTARY.

a. Illustrations of the two cases *implied in the text* are evident enough in my dramatic works.

b. Now of the Actions (vṛitti):

TEXT.

The four dramatic Actions or Styles.

No. 410. The Kais'ikí is used in the Erotic; the Sáttwatí, in the Heroic; the Árabhaṭí, in the Furious; and the action *called the* Bháratí is always employed in the Disgustful Flavour. These are the four actions, the parents of all representations in the Náṭaka and other *sorts of the drama,* being particular performances of the Hero or the like.

COMMENTARY.

a. Of these the Kais'ikí *is defined thus*:—

TEXT.

The Kais'ikí defined.

No. 411. That performance is called the Kais'ikí which is associated with charming vivacity (§91), which is peculiarly delightful from the fascinating dresses worn therein by the heroine and others, in which women abundantly take part, dancing and singing are fully indulged in, and the actings are founded on the enjoyments of love.

* Arising from his jealous suspicion of her unfaithfulness.

The four elements of the Kais'ikí.

It has four elements—(1) Narma (Pleasantry), (2) Narma-sphúrja (Development of love), (3) Narma-sphoṭa (Bloom of love), and (4) Narma-garbha (Covert love).

COMMENTARY.

a. Of these:

TEXT.

(1) The Narma. Its three varieties.

No. 412. The Narma is a witty jest tending to charm the beloved: this again is held to be threefold according as it is used (1) in pure joke, or (2) joke mixed with love, or (3) joke mixed with fear.

COMMENTARY.

The Narma of pure joke.

a. Of these, the Narma employed in simple joke or raillery—as in Ratnávalí *in the following words of Vásavadattá to her husband:*

" *Vásavadattá.*—And this another—*a female shape*—that is portrayed beside you—is this worthy Vasantaka's skill *in painting?*"

Narma of Love.

Narma of love—as in S'akuntalá:

" *S'akuntalá.—(To the king).* If not satisfied, what would he do?

" *King.*—This. *(Determines to kiss S'akuntalá.)*

" *S'akuntalá.—(Turns away her face.)*"

Narma of Fear.

Narma of fear or frightening joke—as, in Ratnávalí, when the king had found the picture—

" *Susangatá.*—I have come to know the matter including the picture, so I am going to inform the queen of it."

Thus has the Narma pertaining to speech been exemplified. So the Narma pertaining to dress and action, *or practical jest.*

TEXT.

(2) The Narma-sphúrja.

No. 413. The Narma-sphúrja (§411) is the first union *of two lovers* in which there is joy in the beginning, but fear in the end.

COMMENTARY.

a. The following is an instance in 'Málaviká and Agnimittra' where *the heroine* Málaviká has resorted to the hero, *her lover* in the appointed place.

" Abandon, O fair one, the delicacy thou feelest in our first union Long have I been expectant in love, and now, as I fancy myself the fragrant mango tree, assume towards me the character of the Atimukta creeper.*

" *Málaviká.*—The fear of the queen prevents me, my lord, from doing my own good, &c."

b. Now of the Narma-sphoṭa :

TEXT.

(3) The Narma-sphoṭa.

No. 414. The Narma-sphoṭa is held to be flavour (the Erotic) slightly suggested by glimpses of love.

COMMENTARY.

a. " Languid is his pace and vacant his sight, his body is beauty-wanting and his respirations increased—what may be the cause of it?—what other than this?—Cupid's command roves through the world, youth is fickle, and those soft and sweet things are ever apt to disturb all fortitude."

Here we have the love of Mádhava for Málatí somewhat manifested by slight indications of love, such as his languid pace, &c.

TEXT.

(4) The Narma-garbha.

No. 415. The Narma-garbha is the action of the *amorous* hero in concealment.

COMMENTARY.

a. For example in the same *drama as quoted above*—the prevention of Málatí from killing herself by Mádhava in the disguise of her female friend.

b. Now of the Sáttwatí (§410) :—

TEXT.

The Sáttwatí defined. Four Kinds of it.

No. 416. The Sáttwatí is a performance abounding in the displays of energy, bravery, generosity, benevolence, and honesty. It is joyful, has little of love in it, is devoid of grief and attended with the Marvellous. The Utthápaka, the Sañghátya, the Sañlápa, and the Parivartaka are declared to be the four kinds of the Sáttwatí.

(1) The Utthápaka,

A speech calculated to excite the enemy is termed the Utthápaka (Exciter).

* 'The Gœrtnera racemosa'—Wilson.

COMMENTARY.

a. As in the Víracharita :—

"To my joy and admiration art thou seen by me, or rather to my grief—how can my eyes be satiated with the sight of thee, *fair, valorous, and virtuous youth.* But the joy of thy friendship is not to be shared by me*—what need then is there of much talk—let this hand illustrious with the victory of Jámadagnya grasp the awful bow."

TEXT.

(2) The Sangháttya. No. 417. The Sanghátya is a breach of alliance under the influence (1) of counsel, (2) of money, or (3) of Fortune.

COMMENTARY.

a. Breach of alliance under the influence of counsel *or machination* —as, in the Mudrá Rákshasa, the division of Rákshasa's allies by the cunning of Cháṇakya.—That under the influence of money is also *exhibited* in the same drama.—That under the influence of Fortune is *exemplified* in the separation of Vibhíshaṇa from Rávaṇa in the Rámáyaṇa.

TEXT.

(3) The Sanlápaka. No. 418. The Sanlápaka (Conversation) is an elevated interlocution embodying a variety of sentiments.

COMMENTARY.

a. For example in the Víracharita :

"*Ráma.*—This, I believe, is that battle-axe which the Great S'iva presented you—his disciple for a thousand years—gratified by your defeat of the War-god together with his attendants.

"*Paras'u Ráma.*—Ráma, child of Das'aratha, this is the same loved battle-axe of my adorable master"†—and so forth.

TEXT.

(4) The Parivartaka. No. 419. Doing of actions other than that commenced is the Parivartaka (Deviation or change).

COMMENTARY.

a. For instance in the Veṇí Sanhára :—

* This clause is obscure and has consequently called forth a variety of readings. I have followed the reading adopted in Pundit Taránátha Tarkavachaspati's edition of the drama, 1857.

† The Heroic Flavour with a mixture of 'love for a deity,' Pride &c. are here suggested.

"*Bhíma.*— Sahadeva, go you and follow the sire (Yudhisṭhira), whilst I am entering the arsenal and furnishing myself with arms—or I must at first take leave of Draupadí."

b. Now of the Árabhaṭí (§410) :—

TEXT.

The Árabhaṭí defined. Its four divisions.

No. 420. The Árabhaṭí is held to be a vehement performance consisting of magic, conjuration, conflict, rage, distraction, imprisonment, slaughter, and other such acts. Vastútthápana, Sampheṭa, Sankshipti, and Avapátana are declared to be the four divisions of the Árabhaṭí.

(1) The Vastútthápana.

Things raised up by magic or the like are spoken of as the Vastútthápana (Conjuration).

COMMENTARY.

a. As in the Udátta Rághava :—

"Whence is this?—that the powerful and glorious rays of the sun himself have suddenly been vanquished by the hosts of night-born darkness covering over the heavens—that these jackals, with bellies puffed up with draughts of blood sucked from the throats of horrible headless corpses, ejecting flames from the caverns of their mouths, utter such sharp *fearful* yells."

TEXT.

(2) The Sampheṭa.

No. 421. Sampheṭa is a mutual encounter of the angry and the agitated.

COMMENTARY.

a. For instance, in Málati Mádhava *the encounter* of Mádhava and Aghoraghaṇṭa.

TEXT.

(3) The Sankshipti.

No. 422. A brief arrangement of some matter, by contrivances of art or otherwise, is termed the Sankshipti;—as also the replacement of a character by another, on the removal of the former.

COMMENTARY.

a. Of the first kind we have an instance in the Udayana Charita, or 'Actions of Udayana' in the contrivance of the straw-made elephant. —The second sort is exemplified *in the Víra-charita* in the replacement of Bálin, on his death, by Sugríva; or in the change of Paras'u Ráma from a haughty to a peaceful character, indicated in *his speech* beginning—'The pure nature of the Bráhman.'

TEXT.

(4) The Avapátana. No. 423. The Avapátana is a medley of entrance, terror, exit, joy, and flight.

COMMENTARY.

a. As in the 6th act of the Krityá-Rávaṇa, the scene opening—'Enter a man sword in hand,' and terminating with the exit.

TEXT.

No. 424. The Bhárati, the fourth of the dramatic actions mentioned in §410, has already been described (see §285).

COMMENTARY.

a. Now of the dramatic phrases:—

TEXT.

Dramatic phrases. No. 425. Something which is not to be heard *or is spoken to one's self* on the stage is called Swagata* or Speech Aside; what may be heard by all is termed Prakás'a or Public. A secret of another uttered by one turning aside is called Apavárita or Speech Apart. The mutual whisper of two persons in the midst of the conversation of the company, preventing, *as it were,* the others *from hearing* by means of the three-bannered hand is termed Janántika. When in the action a person speaks beginning—"What do you say?" without the presence of any addressed, as if hearing something though not really spoken, it is called Ákás'abháshita or Speech in the Air.

COMMENTARY.

a. When any thing is spoken to another away from the person from whom it is to be concealed, the speaker raising his hand in the form called the 'three-bannered' *i. e.* with all the fingers raised but the ring-finger lowered—it is called Janántika. The expressing of another's secret by turning away is Apavárita. The rest *of the text* is clear.

TEXT.

How certain characters to be named. No. 426. The names given to courtezans should contain *the word* 'dattá,' 'siddhá,' or 'sená'; those of merchants should generally end in dattá; and those of male and female servants be the names of things described, for instance, as connected with the Spring.

* Lity.—Self-abiding, inward, secret.

COMMENTARY.

a. A courtesan's name—such as Vasantasená; a merchant's, as Vishṇudatta; a male servant's, as Kalahansa (gander); a female servant's, as Mandáriká.

TEXT.

How the Náṭaka to be named.

No. 427. The Náṭaka should be named so as to indicate the matter contained.

COMMENTARY.

a. Thus, for example, 'Rámábhyudaya' or the Triumph of Ráma.

TEXT.

The Prakaraṇa, &c. how to be named.

No. 428. The Prakaraṇa &c. are to be named after the hero and the heroine *together*.*

COMMENTARY.

a. As for instance—'Málatí and Mádhava.'

TEXT.

The Náṭiká, &c. how to be named.

No. 429. The Náṭiká, the Saṭṭaka, and others are to be designated after the heroine.

COMMENTARY.

a. Thus—Ratnávalí, Karpúramanjarí, &c.

TEXT.

The root 'sádh' for 'gam' used in the dramas.

No. 430. The causal form of the root 'sádh' is generally used instead of 'gam' *in the sense of going*.

COMMENTARY.

a. For instance in S'akuntalá, the two sages say—'sádhayávas távat'—meaning—'We go then.'

TEXT.

The characters how addressed.

No. 431. A king is to be addressed by his servants—'Lord' (swámin) or 'Sire' (deva), and Bhaṭṭa by low persons; by royal sages and the Vidúshaka—'Friend' (vayasya); by saints—'King,' or by a patronymic. A Bráhman is to be accosted by Bráhmans optionally by his patronymic or proper name, and by the other classes—'Sir' (Árya). The Vidúshaka is to be addressed by a king—'Friend' (vayasya), or by his name. The Manager and the Actress are to be mutually addressed by the term

* 'As a general rule,' adds the commentator, 'for we see such a name as Saugandhikáharaṇa.'

A'rya (Sir). The Páripárs'wika or Assistant Manager (see §287. *a.*) should call the Manager 'Bháva,' and the latter should accost the former by the title of Márisha. Equals are addressed—'Hande' among low persons; Vayasya, among men of the highest class; and 'Hanho' among those of the middling class. An elder brother is to be called, 'Sir.' Those who bear the insignia of a Divine Saint (Devarshi) are to be addressed by all—'Bhagavan' (holy sage). The Vidúshaka should give the queen and her female attendant the title of Bhavatí (Madam). A driver should address the chariot-rider—'A'yushman' or 'Sir—long live you.' One not old should call an old man—'Father' (Táta). A son is to be addressed—Vatsa (darling), Puttraka (child), Táta, or by his proper or family name; and so also a disciple and a younger brother. A minister is to be accosted—'Arya' by low men; and 'Minister' (Amátya) or 'Sachiva,' by the Bráhmans. A devotee and one with subdued passions are addressed by the wise—'Sádho' (Holy Sir). A revered person is accosted by his disciple and others by the epithet Sugṛihítábhidha' (Sir of auspicious name). A spiritual tutor is to be addressed—Upádhyáya (master); a monarch—Mahárája (great king); a prince co-regent (yuvarája)—swámin (lord); a prince—Bhartridáraka. A prince is addressed by low men—'Saumya' (gentle sir) or 'Bhadramukha' (You of benign face). The daughter of a king is to be called by his subjects—Bhartṛidáriká. Women are to be addressed in the same manner as their husbands by men of the high, middling and low classes. *Among the women themselves*, an equal is to be accosted—'Halá,' a maid-servant—'Hanye,' and a courtesan—'Ajjuká.' A procuress is to be addressed by her adherents—Amba (mother). Thus also *is* a venerable old woman *to be addressed* by *all* persons. The Páshaṇḍas (infidels) are to be called by their own sectarian names. The S'akas are to be accosted by such names as Bhadṛadatta, &c. Generally a person is to be addressed after his occupation, art, learning, or caste. So according to propriety is it to be understood of others.

COMMENTARY.

a. Now of the division of dialects:

TEXT.

Distribution of dialects.

No. 432. Men not low, and educated, must speak the Sanskrit, and women similarly circumstanced are to speak the S'auraseni *dialect.* These, however, should employ the Maháráshṭrí in songs *or verses.* The Mágadhí is mentioned as the tongue of those who move in the inner apartments of a king. The dialect of servants, princes, and merchants is the half Mágadhí. The Práchyá (Eastern *i. e.* the Gauḍíyá) is the dialect of the Vidúshaka and others; the Avantiká, of gamesters; and the Southern dialect (*i. e.* the Vaidarbhí), of soldiers and citizens while gambling. The Sákárí should be used by left-hand brothers-in-law, the S'akas and others. The Váhlíkí dialect belongs to the people of Northern India; the Dráviḍí to the people of Draviḍa; the Abhírí, to the cowherds; the Cháṇḍálí, to the Chandálas and others. The Ábhírí and the S'ávarí are spoken by those who work upon wood and leaves, as also by charcoal-makers. The Pais'áchí is the tongue of the Pis'áchas and also of female attendants; these latter, if not mean, speak the S'auraseni. This dialect belongs to boys, eunuchs, mean astrologers, and mad and diseased men; and sometimes the Sanskrit. Mendicants and ascetics &c. must employ a Prákrit dialect. The Sanskrit is to be used by noble women, hermitesses, &c., as also, according to some, by a queen, a minister's daughter, and a courtesan. The language of a low person must be that of his country, and men of the highest and middle classes too change their tongue—*the Sanskrit,* when necessary. A woman *in general,* a female friend, a boy, a courtesan, a gambler, and a nymph are to be made occasionally to speak Sanskrit in order to set off their wit.

COMMENTARY.

a. Illustrations of these are to be observed in the Storehouses—the dramas. Descriptions of the different dialects are to be found in the Bháshárṇava or Ocean of Dialects of my adored father.

TEXT.

Further elements of the drama.

No. 433. The thirty-six Lakshaṇas, the thirty-three Dramatic Embellishments, the thirteen Members of the Víthí (see § 521) and the ten divisions of Lásya must be employed in it, with a view to the development of Flavour, where occasion requires.

COMMENTARY.

a. 'Must be employed where occasion requires'—this is the connection.—'In it' *i. e.* in the Náṭaka.

b. Of these, the Lakshaṇas *are the following:*

TEXT.

The 36 Lakshaṇas. No. 434. Bhushaṇa, Akshara-sangháta, S'obhá, Udáharana, Hetu, Sans'aya, Drishṭánta, Tulya-tarka, Padochchaya, Nidars'ana, Abhipráya, Prápti, Vichára, Dishṭa, Upadishṭa, Guṇátipáta, Atis'aya, Vis'eshana, Nirukti, Siddhi, Bhrans'a, Viparyaya, Dákshinya, Anunaya, Málá, Arthápatti, Garhaṇa, Prichchhá, Prasiddhi, Sárúpya, Sankshepa, Guṇakírtana, Les'a, Manoratha, Anuktasiddhi, and Priyavachah.

COMMENTARY.

a. Among these—

TEXT.

Bhúshaṇa. No. 435. The Bhúshaṇa (Ornament) is a combination of Excellences (Chapter VIII.) and Embellishments (see Chapter X.)

COMMENTARY.

a. For example :—

"The Lotuses, O fair one, reflect on the beauty of thy face: what indeed is beyond their power?—furnished as they are with a treasury (kosha*) and a rod (daṇḍa)."

TEXT.

Akshara-sangháta. No. 436. The Akshara-sangháta or Sum of Syllables is a discourse in a few words of charming import.

COMMENTARY.

a. As in S'akuntalá, Act III. :—

"*King.* I hope your dear friend is not too much afflicted by the fever† of her body.

"*Priyamvadá.* It will be soothed, now that it has had its remedy."

TEXT.

S'obhá. No. 437. A speech bearing a striking import in the form of a double-entendre, in which an acknowledged matter is implied along with things *intended to be* established—is called S'obhá or Elegance.

* *Kosha* and *Daṇḍa* respectively mean a bud and a stalk as well as a treasury and a punishing rod. The word *rod* answers well to the Sanskrit *Daṇḍa*.

† The original has *S'arírá-santápah*, or, as is supposed by the commentator of the present work, *as'aríra-santápah* (flame of the Incorporeal one or Káma) which latter might be meant by the king, thus implicitly and explicitly—as the clause is equally resolvable into both these readings.

COMMENTARY.

a. For instance:—

Though born in a good family (or, as the words signify also the properties of a bow—formed of a good bamboo), himself pure *in other respects*, giving ten millions (or, yielding its ends), and possessed of accomplishments (or, bearing a string), a severe master, like the twanging instrument of war, is assuredly to be shunned by the good.

TEXT.

Udáharaṇa. No. 438. When analogous facts are adduced in establishing an intended matter—it is held Udáharaṇa or Example.

COMMENTARY.

a. For example:

"Well hast thou acted in following to the woods thy lord who transcends the world: what is the Beauty of day without the sun, and what is Night without the moon?"

TEXT.

Hetu. No. 439. The Hetu is a brief speech conveying the intended meaning by showing a reason.

COMMENTARY.

a. As in the Veṇí, Act I. *where* the female attendant *repeats* to Bhíma the words she *had spoken to Bhánumatí the wife of Duryodhana:* "I spoke to her thus—How are the locks of our queen to be bound whilst yours, Bhánumatí, are not yet dishevelled?"*

TEXT.

Sans'aya. No. 440. The uncertainty *implied* in the speech of a person not knowing the truth is Sans'aya.

COMMENTARY.

a. For example in the Yayáti Vijaya:—

"Is this the Beauty of the Lord of the heavens, or the daughter of a Yaksha, or is she the goddess of this spot, or Umá herself?"

TEXT.

Drishṭánta. No. 441. Drishṭánta is the showing of a reason for the establishment of a matter or circumstance in respect of the subject *of the discourse.*

* The reason, observes the commentator, of Draupadí's tresses not being bound up is the circumstance of Bhánumatí's not being let down. Under this reason is briefly intimated that Duryodhana must die before the outraged wife of the Páṇdavas should bind her hair—and this is the 'intended meaning.'

COMMENTARY.

a. For example in the Veṇí, Act I.:—"*Bhíma.** Sire, this is quite befitting her, for she is Duryodhana's wife"—and so forth.

TEXT.

Tulyatarka. No. 442. The Tulyatarka is a surmise *made* from a matter coincident with nature's course.†

COMMENTARY.

a. For instance in the same, Act II.:—

"*Bhíma.* Frequently indeed are dreamt dreams both auspicious and inauspicious; but this number of a hundred seems to touch me together with my (99) brothers."

TEXT.

Padochchaya. No. 443. A combination of words echoing to the sense is the Padochchaya.

COMMENTARY.

a. As in S'akuntalá, Act I.:—

"Red like the tender leaf is her under-lip, her hands imitate the soft sprout, and charming like a *full-blown* flower is the *flush of* youth glowing in her members."

Here the words are equally soft with the things implied.

TEXT.

Nidars'ana. No. 444. When well known facts are adduced for the purpose of refuting the opinion of others, it is termed the Nidars'ana.

COMMENTARY.

a. For example:

"Away, princes, away with the duties enjoined to a Kshattriya, in the destruction of a foe: Ráma sent forth his arrow against Balin while turned away in fighting against another person."

* It should be *Sahadeva*, yet the manuscript I have consulted as well as Dr. Roer's edition reads *Bhíma*.

† Thus explains the commentator adopting the reading *prakriti-gáminá* instead of *prakrita-gáminá* as read in Dr. Roer's edition. I should prefer the latter as conforming more to the example (—for our scholiast is not always to be trusted even in his reading and less in his explanation—), and refer the text thus: Tulyatarka (Analogy,) is a surmise made from a circumstance touching the matter in question.

TEXT.

Abhipráya. No. 445. The Abhipráya is the supposition of an impossible* matter under a similitude.

COMMENTARY.

a. For example in S'akuntalá, Act I. :—

"He the saint who wishes to make this unartificially charming body endure the rigors of asceticism verily desires to cut the S'amí tree with the edge of the blue lotus leaf."

TEXT.

Prápti. No. 446. The Prápti is when something is guessed from a certain peculiarity *in the object with respect to which the conjecture is made.*

COMMENTARY.

a. For example in my Prabhávatí :—

"My beloved Prabhávatí must be known by this bee that wanders every where."†

TEXT.

Vichára. No. 447. The Vichára (Argument) is the establishment of an imperceptible matter by reasonable words.

COMMENTARY.

a. For instance in my Chundrakalá :—

"*King.* She certainly conceals in her heart the perturbations of a powerful love, since she smiles without *real* joy, sees not aught though *apparently* staring, and gives an incongruous answer when spoken to by her fair friend."

TEXT.

Dishṭa. No. 448. The description of one under the similitude of time or place is called Dishṭa.

COMMENTARY.

a. For example in the Veṇí, Act I. :—

"*Sahadeva.* Asuredly shall this Draupadí, like the Season of rains,

* Dr. Roer's edition reads अद्भुतार्थस्य (of a marvellous matter) instead a अभूतार्थस्य which is adopted by the MSS. of the text and scholium that I have consulted.

† Wandering everywhere is the peculiarity in the bee, from which is guessed its knowledge of Prabhávatí.

enhance the fire, like lightning, kindled to-day in the angry prince (Bhíma)."

TEXT.

Upadishṭa. No. 449. The Upadishṭa (Advice) is a winning discourse in conformity with the Scriptures.

COMMENTARY.

a. As in S'akuntalá, Act IV. :—

"Serve your superiors, behave like a loving companion towards your fellow-wives, be not sullen even though reproached through anger by your lord"—and so forth.

TEXT.

Guṇátipáta. No. 450. Guṇátipáta is an action opposed to the excellences that one possesses.

COMMENTARY.

a. For example in my Chandrakalá :—

"*Chandrakalá.* (To the moon.) Though thou destroyest darkness, dwellest on the head of Pas'upati,* and thy feet (rays) are touched by all, yet dost thou take the life of women."

TEXT.

Guṇátis'aya. No. 451. The Guṇátis'aya is held to be the superiority *of the compared to what is compared to*, consisting in the *former's* possession of merits in excess over those that are common *to both*.

COMMENTARY.

a. As in the same drama :—

"*King.* (Pointing to Chandrakalá's face.) Where didst thou get, O fair-faced one, that moon, devoid of spot, and ever full, though never associated with Night,† with a couple of full blown fresh blue lotuses quivering within, with a conch shell shining below, and with a collection of bees glowing above?"

TEXT.

Vis'eshokti. No. 452. The Vis'eshokti is the distinguishing *of one of two things compared*, after the declaration of many renowned qualities belonging to the other.

* Lord of the creatures, a name of S'iva.

† In the original विनादोषासङ्गम् which means also—'without connection with a fault.'

COMMENTARY.

a. For example :—

" A pond is pure, a remover of thirst, a dwelling of birds, the native seat of lotuses,* and loved of men, yet it is dull—a place of water (जड़ाशय),† and thou art wise."

TEXT.

Nirukti. No. 453. A declaration of a thing previously effected is termed the Nirukti.

COMMENTARY.

a. For example in the Veṉí, the stanza beginning—" He who has destroyed, one and all, the descendants of Kuru," &c. (—see §380; *a.*)

TEXT.

Siddhi. No. 454. The Siddhi is the declaration of *qualities, severally belonging to* many, *to be in one combined,* for the conveyance of an intended meaning.

COMMENTARY.

a. For example :—

" The strength that belongs to the king of tortoises, and the power that is possessed by Vásuki, reside united in thee, O monarch, in the preservation of the Earth."‡

TEXT.

Bhrans'a. No. 455. The speech of a proud man or the like, being the reverse of what was intended *by him* to be spoken, is the Bhrans'a (slip).

COMMENTARY.

a. For example in the Veṉí :

" *Duryodhana.* (To the eunuch.) Ere long will Páṉdu's son, through his prowess, destroy Duryodhana in battle, with his protégés, with his kindred, with his friends, with his sons, with his brothers."

TEXT.

Viparyaya. No. 456. The Viparyaya is the alteration of a determination under a doubt.

* The three epithets, in the original, corresponding to these mean respectively also—' sinless,' ' satisfier of a thirst of gain,' and ' giver of prosperity.'

† This word means ' of idiotic apprehension,' and, by the allowable exchange of ड for ल, it means ' a place of water' also.

‡ The extolling of the king's protective energy is the ' intended meaning.'

COMMENTARY.

a. For example:

"Those who, deeming the world miserly, resolved to be contented, act not consistently, O King, with respect to your majesty."

TEXT.

Dákshiṇya. No. 457. Dákshiṇya (Complaisance) is compliance with the wishes of others by words or deeds.

COMMENTARY.

a. Complaisance in words—as—

"Protect the city Lanká, thou, Vibhíshaṇa, art the King: to one befriended by the adorable *Ráma* there is no obstacle to prosperity."

b. So Complaisance in deed.

TEXT.

Anunaya. No. 458. Anunaya (Conciliation) is the accomplishment of a purpose by means of kind words.

COMMENTARY.

a. As in the Veṇí, Act III., the speech of Kṛipa to As'wattháman—
"Equal to Droṇa in valour, and versed in the science of heavenly arms, what art thou not capable of?"

TEXT.

Málá. No. 459. Málá (garland or string of things) is an offer of many things *or services* for the attainment of a desire.

COMMENTARY.

a. As in S'akuntalá, Act III.:

"*King.* Shall I move the cooled air with fans of the cool and refreshing lotus-leaves, or shall I, my taper-limbed charmer,* place thy lotus-red feet upon my lap, and knead them to thy comfort?"

TEXT.

Arthápatti. No. 460. Arthápatti is when by the assertion of some thing, some thing else is suggested.

COMMENTARY.

a. As in the Veṇí, Act III., the following speech of the King (Duryodhana) to Karṇa as he was declaring that Droṇa wished to place *his son* As'wattháman on the throne:—

* Lit. One with thighs resembling the part of the metacarpus between the wrist and the little finger.

" *King.* Well *spoken*, monarch of Anga, well *spoken.* How can it be otherwise—if what you say is not *the true reason*, how comes it to be, that the great warrior, having at first bidden him not to fear, should take no heed of Sindhu's King, while he was being killed by Arjuna ?"

TEXT.

Garhaṉa. No. 461. Garhaṉa is a reproach consisting in the proclamation of a fault.

COMMENTARY.

a. As in the same, Act III. :—

" *As'watthâman.* (To Karṉa) Are my weapons powerless, as thine are under the influence of thy master's curse &c. ?"

TEXT.

Prichchhá. No. 462. Prichchhá (Inquiry) is held to be an inquiry after a matter in respectful terms.

COMMENTARY.

a. For example in the same, Act IV. : " *Sundaraka.* Have you, worthy sirs, seen the emperor Duryodhana with his charioteer or not ?"

TEXT.

Prasiddhi. No. 463. Prasiddhi is the announcement of one, under relation to excellent and noted things or persons.

COMMENTARY.

a. As in Vikramorvas'í :

" *King.* He whose grandfathers on the maternal and paternal sides are the sun and the moon ; who was chosen husband of their own accord, by both Urvas'í and Earth."

TEXT.

Sárúpya. No. 464. Sárúpya is a passionate treatment of one mistaken for another through resemblance.*

COMMENTARY.

a. As in Act VI. of the Veṉí, Yudhishṭhira, mistaking Bhíma for Duryodhana, addresses him—" Thou accursed wretch, Duryodhana! &c."

* Dr. Roer's edition of the original has a difference of reading in this text—namely *abhibhútasya* for *anubhútasya* which the scholiast adopts and which I have followed.

TEXT.

Sankshepa. No. 465. It is Sankshepa when one offers himself, in short words, in the service of another.

COMMENTARY.

a. For example in my Chandrakalá :—

" *King.* My beloved, why wouldst thou thus vainly pain thy limbs, tender like the S'irísha flower ?—here *(referring to himself)* is thy servant ready to get thee thy wished-for flowers."

TEXT.

Guṉakírtana. No. 466. Guṉakírtana (Applause) is but the declaration of excellences.

COMMENTARY.

a. As in the same, *the passage* beginning—" O thy eyes mock the wagtail."

TEXT.

Les'a. No. 467. A speech resting upon a similitude is termed the Les'a.

COMMENTARY.

a. As in the Veṉí :—

" *King.* That same glory will be ours which the sons of Pándu acquired having killed the decrepit Bhíshma by placing S'ikhandin* before him."

TEXT.

Abhipráya. No. 468. Abhipráya is the expression of a desire in an indirect manner.

COMMENTARY.

a. As—

" Behold, thou of beautiful brow, behold, the swan, engaged somewhat in caressing sports and languishing with love, fondly kisses his beloved."

TEXT.

Anukta-siddhi. No. 469. An extent of surmise *in speaking of persons or things* in a particular (*i. e.* laudatory) manner is termed the Anukta-siddhi.

* The daughter of Drupada metamorphosed into a male, and hence not a person for Bhíshma to fight with—him whose dread heroic vow would not permit him to cast weapon upon one who had even once been a woman.

COMMENTARY.

a. For example :—

" These two, wise lady, that you behold before the beautiful moon are, *we believe*, Tishya and Punarvasu* of blessed names."

This is addressed to Sítá by her female friends, viewing Ráma and Lakshmaṇa seated before Vis'wámittra the saint, and poetically surmising them to be the said luminaries.†

TEXT.

Priya-vachah. No. 470. Priya-vachah (Agreeable discourse) is a gratifying speech in credencing a venerable person.

COMMENTARY.

a. As in S'akuntalá, Act VII. :—

" The flower first comes to sight, then the fruit ; the clouds rise first, afterwards *descend* the rains : such is the order of the cause and the effect *in nature*, but, *superior over physical causes*, your propitiousness is preceded by blissful fruits."

b. Now of the Dramatic Embellishments (§433) :

TEXT.

The Dramatic Embellishments. No. 471. A's'íh, A'kranda, Kapaṭa, Akshamá, Garva, Udyama, A's'raya, Utprásana, Spṛihá, Akshobha, Pas'cháttápa, Upapatti, A's'ansá, Adhyavasáya, Visarpa, Ullekha, Uttejana, Parivádа, Níti, Artha-vis'eshaṇa, Protsáhana, Sáháyya, Abhimána, Anuvartana, Utkírtana, Yáchná, Paríhára, Nivedana, Pravartana, A'khyána, Yukti, Praharsha, and Upades'a : these are the Dramatic Embellishments, being means of ornamenting the drama.

A's'íh. A's'íh (Blessing) is a friend's benediction.

COMMENTARY.

a. For example in S'akuntalá, Act IV.

" Be thou greatly regarded by thy husband, as was S'armishṭhá by Yayáti, and mayest thou get an imperial son, as she did Púru."

TEXT.

A'kranda. No. 472. A'kranda (Crying) is a lamentation through grief.

* The seventh of the lunar asterisms, Tishya being the eighth.

† So much from the commentator.

COMMENTARY.

a. As in the Veṇí:—

" *Eunuch.* Oh madam, Oh Kunti, glory of the royal house! &c."

TEXT.

Kapaṭa. No. 473. Kapaṭa (Treachery) is when another form is assumed by means of magic.

COMMENTARY.

a. As in Kulapatyanka (the Act of Kulapati):

" Having quitted the form of a deer and assumed a treacherous appearance, that demon, combating Lakshmaṇa, is driving him to a dangerous position."

TEXT.

Akshamá. No. 474. Akshamá (Non-forgiveness) is when even a slight offence is not endured.

COMMENTARY.

a. As in S'akuntalá, Act V.:—

" *King.* O truthful man, we grant this, but what shall we gain by imposing upon her?

" *S'árngarava.* Destruction!"—and so on.

TEXT.

Garva. No. 475. Garva is a speech proceeding from pride.

COMMENTARY.

a. As in the same, Act VI.: " *King.* What, are my houses too infested by spirits?"

TEXT.

Udyama. No. 476. Udyama (Undertaking) is the commencement *or design* of an action.

COMMENTARY.

a. For example in the Kumbha: " *Rávaṇa.* Overpowered as I am by grief, I will meet death."

Here is hinted Rávaṇa's design of fighting.

TEXT.

Ás'raya. No. 477. The having recourse *to any one* for some excellent purpose is termed Ás'raya (Resort).

COMMENTARY.

a. As in the act named "The Reproach of Vibhíshaṇa:" "*Vibhíshaṇa.* To Ráma will I resort."

TEXT.

Utprásana. No. 478. Utprásana (Derision) is a ridicule by a man not good, yet imagining himself to be good.

COMMENTARY.

a. For example in S'akuntalá:—"*Sárngarava.* Supposing, Sir King, your majesty has forgotten the past incidents in the company of others, how should you abandon your wife, afraid as you are of unrighteousness?"

TEXT.

Ákánkshá. No. 479. Ákánkshá (Desire) is a longing for a thing, out of its charmingness.

COMMENTARY.

a. For example in the same:

"*King.* O, the under-lip of my beloved, tender and unbitten, seems, as it quivers so sweetly, to give my thirsty self permission *to suck its nectar.*"

TEXT.

Kshobha. No. 480. Agitation occasioning the use of reproachful terms is styled the same, viz., Kshobha (Agitation).

COMMENTARY.

a. For example:

"Thou ruffian of a devotee, that killest concealed, hast not only destroyed Bálin, but *cut off* thy own soul from the world to come."

TEXT.

Anutápa. No. 481. A repentance for an object slighted through folly is termed so, *i. e.* Anutápa (Repentance).

COMMENTARY.

a. As in the Anutápánka, *or the Act named Repentance, of a certain drama:* "*Ráma.* Did not my angel kiss me then many a time though having blamed me but in jest (?) &c."

TEXT.

Upapatti. No. 482. Upapatti (Argument) is the giving of a reason for the establishment of a matter.

COMMENTARY.

a. As in the Badhya-s'ilá (The Block of the Condemned) :—

" Preserve thyself at the expense of my life, if thou wishest her to be living, who dies if thou diest, and who lives if thou livest."

TEXT.

Ks'ansá. No. 483. A wishing *for one's self* is Ks'ansá (Desire).

COMMENTARY.

a. As *in Málatí and Mádhava,* the desire of Mádhava in the cemetery *shown in these words of his :* " May I then once more see her face, the blissful home of Love !"

TEXT.

Adhyavasáya. No. 484. Adhyavasáya (Resolution) is a vow, *or an expression of determination.*

COMMENTARY.

a. For example in my Prabhávatí : —

" *Vajranábha.* Bruising in a moment his breast with this club, sportively do I destroy both your worlds."

TEXT.

Visarpa. No. 485. Visarpa is an action done, leading to an evil result.

COMMENTARY.

a. As *is indicated* in the Vení *in the couplet beginning*—" Direful has been the effect on the world of that single seizure of hair," (§373. *a.*)

TEXT.

Ullekha. No. 486. A mentioning of a purpose is termed Ullekha (Mention).

COMMENTARY.

a. As in S'akuntalá : " *Ascetics. (To the king).* We proceed to bring fuel. There you see the hermitage of our spiritual tutor, the sage Kanwa, on the bank of the Máliní, *graced* by *the fair* S'akuntalá as by its presiding deity. If no duty be *thus* neglected, do you go in, and accept the services due to a guest."

TEXT.

Uttejana. No. 487. Harsh words uttered to excite *or exasperate* another for the completion of one's own object are called Uttejana (Provocation).

COMMENTARY.

a. For example:

" Of awful valour art thou, Indrajit, powerful only by name: fie! fie! distracted with dread of me, thou fightest concealed."

TEXT.

Parívâda. No. 488. Parívâda (Censure) is a reproof.

COMMENTARY.

a. As in 'Sundara's Act' *or the fourth of the Veṇísanhára:* " *Duryodhana.* Fie, fie, charioteer, what hast thou done! O the evil man will do evil to my boy, wanton by nature, &c."

TEXT.

Níti. No. 489. Níti is acting according to the Scripture.

COMMENTARY.

a. As in S'akuntalá Act I.: " *Dushyanta.* One must enter the sacred wood of holy saints in a humble guise."

TEXT.

Artha-vis'eshaṇa. No. 490. A reprehensive repetition of some thing uttered *by another* is *termed* Artha-vis'eshaṇa (Particularization of a thing).

COMMENTARY.

a. As in S'akuntalá, Act V.: " S'árngarava. *(To the King.)* Ah! what mean you by saying?—' what is this that has been spoken!' Are not you, Sir, well conversant with the manners of the world? A married lady living in her father's house is regarded with suspicion by the people, chaste though she be; a wife, therefore, whether beloved or not, is wished by her relations to be with her husband."

TEXT.

Protsáhana. No. 491. Protsáhana (Exciting) is the urging of any one by stimulative words.

COMMENTARY.

a. As in the Bála Rámáyaṇa:

"She is dreadful like the Night of the universal dissolution—why hesitatest thou, because she is a woman? Do thou, child, strike this female demon Táḍaká, and preserve the triple world."

TEXT.

Sáháyya. No. 492. Sáháyya (Assistance) is the helping of another in danger.

COMMENTARY.

a. As in the Veṇí: "As'watthámau. *(To Kṛipa.)* Be you also attending at the side of the King.

Kṛipa. "I am determined to-day to revenge, &c."

TEXT.

Abhimána. No. 493. Abhimána (Pride) is just what the name implies—*a speech of pride.*

COMMENTARY.

a. As in the same, Act V.: "*Duryodhana.* Unbecoming and poor are thy words, mother"—and so on.

This is the answer given by the unconquerable pride of Duryodhana to the conciliatory words of her mother.

TEXT.

Anuvṛitti. No. 494. Anuvṛitti (Complaisance) is courteous humility.

COMMENTARY.

a. For example in S'akuntalá, Act I.: "*King.* *(To S'akuntalá.)* Are your devotions prospering, lady?

Anasúyá. Yes, by the reception of a particular guest now &c."

TEXT.

Utkírtana. No. 495. By Utkírtana (Rehearsal) is meant the relation of past incidents.

COMMENTARY.

a. As in the Bála Rámáyaṇa:

"Here were we bound in the serpent noose, and here was brought the Droṇa hill by Hanumat, when your brother-in-law (Lakshmaṇa) had been struck by Rávaṇa's dart deep in the heart," &c.

TEXT.

Yáchná. No. 496. A request made personally, as is sometimes the case, or through a messenger, is termed Yáchṇá (Asking).

COMMENTARY.

a. For example:

"Do thou give back Sítá even now: Ráma is gracious towards thee: why wouldst thou make the *fierce* monkeys play the game of balls with thy heads?"

TEXT.

Parihára. No. 497. Begging pardon for a fault committed is termed Parihára (Apology).

COMMENTARY.

a. For example: "Overwhelmed with the pangs of expiration I have uttered improper words; pardon me therefore, lord—and I entrust Sugríva to thee."

TEXT.

Nivedana. No. 498. Nivedana (Announcement) is the intimation of a duty neglected.

COMMENTARY.

a. For example in the Rághavábhyudaya: "*Lakshmaṇa.* What are you about, Sire; are you going to sue the ocean?"

TEXT.

Pravartana. No. 499. Pravartana (Commencement) is the happy commencement of an action.

COMMENTARY.

a. As in the Veṇí, Act VI.: *King.* Eunuch, out of our reverence for the divine son of Devakí, let suitable preparations be commenced for the joyous festivity *to be held* on dear Bhíma's victory."

TEXT.

Ákhyána. No. 500. Ákhyána (Narration) is the declaration of a previous event.

COMMENTARY.

a. As in the same: "This is that place in which ponds were filled with the liquid of the enemies' blood &c."

TEXT.

Yukti. No. 501. Yukti (Reason) is the settlement of a question *by reason.*

COMMENTARY.

a. As in the same, Act III.: "War being shunned, were there no dread of death, fit would it be to fly the field; but if a creature must necessarily die, why would you *thus* vainly taint your glory?"

TEXT.

Praharsha. No. 502. Praharsha (Ecstasy) is an excess of joy.

COMMENTARY.

a. As in S'akuntalá: "*King.* Why then should I not congratulate myself, now that my desires are all fulfilled?"

TEXT.

S'ikshá. No. 503. S'ikshá (Instruction) is advising.

COMMENTARY.

a. As in the same: "It is not proper, friend, for a person dwelling in a hermitage freely to go away, leaving a particular guest unentertained."

b. These Lakshaṉas and Dramatic Ornaments, though generically the same, are spoken of distinctively in pursuance of established custom. And though, among these, some are included severally under the heads of Excellence (Guṉa—see Chap. VIII.), Ornament (Chap. X.), Incomplete Flavour (§ 245) and the members of the Junctures (§ 338 &c.), they have been particularly mentioned here, as they are carefully to be employed in a Náṭaka. That these must be used in the Náṭaka, is established by the following dictum of the sage:

"The poet must compose the Náṭaka thus: It must contain the five Junctures (§ 332), the four kinds of Action (vṛitti), the sixty-four members, and the thirty-six Lakshaṉas. The style must be elevated and embellished with the Ornaments, the use of soft or feeble-sounding words being avoided. It should represent great characters* and good

* Here instead of *mahápurusha-sanchárам*, the reading I have followed, the commentator reads *mahápurusha-satkáram* and explains it—*mahápurushánám satkáro guṉavarṉanam yatra* (—where the excellencies of great men are described). The passage, however, in this and several other places, is extremely obscure, and I have, sometimes, been *forced* to follow the commentator's interpretation.

deeds. It must be full of exquisite relish and noble sentiments. Having its Junctures well connected, it should be suitable for representation, as also interesting and delightful."

c. . The members of the Víthí shall be mentioned *hereafter* (see (§ 521). He states the Members of the Lásya.

TEXT.

The Members of the Lásya. No. 504. Geyapada, Sthitapáṭhya, Ásína, Pushpagaṇḍiká, Prachchhedaka, Trigúḍha, Saindhava, Dwigúḍha, Uttamottamaka, Uktapratyukta: These are the ten members or varieties of the Lásya declared by the learned.

COMMENTARY.

a. Among these—

TEXT.

Geya-pada. No. 505. The Geya-pada (Ballad) is simply a song* sung to the Víṇá by one seated on a seat.

COMMENTARY.

a. For example, listen to Malayavatí singing to the Víṇá in the temple of *the goddess* Gaurí:

" Goddess of radiance yellow like that of the farina powdering the filament of an expanded lotus, O blessed Gaurí, may my desire be fulfilled by thy grace!"

TEXT.

Sthita-páṭhya. No. 506. When a woman, burning with love, stands reciting Prákrit it is designated Sthita-páṭhya (Recitation of one standing).

COMMENTARY.

a. The venerable Abhinava Gupta, however, says—'What *is declared in the text with respect to a woman* is elliptical, the utterance of Prákrit by one infuriate with rage being also Sthita-páṭhya.'

TEXT.

Ásína. No. 507. When a woman under grief and anxiety sits without any ornament on her body, and without any musical instrument, it is termed Ásína (the Seated).

Pushpagaṇḍiká. When songs are sung accompanied with music, and verses of diverse metres *recited,* and when the men and women act contrarily to their nature, this is called Pushpagaṇḍiká.

* *i. e.* not accompanied with dancing.

Prachchhedaka. When a woman considering her lord to be in love with another, and grieved by his infidelity, sings in concert with the Víṇá, it is designated Prachchhedaka (Breach of Affection).

Trigúḍha. The agreeable acting of men in the dress of women is Trigúḍhaka (the Thrice-covert).

COMMENTARY.

a. An example of the last sort occurs in 'Málatí and Mádhava': "*Makaranda.* I here have become Málatí!"

TEXT.

Saindhava. No. 508. When one disappointed in an assignation chants Prákṛit in concert with a clear *musical* performance, it is called Saindhava.

COMMENTARY.

a. 'Performance' (Karaṇa)—*i. e.* a play on the Víṇá or the like.

TEXT.

Dwigúḍhaka. No. 509. A song of harmonious numbers, full of flavour and sentiments, in the shape of an interlocution* is termed Dwigúḍha.

Uttamottamaka. The Uttamottamaka (The Most Excellent) again is a poetical song, sung in anger or grace, charming from a variety of meṭres, containing reflections, and accompanied with *the graces termed, respectively,* 'háva' (see § 127) and helá (§ 128).

Uktapratyukta. A conversation in song, associated with 'vivacity' (see § 91), and containing feigned reproofs is spoken of as the Uktapratyukta (Speech and Reply).

COMMENTARY.

a. Examples *of these* are evident *in the dramas.*

TEXT.

What entitles the Náṭaka to the name of the Great Náṭaka. No. 510. This, when containing all the Patáká Sthánakas or Telling Points (see § 299) and consisting of ten acts, is called by the wise the Great Náṭaka (Mahánáṭaka).

* In the original, *mukhapratimukhánwitam* which the scholiast so interprets, —*mukha* and *pratimukha* meaning, according to him, speech and reply respectively. The Junctures so called have apparently no connection here.

COMMENTARY.

a. This *i. e.* the Náṭaka.—For example, the Bála Rámáyaṇa.

b. Now of the Prakaraṇa:

TEXT.

The Prakaraṇa described. No. 511. The story of the Prakaraṇa must be mundane *or human*, being invented by the poet. Love should be the principal sentiment in it; and the hero must be a Bráhman, or a minister, or a merchant, *of the description called* 'firm and mild' (see § 69), and intent upon meritorious deeds, objects of desire, and wealth, such as are subject to destruction *or bring but transitory pleasure here or hereafter, being sought with selfish motives.**

COMMENTARY.

a. A Prakaraṇa with a Bráhman hero is such, for example, as the Mrichchhakatiká or The Toy Cart; one with a minister for its hero is Málatí and Mádhava; and one with a merchant hero, the drama Pushpabhúshita.

TEXT.

No. 512. The heroine in the Prakaraṇa is sometimes a woman of family, or a courtesan, or both. So there are three divisions of it, the third of which is crowded with such characters as a cheat, a gambler, &c., the 'humble friend' (see § 77) and the 'dependent.'

COMMENTARY.

a. An honourable woman is the heroine, for instance, in the Pushpabhúshita; a courtesan in the Rangadatta; both an honourable woman and a courtesan are heroines in the Mrichchhakatiká.

b. Since it has the Náṭaka for its type, it resembles it in all other respects.

c. Now of the Bháṇa:

TEXT.

The Bháṇa described. No. 513. The Bháṇa is *a piece* in one act, consisting of a variety of incidents *not progressively developed*, being other *than those included under the five stages of the*

* The portion in italics is according to the interpretation of the commentator. He says—Merit is transitory *(sápáya)* when sought as a door to *swarga* or the short-lived bliss of Indra's heaven; Objects of desire are perishable when children or cattle are wished for; and Wealth is so, when desired for enjoyment.

*Deed** (see § 324). In this an expert and learned 'viṭa' (§ 77) must singly represent on the stage what has been experienced by himself or others. He should accost, speak, and reply, as if he were addressing one actually present (*lit.* by the ákás'a bháshita—see § 425); and suggest the Heroic and the Erotic by descriptions of heroism and beauty. The fable must be invented *by the poet*, and the Action (vṛitti—see § 410) should generally be the Bháratí (§ 285). This species has only the Junctures Mukha and Nirvahaṇa, and all the ten members of the Lásya.

COMMENTARY.

a. In the Bháṇa one should make replies and rejoinders, quoting the *suppositious* speeches of another—*technically* called Aerial Discourse.

b. The Erotic and Heroic Flavours are to be suggested by descriptions of beauty† and heroism.

c. Commonly the Action Bháratí, but sometimes the Kais'ikí too is employed.

d. The Members of the Lásya—*i. e.* the Geyapada, &c. (see § 504).

e. The Lílámadhukara is an example *of this class of plays.*

f. Now of the Vyáyoga.

TEXT.

The Vyáyoga described. No. 514. The Vyáyoga must have a well known story for its plot, its *dramatis personæ* consisting mostly of males and but few females. It should be in one Act, and devoid of the Garbha and the Vimarsha (see § 335 and 336). It should represent a contest the occasion of which is not a woman, and should be without the Action Kais'iki. The hero must be a celebrated personage, being a royal saint or a god, of the class styled 'firm and haughty' (see § 67). The principal Flavours *of this variety* are to be other than the Comic, the Erotic, and the Quietistic.

COMMENTARY.

a. For example, the Saugandhikáharaṇa.

b. Now of the Samavakára:

* Such is the explanation of the Commentator, the original having merely—'consisting of a variety of other conditions or stages.'

† In the original, सौभाग्य, which means also 'happiness in love.'

TEXT.

The Samavakára described.

No. 515. Of the Samavakára the fable should be well known, pertaining to gods and demons. It has all the Junctures (§ 332) except the Vimarsha, and consists of three acts, the first of which contains the first two Junctures, and the latter two comprise the others respectively. It has twelve high-spirited heroes, being well known Divinities and Demons, each of whom obtains a separate fruit. The Heroic is to be the most prominent of the Flavours and the Action Kais'ikí is to be seldom employed. The Vindu and the Praves'aka (§ 309 and 319) are not admitted; but the thirteen members of the Víthí (see § 521) may be employed according to occasion. It is composed in a variety of metres, principally the Gáyatrí and the Ushṇih. It must represent the triple Love, the three-fold Circumvention, and the three Vidravas. The business of the first act must occupy twelve Náḍikás; that of the second, three;* and the fourth, two.

COMMENTARY.

a. A couple of ghaṭikás† is called a Náḍiká.—The Vindu and the Praves'aka (see § 309 and 319), though mentioned in *the description of* the Náṭaka, must not be admitted here.

b. Now—

TEXT.

The three species of Love, Circumvention, and Confusion.

No. 516. Love is three-fold, as being (1) conformable to the Law, (2) for the sake of money, or (3) from mere voluptuousness. Circumvention 'or delusion' again is of three sorts, being (1) natural *or caused by natural agencies;* (2) contrived *or effected by the enemy;* and (3) preternatural. And Confusion (Vidrava—see § 377) *also has three varieties,* according as it is caused (1) by things inanimate,‡ (2) by rational beings,§ or (3) by irrational animals.

COMMENTARY.

a. Of these, Lawful Love is love indulged in not in opposition to scripture. Mercenary Love is love made for the purpose of obtaining

* The Das'arúpa has *four* instead of *three* (*tisṛibhiḥ*) which latter reading, however, is evidently from a very natural mistake of the scribes—changing *chatasṛibhiḥ* into *chatisṛibhiḥ.*

† A '*ghaṭiká*' is equal to two-fifths of an hour.

‡ Lit. Things unsentient.

§ Lit. Sentient beings.

money. Voluptuous Love is comic love, ***such as is*** represented ***in the satirical play called*** Prahasana (—see § 533). Of these, the voluptuous love must be described in the first act; as to the others, they say there is no rule.

b. 'Irrational animals' (lit. sentient and unsentient beings) are the elephant and the like.

c. ***The drama in question*** (§ 515) ***is called*** Samavakára (sam + ava + kṛí, to disperse), as a multitude of things is huddled together in it.—The Samudra Mathana or the Churning of the Ocean is a specimen.

d. Now of the Ḍima:

TEXT.

The Ḍima described. No. 517. The Ḍima must have a celebrated story for its plot, and abound with representations of magic, conjuration, war, rage, bewilderment, and eclipses ***of the sun and moon.*** The Furious Flavour should be the principal in it, the others being subservient to it. It is recognized as comprehending four acts; the Vishkambhaka and Praves'aka (see § 308 and 309) are not to be employed in it. Its heroes should be sixteen in number, being extremely haughty, such as a god, a Gandharva, a Yaksha, a Rákshasa, a Serpent (Mahoraga), a ghost, a sprite (Preta), a goblin (Pis'ácha) &c. The Kais'ikí is excluded from among its actions, and the Vimarsha, from among its Junctures. The Quietistic, the Comic, and the Erotic being avoided, it must glow with the six other Flavours.

COMMENTARY.

a. According to the great sage, the Tripura Dáha, or Conflagration of Tripura is an example.

b. Now of the Íhámṛiga:

TEXT.

The Íhámṛiga. No. 518. The Íhámṛiga is described to comprise four Acts founded on a mixed story (see Com.), and to contain the Junctures Mukha, Pratimukha, and Nirvahaṇa. The hero and the rival hero in it may be indifferently a mortal and a god, both illustrious and 'firm and haughty' (§ 67). The other (see Com). covertly commits improper acts. The 'semblance of love' (see § 248) in him, as he endeavours to obtain a divine lady against her will by violent or artful means, is also to be exhibited slightly. The heroes of the Patáká (see § 320) must be ten haughty characters, being either divinities or mortals. The wrath of the enemy being provoked, war, by some artifice, is prevented from taking place. Magnanimous personages, though described in the original story as killed, are not to be so represented here. Some again declare it to be in one Act and to have a divinity for its hero. Others allege that there should be six heroes in it, a war for a divine female *being the subject.*

COMMENTARY.

a. 'Mixed' *i. e.* partly popular and partly invented.—'The other' *i. e.* the rival hero.—The heroes of the Patáká, *or assistants* of the hero and the rival hero, should be altogether ten.—This species is designated the Íhámṛiga, as the hero in it seeks (íhate) a female as unobtainable as a deer (mṛiga). The Kusumas'ekhara Vijaya and the like are specimens.

b. Now of the Anka *or Utsṛishṭikánka*:

TEXT.

The Utsṛishṭikánka. No. 519. The Utsṛishṭikánka is a piece in a single Act, ordinary men being its heroes. The Pathetic is the permanent Flavour in it, abounding, as it does, in lamentations of women and words of self-disparagement. The plot should be a well known story expanded by the poet's imagination. The Junctures, the Actions, and the Members are to be the same with those of the Bhaṇa (§ 513). War, victory and defeat should be verbally represented.

COMMENTARY.

a. Some allege that it is named Utsṛishṭikánka to distinguish it from the Anka (Act), *the common division* of the Náṭaka and other dramas.* Others, however, *deriving the name from ut (trans) and sṛishṭi (creation or plot), explain it* a play whereof the business transgresses (utkrántá) *or contravenes the common rules.* The S'armishṭhá Yayáti is an example:

b. Now of the Víthí:—

* Prof. Wilson seems to have misunderstood this passage, when he says that the Anka is considered by some 'a supplementary Act &c.'—see Hindu Theatre, I. p. 17.

TEXT.

The Víthí. No. 520. The Víthí should be in one Act, and represent any one character who, by means of surprising replies made to speeches called Voice in the Air (§ 425), must suggest the Erotic Flavour in full, as also other Flavours in some degree. Of the Junctures it has the Mukha and Nirvahaṇa, and contains all the Sources of the End (see § 317).

COMMENTARY.

a. 'Any' *i. e.* of the 'best,' the 'middling,' or the 'lowest' description (see § 75).—The piece being full of the Erotic Flavour, the Action Kais'ikí is extensively used in it.

TEXT.

The thirteen elements of the Víthí. No. 521. The learned mention thirteen elements as belonging to it: these are Udghátyaka, Avalagita, Prapancha, Trigata, Chhala, Vákkeli, Adhivala, Gaṇḍa, Avasyandita, Ñáliká, Asatpralápa, Vyáhára, and Mṛidava.

COMMENTARY.

a. Among these, the Udghátyaka* and the Avalagita have been defined and illustrated under the head of the Prastávaná (see § 289 and 293).

TEXT.

Prapancha. No. 522. The Prapancha (Delusion) is held to be a conversation founded in falsehood and exciting laughter.†

COMMENTARY.

a. For example in the Vikramorvas'í, beginning of Act II., the *laughable* dialogue between the Vidúshaka and the female attendant in the turret *on the top of Purúravas' palace.*

TEXT.

Trigata. No. 523. The Trigata is the application of more than one meaning to a sentence from a sameness of sound.

* The definition of it given by our author is quite distinct from that in the Das'arúpa, III. 12.

† This definition too is entirely different from Dhananjaya's, though only one word is changed.

Commentary.

a. As in the same drama, *where Purúravas inquires for his Love, lost in the woods, of a mountain which is called in Sanskrit 'kshiti-bhṛit' (preserver of the earth).*

"*King.* O thou chief of those that preserve the earth, has a woman, all beauteous, separated from me, been seen by thee in this charming wood? *(Hears the echo.)* How! 'seen' he says."

The inquiry itself is here construed into a reply *(—the same words in the original equally serving for both.)*

b. According to some (Dhananjaya), it is to be used only by the three—the Actor &c.,* *the name being a compound of 'tri' (three) and 'gata' (pertaining to).*

Text.

Chhala. No. 524. Chhala (Treachery) is a deceiving by the allurement of words apparently friendly but inimical *in reality.*

Commentary.

a. For example in the Veṇí:—

"*Bhíma and Arjuna.* Where is that proud king, venerated by Duhs'ásana and others—his hundred younger brothers, the friend of Anga's King (Karṇa), who played those tricks at gambling, who set fire to the lac-made house, who was expert in seizing the hair and garment of Draupadí, whose slaves are the Páṇḍavas,—where is that Duryodhana?—give notice, ye men†—we have come to SEE him."

Text.

Chhala as defined by others. No. 525. But others assert that Chhala is a speech uttered, with some object in view, in such a manner as to deceive, amuse, or provoke a person.

Vákkeli. The Vákkeli is a passage exciting laughter by means of two or three rejoinders.

Commentary.

a. *The expression* 'two or three' tropically implies even a greater number.

* By the &c. is meant perhaps, the Manager or the Actress and the Associate (see § 287).

† Dr. Röer reads कथयतु न वषा instead of कथयत पुवषाः which latter might also be rendered simply—'tell (me) ye men.'

b. The following is an example:

"Dost thou eat flesh, mendicant?—What need of it without wine? —Wine too is agreeable to thee?—Ho! agreeable it is, together with harlots.—But a harlot seeks money, and whence gettest thou that?—By gambling and theft.—Your honour then indulges in gambling and theft also?—What else *can be* the course of a reprobate?"

TEXT.

Other definitions of Vákkeli.

No. 526. Some allege it (Vákkeli) to mean a breaking off in a speech commenced,—before its sense is complete. And others define it a single answer to a variety of queries.

Adhivala.

By Adhivala is meant an interlocution of high words in mutual defiance.

COMMENTARY.

a. For example in my Prabhávatí:

"*Vajranábha.* Having bruised even in a moment his (Pradyumna's) breast with this club, I shall sportively destroy both your worlds to-day.

Pradyumna. Enough of this magniloquence, thou wretched demon. Let this earth be in a moment delightful to the flesh-eating fiends—drenched with the blood of the whole multitude of the Titans under the showers of arrows issuing from the mighty bow grasped by my rigid hand."*

TEXT.

Gaṇḍa.

No. 527. The Gaṇḍa is a hurried *or sudden* speech, casually connected with a matter in hand—though having a different signification (*i. e.* having no real reference to what it chances to be connected with).

COMMENTARY.

a. For example in the Veṇí:

"*King.* My thighs indeed, O thou of taper thighs,† are fit long to be occupied by thy loins.

Enter Eunuch.

Eu. Broken, Sire, broken &c." (see § 302, *d.*)

* Lit. Fixed on the rod of my hand.

† Lit. One with thighs like the lower part of the hand *(Karabha)*.

Here the words importing the breaking of the chariot-flag are construed into the sense of the breaking of Duryodhana's thighs, *which actually happens to take place towards the end of the drama.*

TEXT.

Avasyandita. No. 528. Avasyandita is the interpretation of a speech contrary to the sense in which it was *first* spoken.

COMMENTARY.

a. For example in the Chhalita Ráma:

"*Sítá.* To-morrow, child, thou art to go to Ayodhyá: thou must please the King with thy humility.

Lava. Are we two, henceforth, to be the dependents of a King?

Sítá. He is your father, child.

Lava. Is the lord of the Raghu family our father?

Sítá. Apprehend not otherwise—he is not only the Father of you two, but of the entire Earth."

TEXT.

Náliká. No. 529. The Náliká is but an enigma (prahe-liká) associated with pleasantry or jest.*

COMMENTARY.

a. An answer concealing *the real meaning* is a 'prahelliká.'—The following is an example of it (Náliká) from the Ratnávalí:—

"*Susangatá.* Even here, my friend, stands he for whom thou hast come.

Ságariká. For whom have I come?

Susan. Nay, for the picture."

Here is concealed the meaning—'Thou hast come for the King's sake."

TEXT.

Asat-pralápa. No. 530. An irrelevant (1) speech, or, (2) reply, or (3) salutary words spoken to an unwise person, though not accepting them, are termed Asat-pralápa (empty speech).

COMMENTARY.

a. Of these the first *description* is exemplified in the following lines from my *drama* Prabhávatí:—

* The circumstance of its being attended with joke, says the Commentator, constitutes its distinction from Avasyandita.

"*Pradyumna.* (*Rejoicing at the sight of the mango plant.*) Aha! how! Is it here that she with hair beautiful like the bee-swarm, breathing sweet fragrance, with hands soft like the tender leaf, speaking with the Kokila's sweet voice—is it here that my slender-formed beloved dwells?"

So an irrelevant reply. The third *sort* is such, for example, as in the Veṇí, the speech of Gándhárí to Duryodhana.

TEXT.

Vyáhára. No. 531. Words spoken for the sake of another, exciting laughter and desire, are *termed* Vyáhára.

COMMENTARY.

a. For example in 'Málaviká and Agnimitra':—

"(*Málaviká, at the end of her dancing performance, wishes to go out.*)

Vidúshaka. Nay, thou shalt not go untaught.

Slave. (*To the Vidúshaka*) Say, sir, what violation of the rules of propriety you have observed *in her behaviour.*

Vidú. A Brahman must first be entertained, and this *duty* has been neglected by her.

Málaviká. (*Smiles*)."—and so forth.

These words *of the Vidúshaka* exciting, as they do, joy and desire in the hero, as he thereby observes the purity of the heroine—are an instance of the Vyáhára.

TEXT.

Mṛidava. No. 532. When (1) faults *turn into* merits, or (2) merits into faults, it is termed Mṛidava.

COMMENTARY.

a. *The following are* examples, respectively:—

"Love of life and cruelty, ingratitude and want of affection—these in me have become merits, now that I see him (my lord) again."

"O! that beautiful form of her, ornamented with the lustre of youth, O! that sole diffuser* of joy in me has now turned to be my affliction."

* 'Sole *abode* of my joy'—if सुखैकायतनं instead of सुखैकतायनं be the reading adopted.

These elements, though also occurring in the Náṭaka and others, and expressly admitted therein, are here illustrated, because they are necessarily to be admitted into the Víthí.

As to the *name* Víthí (garland), this kind is so designated, as a variety of sentiments resides in it, as it were, in the shape of a garland, *or, in other words, as it is a garland wreathed with sentiments.*

The Málaviká is an example. Now of the Prahasana:

TEXT.

The Prahasana described.

No. 533. The Prahasana is a representation of reprobates invented by the poet, resembling the Bháṉa in the number of its acts, in its Junctures, and Members of the Lásya.

COMMENTARY.

a. Herein is not to be admitted the Action A'rabhaṭí (§ 420), nor the Introductory Scenes Vishkambhaka and Praves'aka (§ 308).

TEXT.*

The Pure Prahasana.

Nos. 534-35. The Comic is the principal Flavour in it, and the members of the Víthí (§521) may or may not be introduced. When the hero in it is an impudent character, being an ascetic, a mendicant, a Bráhman, or the like, it is called Pure Prahasana.

COMMENTARY.

a. The Kandarpa-keli or 'Sports of Love' is an instance.

TEXT.

The Mixed Prahasana.

No. 536. When founded on any character whatever, it (the Prahasana) is known as the Mixed Prahasana.

COMMENTARY,

a. For example the Dhúrta-charita or 'Action of the Rogue.'

TEXT.

The Mixed Prahasana.

No. 537. Some call that the Mixed *Prahasana* which represents the character of a multitude of reprobates. This again may either consist of two Acts or merely of one act.

* Roer's edition has this divided into two distinct texts, and inserts, as commentary to the first, the word तत्र which can have no meaning here, nor is it found in my MS.

COMMENTARY.

a. For example the Náṭakamelaka or the like.

b. But the sage declares—"That in which a courtesan, a slave, a eunuch, a gallant, a rogue, and a harlot are represented without a change in their appearance, dress, and proceedings—is *named* Mixed *Prahasana.*"

TEXT.

The Vikṛita Prahasana.

No 538. That they call the Vikṛita *Prahasana or Farce of Disguise*, in which an imbecile, a eunuch, and an ascetic are *represented* with the guise and language of a gallant, dancer, soldier, &c.

COMMENTARY.

a. This *sort* being implied in the division of the 'Mixed' is not separately mentioned by the sage.

b. Now of the Uparúpakas *or minor forms of the Drama.*

c. Of these:

TEXT.

The Náṭiká described.

No. 539. The Náṭiká is founded on an invented story, consisting of four acts, and abounding with female characters. The hero in it should be an illustrious prince, and *a character* 'gay and thoughtless, yet firm' (§ 68). The heroine should be a maid of royal family, newly in love, belonging either to the inner apartment *of the hero, as an attendant of the queen,* or employed as a musical performer. The hero, *fallen in love with her*, conducts herself restrainedly from fear of the queen. The queen, older than the other lady and also of royal family, should be a bold woman, every moment in indignation. The union of the two is to be under her control. The Kais'ikí must be the action employed in it, and the Junctures should be without the Vimarsha.*

COMMENTARY.

a. 'Of the two'—*i. e* of the hero and the heroine.—The Ratnávalí, Viddha-s'álabhanjiká and the like are examples *of this kind.*

b. Now of the Troṭaka:—

* So explains the commentator the expression—स्वल्पविमर्षाः सन्धयः, which would be more naturally rendered—"The Junctures with but a scanty Vimarsha."

TEXT.

The Troṭaka described.

No. 540. A performance in five, seven, eight, or nine acts, founded on *the story* of a demigod, and representing the Vidúshaka in every act, is designated Troṭaka.

COMMENTARY.

a. From the very circumstance of the Vidúshaka's being represented in every act, *it is to be inferred* that Love is the chief sentiment in it.

b. Of the Troṭaka in seven acts the Stambhita-rambha is an example, and the Vikramorvas'í, of that in five acts.

c. Now of the Goshṭhí :—

TEXT.

The Goshṭhí described.

No 541. The Goshṭhí is graced with nine or ten common characters, does not contain lofty discourse, and employs the Action Kais'ikí (§ 411). It is devoid of the Garbha and Vimarsha (§ 335 and 336) and represents five or six female characters; it represents love and enjoyments, and consists of one act.

COMMENTARY.

a. For example the Raivata Madaniká.—Now of the Saṭṭaka :—

TEXT.

The Saṭṭaka described.

No. 542. The Saṭṭaka has all its recitations, *or speeches*, in Prákrit, and is without the Praves'aka (§ 309) and Vishkambhaka (§ 308). The Marvellous Flavour prevails in it. Its acts are named Javaniká. It is like the Náṭiká in other particulars.

a. The Karpúra-manjarí is an example.

b. Now of the Náṭya-rásaka :

The Náṭya-rásaka described.

No. 543. The Náṭya-rásaka is in one act and abounds in dancing and music. A 'high-spirited' personage (see § 65) is to be the hero in it, and his 'comrade' (§ 76), the secondary hero. The Comic and the Erotic Flavours are chief in it. The heroine is to be one 'prepared in her house' (§ 120). It contains the Junctures Mukha and Nirvahana and the ten Members of the Lásya (see § 504). Some would exclude from it the Juncture Pratimukha alone.

COMMENTARY.

a. Of these *two descriptions, as answering to the two different opinions mentioned in the Text*, the 'Narmavatí' is an example of the kind with two Junctures; and the Vilásavatí, of that with four Junctures.

b. Now of the Prastháná.

TEXT.

The Prastháná described.

No. 544. In the Prastháná, the hero and the heroine should be slaves or servants, and the secondary hero a low person, and the action *must be that called* Bháratí (§ 285). Drinking of wine leads to the consummation of the end *in the drama.* It is in two acts. Music and song and festivity are plenteously indulged in.

COMMENTARY.

a. The S'ṛingáratilaka is an example.—Now of the Ullápya.

TEXT.

The Ullápya described.

No. 545. The Ullápya should have a divine plot, a 'high-spirited' hero, and consist of one act. It is associated with the Members of the S'ilpaka, and with the Comic, Erotic, and Pathetic Flavours. The Ullápya, according to some, should be in three acts, have four heroines, abound in combats, and be delightful with songs in triplets.

COMMENTARY.

a. The Members of the S'ilpaka shall be stated hereafter.—The Deví Mahádeva is an example *of this kind.*

b. Now of the Kávya.

TEXT.

The Kávya described.

No. 546. The Kávya is in one act, devoid of the Action Árabhaṭí (§ 420), and full of the Comic. It is graced with songs named Khaṇḍamátrá, Dwipadiká (distich) and Bhagnatála. It employs also the metres Varṇamáttrá, and Chhaḍḍaliká. It is a love-story with a high-spirited hero, and similar heroine, using the first two and last Junctures (viz. Mukha, Pratimukha, and Nirvahaṇa).

COMMENTARY.

a. The 'Yádavodaya' *or Rise of Yádava* is an example.

b. Now of the Prenkhaṇa.

TEXT.

The Prenkhana described. No. 547. The Prenkhana is in one act, devoid of the Garbha and Vimarsha (§ 335 and 336) as also of the Vishkambhaka aud Praves'aka; the hero being a low person. Angry interlocution and single combats form its subject. It employs all the kinds of dramatic Action (see § 410). It is without *the peculiar performance* of the Manager (see § 281), the Benediction (§ 282) and Propitiation (§ 286 *a.*) being performed behind the scene.

COMMENTARY.

a. For example the Báli-vadha. Now of the Rásaka :—

TEXT.

The Rásaka described. No. 548. The Rásaka has five principal characters and contains *the Junctures* Mukha and Nirvahana. It employs a variety of languages and dialects,* and *the Actions* Bhárati and Kais'iki. It is in one act, without the Manager's performance (§ 281), containing the Members of the Víthí (§ 521) and musical performances. It has a Benediction (§ 282) with a *double entendre*, and a foolish man and noted woman for its hero and heroine. Its representations must be more and more dignified as it progresses. Some admit into it also the Juncture Pratimukha.

COMMENTARY.

a. The Menakáhita is a specimen of it. Now of the Sanlápaka.

TEXT.

The Sanlápaka described. No. 549. In the Sanlápaka there may be three or four acts, the hero being a heretic, and the flavours other than the Erotic and the Pathetic. Blockade of a city, treachery, combat, and confusion are represented. Neither the Action Bhárati nor Kais'iki is employed.

COMMENTARY.

a. For example the Máyákápálika. Now of the S'rígadita.

* In the original—भाषा and विभाषा, the former, according to the commentator, including under it the Sanscrit and the different forms of Prákrit proper, the latter denoting those corrupt dialects of the Prákrit, called अपभ्रंश.

TEXT.

The S'ríga̤dita described.

No. 550. The S'ríga̤dita is held to be a species of the Minor Drama (Uparúpaka—see § 276) consisting of one act, founded on a celebrated story, with a famous high-spirited hero and a celebrated heroine. It is wanting in the Garbha and Vimarsha (§ 335 and 336). The Action Bhárati is chiefly employed, and the word S'rí (prosperity) comes frequently into its vocabulary.

COMMENTARY.

a. The Kríḍárasátala is an example.

The S'rígadita according to another description.

b. Some declare the S'rígadita to be a play in which S'rí, or Lakshmí, (the Goddess of temporal and spiritual prosperity) seated, sings and recites something; consisting of one act and employing chiefly the Action Bháraṭí. An example of it may be imagined. Now of the S'ilpaka.

TEXT.

The S'ilpaka described.

No. 551. The S'ilpaka has four acts and uses all the four Actions; the Flavours are without the Quietistic and Comic; the hero is a Brahman, and the secondary hero a low character. A cemetery or the like forms the subject of its representation. It comprises twenty-seven elements, which are these: Expectation, Surmise, Doubt, Pain, Anxiety, Inference (Prasakti), Effort, Intimation of purpose, Longing, Dissimulation, Belief or Conviction (Pratipatti), Voluptuousness, Indolence, Perverseness, Rapture, Indecency, Folly, Seeking of means (sádhanánugama), Relaxation, Surprise, Obtainment (prápti), Gain (lábha), Forgetfulness, Angry speech, Expertness, Instruction, and Astonishment. These are not defined because of their clearness.

COMMENTARY.

a. The Sampheṭa and Grathana, spoken of before (§ 421 and 394), have been already defined.

b. The Kanakávatí Mádhava is a specimen. Now of the Vilásiká:

TEXT.

The Vilásiká described.

No. 552. The Vilásiká is defined a play in one act, with Love for its leading sentiment, containing the ten Members of the Lásya (see § 504) and graced by the

Buffoon (see § 77), the 'humble friend' (§ 77), and the 'Comrade' (§ 76). It is without the Junctures Garbha and Vimarsha; it has a low hero, a short fable, and a beautiful toilet.

COMMENTARY.

a. Some read 'Lásiká' instead of Vilásiká, and others include it in the Durmallí. Now of the Durmalliká.

TEXT.

The Durmalliká described.

No. 553. The Durmalliká is *an entertainment* in four acts, with a hero of an inferior character, employing the Actions Bhárati and Kais'ikí, and wanting the *Juncture* Garbha. Its *dramatis personæ* are composed of men of pleasure. The first act, occupying three 'náḍikás' (§ 515 *a.*), should represent the sports of the 'humble friend' (§ 77); the second, of the duration of five náḍikás, should contain the enjoyments of the 'buffoon' (§ 77); the third, of six náḍikas' duration, those of the 'comrade' (§ 76); and the fourth, extending over ten náḍikás, should represent the sports of the hero.

COMMENTARY.

a. The Vindumatí is an example. Now of the Prakaraṉiká.

TEXT.

The Prakaraṉí described.

No. 554. The Náṭiká is termed Prakaraṉí, when it has, for example, a merchant for its hero, and a heroine of a family similar to the hero's.

COMMENTARY.

a. Let an example of it be searched out *by the reader for himself.* Now of the Hallís'a.

TEXT.

The Hallís'a described.

No. 555. The Hallís'a is *a piece* in one act, with one male, and seven, eight, or ten female characters; the language being elevated, the Kais'ikí its chief Action, the Mukha and Nirvahaṉa its Junctures. It uses music and song in abundance.

COMMENTARY.

a. The Keli Raivataka is an example. Now of the Bháṉiká.

TEXT.

The Bhánika described.

No. 556. The Bhánika is a play in one act, in which the actors dress themselves beautifully, containing the Mukha and Nirvahana (§ 333 and 337) and the Actions Bhárati and Kais'ikí, with a heroine of high family and a vulgar hero. The following are its seven elements: Upanyása, Vinyása, Vibodha, Sáddhwasa, Samarpana, Nivṛitti, and Sanhára. Upanyása is a casual declaration of the end. An utterance of self-disparaging words is called Vinyása. Vibodha is the removal of error, and Sáddhwasa is a false statement. Reproachful words uttered under the agitation of grief are *termed* Samarpaṇa. A mentioning of an example is called Nivṛitti. The accomplishment of the object is styled Sanhára

COMMENTARY.

a. Examples *of these* are evident *in the dramatic works.*—The Kámadattá is a specimen *of this species of drama.*

b. The peculiarities spoken of as belonging to the Náṭaka may be admitted, only if proper and possible, into these *other kinds beginning with the Prakaraṇa,* though generically they all are of the nature of the Náṭaka. But such elements, mentioned in the Náṭaka, as have been repeated *in the several descriptions of them* are, as a rule, to be introduced into them.

c. Now of Audible Poetry (see § 272.)

TEXT.

Audible Poetry, twofold, viz. (1) Metrical, or (2) in Prose.

No. 557. Audible Poetry, or Poetry that is merely to be heard, is twofold, being (1) Metrical (padya), or (2) in Prose (gadya.)

COMMENTARY.

a. Of these, he speaks of Poems in Metre.

TEXT.

Metrical Poetry, defined.

No. 558. Metrical Poetry is that in which the words are regulated by metre, *generally making up four lines which constitute what is termed a 'padya' (stanza). A piece of Poetry,* complete in a single stanza, is called Muktaka (*Free, or independent as to the completion of its sense, on the succeeding stanza).* Complete in a couple of stanzas, it is termed

Yugmaka (couplet); in three stanzas, Sandánitaka (triplet); in four, kalápaka; and in five, Kulaka.

COMMENTARY.

a. Of these, the Muktaka is exemplified in the following verses of mine:

"Him of Perfect Bliss, Infinite, Immutable, and Unborn, whom devotees, absorbed in meditation, unceasingly adore in order to behold him in *beatific vision* even for a moment—blessed were those young women of Mathurá who would sportively draw away that Supreme Brahma, talk to him a hundred ways, embrace him, and kiss him!"

b. A Yugmaka, as these verses of mine:

"'Why dost thou, love, thus recline thy cheek on thy hand—anger, in extreme, is not proper towards a lover yielding in affection'—thus as I would speak to the deer-eyed one, the sweet hum of the honey-maker rose on the mango tree."

Similarly the others.

TEXT.

The Mahákávya or Great Poem, described.

No. 559. The Great Poem (*Mahákávya*) is a poetical composition in a number of cantos. The hero thereof should be a deity, or a Kshattriya of noble family, characterized by firmness and generosity of heart. Or a number of kings belonging to the same noble family may be its heroes. Of the Erotic, Heroic, and Quietistic any one flavour should be the principal in it, all the *other* flavours being ancillary thereto. It should contain all the dramatic Junctures (§ 332). The story, pertaining to some virtuous character or characters, must be derived from history *such as the Mahábhárata*, or from any other source. It has for its fruits (*i. e. the final objects obtained by the hero or the like*) all the four of the class *consisting of the great objects of human desire, viz. Merit, Wealth, Enjoyment and Liberation*, or it has only one of them. It begins with a salutation to a deity or a benediction, or simply with the mention of a matter* *leading into the main story of the poem.* Sometimes it

* In the original, वस्तुनिर्देशः which I have translated in accordance with the common acceptation of the term वस्तु, as Mallinátha has explained the expression in the beginning of his commentary on the Kumára Sambhava. The commentator of the present work, however, explains the term to mean the leading personage of the poem. Premachandra Tarkavágís'a adopts this interpretation, but includes under the term also one related to the hero. (See Kávyádars'a, p. 16 Bib. Ind.)

begins with a reproach of the malicious or the like, and an eulogium of the good. It consists of cantos, more than eight in number, neither too short nor too long, *each canto* comprising stanzas composed in some particular metre, but ending in those of a different one. Sometimes, however, we find a canto composed in a vaṛiety of metres. At the end of each canto should be hinted the subject of the succeeding canto. The sun and moon, day and night, morning and evening, noon, twilight, and darkness, ocean and mountain, woods, and hunting, the seasons, the enjoyment and separation *of lovers*, saints, heaven' city, sacrifice, military march, counsel, marriage, birth of a son, &c.: these are to be described in it, according to occasion, together with their attendant incidents and circumstances.* It is to be named after the poet, the story, the hero or the like, whilst the designation of a canto is to be after the principal matter contained therein.

COMMENTARY.

a. The Members of the Junctures (§ 338—405) are to be admitted into it as occasion may require.

b. 'Ending in those of a different one' (see Text)—here the plurality *implied in 'those'* is not necessarily intended.

c. 'Together with their attendant incidents and circumstances'—implying, for instance, sporting in water, carousal and the like, *which must be described in connection with evening and night.*

Specimens of the Great Poem.

d. The Raghuvaṇs'a, the S'is'upálavadha, the Naishadha and others are specimens *of the Great Poem*. Or my own Rághava-vilása and other *poems* might be instanced.

TEXT.

A Great Poem by a saint.

No. 560. The cantos of this again, when composed by a saint (*ṛishi*), are designated Ákhyána (Narration).

COMMENTARY.

a. 'Of this'—*i. e.* of the Great Poem.—The Mahábhárata is an example *of a Great Poem composed by a saint.*

TEXT.

A Prákṛit Great Poem.

No. 561. The cantos belonging to that composed in any of the Prákṛit dialects are named

* Lit. Together with their members and by-members.

A'swása. This (a Prákṛit Great Poem) is generally composed in the metre *called* A'skandaka, and sometimes also in those named Galitakas.

COMMENTARY.

a. The Setubandha (Bridging of the Sea) or my own Kuvalayás'wa-charita (Actions of Kuvalayás'wa) is an example.

TEXT.

A Great Poem in a corrupt dialect (Apabhrans'a.)

No. 562. The cantos belonging to a Great Poem written in any of the corrupt dialects (Apabhrans'a) are styled Kaḍavakas. A variety of metres befitting the corrupt dialects *are employed in it.*

COMMENTARY.

a. The Karṇa-parákṛama, or the Valour of Karṇa, is an instance.

TEXT.

The Kávya, or Poem simply so called, described.

No. 563. The Kávya, *or Minor Poem,* is one in which, as a rule, the pure and corrupt forms of Prákṛit as well as the Sanskrit are to be employed, which is without *the division into* cantos, consisting of stanzas tending to one object, and not comprising a totality of Junctures (§ 338—405).

COMMENTARY.

a. For instance, the Bhikshátana or the A'ryávilása.

TEXT.

The Khaṇḍa Kávya described.

No. 564. The Khaṇḍa Kávya, or Partial Poem, *is a composition* partially* resembling the Kávya.

COMMENTARY.

a. The Meghadúta *of Kálidása* and the like are examples.

TEXT.

The Kosha described.

No. 565. The Kosha, *or Poetical* Treasury, is a collection of independent stanzas arranged in the order of classification; and this is indeed extremely charming.

COMMENTARY.

a. 'Classification' (vrajyá) is the putting together of things of the same species.

b. The Muktávalí and the like are specimens of the Kosha.

* Hence, says the Commentator, it comprises Sanskrit verses only, unlike the Kávya which admits the various forms of Prákrit along with Sanskrit.

c. Now *we have to speak* of 'Poems in Prose,' *and therefore, as being essentially* connected therewith, *we shall first define* Prose *and its varieties.*

TEXT.

Prose and its four varieties defined.

No. 566. Prose (Gadya) is speech not regulated by metre, and this is fourfold, viz. the Muktaka, the Vṛittagandhi, the Utkalikápráya and the Chúrṉaka. The first *of these kinds* is devoid of compounds, the second contains portions of metre, the third abounds in long compounds, and the fourth is characterized by short compounds.

COMMENTARY.

The Muktaka.

a. The Muktaka, or Free Prose; as—

गुरुर्वचसि पृथुरुरसीत्यादि (Grave of speech and wide of breast, &c.)

The Vṛittagandhi.

b. The Vṛittagandhi, or Prose smelling of Metre, is instanced in this line of mine—

समरकण्डूलनिबिडभुजदण्डकुण्डलीकृतकोदण्डशिञ्जिनीटङ्कारोज्जागरितवैरिनगर (O thou, whose foeman's city is startled by the twang of the string of thy bow, as it is drawn into the form of a ring by those rods—thy brawny hands, eager for war.)

Here, कुण्डलीकृतकोदण्ड is a *complete* line of the Anushtubh metre, and समरकण्डूल is another line of the same metre, without its first two syllables.

The Utkalikápráya.

c. The Utkalikápráya is illustrated in the following line also of mine:—

अणिसविसुमरणिसिदद्दरसरविसरविदलिदसमरपरिगदप्पवरपरबलेत्यादि—(O thou the fighting forces of whose enemy, powerful as they are, are torn by the multitude of thy excessively sharp arrows, flying incessantly.)

The Chúrṉaka.

d. The Chúrṉaka, as this line of mine—

गुणरत्नसागर जगदेकनागर कामिनीमदन जनरञ्जनेत्यादि (O ocean of the gems of excellence, gallant unique in the world, O charmer of the fair ones and gladdener of the people.)

TEXT.

The Kathá described.

No. 567. In the Kathá (Tale), *which is one of the species of poetical composition in prose,* a poetical matter is represented in verse, and, sometimes, the Áryá and, sometimes, the Vaktra and Apavaktraka are the metres employed in it. It begins with stanzas in salutation to some divinity, as also descriptive of the behaviour of bad men and others.

COMMENTARY.

a. The Kádambarí *of Váṇa Bhatta* is an example.

TEXT.

The Ákhyáyiká described.

No. 568. The Ákhyáyiká (Narrative) resembles the Kathá, but it has these distinctive peculiarities. The genealogy, &c. of the poet *of the composition* and, sometimes, an account of other poets also are given. The divisions of the story are distinguished by the name of Ás'wása. The matter to be related in an Ás'wása should be hinted in its beginning, in any of the metres Áryá, Vaktra and Apavaktraka, under the artifice of describing something else.

COMMENTARY.

a. The Harsha-charita and others are instances.

The opinion of some that the story of the Ákhyáyiká is to be related by the hero—refuted.

b. Some assert that the story of the Ákhyáyiká must, as a rule, be related by the hero,—which is not right, as is evident from the declaration of Daṇḍin, the Áchárya (Great Doctor), viz. "We find that there is no rule as to this (*i. e.* the relation of the story by the hero), for other personages also than the hero do relate *it in the Ákhyáyiká.*"

Other divisions of 'Poetry in Prose' fall under the Kathá and Ákhyáyiká.

c. The Ákhyána (Narration) and other *divisions of Poetry in Prose,* being included under the Kathá and Ákhyáyiká, have not been separately spoken of; as has been said by the same *author,* Daṇḍin—"Under these will be included the remaining descriptions of Narrative." The Panchatantra and others are examples *of these latter kinds.*

d. Now of 'Poems in prose and verse.'

TEXT.

The Champú defined.

No. 569. A Poem composed in prose and verse is designated Champú.

COMMENTARY.

a. For example, the Des'arája-charita or Adventures of Des'arája.

TEXT.

The Viruda described. No. 570. A eulogium of a king, in prose and verse, is styled Viruda.

COMMENTARY.

a. For example, the Virudamaṇimálá, or Gem-garland of Royal Praise.

TEXT.

The Karambhaka. No. 571. *A Champú* composed in a variety of dialects is *called* the Karambhaka.

COMMENTARY.

a. Such is my Pras'asti-ratnávalí, composed in sixteen dialects.

b. Other such divisions *of the Champú*, known merely by name and not falling beyond the said distinctions, have not been specified.

So much for the sixth chapter of the Mirror of Composition—entitled the 'Declaration of *Poetry to be seen* and *Poetry to be heard*.'

CHAPTER VII.

The Declaration of Blemishes.

It was shown in the beginning *of this treatise* how in Poetry reside Faults, Excellences, Style and Ornaments. Now the question arising —What are they? he declares the nature of Faults, as coming first in the order of mention.

TEXT.

Faults defined. No. 572. Faults are depressers of Flavour.

COMMENTARY.

a. The sense of this has been already cleared (see § 4 *a.*)

b. He states their divisions.

TEXT.

And divided. No. 573. They are held to be fivefold, inasmuch as they occur in (1) a word (pada), (2) a part of a word (padáns'a), (3) a sentence or phrase, (4) the sense, and (5) the Flavour.

COMMENTARY.

a. Of these—

TEXT.

Faults of a word, part of a word and a sentence or phrase—specified.

No. 574. Unmelodiousness, the threefold Indecency, Improper Signification, Unemployedness, Vulgarism, Unintelligibility, Ambiguity, a Meaning to be guessed out, Obsoleteness or a Sense overpowered by another, Inexpressiveness, Obscurity, Repugnant Suggestion, and Non-discrimination of the Predicate, the Apodotic or the Emphatic (vidheya)* belong to words and sentences, some of them occurring in a part of a word also.

Faults exclusively of a word.

And Unmeaningness, Powerlessness and Solecism occur only in a word.

COMMENTARY.

Unmelodiousness.

a. UNMELODIOUSNESS, *as a fault of a word or phrase*, is its painfulness to the ear arising from harsh syllables; as—

कार्त्तार्थ्यं यातु तन्वङ्गी कदाऽनङ्गवशंवदा ।

(O when may that slender-bodied lady, subjugated by Cupid, have her desires fulfilled !)

The threefold Indecency.

b. INDECENCY is threefold, as being suggestive of (1) shame, (2) disgust and (3) inauspiciousness. These *three forms* are, in their order, exemplified *as follows :—*

दृप्तारिविजये राजन् साधनं सुमहत्तव ।

"Great are thy resources (sádhana), O Monarch, in vanquishing the proud enemy."

प्रससार शनैर्वायु र्विनाशे तन्विते तदा ।

"The wind then flowed languidly, O slender one, at thy loss."

Here, the words *sádhana*, *váyu* (wind) and *vinás'a* (loss by separation or death) are respective instances of the three sorts of Indecency.

* It is necessary to remark here that the Sanskrit word विधेय is not restricted to the sense of 'predicate,' but is used also in the signification of a word that gratifies the expectation raised by a previous word, as also in the sense of one on which a stress is laid. In the absence of any English word conveying the second sense, I have been obliged to coin the adjective *apodotic* from Apodosis, which in Greek Rhetoric means the completive part of a sentence, which gratifies the expectation raised by the Protasis, or the introductory part.

Improper Signification.

c. "Heroes attain to the state of immortals—as animals killed in the sacrifice of war."

Here the word 'animals' conveys the *improper* notion of wretchedness with reference to the heroes; so it has the fault of Improper Signification.*

Unemployedness

d. UNEMPLOYEDNESS is when a word is used in a form, which, though admitted as correct, is not approved by the poets; as—"There shines the lotus (पद्मः) in the pond." Here the word पद्मः is *used* in the masculine gender, *which is against the practise of the poets, though the word is well known as both masculine and neuter.*

Vulgarism.

e. VULGARISM is instanced in—'Thy buttock (kaṭi) ravishes my heart,' where the word *kaṭi* is vulgar.

Unintelligibility.

f. UNINTELLIGIBILITY is when an expression is used in a sense *which is not recognized in Poetry*, but only in some particular department of learning. As,—'With his deserts (ás'aya) destroyed by divine meditation.' Here the word ás'aya is employed in the sense of 'desert' which it has only in the Yoga Philosophy.†

Ambiguity.

g. "Admit in your ear the series of his benedictions (ás'íh-parampará) and have mercy on the prisoner (vandyám)."

Here the word 'vandyám' is Ambigious, since it is doubtful whether it *is the Locative of Vandí and* means 'on the prisoner' or *the Accusative of 'vandyá' and an epithet of 'as'íh-parampará,'* signifying laudable.'

A Meaning to be guessed out.

h. 'A MEANING TO BE GUESSED OUT' is the fault of an expression employed, from the poet's inability *to find a better one*, to convey an Indicated sense *which it cannot properly do* because of the absence of Notoriety or a Motive necessary to Indication (see chapter II. § 13). As—'Thy face, O fair-faced one, has kicked the lotus.' Here by 'kicked' is indicated 'vanquished' or 'excelled,' the term, therefore, is faulty, inasmuch as it is neither (1) notorious, or established by Usage, as indicative of such a sense, nor (2) is there any Motive for such an Indication.

* Simple as this sentence is in the original, Prof. Goldstücker understands it in a sense the very reverse of what is really meant, and thus confounds the present fault with Unintelligibility or Technicality (§ *f.*) See the word अनुचितार्थं in the enlarged edition of Wilson's Sanskrit Dictionary.

† See Dr. Ballantyne's Aphorisms of the Yoga, I. § 24, *a.*

Obsoleteness. *i.* **Obsoleteness** is the employment of a word with two senses in the obsolete meaning. For example—

"The waters (s'ambara) of Yamuná overspread the sky."

Here the word 's'ambara,' generally known to mean the demon *so called*, is used in the obsolete sense of 'water.'

Inexpressiveness. *j.* 'He gives (ádatte) ear to songs:' the verb 'dá' with the prefix *á*, used here in the sense of 'giving,' is Inexpressive of that sense, *as it signifies 'to take.'* Or for example—

"Night, though covered with darkness, is day (dina) to me when thou hast come.'

Here, the word 'dina' is inexpressive of the sense of 'luminous' in which it is used.

Obscurity. *k.* **Obscurity** is the circumstance of the meaning's being far-fetched, as is exemplified in this line—

"The native regions of the dwelling of her *who was* born of the milky ocean are lucid."

She who was born of the milky ocean is Lakshmí, her dwelling is the lotus and its native regions are the waters.

Repugnant Suggestion. *l.* **Repugnant Suggestion** *is instanced thus:*—

"May the lord of Bhaváni (etymologically, the wife of Bhava or S'iva) be for our prosperity!"

Here the word 'Bhavánís'a' (lord of Bhaváni), bringing in, as it does, the notion of another lord of Bhaváni, conveys a repugnant suggestion.

Non-discrimination of the Predicate. *m.* **Non-discrimination of the Predicate** *is exemplified in the following:*—

"Or what from these arms that in vain swelled (वृथोच्छूनैः) with *the pride of carrying off* the spoils of the poor villages of heaven" (§ 2, *f.*)

Here, 'vanity' is intended to be **predicated** of the 'arms,' but losing its prominence in the compound *epithet applied to the subject*, it looks as if it were meant only to be collaterally attributed.

Non-discrimination of the Emphatic. *n.* Or, *to exemplify* "**Non-discrimination of the Emphatic**" *which, in the original, is included under the same name* (§ 574):—

"Are even demons able to stand before me—Ráma's brother (रामानुजस्य)."

Here instead of using the compound word रामानुजस्य we should say *separately* रामस्यानुजस्य, *for the genitive termination* स्य (*which is lost in the compound*) *is particularly significant here, as marking distinctly the relationship of the speaker (Lakshmaṇa) to Ráma.*

The same. *o.* Or the same fault may be illustrated by this line from the first canto of the Raghuvans'a—" Of the lords of the earth to the ocean's verge (आसमुद्रक्षितीशानाम्)." Here the poet should have said आसमुद्रं क्षितीशानाम्, *and thus given a separate, and thereby a prominent and emphatic expression to the circumstance implied in* आसमुद्रम्, *for it is this circumstance that, as heightening our idea of the extension of the rule of the kings, the poet wishes particularly to direct our attention to.*

The same. *p.* Or, for example :—

" Wherever falls thy glance, fair-browed lady, like a sixth arrow (षष्ठबाण इव) of Him of the five arrows (Káma)—."

Here *a stress being evidently laid upon* षष्ठ (*sixth*), *it should not be compounded with* बाण (*arrow*), *but* the poetical fancy *of the maiden's glance being a sixth arrow* should be expressed *by the words separated,* thus—षष्ठ इव बाणः

The same. *q.* Or, to exemplify *the same fault in a negation*—

" My lord, she was unquitted (अमुक्ता) by you, even for a moment, before."

Here the denial in अमुक्ता bearing, as it does, the character of an Express, or Pominent Negation, ought to be directly or emphatically expressed. As it has been said—

An Express Negation what. " When the affirmation is not principal, but the denial is so, the latter is termed an Express Negation (प्रसज्यप्रतिषेध), in the case of which the negative associates with *i. e.* qualifies the VERB :" *e. g.*

" It is a new cloud risen ready, NOT a proud demon."*

In the *former* example, the denial has not the appearance of an emphatic negation, being reduced to an unprominent condition in the Tatpurusha compound अमुक्ता, and hence faring like *what is called* a Privation. To this effect it has been said—

* न दृप्तनिशाचरः, not अदृप्तनिशाचर (non-proud-demon), which, like अमुक्ता in the former example, would be improper.

A Privation what. "When the affirmation is chiefly intended and not the denial, it is to be recognized as *that case of denial which is termed* Privation (पर्युदास), where the negative is compounded with another word." Hence—

"Undaunted he protected himself, undiseased* he cultivated virtue, ungreedy he exacted tribute, and unaddicted he enjoyed pleasure."

Here, since it is the protecting of self &c. that are meant to be predicated of the king, having COLLATERALLY ATTRIBUTED to him the qualities of undauntedness &c., the reduction of the negative to one of Privation is proper.

An objection to the above illustration of the fault repelled.

r. But then, *if an objector should say*, the expression अमुक्ता WOULD imply an Express Negation, just like the phrases अश्राद्धभोजी ब्राह्मणः (a Bráhman not-eating at a funeral ceremony), असूर्यम्पश्या राजदाराः (a princess not seeing *even* the sun) &c. We would reply—No, for even in these cases then only would we acknowledge an instance of Express Negation, if (—to take the former example—) the negative applied to that portion *of the meaning of s'ráddha-bhojí (eating or eater at a funeral anniversary)* which consists in the ACT —'eating,' but this is not the case, inasmuch as the negative relates to the portion AGENT, viz. the eater, since it is this which is the qualified, and therefore the most prominent part of the expression. To this effect it has been said: '—Since the AGENT—the eater at funeral anniversaries, and not simply the ACT of eating is thought of, because of the employment of 'ini,' a suffix of agency." In 'amuktá,' however, the relation *of the negative* being to the act, there is of course a fault.

s. These faults, Obscurity, &c. are blemishes of a word, only in composition.

Unmelodiousness in a Sentence.

t. Unmelodiousness in a sentence; as, स्मरार्त्तान्धः कदा लप्स्ये कार्त्तार्थ्यं विरहे तव. (Blind, at thy separation, with the torments of love, O when shall I have my wishes fulfilled!)

Indecency in a Sentence.

u. "The poet who takes to another's sentiment eats vomit."

Here we have Indecency suggestive of Disgust *exemplified in a sentence.*

* Unlike the great majority of mankind who think of religion, only when distressed.

A "Meaning to be guessed out" in a Sentence.

v. "Their bodies were adorned by the fair ones (vakrá) with orient rubies (kamala-lauhitya)."

Here, 'kamala-lauhitya' and 'vakrá' *are* GUESSED, *by the sameness of the etymological sense in the one case and that of the primary meaning in the other, to indicate the words* 'padmarága' and 'vámá,' *which latter words respectively signify a ruby and a woman. The sentence, therefore, has the fault of a "Meaning to be guessed out."*

Obscurity in a Sentence.

w. धम्मिल्लस्य न कस्य प्रेक्ष्य निकामं कुरङ्गशावाक्ष्याः ।
रज्यत्यपूर्व्वबन्धव्युत्पत्तेर्मानसं शोभाम् ॥

(Whose heart is not completely warmed to see the beauty of the locks of her with eyes like the young deer's—locks bound up with an unprecedented art?)

The construction of the line is Obscure, the connection being this —धम्मिल्लस्य शोभां प्रेक्ष्य कस्य मानसं न रज्यति.

'Nondiscrimination of the Predicate' in a Sentence.

x. The fault of 'Nondiscrimination of the Predicate' in a sentence is exemplified in—न्यक्कारो ह्ययमेव यत् &c. (For, this indeed is an utter contempt of me &c.—see § 2. *f.*) Here न्यक्कारः (contempt) is meant to be the predicate, *and should, therefore, be placed after the subject,* thus—ह्ययमेव न्यक्कारः, but from the reversed order of the sentence, the word's character, as a predicate, is rendered less clear. The fault is that of a sentence or phrase, inasmuch as it arises from the reversed collocation of TWO words.

'Nondiscrimination of the Apodotic' in a Sentence.

y. 'Nondiscrimination of the Apodotic' in a sentence; as—आनन्दयति ते नेत्रे यो (who) ऽसौ (he) सुभ्रु समागतः (*The one* who cheers thy eyes, O thou of fair brows,—he has arrived.) In expressions such as this, according to the rule that there is an invariable correlation between *the relative* यद् (who or which) and *the personal pronoun* तद् (he or it), the pronominal words इदम्, एतद्, अदः, used in the same sense with *the pronoun* तद्, in order to the fulfilment of the expectation raised by the relative यद्, must, properly, belong to the Apodosis. But here the

The Personal pronoun, immediately following the Relative, merely emphasizes the latter.

Personal pronoun, being placed immediately after the Relative, appears as if it belonged to the Protasis. The word तद् also, immediately following the word यद्, merely implies that the person or thing which it qualifies or points to, is well known; *e. g.*,

यः स* ते नयनानन्दकरः सुभ्रु स आगतः

(That *person* who is the joy of thy eyes—he has come.)

z. These words (इदम्, एतद्, अदः, तद्), however, not immediately following *the Relative* यद्, do gratify our expectation ; as,

आनन्दयति ते नेत्रे योऽधुना ऽसौ समागतः (He who cheers thy eyes has now arrived).

So also in the case of the employment of इदम् &c.,—*the use of* अदः (—*which makes* असौ *in the nominative singular*—) *being exemplified here.*

aa. Where, of the Relative and Personal pronouns—यद् and तद् &c., one may be understood, there the expectation is fulfilled, though one only, *i. e.* either the relative or personal pronoun, be used: hence in such a case there is no fault.

When the Personal pronoun may be understood.

bb. Thus, the *relative* यद् being used in the latter clause, the personal pronoun तद् may, from the context, be understood in the former ; as, आत्मा जानाति यत् पापं.—" The soul knows (that) which is a sin."† So also in such instances as the following—

यं सर्व्वशैलाः परिकल्प्य वत्समित्यादि ‡

(Whom all the mountains made the calf, when, by Prithu's command, they milked radiant gems and herbs out of Earth bearing the form of a cow—while Meru, dexterous in milking, acted as the milker.)

When the Relative pronoun may be understood.

cc. When the term तद् refers to one that (1) is the subject of discourse, or (2) well known, or (3) known by one's self, then the term यद् is understood. For examples in their order :—

" Having slain the brave Bálin, HE (सः) placed Sugríva on the throne so long wished for by him (the latter), as *the Grammarian substitutes* a distinct syllable (—technically called ádes'a—) in the room of a radical."

" May HE (सः) with a lunar digit on his head help you to Divine Identity, *or the union of your soul with Him !*"

* This form of expression cannot be translated into English.

† Or, for instance : 'But he who found not whom his soul desired, &c.'—*Pope's Iliad.*

‡ Kumára-sambhava, I. 2.

"HER (तां) of the moon-enchanting face I meditate in my heart."

The Personal pronoun, when of a different gender or case, may immediately follow the Relative.

dd. But where the personal pronouns इदम् &c., though standing close to the relative यद् (see § *y*.), have a different (1) gender or (2) case *from that of the latter*, there also is the sense complete. For examples in their order :—

विभाति मृगशावाक्षी या इदं भुवनभूषणम्।

(The lady who shines—she, with eyes like those of the young deer, is an ornament of the world.)

इन्दुर्विभाति यस्तेन दग्धाः पथिकयोषितः।

(This moon that shines—by him have the separated wives of travellers been burnt.)

The personal and relative pronouns may, sometimes, be both understood.

ee. Sometimes even both of these (viz. the relative and the personal pronoun), when not expressed, are understood from the context of the sentence. As—

"'Alas! there is none to relieve my burden'—lament not thus, O Earth: there is, in the house of Nanda, a boy of marvellous prowess."

Here is understood—'HE WHO is *such* will relieve thy burden.'

ff. यद् यद् विरहदुःखं मे तत् को वाऽपहरिष्यति।

(The pangs of separation that I feel, alas, who will remove them!)

It is not to be asserted that one of the relatives, in this example, leaves the sense incomplete,* since, by the repetition of यद्, the thing *(viz. pain,)* is indicated in all its forms, whichever they be, and the personal pronoun तद् (it) refers to it as of such a character.

gg. So may the illustration of the other *faults* (§ 574), as belonging to a sentence, be understood *by the reader*.

Unmelodiousness in a *part of a word.*

hh. Unmelodiousness in a PART OF A WORD (§ 574) is exemplified in *the harsh combination of three consonants, viz.* द्ध्यै *(ddhyai), the inflected portion of the word* सिद्ध्यै *in*—तद्गच्छ सिद्ध्यै कुरु देवकार्य्यं.† (Go, act in behalf of the gods and prosper!)

Obsoleteness in a *part of a word.*

ii. Obsoleteness in a part of a word; as धातुमत्तां गिरिर्धत्ते. (The mountain bears the nature of being metalline.)

* Lit. is expectant.

† Kumára Sambhava, III. 18.

Here *the part* मत्ता *of* धातुमत्ता has its sense overpowered by the *more common* meaning of 'intoxicated' *which sense it bears as the feminine of* मत्त.*

Inexpressiveness in a *part of a word.* *jj.* "How can Mahásena (the War-god), by whom was conquered (विजेयः) the demon Táraka, be described?"

Here, in the word विजेय, the suffix कृत्य, *(a sign of the future passive participle)*, is INEXPRESSIVE of the sense *in which it is used*, viz. that of the suffix क्त *(of the past participle)*.

Indecency in a *part of a word.* *kk.* पाणिः पल्लवपेलवः (Hand soft like the tender leaf.)

Here the first two syllables of the word पेलव are INDECENT, *as they form a Sanskrit word of an indecent import.*

'A meaning to be guessed out' in a *part of a word.* *ll.* "Heroes, slain in battle, attained to the state of a god (वचोवाण)."

Here the word वचः *(word)* is to be GUESSED OUT as signifying the *synonymous* word गीः *and thus, in composition with* वाण, *suggesting the term* गीर्वाण *(a god). So the fault might be exhibited* by substituting the *synonymous* word शर *(arrow)* for वाण in the same word गीर्वाण, so that neither of the component words in गीर्वाण would bear being exchanged for a synonymous word. In such compounds, however, as जलधि (sea), the latter word (धि) only, and in such as वाड़ावानल (submarine fire), the former (वाडव) only are not exchangeable.

mm. Similarly may other faults, possibly occurring in a part of a word, be understood *by the reader for himself.*

Unmeaningness. *nn.* And the three faults commencing with Unmeaningness† may occur in our subject (*i. e.* Poetry), only as residing in a WORD; as—मुञ्च मानं हि मानिनि (Proud one, do quit thy pride).

Here the word हि is an UNMEANING *expletive* used for the purpose of merely filling up the metre.

* The proper reading seems to be चीवार्थेन, as the printed *Kávya-prakás'a* has, instead of चौवार्थे. Röer's *Sáhitya-darpana* and my own MS., however, have the latter reading.

It is necessary to remark here that the fault denoted by निहतार्थत्व is not exactly represented by the term 'obsoleteness' (see § *rr.*) निहतार्थत्व literally means 'the state of having a sense overpowered or borne down by another *more common meaning.*'

† See text 574.

Powerlessness. *oo.* कुञ्जं हन्ति कृशोदरी (To the grove resorts the slender-waisted lady). Here हन्ति, though read in Root-books in the sense of going, is POWERLESS *in that meaning.*

Solecism. *pp.* "He of the Gáṇḍíva *bow* (Arjuna) struck (आजघ्ने) with his hands the breast of the Uneven-eyed* *God* (S'iva), shining like a golden slab."

Now on the authority of the rule—"Of the verbs यम् and हन् with the prefix आ there is to be the Átmanepada termination, when one's own body is the object governed by them" (Páṇini, I. 3, 28)—the Átmanepada termination is directed of हन with the prefix आ, only when the body of the agent is the object. This rule is transgressed here *in the use of the word* आजघ्ने, hence it has the fault of Solecism, as being without its grammatical characteristic.

An objection to the above fault belonging to a word—confuted. "But then," an objector would say, "since the word आजघ्ने is not in itself faulty, but in relation to other words (viz. '*the breast of the Uneven-eyed god*'), the fault is that of a SENTENCE, *not a* WORD." I answer—Say not so: for the reason, *or condition*, of an excellence, a fault and an ornament being held as belonging, *for instance,* to a word or meaning is the circumstance of the fault, &c., appearing and disappearing with the word or meaning. Now here *in the above example*, the fault appears and disappears simply with the word आजघ्ने—for it remains as it is, even on the alteration of the other words, hence it is no other than a fault of a word. Likewise, since the fault disappears as well on the change of the root हन् as that of the Átmanepada inflection, it is not a fault of a PART of a word.

Similarly in पद्मः (see § 574, *d.*), Unemployedness is to be recognized as a fault of a word, *not a part of a word.*

qq. As in Sanskrit so in Prakrit or other dialects is *the fault of* Solecism to be understood, when words want the peculiarities assigned to them by the respective Grammars.

Powerlessness, &c. distinguished. *rr.* Powerlessness (असमर्थत्वं),† *spoken of* in the text *as a fault of a word*, is when a vocable is used in a sense never applied to it; and Obsoleteness (निहतार्थत्वं) is when it is employed in a rare meaning. Obsoleteness can occur *only*

* *I. e.* With an odd number of eyes, or three-eyed.

† The author of the *Kávya-prakásá* owns that "the Unemployed, &c. are only certain varieties of the Powerless" though he has treated of them distinctively in pursuance of general custom. *Calcutta edition*, p. 82.

in words bearing more than one signification. Unintelligibility (अप्रतीतत्वं) may occur even in a word having but one sense, but not of universal application. Words conveying one meaning are the subject of Unemployedness (अप्रयुक्तत्वं), and those bearing more than one sense, of Powerlessness (असमर्थत्वं). Under Powerlessness *come* such *blemishes* as *the use of* हन्ति in the sense of going, which we do find in the Dictionary; but under Inexpressiveness we have such faults as दिव employed in the sense of 'luminous,' which is not given in the Dictionary. Such is the difference between them.

88. Thus have the faults of a sentence, homogeneous to those of a word, been declared. Those of a different class are now stated.

TEXT.

Faults peculiarly of a sentence or phrase—specified.

No. 575. Repugnance or Incongruity of Letters; Rejection, and Blunting, of the 'Visarga;' Redundancy, Deficiency, and Repetition, of a word; Lameness of Metre; Excellence falling off; Disjunction, Indecency, and Harshness, of 'Sandhi;' Isolation of a word in a distinct half; Resumption of the concluded; Failure of an intended connection; Syntactic Irregularity; an Unacceptable second sense; Omission of what must be said; Violation of Uniformity or Incongruity of Expression; Disregard of Usage; Misplacement of a word; a Compound (समास) out of place; Confusedness; the use of a Parenthesis: these are faults residing only in a sentence or phrase.

COMMENTARY.

Repugnance of Letters.

a. Repugnance of Letters is their inconsonance with the flavour *of the piece in which they occur, as is exemplified in these verses of mine:—*

ओवट्टइ उल्लट्टइ सअणे कहिम्पि मोट्टाअइ णो परिहट्टइ ।
हिअएण फिट्टइ लज्जाइ खुट्टइ दिहीए सा ॥*

(She turns over and rolls on the bed, towards none does she display gestures of love, she is confounded with shame, and her constancy keeps her stubborn.)

* This is not cited as an instance of Unmelodiousness (see § 574, *a.*) though the letters are unmelodious, the distinction between it and Literal Incongruity being this, that the former is simply harshness, whilst the latter fault may consist even in the smoothness of the letters, when the flavour, for instance, is the Heroic, or in other words the description is martial: For,

Here the ṭ's (ट) are opposed to the Erotic flavour (§608), being used merely for a display of skill *in alliteration.* It is, however, no fault when the letter occurs once, twice, thrice, or *even* four times, inasmuch as this does not so much injure the flavour.

The Rejection of the Visarga.

b. The REJECTION OF THE VISARGA is exemplified in गता निशा इमा बाले (Passed are these nights, O girl !)

The Blunting of the Visarga.

c. The BLUNTING OF THE VISARGA means its change into ओ, as *is shown in* धीरो वरो नरो याति (The gentle and excellent man goes).

The Redundancy of a word.

d. The REDUNDANCY OF A WORD is exhibited in पल्लवाकृतिरक्तोष्ठी (she with lips ruddy like the form of the new leaf), where the word आकृति (form) is redundant. So in सदाशिवं नौमि पिनाकपाणिम् (I adore S'iva, the holder of the Pináka bow) the epithet पिनाकपाणिम् ('holder' &c.) is superfluous. In such a sentence, however, as कुर्यां हरस्यापि पिनाकपाणेर्धैर्यच्युतिम्* (I can overthrow the fortitude even of S'iva, the holder of the Pináka bow) *the epithet* is proper, being used to convey a particular sense, *viz. the excessive valour of the speaker, Káma of the flowery bow, defying the Terrible God armed with the Pináka.* Or, *the same fault might be instanced* in "Kautsa spoke a speech" where the word 'speech' is unnecessary, the word 'spoke' being sufficient for the sense. Sometimes, however, its use is proper, when it is for the purpose of adding an epithet, as—'He spoke a sweet speech.' But some say that there too its employment is out of place, where the attributive may be used in an adverbial form, as—"Sweetly spoke the wise one."

The Deficiency of a word.

e. The DEFICIENCY OF A WORD is instanced in—"If a glance be cast on me, what need should I have of Indra's rank ?" where the word त्वया (by thee) is wanting.

"'Tis not enough no harshness gives offence,
The sound must seem an echo to the sense."

Literal Incongruity when the letters are smooth is exemplified in the following stanza, addressed by Ráma to Rávaṇa :—

वृन्दारकप्रकरमद्य करोम्यशङ्क
मानन्दयामि मुनिवृन्दममन्दमङ्ग ।
भङ्गं भुजङ्गमगणस्य भयं नयामि
त्वामन्तकातिथिमसन्तमहं विधाय ॥

* Kumára Sambhava, Canto III., stanza 10.

The Repetition of a word.

f. The **Repetition of a word** is shown in—"The wind, sportively blowing, breaks the languor of amorous sports," where the word लीला (sport) is repeated. So—अद्यु बिसं धृतविकासिबिसप्रसूना (They ate the fibres, holding an expanded lotus). Here बिस, *instead of being repeated*, should be referred to by a pronoun thus—धृतपरिस्फुटतत्प्रसूना.

Lameness of Metre. Its three kinds.

g. **Lameness of Metre**, *or lit., Dead Metre:* Metre is lame (1) when it is harsh, though conformable to its *prosodial* definition, or (2) when it is inconsonant with the flavour, or (3) when a verse ends in a short syllable that is not, *according to Prosody*, to be reckoned long. These are exemplified in their order :—

Metre harsh, though conformable to the definition.

(1) हन्त सततमेतस्या हृदयं भिन्ते मनोभवः कुपितः (Alas! the angry god of love constantly pierces her heart.)

Metre inconsistent with the Flavour.

(2) अयि मयि मानिनि मा कुरु मानम् (My proud lady! be not indignant against me.)

This Metre suits only the Comic Flavour.

Anomalous Metre.

(3) विकसितसहकारभारहारिपरिमल एष समागतो वसन्तः (The spring has arrived, delightfully fragrant with the exuberance of blooming mango trees.)

Here रि, *the final syllable of the first line, is short.*

h. As for the rule *of Prosody* that the final short syllable of a stanzaic line is reckoned long, it always respects only the second and fourth lines, except in the metre 'vasantatilaka' or the like, where it relates to the first and third lines *also.* In the above line, *instead* of परिमल एष समागतो वसन्तः, it would be proper to read प्रमुदितसौरभ आगतो वसन्तः, *as* रि *would be accented long being followed by the compound consonant* प्र.

i. Or we may take the following example—

अन्यास्ता गुणरत्नरोहणभुवो धन्या मृदन्यैव सा
सम्भाराः खलु तेऽन्य एव विधिना यैरेष सृष्टो युवा ।
श्रीमत्कान्तिजुषां द्विषां करतलात् स्त्रीणां नितम्बस्थलात्
दृष्टे यत्र पतन्ति मूढमनसामस्त्राणि वस्त्राणि च ॥

(Other are those lands which produce such gems of excellence, other is that blessed earth, other are those materials whereby the

Creator formed this youth, whom if his enemies or women of resplendent beauty but behold, down slip from their hands or hips the weapons or garments, agitated as they are *with fear or love.*)

Here the composition वस्त्राणि च sounds flaccid to the ear. If, however, we read वस्त्राण्यपि, it would sound strong and the fault be removed. The author of the Kávya Prakás'a *declares* it *to be an instance of a verse* ending in a short syllable not to be reckoned long. Others say—"it is properly *an instance of* the 'Harsh though conformable to the Definition' (§ 575, *g.*)"

Excellence falling off.

j. EXCELLENCE FALLING OFF *is shown in*—

प्रोज्ज्वलज्ज्वलनज्वालाविकटोरुसटाच्छटः ।
श्वासक्षिप्तकुलक्ष्माभृत् पातु वो नरकेसरी ॥

(May He of the half human and half leonine form preserve you—the glory of whose mighty mane is terrible like the blaze of the flaming fire—whose breath blew off the seven principal mountains!)

The alliterative excellence in this verse gradually falls off.

Disjunction of Sandhi.

k. DISJUNCTION OF SANDHI *is exhibited in*—

दलिते उत्पले एते अक्षिणी अमलाङ्गि ते ।

(O thou of bright form, these thy eyes are expanded blue lotuses.)

l. Such a disjunction of Sandhi, *conformable to grammar, as is illustrated here*, is a fault only when occurring more than once. The same, however, resorted to even once, to the violation of a Grammatical rule, merely for fear of violating the Metre, is a fault; *e. g.*

वासवाशामुखे भाति इन्दुश्चन्दनबिन्दुवत्

(The moon shines on the face of Indra's Quarter like a round *ornamental* mark of sandal.)

Indecency of Sandhi.

m. INDECENCY OF SANDHI is exemplified in चलण्डामरचेष्टितः. The Sandhi, here, *giving rise, as it does, to the word* लण्डा, is suggestive of disgust.

Harshness of Sandhi.

n. HARSHNESS OF SANDHI *is shown in*—

उर्व्यसावत्र तर्वाली मर्वन्ते चार्ववस्थितिः ।

(Yonder, at the end of this desert, there is a long line of trees beautifully situated.)

Here the Sandhis between उर्व्यां and असौ &c. are Harsh.

Isolation of a word in a distinct half.

o. Isolation of a word in a distinct half *is shown in this couplet* :—

इन्दु र्विभाति कर्पूरगौरै र्धवलयन् करैः ।
जगन्मा कुरु तन्वङ्गि मानं पादानते प्रिये ॥

(The moon shines whitening the world with camphor-white rays—be not unkind, O thou of slender form, to thy lover who is fallen at thy feet.)

The *word* जगत्, here, ought to be read in the first half *of the distich.*

Resumption of the Concluded.

p. Resumption of the Concluded *is exhibited in*—

नाशयन्तो घनध्वान्तं, तापयन्तो वियोगिनः ।
पतन्ति शशिनः पादा, भासयन्तः क्षमातलम् ॥

(Destroying the thick darkness and scorching the separated *lovers*, the beams of the moon fall—illuminating the earth.)

The fourth line in this stanza, (*viz.* भासयन्तः क्षमातलं) takes up again the sense already concluded.

Failure of an intended connection.

q. Failure of an intended connection* *is exemplified in the following* :—

* Prof. Goldstücker speaks of this fault under three heads, viz. (*a*) "connecting syntactically words which have no logical relation to each other," (*b*) "disconnecting syntactically words which are logically connected," and (*c*) "erring in the mode of connection." The example, however, which he cites from the Kávyaprakás'a in illustration of the first sort, does not, in kind, differ, in the slightest degree, from the instance here given, which he quotes to illustrate his second sort. The following is the example in the Kávyaprakás'a :—

येषां तास्त्रिदशेभदानसरितः पीताः प्रतापोष्मभि-
र्लीलापानभुवश्च नन्दनतरुच्छायासु यैः कल्पिताः ।
येषां हुङ्कृतयः कृतामरपतिक्षोभाः क्षपाचारिणां
किं तैस्त्वत्परितोषकारि विहितं किञ्चित् प्रवादोचितम् ॥

—which, retaining the fault, may be rendered in English thus :—

"They, the flames of whose triumphant energy drank up those streams of liquid *flowing from the temples* of the divine elephants, who made the shades of Indra's garden the places of their mirthful carousals, whose—the night-prowlers'—roarings troubled the prince of the gods, what have they done to thy satisfaction and in accordance with the report *of their prowess?*" (The printed Kávyaprakás'a reads चन्दनतरुच्छायासु instead of नन्दनतरु—, no doubt, by mistake.)

Now the Professor does not seem to have paid sufficient attention to the sense of the stanza, when he so strangely remarks upon it that "there is no logical relation between the words in the relative and those in the correlative sentence."

या जयश्री र्मनोजस्य यया जगदलङ्कृतं।
यामणाक्षीं विना प्राणा विफला मे कुतोऽद्य सा॥

(She who is the very glory of Cupid's victory, who is an ornament of the world, without whom—the fawn-eyed—my existence is vain, alas! where is she now?)

Here, since the three clauses marked by the relative यद् (who), are independent, or irrespective, of each other, the word एणाक्षी (fawn-eyed) occurring in one of them cannot have a connection with the others, though meant so by the poet. *If for the second verse of the above couplet* we read—

यां विना ऽमी वृथा प्राणा एणाक्षी सा कुतो ऽद्य मे।

—then the word एणाक्षी falling within the clause marked by the term तद् (she), *i. e. the correlative clause*, can be related to all the foregoing clauses marked by the term यद्, *i. e. the relative clauses.*

r. Or we may take another example:—

Another example. ईक्षसे यत् कटाक्षेण तदा धन्वी मनोभवः

(As thou lookest with the corner of thy eye, then holds Cupid his bow.)

Here the word यत् *(as* or *since)* can have no correlation with the word तदा (then.) The proper reading would be ईक्षसे चेत् (if thou lookest.)

s. Or for example:—

Another example.

ज्योत्स्ना च यः पयःपूरस्तारकाः कैरवाणि च।
राजति व्योमकासारराजहंसः सुधाकरः॥

(The moon-light is the flood of water, the stars are the lilies,—the moon shines as a noble swan in the lake of ether.)

Here the word कासार (lake) being reduced to a subordinate position in the compound, the object denoted by it cannot be connected with those meant by the other words, *viz.* पयःपूर &c., *which, however, are intended to be connected therewith, as its essential and adjuncts.*

How "Nondiscrimination of the Predicate, &c." differs from the above fault.

t. In "Nondiscrimination of the Predicate, the Apodotic or the Emphatic" (§ 574 *m & n*) that *word or phrase* only is faulty which, *though it ought to be*, is not, discriminated. Whilst, here, since the object 'कासार' (lake), chief as it is, is not so apprehended, all the *other* objects such as the पयःपूर (watery flood) and the like are not understood as subordinate thereto, and hence the whole sentence conveys an incongruous meaning. This is the difference between the two *faults.*

u. The following also, is, by some, considered an instance of the same fault :—

Another example according to some.

"My sword, O Bhṛigu's son, is ashamed in being resolved to cope with this battle-axe of thine that cut off the head of thy mother."*

Here, in reproaching Paras'u Ráma, it is not proper to ascribe to the AXE the agency in cutting off† the head of his mother. So say the ancients. But the moderns declare that it is this *form of expression* that displays wit,‡ for the reproach against Paras'u Ráma is more strongly felt, *being reflected* through the blaming of the axe.

Syntactic Irregularity.

v. SYNTACTIC IRREGULARITY ; as—

समय एव करोति बलाबलं प्रणिगदन्त इतीव शरीरिणां।
शरदि हंसरवाः परुषीकृतस्वरमयूर मयू रमणीयताम्॥

('Time it is that is the cause of power and weakness among creatures'—thus proclaiming, as it were, the cries of the swan in autumn, attained to a charmingness that made the peacock's voice harsh.)

Here, the particle इति ('thus') should be used just after the sentence it refers to, not after प्रणिगदन्तः.

Another example.

w. Similarly—

द्वयं गतं सम्प्रति शोचनीयतां
समागमप्रार्थनया कपालिनः।§
कला च सा कान्तिमती कलावतस्
त्वमस्य लोकस्य च नेत्रकौमुदी॥

(Two have now made themselves pitiable by wishing for an association with Him of the human skull (S'iva)—that lovely digit of the moon, and thou the moon-light to the eye of this world.)

* In this stanza, instead of बद्धस्पर्द्ध Prof. Goldstücker wrongly reads बद्धस्पर्श, and makes the following not very intelligible remark upon the example:—"—the word परशु, although intended to express the reason, (?) has no logical connection with the blame uttered against Paras'u Ráma."

† Here instead of मातृकण्ठच्छेदनकर्तृत्वस्य, as read in Roer's edition, my MS. has simply मातृकण्ठच्छेदनस्य which the commentator indeed explains by—छेदनकर्तृत्वस्य.

‡ My MS. here leaves out the वैदग्ध्य of Roer's edition.

§ The Calcutta edition of the Kumára-sambhava, to which belongs this stanza, reads पिनाकिनः instead of कपालिनः

Here the च (*que*) should come immediately after त्वं ('thou.')

An Unacceptable second sense.

x. An UNACCEPTABLE SECOND SENSE;* as, 'Wounded in the heart by the irresistible arrow of that Cupid Ráma,' &c. (§ 182, *a.*)

Here the second sense suggestive of the Erotic Flavour is not acceptable, being opposed to the proper Relish of the piece, *viz. the Heroic or Disgustful* (see § 242.)

The Omission of what must be said.

y. The OMISSION OF WHAT MUST BE SAID; as—

"What particle of impropriety having seen in me, dost thou become angry, my fair-eyed lady?"

Here अपि ('even') is omitted, though it must necessarily be said, *thus*—'What particle EVEN' &c.

Difference between this fault and 'Deficiency of a word.'

z. In the *fault termed* 'Deficiency of a word' (§ *e.*) the deficiency meant is that of a SIGNIFICANT word, whilst अपि, *the word omitted in the present instance*, is not such: this is *what makes the* difference between the two *faults*. So in other cases.

aa. Or (if the above-mentioned distinction be not admitted) we may take another example:—

Another example.

चरणानतकान्तायास्तन्वि कोपस्तथापि ते

(Having thy lover fallen at thy feet, thou art still angry, slender one.)

Here the proper expression would be चरणानतकान्ताऽसि (Thou hast thy lover fallen at thy feet.)

Violation of Uniformity.

bb. VIOLATION OF UNIFORMITY, OR INCONGRUITY OF EXPRESSION: For example—

एवमुक्तो मन्त्रिमुख्यै रावणः प्रत्यभाषत।

(Thus spoken to by his chief counsellors, Rávaṇa replied.)

* Prof. Goldstücker explains अमतपरार्थ, or a sentence with the present fault,—"Having another sense (viz. one) which is at variance *with (that of!) the subject-matter*"—instead of saying "—with the principal meaning, or the sense connected with the subject." The stanza here cited is the 20th of the 11th canto of the Raghuvans'a, and the Professor is again wrong in remarking upon it—"The erotic character of which sentence, as the Kávyaprakás'a observes, is at variance with the character of the poem where it occurs." Neither is the sentence of an erotic character, nor would its character, if supposed to be erotic, be at variance with the character of the poem, nor—if its character *were* at variance with that of the poem—would the circumstance constitute the fault in question, nor does the author of the Kávyaprakás'a say all this.

Here, at first, Rávaṇa's being spoken to is expressed by the verb वच्, so his replying also should be expressed by the same verb.* Thus, रावणः प्रत्यवोचत would be the proper reading. Nor in such a case would there be the fault of 'Repetition of a word' (§ 575 *f.*), for the case where something is mentioned and re-mentioned is beyond the sphere of such a fault, and here the speaking (or being spoken to) and replying have *respectively* the characters of 'something that is mentioned' and 'something that is re-mentioned, or referentially mentioned.' For instance, 'Red rises the sun and red it sets'—here if the same meaning *of red* were to be expressed by another word, then this distinct word, seeming as if it conveyed a distinct sense, would obstruct our apprehension of the meaning *of the sentence*.

cc. Or for example—

Another example.

ते हिमालयमामन्त्र्य पुनः प्रेक्ष्य च शूलिनं ।
सिद्धञ्चास्मै निवेद्यार्थं तद्विसृष्टाः खमुद्ययुः ॥

(Having taken leave of Himálaya, visited again the God with the trident, and announced to him that his object had been gained, they, dismissed by him, ascended the heavens.)

Here what is first spoken of by *the pronoun* इदम् (अस्मै in the Dative) should be referred to by the same word or by *one of* its equivalents एतद्, अदः, not by the word तद्.

dd. Or to take another example:—

Another example. "The earth is bounded by the ocean and this Lord of waters *extends* a hundred *yojanas*."

Here it would be proper to read—'The earth is measured by the Lord of the waters and this Lord of the waters' &c.

ee. Similarly—

Another example. "Whether it be to acquire fame, or with a wish to obtain happiness, or even to transcend being counted among mortals—*be it for whatever purpose*—whoever resort to patient application—Prosperity comes, as with eagerness, into their laps."

Here instead of—'with a wish to obtain happiness' we should properly read, *simply*—'to obtain happiness.'

* My MS. as well as Roer's edition reads here—अत्र वचधातुना प्रक्रान्तं प्रतिवचनमपि तेनैव वक्तुमुचितम्, which can scarcely make sense unless we suppose वचनमिति to be omitted after प्रक्रान्तं, through a mistake of the scribes. My translation is according to this corrected reading.

ff. Among these *examples*, in the first two we have Violation of Uniformity* in a Radical; in the third we have the fault occurring in a Synonym; and in the fourth, in an affix. Similarly of other *cases than those illustrated here.*

Disregard of usage.

gg. DISREGARD OF USAGE; as—"The dire croaking (रव) of the clouds." The usage is to speak of the roaring of the clouds and this is here disregarded. To this effect has it been said:—

"*The sound* of an anklet (मञ्जीर) or the like, *it is the custom to call* 'tinkling' (रणित); that of birds' voice, 'warbling;' that in dalliance, muttering (स्तनित) or murmuring (मणित); and that of clouds 'roaring' (गर्ज्जित) or the like."

hh. MISPLACEMENT OF A WORD is exemplified in—

Misplacement of a word.

तीर्थे तदीये गजसेतुबन्धात् प्रतीपगामुत्तरतोऽस्य गङ्गां ।
अयत्नबालव्यजनीबभूवु र्हंसा नभोलङ्घनलोलपक्षाः ॥

("As he crossed the Ganges, that flowed westward from the bridging of elephants along its ford, swans moving through the air with waving wings became his *chowries—chowries brought about* without the aid of art." *Raghuvans'a*, XVI. 33.)

Here गङ्गा should properly be read BEFORE the word तदीये† *which refers to it.*

Another example.

ii. Similarly—"Bad is that master who does not hear his friends (हितान्न यः संशृणुते)." *Kirátárjuniya*, I. 5.

Here the collocation of the negative (नञ्) should properly be *immediately* before *the verb* संशृणुते.

* The *Kávya-prakás'a* reckons 'incongruity of order' also under प्रक्रमभङ्ग and cites the following example from Rhavabhúti's Víracharita:—

अकलिततपस्तेजोवीर्य्यप्रथिम्नि यशोनिधा-
ववितथमदाध्माते रोषान्मुनावभिधावति ।
अभिनवधनुर्विद्यादर्पक्षमायच कर्म्मणे
स्फुरति रभसात् पाणिः पादोपसंग्रहणायच ॥

The following celebrated lines of *Hamlet* are an example of the same fault—

"O, what a noble mind is here o'erthrown!
The courtier's, soldier's, scholar's eye, tongue, sword;" &c.

† Mallinátha, however, removes the fault by interpreting तदीये by वैन्ध्ये *i. e.*, making it refer to Vindhya, spoken of in the foregoing stanza.

Why this is counted a fault of a sentence.

jj. The fault *instanced in these two examples*, is *spoken of as* a blemish of a sentence, since the whole of the sentence is slow in conveying the intended meaning, though only one word is inserted in a wrong place. Similarly *should it be understood* of others *of the faults here reckoned, that at first sight seem to be only blemishes of a word.*

This, according to some, pertains only to a word significant in itself.

kk. With respect to the just-mentioned example, some say—'By the term पद (word) *in the compound* अस्थानस्थपदता (the designation of the fault in question) is meant an expression significant *by itself*, but *the negative particle* नञ् (not) has not this character, as its incapability *of conveying a sense independently of other words* is undisputed; hence, as in the stanza beginning—द्वयं गतं (§ 575 *w.*) there is the fault of Syntactic Irregularity, so also is it here.'

ll. A Compound out of place: For example—

A Compound out of place.

अद्यापि स्तनशैलदुर्गविषमे सीमन्तिनीनां हृदि
स्थातुं वाञ्छति मान एष धिगिति क्रोधादिवालोहितः ।
प्रोद्यन्* दूरतरप्रसारितकरः कर्षत्यसौ तत्क्षणात्
फुल्लत्कैरवकोषनिःसरदलिश्रेणीकृपाणं शशी ॥

"O fie! Does this Pride yet wish to dwell in woman's heart inaccessibly fortified as it is with that mountain of her breast'—thus exclaiming, yon rising Moon, red with rage, stretching far his hands (or rays कर), in a moment draws his sword—the series of bees issuing out of the opening bud (or sheath—कोष) of the water-lily."

Here, *long* compounds are not used in the *supposed* speech of the angry *Moon* (*—where they would have been appropriate as being suggestive of the ardour and vigour of the speaker—*), but they are used in the words of the poet.

Confusedness.

mm. Confusedness is the insertion into a sentence, of words belonging to a distinct sentence. As—

"Forego the moon, fawn-eyed one, and behold *thy* pride in the celestial court.

Properly here—'Behold the moon in the celestial court and forego thy pride.'

* The printed *Sáhitya-darpaṇa* and *Kávya-prakás'a* have both here प्रोद्यत्, in composition with the next word. My MS. prehaps rightly reads प्राद्यन apart.

Its difference from Obscurity.

nn. 'Obscurity' respects only one sentence, *or a sentence independently of another*, so it is distinct from the present fault.

A Parenthesis.

oo. A PARENTHESIS is a distinct sentence *wholly* inserted into a *principal* one. As—

"Towards thy lover now humbly bending at thy feet, (I tell you, my fair friend, the truth), anger is by no means proper."

pp. He *now* mentions the faults of the Sense :—

TEXT.

The faults of Sense specified.

No. 576. Irrelevancy, Impropriety of Order, Rusticity, Contradiction or Inconsistency, Indecency, Obscurity, Monotony or Want of Variety, Inconsequentiality, Repugnant Suggestion, Dubiousness, Tautology, Opposition to Notoriety, Opposition to Science, Incompleteness, Dissimilitude of the Associated, Introduction into a Wrong Place, a Specification where there is no particularity, a Limitation where no restriction is required; Contraries of these, Impropriety of Predication, Impropriety of Attribution, and Resumption of the Concluded : These are declared to be the Faults of the Sense *or Idea.*

COMMENTARY.

a. 'Contraries of these'—*i. e.* Non-specification where there is a Particularity and Non-limitation where there is a Restriction.

Irrelevancy.

b. Of these faults *above enumerated*, IRRELEVANCY consists in not being auxiliary to the principal sense. As—

"Behold, my love, the moon in the expanded heaven, and give up thy anger."

Here *the notion conveyed by* the word 'expanded,' *i. e. the circumstance of the heavens being spread out*, does not in any way contribute towards *the lady's* quitting her indignation.

How, different from 'Redundancy of a word.'

c. In the case of 'Redundancy of a word,' the blemish becomes evident simultaneously with the apprehension of the connection among the meanings of the *several* words, whilst here *it comes to be recognized* afterwards. This *makes* the difference.

d. IMPROPRIETY OF ORDER; *e. g.*

Impropriety of order. "Give me a horse, O king, or a mighty elephant, majestically slow."

Rusticity. *e.* RUSTICITY; as, "Do thou lie down by me"—"My Lord, I am presently lying down."

Here the idea is rustic, or coarse.

Contradiction. *f.* When having at first declared the excellence or inferiority of an object, we speak otherwise afterwards, it is *termed* CONTRADICTION. For example—

"The digit of the new moon and other *such fair* things charm not the heart of those young men who behold this slender-bodied *lady*, the moon-light to the eyes of the world."

Here the lady is represented as the moon-light for her charming those very persons to whom the lunar digit is not a cause of delight.

Indecency. *g.* INDECENCY; as—

हन्तुमेव प्रवृत्तस्य स्तब्धस्य विवरैषिणः ।
यथाऽऽशु जायते पातो न तथा पुनरुन्नतिः ॥

(That *man* rises not again so soon as he falls, who is ever rigidly bent on striking and is always seeking for holes, *or the faults of others.*)

Here the *second* sense is indecent, *and suggested as it is by the principal* MEANING *of the sentence and not by the mere words, it is a fault of the* SENSE, *and is therefore distinguished from the same fault, occurring in a word,* sentence or Sandhi (see § 574 *b.* and *t.* and § 575 *m*).

h. OBSCURITY; *as*—

Obscurity. "It is the God of day, not the clouds, that rains pure water out of its rays. Verily is she (*Yamuná*) the daughter of the Sun who has swelled the floods of the Celestial Stream (Gangá). And is there the being who believes not in Vyása's Word (the Puráṇas), or has no faith in the Scripture? yet this deluded doe would see no water in the beams of the Glorious *luminary.*"

Here *what is meant is this:* 'Since the origin of the rain and the *personified river* Yamuná is the sun, their waters too are *directly* generated by the sun; hence it is proper that the sun's rays should cause the preception of water, yet the doe, deluded as she is, perceives no water in them.' This sense, which is not principally intended, is itself hard to be understood, and the more difficult is it, through it, to understand the principal sense* *thus allegorically represented.* So *we have here the fault of* Obscurity.

i. " The sun always traverses the heavens, the wind always blows, *the serpent* Vasuki always bears the earth, and the brave are always free from bragging."

Monotony.

Here the invariability is not expressed *in each of the four cases* by varied language. We admit the existence of this fault, Monotony, in this passage, inasmuch as no beauty is added to it by the mere removal of the repetition of 'always' by the use of equivalents. Thus it is distinguished from the fault termed Repetition of a word. (§ 575 *f.*). *To convey a clear idea of this fault,* we shall exemplify *its opposite,* viz. Diversity of expression :

" The Sun has yoked his horses once for all, the wind blows day and night, the Serpent ever bears the earth, and such is also the duty of him (the king) who lives upon the produce of the sixth part of the land."

Diversity of expression.

j. " Farewell to thee, Weapon, since I too will quit thee—thou weapon that wast abandoned, from grief for his son (falsely reported to be dead), not from timidity—even by him who bore thee, (improper though it was for a Brahman to bear arms), for fear of being overcome by his enemy Drupada,—by whose prowess none there was who has not been thy mark."

Inconsequentiality.

Here the reason for the second laying aside of the weapon is not stated, so there is an instance of Inconsequentiality.

Repugnant Intimation.

k. " May thy son, O Lord of men, obtain royalty."

Here we have a Repugnant Intimation,† since the passage suggests the repugnant thought, ' Do thou die.'

Obscurity.

l. " Say, ye wise, whether mountains or women are to be resorted to."

Here, there being nothing particular for the subject-matter, there is an absence of certainty as to which of the two characters the

* This, according to the commentator, is the unwillingness of a newly married coy lady to believe that she would obtain what she could desire, in the company of her lord.

† Its difference from Repugnant Suggestion [P. 574. *b.*], according to the commentator, consists in the fact that the repugnant notion in the present fault is suggested by the *sense* of the sentence, while that in the other is suggested by the *words*.

speaker may be, a quietist or a lover. There is, therefore, the fault of Obscurity.

Repetition.

m. "Let not a man heedlessly do a deed: indiscretion is the principal resting-place of evils. For merit-loving Prosperity, of her own accord, chooses the man who acts with prudence."

Here the second half of the stanza conveys contrariwise the same sense as the second line, and hence there is a Repetition.

Opposition to notoriety; e. g.—

Opposition to notoriety.

n. "Then did Hari move in the battle, bearing a sharpened trident."

Here the trident of Hari, which people do not know respecting this deity, he being always represented with a discus, is spoken of faultily.

o. Or for example:—

Another example.

"The As'oka, by the stroke of thy feet, bristles with newly sprouted shoots."

It is notorious, *according to the fancy of the poets*, that flowers, and not new shoots, are produced in the As'oka tree by the stroke of women's feet. There is here consequently an Opposition to the conventional usage of the poets.

Opposition to Science.

p. "The wound of the nail in the under-lip of the fawn-eyed lady."

Here we have an Opposition to Science, *the wounding of the under-lip by the nail* being opposed to the erotic science.

Incompleteness.

q. "The breaking of [Is'a's] S'iva's bow, and the rise of a Kshattriya, and that gem—a fair woman—, how can Paras'u Ráma bear *these* now?"

Here the word 'to overlook' is wanting after 'that gem—a fair woman—.' We have, therefore, the fault of Incompleteness.

r. "A good man fallen into adversity, a woman with her breasts fallen, and a bad man respected in an assembly are to my heart's distress."

Here a 'good man,' and a 'woman' are agreeable objects, and a 'bad man' associated with them is disagreeable; hence there is in the passage the fault termed 'Dissimilarity of the associated.'

Introduction into a wrong place.

s. "His authority is familiar with the crest-gem of Indra; the scripture is to him a new eye, his devotion is to the Lord of beings who bears the Pináka bow (S'iva); his habitation is Lanká the heavenly city; and his birth is in the family of Brahmá. Such a bridegroom then is indeed not to be found, were it not that he is Rávana, and how can all excellences be expected everywhere?"

Here *the passage* ought to be concluded at *the word* Rávana.

Improper Specification. *t.* "How may we describe the ocean, the receptacle of diamonds?"

Here should be said in general 'the receptacle of gems.'

Improper limitation. *u.* "Thy navel is but an eddy, thine eyes are blue lotuses, the wrinkles in thy waist are the waves. Therefore thou art a lake full of the water of loveliness."

Here the limitation *implied* in '*but* an eddy' should not be made.

Improper non-specification. *v.* "Ladies resorting to their lovers go in the night covered with a blue wrapper."

Here the night should be particularly specified thus—'in the dark nights.'

Improper non-limitation. *w.* "What do not men do immersed in pleasure affording present gratification."

Here there should be a limitation made thus—'affording *but* (एव) present gratification.

x. 'But,' *somebody might object*, in *the fault termed* 'Omission of what must be said' there is the absence, for instance, of अपि in such examples as, 'What particle of impropriety' &c. (§. 575. y), and here there is the absence of एव, what then is their difference? To this reply some: 'It is the omission of a limitation separately taken, that is the subject-matter of the *present fault of* non-limitation.' This is not the case, since, were it even so, *i. e. if Non-limitation were really only a species of Omission of what must be said*, there would be no criterion for the two being reckoned respectively as the faults of a word and of sense. "Then what is to be our alternative? how are we to escape *from the dilemma?*" Well, the difference is this, that in the line व्यतिक्रमलवं कं मे वीक्ष्य वामाक्षि कुप्यसि, for example, the fault becomes manifest on the mere utterance of the words, but here it is perceived after the apprehension of the *whole* meaning. So that the *two* divisions of faults of word and sense, though held by the ancients as founded upon the circumstance of their bearing or not bearing an ex-

Criterion of fault of the word and that of the sense.

change of words, terminate in this :—The fault that does not bear (i. e. disappears on) an exchange of the words is of course the fault of a word; but that too is the fault of a word which is perceived before the apprehension of the logical connection of words. And that fault which is apprehended after the sense is understood, pertains to the sense. Similarly is to be understood the distinction of Improper Limitation (§. 576, *u*), &c. from the Redundancy of a word &c. As to *the fault named* an Unacceptable second sense, for instance in रामसन्मथ इत्यादि (§. 182, *a*), from the consideration of its pervading, of necessity, the whole sentence, it is held to be a fault of the whole sentence. But Indecency and others do not of necessity pervade the sentence.

Impropriety of Predication.

y. "He will kill his enemies, while he has gladdened his friends."

Here what is intended to be predicated is that having killed his enemies, he will gladden his friends.

Impropriety of Attribution.

z. "Crest-ornament of the lord of Chaṇḍí (or Durgá), O Moon, who dispellest the darkness of the world, and takest the life of the absent lover, torment me not in vain."

Here in the speech of an absent lover, that which is denoted by the third quarter of the stanza, *i. e. the fact of his taking the lives of separated lovers*, should not be attributed to the subject, *the moon, who is propitiatorily addressed.*

"'That Sword, its whole length covered with blood (or, her frame filled with the warmth of passion), which clung to the enemy's neck, which was seen by the enemy falling upon the elephants (or seen by others falling upon libidinous men),—attached to that Sword this man heeds not aught. Be it known to you, by him have I been given up to his retainers.' Thus to speak, by Lakshmí's appointment, as it were, his Fame has gone to Ocean *(her father)*."

Here the sentence, though concluded by 'be it known to you,' is again taken up with 'by him' &c.

He now states the faults of Flavour.

Text.

The Faults of Flavour specified.

No. 577. The expression of Flavour (1) by its own term, (2) as also that of a Permanent, or (3) Concomitant (i e. Accessory) Mood, the admission of the elements of a conflicting Flavour such as an Excitant or the like belonging to it, a Far-fetched Ensuant or Accessory, an Unseasonable Introduction, Unseasonable Interruption, or a Repeated Heightening of Flavour, Overlooking of a Principal Element, Celebration of an Unimportant Object, Excessive Expansion of a Subordinate Element, Perversion of Character, and improprieties of other kinds are held to be Faults pertaining to the Flavour.

COMMENTARY.

a. 'The expression of Flavour by its own term,' i. e. by the word Flavour or Relish (रस) or such words as Amorous Desire (शृङ्गार) and the like. For examples in their order :—

a. तामुद्वीक्ष्य कुरङ्गाक्षीं रसो नः कोऽप्यजायत

(Having beheld that fawn-eyed lady there was experienced by us an inexpressible relish.)

b. चन्द्रमण्डलमालोक्य शृङ्गारे मग्नमन्तरम् ।

('Having seen the lunar orb, my heart was sunk in amorous desire.')

c. The expression of a Permanent Mood by its own term, as—

"Love (रति) was excited in her when thou wast before her eyes."

d. The expression of an Accessory by its own term, as—

"The coy lady was ashamed on being kissed by her lover."

Here in the first quarter of the stanza, it would be proper to describe the shame through its Ensuant *or effect* (see § 162) and read thus, 'she closed her eyes.'

Admission of Elements of a conflicting Flavour. *e.* "Be not indignant, lady of the slender frame, seeing that youth is not lasting."

Here the announcement of the transitoriness of youth is an element of the Quietistic Flavour (see § 238) which is opposed to the Erotic (§ 210), and it is an Excitant (§ 61) of the same Quietistic Flavour alone, so that its admission into the Erotic is improper.

Far-fetched Ensuant. *f.* "Behold the slender lady with smiling face, slightly casting a side-glance, as the cool-rayed moon, delighting the eyes of the world, whitens the earth."

Here the Substantial and Enhancing Excitants (see § 62) of the Flavour terminate in an Ensuant, but it is a forced Conception.

Far-fetched Excitant. *g.* "He shuns pleasure, loses all self-possession, frequently falls down and rolls about; thus, alas, a hard fate violently overcomes his frame. How can we help it?"

Here, the shunning of pleasure &c., being also possible in the Pathetic or the like, such an Excitant as a woman is implied in a forced manner.

h. An Unseasonable Introduction; as in the second act of the Veṇísaṇhára, the representation of Duryodhana's love towards his wife Bhánumatí at a time when so many heroes were perishing in war.

i. An *Unseasonable* Interruption; as in the Víra Charita, the speech of Rama, *viz.* 'I am going to take off my bracelet,' when the fight between Ráma and Parasu Rama was just about to begin.

j. A Repeated Heightening; as, *for instance,* in the Kumára Sambhava, *the too frequent heightening of pathos* in Rati's lament.

k. Overlooking of a Principal Object; as, in the fourth act of Ratnávalí, the forgetting of Ságariká on the arrival of Bábhravya.

l. Celebration of an Unimportant Object; as in the Karpuramanjari, the praising of the bard's description of the spring, to the neglect of that by the king and the heroine themselves.

m. An Excessive Expansion of a Subordinate Element; as in the Kirátárjuníya, the sports of the celestial nymphs.

Perversion of Character. *n.* The characters are divine, human, and both human and divine; these are subdivided (§ 66) into 'high-spirited but temperate and firm,' 'firm and haughty,' 'gay and thoughtful yet firm,' and 'firm and mild;' and these again are further subdivided into the 'best,' 'middling,' and 'lowest.' The representation of any of these, not in accordance with what they are, is the fault termed the 'Perversion of Character.' As for example, Ráma's killing Bálin, by artifice, like a 'firm and haughty' character, though he was 'high-spirited, but temperate and firm.' Or as in the Kumára Sambhava, the description of the amorous enjoyments of the supreme divinities Síva and Párvatí. They (*i. e.*, the author of the Kávyaprakása) remark upon it that this, like the description of the enjoyment of our parents, is infinitely improper. Other improprieties are representations of time or place or the like otherwise than as they are; for in such cases there is an impossibility of teaching those that are to be taught (see § 2), from the poems seeming untrue.

Text.

No. 578. Apart from these there is no possibility of Faults of Ornament.

Commentary.

a. 'From these,' *i. e.*, from the said faults. Such a blemish, for instance, in the ornament of Simile, as a dissimilarity, or impossibility, or an inferiority, or superiority of the comparison, as to genus or size, and *such a fault in the ornament termed* Transition as the confirmation of a poetically fancied fact, are *no other than that spoken of as the blemish of a word and sentence under the title of* Improper Signification (§§ 574, 575). For examples in their order:

Dissimilarity in Simile. *b.* "I wreathe a poetical moon with the extended strings or rays (रश्मि) of sense."

Impossibility in Simile. *c.* "Thy arrows fall like a burning shower of rain."

Inferiority in Simile. *d.* "Like an outcast that king has exceeding bravery in war."

"The lunar orb shines like a lump of camphor."

Superiority in Simile. "Like S'iva this peacock shines with an azure throat."

Confirmation of a poetically fancied fact, a fault. *e.* "Who (Himalaya) protects from the sun darkness, like an owl, lying hidden in the mountain caves: great indeed is the tenderness of those of lofty souls (lit. elevated heads) even to a low person who has resorted to them for refuge."

In such cases as the above, the matter mentioned being no real fact, its proper character consists in its merely appearing to be so; its confirmation therefore is improper.

Incomplete Rhyme. *f.* The fault of a Rhyme occurring only in three lines of a stanza is that termed Unemployedness (§ 574*d*). For example:—

सह साऽऽलिजनैः स्निग्धैः सहसा कुञ्जमन्दिरम् ।
उदिते रजनीनाथे सहसा याति सुन्दरी ॥

('On a sudden, as the moon rose, that beautiful one, with her affectionate friends, goes out, smiling, to the grove-house')

g. In the Ornament of Poetical Fancy, the word यथा has the fault of Inexpressiveness (§ 574 *jj.*), when used to imply a fancy. For example:—

एष मूर्त्तो यथा धर्मः क्षितिपो रक्षति क्षितिम्।

('This monarch preserves the earth, as if he were Justice, embodied in a material form.')

h. So in the case of the ornament of Alliteration (अनुप्रास), when it is opposed to the proper style, *i. e., the peculiar literal style agreeable to the flavour of the piece,* it has *the fault named* Repugnance of Letters (see § 575*d.*). As for instance in ओवट्टइ उल्लट्टइ सअणे &c. ('She rolls over and turns on the bed,' &c.)

i. And in a Simile, when there is a redundancy or deficiency in the common attribute, there is *the fault termed* Redundancy of a Word or Deficiency of a Word (see § 575. *d. e.*). For examples in their order:—

Redundancy in a Simile. "S'iva with a radiance white from Vibhúti (the sacred ashes that smear his body), shines with the splendour of his eyes, as an autumnal cloud with the lightning flash, bearing a fragment of blue cloud (नीलवारिदखण्डक)."

Here the Holy One not being represented as having an azure throat, the fourth quarter of the stanza is redundant.

Deficiency in the same. "Embraced by Lakshmí and charming with a necklace of radiant pearls, the foe of Mura (Vishṇu) shines like a blue cloud adorned with lightning."

Here that which Vishṇu is compared to, *viz.*, the 'blue cloud,' should be represented as attended with cranes, *in correspondence to the circumstance of the deity's being ornamented with a pearl necklace.*

Incongruity in Simile. *j.* In the same ornament, the difference between the thing compared and that to which it is compared, as to gender and number, as also that as to tense, person, predication or the like, come under the fault termed Incongruity of Expression (see § 575 *bb.*) For examples in their order:—

(1). सुधेव विमलश्चन्द्रः ('The moon pure as ambrosia.')

(2). ज्योत्स्ना इव सिता कीर्त्तिः ('Fame white as moonbeams.')

(3). "Inexpressible was the lustre of the two, as they were travelling, dressed in pure garments, like the splendour of the moon and Chitrá (the star) at the conjunction, when they are freed from mist."

Here the fact is not that the splendour of Chitrá and the moon so circumstanced WAS only *in past time*, but that it also IS constantly taking place.

(4). लतेव राजसे तन्वि ('Like a creeper shinest thou, O tender lady.')

Here *the verb* राजसे ('shinest') *used for* त्वम् ('thou') cannot be, as it is meant to be, construed with लता ('a creeper') which should take the third personal verb राजते ('shines'), *an ellipsis of the same being here inadmissible.*

(5). चिरं जीवतु ते सूनुर्मार्कण्डेयमुनिर्यथा ।

('Long live thy son as the saint Márkaṇḍeya.')

The saint Márkaṇḍeya lives and this fact ought not here to be predicated of him by the rb *of the benedictive mood* जीवतु ('may live') which is syntactically to be construed with Márkaṇḍeya.

k. In the present case, however, *viz., that of the ornament of Simile*, where *the expression denoting* the common property, in spite of the difference of gender or number in the object to which the comparison is made, is not incongruous, there is no fault. For examples in their order:—

(1). "The face shines as the moon."

(2). तद्वेषोऽसदृशोऽन्याभिः स्त्रीभिर्मधुरताभृतः ।
दधते स्म परां शोभां तदीया विभ्रमा इव ॥

('Unlike that of other women, her dress, laden with sweetness, exhibited the highest splendour, as her blandishments.')

In the former examples, since *the expression* of the common property comes to be logically connected with only one of the two objects compared together, the intended sense is evidently not properly conveyed.

Irrelevant Alliteration.

l. Similarly when the alliteration is useless *or does not minister to the heightening of the sentiment*, it has the fault of Irrelevancy. For instance—

स्वनपुरणन्मणिमेखलमविरलसिञ्जानमञ्जुमञ्जीरम् ।
परिसरणमरुणचरणे रणरणकमकारणं कुरुते ॥

('Thy ramble, crimson-footed lady, excites but in vain fancies of love, as thy girdle of gems sharply sounds, and continuously tinkles thy musical anklet.')

This, according to the commentator, is a speech of disaffection, and the musical assonance of soft consonants employed in the couplet is of no use and therefore irrelevant in this place, being favourable only to the Erotic Flavour.

m. Similarly the Modal Metaphor (समासोक्ति) has the fault of Tautology, when the second object (*i. e.*, the object to which the comparison is made), is expressed, though understood by the force of the attributes equally applicable to both objects of comparison; and the Indirect Description (अप्रस्तुतप्रशंसा) has the same fault when the principal sense though apprehended by suggestion is verbally mentioned. For examples in their order :—

(1). अनुरागवन्तमपि लोचनयोर्दधतं वपुः सुखमतापकरं

निरकासयद्रविमपेतवसुं वियदालयादपरदिग्गणिका ।

('Though he was in love [or red], gave no pain [or heat], and bore a form pleasant, *or not dazzling*, to the eyes, that courtesan, the Western Quarter, as his wealth was exhausted [or as he was shorn of his rays], drove the Sun out of the mansion of ether.')

Here by the expression 'Western Quarter' alone the character of a courtesan would be understood in respect of it, *the addition therefore of the term 'courtesan' is tautological.*

(2). 'The musquito, coming forward when the wanderers of the heavens are invited, is not prevented; amber dwelling in the midst or in the front of the gems takes their lead; even the glow-worm trembles not to intrude among luminaries: Fie to the common property that, like a senseless master, recognises not the difference of things.'

Here the actual mention of 'a senseless master' is improper.

n. So in the Embellishment named Alliteration अनुप्रास (see 633) the absence of notoriety has the character of the fault 'Opposition to Notoriety.' As :—

चक्राधिष्ठिततां चक्री गोत्रं गोत्रभिदुच्छ्रितम् ।

वृषं वृषभकेतुश्च प्रायच्छद्यस्य भूभुजः ॥

(‘The Wielder of the Discus bestowed upon this monarch the dominion of an emperor, the Render of the Mountains the lofty umbrella, and He with the bull on his banner endued him with holiness.’)

o. The said faults are sometimes no faults, and sometimes positive merits. So he declares:—

TEXT.

Harshness, when a merit.

No. 579. When the speaker is enraged, or the theme lofty, Unmelodiousness becomes a merit, but it is absolutely so, when the Flavour is the Furious or the like.

COMMENTARY.

a. The designation of ‘merit’ or ‘excellence’ (see Chapter VIII) given to these qualities,—*Unmelodiousness and the like,*—is only secondary, being applied to them only because of their ministering to the heightening of the chief excellence, (*i. e. the merit properly so called*) which consists in a particular species of poetical Relish (see § 33.) The following are the respective examples *of the three cases of Unmelodiousness assuming the nature of a merit, mentioned in the text.*

Harshness, when the speaker is enraged.

(1.) तद्विच्छेदकृशस्य कण्ठलुठितप्राणस्य मे निर्दयं
क्रूरः पञ्चशरः शरैरतिशितैर्भिन्दन् मनो निर्भरम् ।
शम्भोर्भूतकृपाविधेयमनसः प्रोद्दामनेत्रानल-
ज्वालाजालकरालितः पुनरसौ नास्तां समस्तात्मना ॥

b. (‘That cruel deity of the five shafts who mercilessly and incessantly pierces my heart with the keenest shafts, emaciated as I am by separation from my beloved, and while my spirit trembles in my throat,—O may the tyrant’s whole self be annihilated, consumed again by the fierce flames of the eye of S′ambhu, as his mind is subdued by compassion for his creatures.’)

Here in the Erotic Flavour an angry person is the speaker.

Harshness, when the theme is lofty.

(2.) मूर्धव्याधूयमानध्वनदमरधुनीलोलकल्लोलजालो-
द्भूताम्भःक्षोददम्भात् प्रसभमभिनभःक्षिप्तनक्षत्रलक्षम् ।
ऊर्ध्वन्यस्ताङ्घ्रिदण्डभ्रमिभवरभसोद्यद्ब्रह्मभस्त्रप्रवेश-
भ्रान्तब्रह्माण्डखण्डं प्रवितरतु शिवं शाम्भवं ताण्डवं वः ॥

('May the awful dance of S'ambhu bestow felicity upon thee; that dance which impetuously hurls up to the heavens myriads of stars in the disguise of those particles of water that are sent up by the tumultuous waves of the river of the gods, roaring in agitation on His head; that dance in which the upper portion of the universe is whirled by the wind rising in fierce whirlwind from the revolution of His mighty feet which he tosses up.')

Here the theme is lofty, being the terrific dance of Mahádeva. The two preceding stanzas are mine.

c. In such a Flavour as the Furious and the like, Unmelodiousness is a merit in a far higher degree than in the two instances above. For example, take the verses beginning उत्कृत्योत्कृत्य कृत्तिमित्यादि (3) ('Having first torn and stripped off the skin,' &c., see § 236. *a.*) the Flavour of which is the Disgustful.

TEXT.

Indecency, when a merit.

No. 580. Indecency again is such in an erotic gossip, &c.

COMMENTARY.

a. Again is such; *i. e.*, is a merit; *e. g.*

करिहस्तेन संबाधे प्रविश्यान्तर्विलोडिते ।
उपसर्पन् ध्वजः पुंसः साधनान्तर्विराजते ॥

"The elephants having entered and agitated the arrays with their trunks, the banner of the hero shines in the midst of the army."

Here in the amatory colloquy there is followed a rule of the erotic art—"One should intimate a secret purpose by equivocal words."

b. By the words '&c.' the same is to be understood with regard to a discourse on quietism or the like.

TEXT.

Obsoleteness and Unemployedness, when not faulty.

No. 581. Obsoleteness (see 571. *i. i.*) and Unemployedness (see 571. *r. r.*) are no faults in a Paronomasia (see 705) and the like.

COMMENTARY.

a. For example:—

पर्वतभेदि पवित्रं जैत्रं नरकस्य बहुमतं गहनं ।
हरिमिव हरिमिव हरिमिव सुरसरिदम्भः पतन्नमत ॥

"Worship ye the adored waters of the Divine River (Ganga) as they fall—the waters that are hard to be approached, that divide mountains, that are holy and vanquish Naraka (Hell)—thus resembling Hari (Indra) and Hari (Vishṇu, the destroyer of the demon Naraka) and Hari (the lion which destroys elephants).

Here the word पवित्र (pavitra) has an obsolete sense when used for Indra. In the case of a lion, the word मतङ्ग is Unemployed in the sense of मातङ्ग (elephant).

TEXT.

Unintelligibility when a merit.

No. 582. Unintelligibility is a Merit when the speaker and the person spoken to are wise.

For example :

"They declare Thee Nature that energises for the sake of the Soul, and thee they know to be the soul—the passionless Spectator of Nature."

TEXT.

The same when again a merit.

583. Or when one thinks by himself.

COMMENTARY.

Unintelligibility is a merit—so much is to be supplied in the text.

E. g. युक्तः कलाभिस्तमसां विवृद्ध्यै
क्षीणश्च ताभिः क्षलयेय एषाम् ।
शुद्धं निरालम्बपदावलम्बम्
तमात्मचन्द्रं परिशीलयामि ॥

"I meditate upon that pure moon, the Soul, that rests in the Unsustained, who when associated with the attributes of Nature (कला)* sustains this Universal Darkness (*i. e.*, mundane illusion)—who, when devoid of those attributes, dispels it."

TEXT.

Repetition, when a merit.

No. 584. A repetition (again is a Merit) when (1). something predicated is referred to; as also (2) in grief; (3) in surprise; (4) in anger; (5)

* कला means the digit of the moon also. निरालम्बपद means the सहस्रारपद्मं or the lotus of a thousand petals supposed to exist in the brain by the Hindu Ascetics (Yogis).

in misery; (6) in the Látánuprása (7) in mercy, (8) in propitiation; (9) when the expressed meaning is transferred to another; (10) in joy; (11) and in decision.

COMMENTARY.

(*a.*) Supply in the text "is a Merit."

E. g. "Red rises the sun and red it sets." Here the epithet "red" which was predicated is referred to.

(*b.*) 'Alas! alas! My love has gone and come not back in the spring!' Here we have grief exemplified.

(*c.*) "O wonder! O wonder! How fair-faced lady there is here the moon without a firmament!"

Here we have "wonder."

(*d.*) "Lady with the charming eyes, turn thy eyes, &c." Here there is the Látánuprása.

(*e.*) "His eyes indeed are eyes &c." Here the second "eyes" is used suggestively with its expressed or literal sense passing into another.

So of the other cases.

TEXT.

Dubiousness when a merit.

585. So is Dubiousness (§ 576), if it terminates in the ornament named Artful Praise (vyája-stuti, § 707).

COMMENTARY.

Supply "is a Merit" *e. g.* पृथुकार्तस्वरपात्रं &c. (§ 643. *e.*)

TEXT.

When obscurity and unmelodiousness are merits.

No. 586. Obscurity and Unmelodiousness are so, when a great grammarian is addressed or is himself the speaker.

COMMENTARY.

(*a.*) They are Merits. *E. g.*

दीधीवेवीसमः कश्चिद्गुणवृद्ध्योरभाजनं ।
क्विप्_ प्रत्ययनिभः कश्चिद् यत्र सन्निहिते न ते ॥

"There at thy presence, some fared like the roots 'Dídhí' and 'Véví,' bearing neither गुण* (merit) nor वृद्धि* (excellence) and some resembled the affix 'kwip,' *that disappears entirely.*

* Technical terms for grammatical augments.

Here the sense is obscure and a grammarian is the speaker. So also in the case of his being addressed.

TEXT.

Rusticity, when a merit.

587. So is Rusticity in the words of a low man.

COMMENTARY.

It is a Merit. For example take my verses :—

"Yonder orb of the moon looks like a lump of butter, and these troops of horses flying all around appear like streams of milk."

This is the speech of the विदूषक (Fool).

TEXT.

When Inconsequentiality, or an absence of reason, is no fault.

No. 588. Inconsequentiality does not attain to the nature of a fault when the notion expressed is established.

COMMENTARY.

a. For example.

"Now the time of evening separates the couples of herons."

TEXT.

When 'Opposition to notoriety' is a merit.

No. 589. In a well known convention of the poets 'Opposition to Notoriety' is a Merit.

COMMENTARY.

a. The following are established by the convention of the poets :

TEXT.

Poetical conventions.

No. 590. The sky and sin are described as black ; fame, laughter and renown as white ; anger and love as red. Red and blue lotuses are spoken of as growing even in rivers and seas, and birds such as the duck and others invariably haunt all receptacles of water. The Chakwás drink the moonlight ; and in the rainy season the ducks emigrate to the Mânasa lake (*Manassarovara*). The Asoka flowers from the stroke of fair women's feet and so does the Vakula from the wine of their mouths. The necklaces on the breast of youthful lovers along with their hearts burst from the flames of separation. The God of Love bears a flowery bow furnished with flowery shafts and strung with a string of bees. His arrows pierce the heart of the young and so does the glance of a woman. The lotus blooms in the day and the lily during the night; there is always the moonlight in the white fortnight. The peacocks dance at the grumbling of clouds and the Asoka does not bear fruit. The Játi blooms not in the spring and fragrant trees neither flower nor fructify, and so forth. Other poetical conventions are to be found out in the compositions of good poets.

COMMENTARY.

a. Illustrations of these are clear in the poems.*

TEXT.

No. 591. In such expressions as धनुर्ज्या (the bowstring of a bow) and the like, the words धनुः &c. are to denote that the bow is strung, &c.

Pleonasm, when allowable.

COMMENTARY.

For example.

"Heaven and Earth were filled with the clangour arising from the twanging of the bowstring (धनुर्ज्या)." Here though the word ज्या (bowstring) suffices to convey the meaning, the *pleonastic use of* the word धनुः (bow) is intended to signify the tension of the bowstring upon the bow. The words "and the like" refer to such expressions as कर्णावतंस &c., in such examples as भाति कर्णावतंसस्ते (the earring in thy ear shines); where the word कर्ण (ear) is employed to denote that the earring is worn in the कर्ण. Similarly श्रवणकुण्डल, (the earring in the ear) शिरःशेखर (the crest gem of the head) &c.

In like manner though the term माला (garland) without an antecedent qualification denotes a wreath of flowers, the word पुष्प (flower) in the example पुष्पमाला विभाति ते ('thy flower garland shines') is intended to imply excellent flowers. So in the example मुक्ताहार (a necklace of pearls) the word मुक्ता (pearl) signifies its being unmingled with other gems.

TEXT.

No. 592. These may be employed when already existent.

COMMENTARY.

Such expressions as धनुर्ज्या (the bowstring of a bow), warranted by usage in good poetry may be used in poetical composition; not such

* आकर mines or original sources from which these rules of composition were derived.

as जघनकाञ्ची (girdle of the loins) करकङ्कण (bracelet of the arm) which are not so justified.

TEXT.

Verbal Deficiency, when a Merit.

No. 593. Verbal Deficiency would be a Merit in the speech of one immersed in Joy or other *Emotion.*

COMMENTARY.

For example.

"गाढालिङ्गनवामनीकृतकुचप्रोद्भिन्नरोमोद्गमा
सान्द्रस्नेहरसातिरेकविगलच्छ्रीमन्नितम्बाम्बरा ।
मा मा मानद माति मामलमिति क्षामाक्षरोल्लापिनी
सुप्ता किं नु मृता नु किं मनसि मे लीना विलीना नु किं" ॥

(Was she asleep or was she dead, melted in my soul or dissolved away, when, with breasts dwarfed by my close embrace, with horripilation excited, the vesture of her beauteous loins slipping off from the excess of passionate love, she breathed out feebly in broken accents—"Nay, nay, my lord, me—not too much, enough.")

Here there is a deficiency of the word पीडय (*press*).

TEXT.

Sometimes neither a merit nor a fault.

No. 594. Sometimes it is neither an excellence nor a blemish.

COMMENTARY.

'It' *i. e.* verbal deficiency; for example:

तिष्ठेत् कोपवशात् प्रभावपिहिता दीर्घं न सा कुप्यति ।
स्वर्गायोत्पतिता भवेन्मयि पुनर्भावार्द्रमस्या मनः ।
तां हर्तुं विबुधद्विषोऽपि न च मे शक्ताः पुरोवर्त्तिनीं ।
सा चात्यन्तमगोचरं नयनयोर्यातेति कोऽयं विधिः ॥

(Perhaps she may be staying in anger, concealed by her superhuman power—she is not angry long; perhaps she has flown away to paradise—her mind is tender in affection. Not the enemies of the gods themselves could ravish her in my presence; yet she is altogether passed from before my eyes: What can this be!)

In this example the words 'It cannot be so, because' are deficient after the words "concealed by her superhuman power" and "has flown away." In the deficiency of these words there is no excellence, because it does not heighten the Accessory Mood designated Debate, (see text 202) which is suggested by the above example. On the other hand, the repugnance of the fact implied by the words 'may be staying' to the fact implied by the sentence 'she is not angry long' is clearly apparent, and therefore there is no blemish.

TEXT.

Verbal Redundancy, sometimes a merit.

No. 595. Sometimes a redundant word is a Merit.

COMMENTARY.

For example:

"That an evil man, all on a sudden, does things never even to be imagined, it is not that I do not know—I know; Yet my heart feels no unkindness." Here by *the clause* "it is not that I do not know" there is the exclusion of negation. In the second phrase "I know," there is a especially striking point *viz.*, 'I know and I only,' through the exclusion of the attribution of knowledge in regard to others.*

TEXT.

Resumption of the Concluded, sometimes neither merit nor demerit.

No. 596. Resumption of the Concluded (§ 575 *p*) is sometimes neither an excellence nor a blemish.

COMMENTARY.

For example—अन्यास्तागुणरत्नेत्यादि (Other are those lands which produce such gems, &c., see § 575. *i.*)

Here though the sentence is completed by the former half of the stanza, yet in the latter it is resumed. Thus, it is to be understood that there is the fault of the Resumption of the Concluded when only a qualification is resumed, *that is to say, takes up again the sense already completed;* but such is not the case when a distinct sentence or clause is added.

TEXT.

A Parenthesis, sometimes a merit.

No. 597. The Use of a Parenthesis (§ 575) is sometimes an Excellence.

* This farfetched explanation can hardly be admitted as correct, as the repetition is evidently and naturally for the addition of force.

COMMENTARY.

a. For example.

"The Earth is conquered, whose four bounds are divided by the Elephants of the Quarters? Conquered—lo! even while we say it, our hairs stand on end—it is bestowed upon a Brahmana (Kásyapa)! What more? Glory to that Ráma from whom arose this wondrous tale and in whom again it set." Here the clause "even while we say it," parenthetically inserted in the pregnant sentence, displays an excess of brilliance.

TEXT.

Excellence falling off, sometimes a merit.

No. 598. Likewise Excellence falling off. (See § 575. *g.*)

COMMENTARY.

a. 'Likewise' *i. e.*, it is sometimes a merit. For Example:—

चञ्चद्भुजभ्रमितचण्डगदाभिघात-
सञ्चूर्णितोरुयुगलस्य सुयोधनस्य।
स्त्यानावनद्धघनशोणितशोणपाणि-
रुत्तंसयिष्यति कचांस्तव देवि भीमः॥

Here, in the 4th verse, the avoidance of grandeur of language on account of the softness of the sense is an Excellence.

TEXT.

Naming of an Accessory, sometimes no blemish.

No. 599. Sometimes the mention of an Accessory by its proper name (see § 577 *a, b, c,*) is not a blemish where the composition is not proper to be elaborated by *Excitant* and *Ensuant*.

COMMENTARY.

a. Where there is not a distinct apprehension in setting forth the object matter by means of the Excitant and Ensuant, and where the absence of the elaboration effected by them is favourable to the composition, there is no blemish in the mention of the Accessory by its own name.

b. For example:

"She who, at the first union, had made haste in her eagerness, but was turning aside from native modesty, who, on being made to turn towards her husband again, by the repeated urgings of her fair friends, seeing him before her, was seized again with timid emotion, was embraced by smiling Siva and was thrilled—may that Gaurí be for your felicity!"

c. In this Example, if the *Accessory Mood, viz. Eagerness, instead of being actually mentioned,* had been represented, or *left to be understood,* by means of the Ensuant "*haste,*" the sense would not have been readily understood. For "*haste*" may also be occasioned by fear and the like. 'Turning aside', *here,* the Ensuant of bashfulness, may also result from anger or other emotion. While the development of fear and the comic sentiment by means of the Accessories would be almost unfavourable to the present Flavour: So it is legitimate to mention all these sentiments by their proper titles (instead of leaving them to be suggested).

TEXT.

No. 600. The mention of a conflicting Accessory or the like in such a manner that it may be sublated, is an Excellence.

A conflicting Accessory, how to be admitted.

COMMENTARY.

a. "O! a bad action and the offspring of the moon, how inconsistent" &c. (see § 249 *d.*)

In this example, the obscuration or sublation of Debate, Resolve, Apprehension, Equanimity, which are subsidiary to Quietism, by Recollection, Depression, and Painful Reflection—subsidiaries of Desire—terminates in giving rise to an Excess of Relish in which Painful Reflection predominates.

TEXT.

No. 601. There is no incongruity where a conflicting flavour is (1) recalled or (2) described under a comparison or (3) where two or more flavours stand in the relation of principal and subordinate.

Conflicting Flavours, how to be admitted.

COMMENTARY.

a. For examples in their order:—

"This is that hand that drew my girdle" &c., (§ 266 *b*) Here the exciting cause, *viz.*, the *husband of a lamenting widow,* being destroyed, Love is no longer a Relish, and its subsidiaries being recalled to heighten Sorrow, harmonize with the Pathetic.

b. सरागया स्रुतघनघर्म्मतोयया
कराहतिध्वनितपृथूरुपीठया ।
मुहुर्मुहुर्दशनविलङ्घितोष्ठया
रुषा नृपाः प्रियतमयेव भेजिरे ॥

(There was the burning passion, there was the profuse flow of the heat-drops, there was the resonance of the massy thighs struck with the hand, there was the biting of the lips with the teeth, ever and anon : thus the princes were served by Wrath as by their beloved.)

In this example, the sentiment of "love in union" is suggested under a similitude to the Ensuant of Anger which is an Accessory of the Heroic Flavour here represented.

c. "May the three eyes of S'ambhu protect you—eyes showing different emotions during abstract contemplation—one closed like a bud in meditation ; the second, languid with love, fixed on the lotus-face and swelling breast of Párvatí ; the other kindled with a flame of wrath against Káma who had drawn afar his bow."

Here Love for the Deity is intensified by the Quietistic, Erotic and Furious Flavours.

d. Or for example :

"May the fire of Sambhu's arrows consume your sins—that fire which resembled a lover that has recently offended, for, as it touched the hand, it was cast away ; as it caught the hem of their garments, was with force repelled ; as it seized their hair, was tossed away ; as it fell at their feet, in their flurry was not looked at ; as it clasped them around, was thrown off by the ladies of Tripura, their lotus eyes suffused with tears."

In this example, Love, conceived by the poet towards the Deity predominates. This is developed by the Divine Energy in the destruction of Tripura, and the Pathetic is ancillary to this Energy, which not being fully developed has not attained the rank of Flavour Proper, but is only an Incomplete Flavour. To this Pathetic again the Erotic is ancillary, being suggested by the force of the similitude 'resembling a lover.' Thus, inasmuch as the Pathetic is not the ultimate sentiment, it is merely subordinate. The two Flavours, therefore, *viz.* the Erotic and the Pathetic, do not conflict with one another, as they both elevate the Relish consisting in the sentiment of Divine Love, developed by the Energy of the Deity, and as they exist simultaneously as ancillary to them. 'How can an incongruity,' it may be asked, 'be suspected between two Flavours which both consist in the fulness of unintermitted Joy composed of the *three-fold emotional* apparatus, *viz*, the Exitants, the Ensuants, and the Accessories, since they could not thwart each other—not being manifested simultaneously in the same sentence. Nor is there the relation of the Principal and the Subordinate, since they are both absolute and complete in themselves.' True, we reply; hence to such Flavours as are other than the principal, there is customarily applied by the Ancients the name of Concomitant Flavour, inasmuch as they cannot terminate absolutely in themselves and are distinct from a fully developed Flavour and a mere *undeveloped* sentiment. And my grandfather's younger brother—himself a leading poet and a scholar—the Venerable Chandídása gives the name of Partial Flavour. Thus he says:

An Objection as to the incongruity of Flavours.

Name of Concomitant Flavour given to the so-called incongruous Flavours in a composition.

"If in the midst of a Flavour there is another as (1) ancillary or (2) as one to be sublated or (3) as a Concomitant Flavour—which is not relished n its integrity—this is called a Partial Flavour."

The same named by some Partial Flavour.

e. It may be objected: How can the Heroic and the Erotic which are incongruous according to the rule formerly laid down, *viz.* 'The Erotic is incompatible with the Pathetic, the Disgustful, the Furious, the Heroic, and the Fearful (§ 242)' be employed in the same place as in the Stanza:

"Repeatedly beholding the lotus face of Jánakí thrilled and throbbing with smiling love, and the cheeks which stole the splendour of the tusks of the young elephant—and hearing the confused clamour of the Demon Army, the Prince of the Raghus binds fast the knot of his matted hair."

f. We answer: There may be congruity or incongruity among Flavours in three ways; in some cases by reason of the identity of the Exciting cause; in others by reason of the identity of the subject of the Emotion; and in others by reason of immediacy of succession. The Erotic and the Heroic are incompatible, if the Exciting Cause is *supposed*

Congruity and incongruity of Flavours determined.

to be the same; so also 'Love in union' is incompatible with the Comic, the Furious, and the Disgustful; and 'Love in separation' is incompatible with the Heroic, the Pathetic, the Furious, &c. *if the same object be supposed to excite these sentiments.* There is an incongruity between the Heroic and the Fearful where the Exciting cause or the Feeling subject is the same. The Quietistic and the Erotic are rendered incompatible by immediacy or identity of the Excitants. The Heroic is compatible, in each of the three modes, with the Marvellous as well as with the Furious; the Erotic, with the Marvellous; the Fearful, with the Disgustful. In the above example, therefore, there is no incompatibility between the Heroic and the Erotic, because the Exciting causes are different. In like manner where the Heroic exists in the hero and the Fearful in the rival hero of the composition, there is no incompatibility, since the Subjects of the Emotions differ. As respects the Love displayed towards Malayavatí by Jímútaváhana though a subject of Quietism, in the Nágánanda, since the Marvellous in the words 'How she sings and how she plays' is introduced intermediately, there is no immediacy of succession, and hence there is no incompatibility between the two Flavours. In like manner other places are to be understood. In the example 'The pale and emaciated countenance' &c., paleness &c., are ancillary to 'love in separation' as well as to the Pathetic; hence there is no incompatibility.

TEXT.

No fault is fault in imitation.

No. 602. All Faults cease to be such where there is imitation.

COMMENTARY.

a. 'All' *i. e.*, Unmelodiousness and others.

b. For example—

एष दुश्च्यवनं नौमीत्यादि जल्पति कश्चन।

(A certain one babbles. Lo! I bow down before Dus'chyavana, &c.) Here the word Dus'chyavana (Indra) is Unemployed (§ 574 *d.*)

TEXT.

Faults, generally so called,

No. 603. Similarly it is to be determined, according to propriety, by the critics, that the other Blemishes also are sometimes no faults and sometimes merits.

are sometimes blemishes, sometimes positive merits, and sometimes neither, as the case may be.*

Commentary.

a. 'Neither' means neither blemishes nor positive merits.

b. So much for the *Declaration of Blemishes*, the seventh chapter of the Mirror of Composition.

* In Röer's Sáhitya, read अदोषताथगुणता instead of अदोषतापगुणता.

CHAPTER VIII.

The Declaration of Merits, or Excellences.

He states the Excellences.

TEXT.

No. 604. Excellences are to the Flavour, the essence of Poetry, what heroism and the like are to the Soul.

Excellence defined.

COMMENTARY.

a. As heroism and the like are designated by the term Merit, inasmuch as they cause the exaltation of the soul viewed essentially, so in like manner are Sweetness and the like which are the qualities, or particular modes, of Flavour, the essence of poetry. It is these attributes of Flavour that constitute the claim to the designation of Poetry, of a composition communicating its essence, viz. relish. It has already been shown that they are attributes of the Flavour only.

TEXT.

Its three varieties.

No. 605. These are of three kinds—Sweetness, Energy and Perspicuity.

COMMENTARY.

a. 'These' means the Excellences. Of these—

TEXT.

No. 606. Joy consisting in the melting of the heart is called Sweetness, or Tenderness.

Sweetness defined,

COMMENTARY.

a. As for the assertion of some (the author of Kávyaprakása) that Sweetness is the CAUSE of melting, it is not so; for the melting being identical with the joy consisting of the Relish of poetry, cannot be its effect. Melting is

Sweetness, or softness, in Poetry, is not the cause of, but the same with the melting of the heart.

then, the softening, as it were, of the heart of a man of sensibility, by absence of hardness or a natural unimpassionedness, of the inflammation produced by resentment, anger and the like, and of agitation caused by surprise, mirth and so forth,—and by the excitement of joy impregnated with the emotions of love, &c. This again—

TEXT.

Sentiments in which it is successively developed, in a higher degree.

No. 607. Is successively higher in Love in Union, the Pathetic, Love in Separation and the Quietistic.

COMMENTARY.

a. Love in Union and the other terms are used in a general sense. It is to be understood therefore that Sweetness may reside also in Semblances of Love in Union, &c.

TEXT.

What manifest Sweetness.

No. 608. र (*r*) and ण (ṇ) short, and such letters, excepting *the cerebrals* (ट ठ ड ढ), as are preceded by the last of the series, *i. e. the dentals*, cause the manifestation of Sweetness, as also an absence or a paucity of compounds and a melodious style.*

COMMENTARY.

a. For example.—

Sweetness in short compounds, exemplified.

अनङ्गमङ्गलभुवस्तदपाङ्गस्य भङ्गयः ।
जनयन्ति मुहुर्यूनामन्तस्सन्तापसन्ततिम् ॥

(Her beautiful side-glances, Love's auspicious abode, ever and anon beget in the heart of youths a series of pangs.)

b. Or, for example, my own verses:—

Another example of Sweetness.

लताकुञ्जं गुञ्जन्मदवदलिपुञ्जं चपलयन्
समालिङ्गन्नङ्गं द्रुततरमनङ्गं प्रबलयन् ।
मरुन्मन्दम्मन्दं दलितमरविन्दं तरलयन्
रजोवृन्दं विन्दन् किरति मकरन्दं दिशि दिशि ॥

* For instance, the verses of Gítagovinda which are not wanting in large compounds and are yet exquisitely sweet, from an absence of harsh letters. According to the commentator, 'melodious style' means a composition soft both as to sound and sense, for notwithstanding the presence of smooth words, we perceive no sweetness, where the sentiment is not delicate or tender.

(Agitating the bower of creepers resonant with the hum of joyous bees; embracing the body and quickly awakening love; gently shaking the blooming lotus and wafting the pollen, the wind scatters abroad the nectareous dew.)

TEXT.

No. 609. The state of being fired or, in other words, an expansion of the mind is what is termed Energy: Of this there is a successively higher development in the Heroic, the Disgustful and the Furious.*

Energy defined.

COMMENTARY.

a. 'Of this' means 'of Energy.' Here also the terms Heroic, &c. are used in a comprehensive sense, and so it may reside in the Semblance of the Heroic and the like.

TEXT.

No. 610. The first and the third letters joined with the second and fourth of any series, that is to say, with any of the *aspirates*, such letters as are combined with *r* (र) preceding or following or both, the *cerebrals* (ट ठ ड ढ) even though uncombined with another consonant, and *the hard sibilants* श and ष serve to manifest this Energy; as also an ample use of compounds and an exalted style† of composition.

Causes of its manifestation.

COMMENTARY.

a. For example: चञ्चद्भुजेत्यादि (see §598 *a*).

TEXT.

No. 611. Perspicuity is that, which existing in all the Flavours and the *four* styles of composition, pervades the heart, as fire spreads itself through dry fuel.

Perspicuity defined.

* Our commentator gives the following different view, which we ourselves should prefer, of Chandídása who taking that of the author of Dhwani-siddhánta-sangraha observes: In the Heroic and the Furious, Energy is unopposed; in the Disgustful, it is slightly impregnated with sweetness, or softness; while in the Comic, Marvellous and Fearful there is an admission of both. According to this opinion, there is greater energy in the Furious and the Heroic than in the Disgustful.

† Exalted style, says the scholiast, means lofty as to sentiment.

COMMENTARY.

a. 'Pervades' means 'excites its sensibility.'

TEXT.

Perspicuity how manifested.

No. 612. Words conveying their meaning as soon as they are heard serve to manifest it.

COMMENTARY.

a. For example :—

Perspicuity exemplified.

सूचीमुखेन सकृदेव कृतव्रणस्त्वं
मुक्ताकलाप लुठसि स्तनयोः प्रियायाः ।
बाणैः स्मरस्य शतशो विनिकृत्तमर्मा
स्वप्नेऽपि तां कथमहं न विलोकयामि ॥

(Thou necklace of pearls, though pierced but once by the needle's point, rollest in the bosom of my beloved; I, cut to the quick a hundred times by Love's arrows, see her not so much as in my dreams.)

TEXT.

Excellence figuratively attributed to words.

No. 613. It is by a trope that these Excellences are spoken of by the learned* as belonging to the words.

COMMENTARY.

a. Add 'As heroism and other qualities are tropically attributed to the body.'

TEXT.

Merits of words, recognised by the ancients, discussed.

No. 614. As for the Merits, declared by the ancients, Consonance (*s'lesha*), Harmony (*samádhi*), Sprightliness (*audárya*) and Brilliance (*prasáda*),† these are included in Energy.

COMMENTARY.

a. 'In Energy' *i. e.* in attributes of word or meaning TROPICALLY designated by the term 'energy,' (*which* PROPERLY *means an expansion of mind*).

* 'By Vámana and others,' explains the scholiast.

† These four and the following five, *viz.*, Simplicity (*mádhurya*), Lucidness (*artha-vyakti*), Elegance (*kánti*), Softness (*sukumáratá*) and Evenness (*samatá*) were recognised by Vámana and others as merits of word.

Consonance.

b. Among these, Consonance consists in the sounding of many words as one; for example:—

उन्मज्जज्जलकुञ्जरेन्द्ररभसास्फालानुबन्धोद्धतः
सर्व्वाः पर्व्वतकन्दरोदरभुवः कुर्व्वन् प्रतिध्वानिनीः ।
उच्चैश्चरति ध्वनिः श्रुतिपथोन्माथी यथाऽयन्तथा
प्रायः प्रेङ्खदसङ्ख्यशङ्खधवला वेलेयमुद्गच्छति ॥

(As there arises on high a sound excited by the continuous and furious lashing of the mighty sea-elephants emerging from the deep, which fills with echoes all the hollow grottos of the mountain, distracting the passage of the ear; so rises yonder wave white with unnumbered shells rolling incessantly.*)

This is no other than Energy, consisting, as it does, in the roughness of the composition.

Harmony.

c. Harmony consists in alternate rising and falling. Rising and falling mean elevation and declension, *i. e. an increase and decrease of sonorousness;* the alternation of these is their arrangement in a manner not marring the relish. As, चञ्चद्भुजेत्यादि (see §598. *a*).

Here in the first three verses, there is a gradual increase of sonorousness in the composition; in the fourth line, a decrease, though this too is forcible, inasmuch as it is pronounced with strong effort.

Sprightliness.

d. Sprightliness is briskness of style. It consists in what may be called a dancing movement of the words; *e. g.*

स्वचरणविनिविष्टैर्नूपुरैर्नर्त्तकीनां ।
झणिति रणितमासीत्तत्र चित्रं कलञ्च ॥

(There was the varied and melodious jingling of the anklets which the dancing girls wore on their feet.)

Here also, according to the teaching of the ancients, without a reference to the Relish, there is Energy resulting from the liveliness o the expression.

Brilliance.

e. Brilliance consists of simplicity, mingled with energy; for example:—

* The scholiast reads प्रायप्रेङ्खत् for प्रायः—and interprets it 'rolling from being dead,' which is evidently a mistake, for shells living or dead must roll with the rolling waves.

यो यः शस्त्रं बिभर्त्ति स्वभुजगुरुमदात् पाण्डवीनां चमूनां
यो यः पाञ्चालगोत्रे शिशुरधिकवया गर्भशय्यां गतो वा ।
यो यस्तत्कर्मसाक्षी चरति मयि रणे यश्च यश्च प्रतीपः
क्रोधान्धस्तस्य तस्य स्वयमिह जगतामन्तकस्यान्तकोऽहम् ॥

(Whoever holds a weapon, &c. see §368, *a*).

TEXT.

No. 615. In declaring that Sweetness is manifested by an absence of compounds, we have already admitted the 'Simplicity' *of the ancients* defined to be 'a separateness of words.'

Simplicity.

COMMENTARY.

a. For example:—

श्वासान्मुञ्चति भूतले विलुठति त्वन्मार्गमालोकते
दीर्घं रोदिति विक्षिपत्यत इतः क्षामां भुजावल्लरीं ।
किञ्च प्राणसमान काङ्क्षितवती स्वप्नेऽपि ते सङ्गमं
निद्रां वाञ्छति न प्रयच्छति पुनर्दग्धो विधिस्तामपि ॥

(She pours forth sighs &c., see §147, *a*).

TEXT.

No. 616. Lucidness is included under the merit named *by us* Perspicuity, for lucidness of words is no other than their conveying the meaning immediately.

Lucidness.

COMMENTARY.

a. Examples are obvious.

TEXT.

No. 617. Elegance and Softness (are admitted by us) in the negation of Vulgarism (§574, *e.*) and Unmelodiousness (§574, *v*) respectively.

Elegance and Softness.

COMMENTARY.

a. Supply 'are admitted by us' to complete the sentence.

b. Elegance is refinement. It consists in brilliancy of language, contradistinguished from familiar *speech* and opposed to expressions used by rustics and others.

c. Softness is the absence of harshness.

d. Examples of these are obvious.

TEXT.

No. 618. As for Evenness which consists in an uniformity of style, it is sometimes a blemish. In other cases it is to be included, according to propriety, under the Merits specified.

Evenness.

COMMENTARY.

a. Uniformity of style is the completion of a composition in the soft or harsh style in which it is begun. This is in certain cases a fault, *which we shall illustrate by* an example *of its contrary* :—

Uniformity of style.

अव्यूढाङ्गमरूढपाणिजठराभोगश्च बिभ्रद्वपुः
पारीन्द्रः शिशुरेष पाणिपुटके सम्मातु किन्तावता ।
उद्यद्दुर्द्धरगन्धसिन्धुरशतप्रोद्दामदानार्णव-
स्रोतःशोषणरोषणात् पुनरितः कल्पाग्निरल्पायते ॥

(It matters not that this young lion, in whose frame the limbs are undeveloped, the fulness of whose paws and belly is unformed, can be contained in the hand; for the fire of universal dissolution is small in comparison with it, when its fury dries up the powerfully streaming flood of exusion of a hundred elephants, the odour rising from which is intolerable.)

Here the dropping of the soft style *in the third and fourth lines* where the subject-matter is exalted, is a merit. When the case is different from the above, *i. e. where the sentiments in a single piece of poetry do not vary as to magnificence or mildness, a consistency of style* would be included under Sweetness or Energy, *as the composition is smooth or rough.* As लताकुञ्जं गुञ्जदित्यादि (see §608, *a*).

TEXT.

No. 619. Force or Vigour (*ojas*), Perspicuity (*prasáda*), Beauty (*mádhurya*), Mildness (*saukumárya*), and Elegance (*udárata*),* *recognised by the ancients as* merits of the sense, have been admitted by us, inasmuch as their contraries *have been noticed as* blemishes.

Merits of sense recognised by the ancients, discussed.

* These and the five discussed next, viz. Manifestation of nature (*artha-vyakti*), Loveliness (*kánti*), Ingenious Collocation (*s'lesha*), Consistency (*samatá*), and Imagination (*samádhi*) were the merits admitted by Vámana and others as belonging to the sense or sentiment.

COMMENTARY.

a. Force consists in pregnancy of meaning; Perspicuity is clearness of sense; Beauty is diversity of expression; Mildness is an absence of harshness; Elegance is freedom from rusticity. These five excellences of sense are admitted by merely rejecting respectively *the faults*, Irrelevancy (§575, *a.*), Redundancy of a word (§576, *d*), Monotony (§576, *i.*), Indecency of inauspiciousness (§576, *h.*) and Rusticity (§576, *e.*). Illustrations are obvious.

TEXT.

Manifestation of Nature and Loveliness.

No. 620. Manifestation of Nature (has also been admitted) under the ornament of Natural Description (§750), and the Merit named Loveliness, under Suggestive Poetry and Poetry of Subordinate Suggestion.

COMMENTARY.

a. The words 'has been admitted,' complete the construction. Manifestation of nature is fidelity of representation. Loveliness is fulness of Flavour. Examples are obvious.

TEXT.

Ingenious Collocation and Consistency.

No. 621. Ingenious Collocation is merely strikingness of description; and Consistency again is only the absence of a blemish, *or a negative merit.*

COMMENTARY.

a. Ingenious Collocation is a composition consisting of a combination of *krama* (a succession of acts), *kautilya* (cunningness), *anulvaṇatwa* (absence of extravagance) and *upapatti* (probability). Of these, *kṛama* is a series of actions; *kautilya*, ingenious behaviour; *anulvanatwa*, an absence of far-fetched representation; *upapatti*, an adjustment of reasonable circumstances conducive to probability. A combination, or commixture, of these *four elements* forming what is termed *s'lesha* produces only a striking effect, *and it cannot be admitted as a particular excellence of poetry*, for it does not serve to heighten the Flavour in a manner not common to other *innumerable circumstances that may be imagined by the poet.* For example: 'Seeing his two dearest ones' &c. (§107). Here the actions are 'seeing' and so forth; the cunningness is the paying attention to both; an absence of extravagance consists here in the natural behaviour; the circumstances conducive to probability are expressed in the words 'seated together,' 'having approached from behind,' 'having closed the eyes,' and 'gently turning his neck.' Inasmuch as in this combination, the reader's attention is engrossed in apprehending the probable circumstances mentioned, the tasting of the flavour is postponed in some measure, and consequently there is no positive merit.

b. Consistency is an absence of incongruity in the meaning of the whole, by non-violation of uniformity in respect of the grammatical radicals and suffixes employed, and this is a mere absence of the fault termed Violation of Uniformity (§575. *bb.*) Exemplification is superfluous.

TEXT.

Imagination.

No. 622. Nor is Imagination (*samádhi*) a Merit.

COMMENTARY.

a. Imagination consists in the conceiving of a new thought (*ayonyartha*) or of a thought based upon that of another poet (*anyachchháyáyonyartha*). An original thought is exemplified in 'The orange vieing with the chin of a drunken barbarian (*húna*) just shaven.' A thought based upon that of another is illustrated *in the following couplet:*

'The fair gatherer of flowers oft deceived by the reflection of her own eyes in the water, hesitates to extend her hand even to the real blue lotus.'

In this example, the trite comparison of eyes to the blue lotus is expressed by a peculiarly striking circumstance. This twofold *Imagination*, inasmuch as it gives rise to no peculiar beauty, is no Merit, but simply serves to sustain the poetical character* of the composition.

Periphrasis and Conciseness, Amplification and Condensation, defined.

b. In some cases, where a single object, for instance, the moon is to be spoken of, it is represented periphrastically as 'the light which sprang from Atri's eyes.' In other instances where the meaning of a whole sentence is to be expressed, as 'a lady whose tender limbs are cool in summer and warm in winter,' it is conveyed by a single term *vara-varṇiní*. In other cases, where the

* Lit. composes the mere body of the poetry, viz. words and sense, relish being the soul.

meaning of a single sentence is enounced in several sentences by inserting qualifications, there is Amplification (*vyása*); where the meaning of several sentences is expressed by a single sentence, there is Condensation (*samása*).* These† and other excellences mentioned by other authors are not properly speaking merits, but merely minister to striking effect.

TEXT.

No. 623. Therefore the Merits of sense are not distinct.

COMMENTARY.

a. 'Therefore,' for the reasons above mentioned. 'Merits of sense,' *i. e.* Force and the rest, discussed above (§ 619).

So much for the 'Discussion of Merits' the eighth chapter of the MIRROR OF COMPOSITION.

* Amplification and Condensation are exemplified by the scholiast in the following two stanzas respectively:

असौ नानाकारो भवति सुखदुःखव्यतिकरः
सुखं वा दुःखं वा भवति न भवत्येव च ततः ।
पुनस्तस्मादूर्द्ध्वं भवति सुखदुःखं किमपि तत्
पुनस्तस्मादूर्द्ध्वं भवति न च दुःखं न च सुखम् ॥

श्रूयतां धर्म्मसर्व्वस्वं श्रुत्वा चाप्यवधार्य्यताम् ।
आत्मनः प्रतिकूलानि परेषां न समाचरेत् ॥ (*Mahábhárata.*)

These latter verses I insert here the more, as they show that the Indian lawgivers had not a *distant* perception, as Prof. Max Müller supposes, of the truth of the maxim 'Do to others as ye would that others should do to you,' but that they were aware that it forms the essence, the sum-total, the *sarvaswa* of all our duties to our neighbours.

† These four peculiarities of expression, says the commentator, were recognised by the ancients under the title *ojas* (force or vigour) which was one of the merits of sense (see § 619).

Chapter IX.

The Discrimination of Style.

a. Here the author, postponing the description of Ornaments which come next in the order of enumeration (see § 5), as requiring a detailed treatment, proceeds to describe Style.

Text.

Style defined.

No. 624. Style is an arrangement of words, auxiliary to Flavour, &c., as the conformation of the body *is to the soul.*

Commentary.

a. 'To Flavour &c.' which are the soul of poetry, while the words and the meaning are its body.

Text.

No. 625. Of this, there are four varieties, *viz.* the Vaidarbhí, the Gauḍí, the Pánchálí, and the Látí, *prevalent respectively in Vidarbha, Gauḍa, Panchála* and *Láta.*

Its four varieties.

Commentary.

a. 'Of this' *i. e.* of Style. Among these *varieties :—*

Text.

The Vaidarbhí style defined.

No. 626. A dulcet composition with letters manifesting Sweetness (§ 606), with few or no compounds, is designated the Vaidarbhí style.

Commentary.

a. For example—अनङ्गमङ्गलभुव इत्यादि (see § 608 *a.*)

b. But Rudraṭa says: 'The Vaidarbhí contains no compounds or but few, has the ten Merits, abounds in the second letter of each series in the alphabet (*viz.* ख छ ठ थ फ), consists of letters pronounced with little effort; and is of easy construction.' Here the ten Merits are those enumerated in his system, *s'lesha* (compactness) and the rest.*

* These are probably the same with those mentioned by Daṇḍin in his Kávyádars'a, Chap. I. s'loka, 41.

TEXT.

The Gaudí style defined.

No. 627. The *Gauḍí* is a grand style, composed of letters manifesting energy, and abounding in compounds.

COMMENTARY.

a. For example: चञ्चद्भुजेत्यादि (see § 598 *a.*)

b. But Purushottama says: 'A style comprising numerous compounds and consisting of letters pronounced with vigorous effort is *termed* the Gauḍí; as also a composition of languid sentences,* dependent upon a profusion of alliteration.'

TEXT.

The Pánchálí style defined.

No. 628. A composition, comprising other letters than those of the two (foregoing) styles, and containing compounds of five or six words, is held the Páncháliká.

* The original has अनुप्रासमहिमपरतन्त्रा स्तोभवाक्या च which Premachandra in his commentary on the Kávyádarsa, reads— अस्तोभवाक्या, overlooking this second peculiarity of the Gáuḍí style. My translation is according to the interpretation of Rámachandra the commentator of the present work. He cites the authority of the Kávyádarsa itself—

श्लिष्टमस्पृष्टशैथिल्य; मल्पप्राणाक्षरोत्तरं ।
शिथिलं मालतीमाला लोलालिकलिला यथा ॥

"The compact style is one untouched by languidness; a languid style being composed of syllables pronounced with little effort;" as, (to give Pope's example, though harsh enough, judged by the Sanskrit standard)—

'The line too labours and the words move slow.'

Or, 'That like a wounded snake drags its slow length along.'

Premachandra makes शिथिलं the epithet of श्लिष्टं and construes the example to be one of the compact or firm style. This forced explanation is undoubtedly a mistake as is still more clear from *sloka* 69th of the same work. It may not be out of place to remark here that Ácharya Danḍin entirely concurs in the precept of Pope—

'And praise the easy vigour (s'lesha) of a line,
Where Denham's strength and Waller's sweetness join.'

—and that it is not too much to suspect that many of the songs of Jayadeva, a Gauḍa, would sound languid in his ear. Indeed, Danḍin is sometimes unfairly opposed to the Gauḍa style of composition, though he rightly condemns its principal faults.

COMMENTARY.

a. 'Of the two' *i. e.* of the Vaidarbhí and the Gauḍí.

b. For example:

मधुरया मधुबोधितमाधवीमधुसमृद्धिसमेधितमेधया ।
मधुकराङ्गनया मुहुरुन्मदध्वनिभृता निभृताक्षरमुज्जगे ॥

(The sweet female bee, with joyous melody, softly hummed ever and anon,—her sensibility expanded by the exuberant nectar of the Mádhaví creeper blooming in spring.)

c. But Bhoja says: A sweet and soft style characterised by force (ojas) and elegance (kánti), containing compounds of five or six words, the learned designate the Pánchálí?

TEXT.

The Láṭí style defined.

No. 629. The Láṭí is a style intermediate between the Vaidarbhí and the Pánch.lí.

COMMENTARY.

a. For examp'e:—

अयमुदयति मुद्राभञ्जनः पद्मिनीना-
मुदयगिरिवनालीबालमन्दारपुष्पम् ।
विरहविधुरकोकद्वन्द्वबन्धुर्विभिन्दन्
कुपितकपिकपोलक्रोडताम्रस्तमांसि ॥

(Yonder rises the cause of the expansion of the lotuses; the new-blown Mandára flower in the extended forest of the Eastern mountain; the friend of the separated couple of ruddy geese sorrowing in separation; dispelling the gloom and glowing like the middle of an angry quadruman's cheek.)

b. A certain *authority* has said: 'The Láṭí is a style agreeable from the simplicity of its compounds, not superabundant in conjunct letters, and describing things by a number of appropriate epithets.' Others have said: 'The Gauḍí is a grand composition; the Vaidarbhí sweet, the Pánchálí mixed, whilst the Láṭí is composed of simple words.'

TEXT.

The modification of style.

No. 630. Sometimes the style &c. should be modified or adjusted for the sake of appropriateness as to the speaker and the rest.

COMMENTARY.

a. 'The speaker and the rest:' 'The rest' refers to the subject-matter and the particular species of poetical composition. 'Style &c.'—the *et cetera* includes *the use of* compound words and the harsh or soft letters.

b. Of these *several cases, a modification* for appropriateness as to the speaker is exemplified in मन्थायस्तार्णवाम्भ इत्यादि.* Here though the subject-matter, *the sound of a kettle-drum*, does not manifest anger or the like, the style &c., are lofty, *the haughty* Bhímasena being the speaker.

c. For appropriateness as to the subject-matter, as in the verses already cited—मूर्द्धव्याधूयमान &c.

d. An adjustment of diction suitable to the species of Composition; as, in the drama, compound words, for instance, are not used even *where the sentiment is lofty as* in the Furious Flavour, for they are unfavourable to acting, *being hard to articulate as well as to under-*

* मन्थायस्तार्णवाम्भःप्लुतकुहरवलन्मन्दरध्वानधीरः
कोणाघातेषु गर्ज्जत्प्रबलघनघटान्योन्यसंघट्टचण्डः ।
कृष्णाक्रोधाग्रदूतः कुरुकुलनिधनोत्पातनिर्घातवातः
केनास्मत्सिंहनादप्रतिरसितसखो दुन्दुभिस्ताडितोऽयम् ॥ *Vení Sanhára*

The reader will observe that our author rather hastily thinks that the style of these verses corresponds to the haughtiness of the speaker rather than to the loftiness of the thought. The following is a translation:

Who is it that thus beats the kettledrum, the sound whereof is so akin to the resonance of my own leonine roar;—which seems as if it were an ominous whirlwind foreboding the destruction of the hundred Kauravas and the harbinger of the wrath of Draupadi;—which, at these violent strokes, imitates the fierce rattle of heavy thunder-clouds clashing against each other, and is grave again like the sound emitted by the Mandara mountain whirled in the churning of the ocean, as its waters rushed into its hollow caves.

stand. Similarly, in the Áḳhyáyiká (§ 568) smooth letters, for instance, are not to be *profusely* introduced even where the Flavour is Erotic, and in the Kathá (§ 567) they ought not to be too rough even when the Flavour is Fúrious. Thus other particulars are to be understood.

So much for the 'Discrimination of Style,' the ninth chapter of the Mirror of Composition.

CHAPTER X.

The Declaration of Ornaments.

He now declares the Ornaments, the occasion *for treating of them* having arrived, *after the discourse on Faults, Excellences and Styles, the other accompaniments of Poetry.*

TEXT.

Ornament defined.

No. 361. Those non-permanent attributes of a word and its sense, that add to their beauty and aid the flavour or the like,* are styled Ornaments, being like bracelets and the like, *that adorn the human form.*

COMMENTARY.

a. As bracelets and the like, by promoting the beauty of the person, advantage the man, so Alliteration, Simile and other figures, which, by adding to the beauty of word and sense, serve to aid the flavour or the like, are termed Ornaments.

b. 'Non-permanent'—*i. e.* their (the ornaments') presence is not necessary like that of the excellencies, or the merits of Sweetness, Energy, and Perspicuity (see Chapter VIII).

c. Since of a word and its sense, the word becomes first the o bjet of apprehension *and then the sense*, it is proper to speak first of the ornaments of word; and the semblance of Tautology, though an ornament of word and sense, being by the ancients defined among ornaments of word, he declares first.

TEXT.

Semblance of Tautology.

No. 632. What at first sight appears to be the repetition of a sense, is called the Semblance of Tautology,† and this consists in the use of different words *of the same apparent import.*

* 'The like' sums up all those sentiments that excite poetical delight, though they are not fully developed, from the want of some of its requisites into Flavour or Relish properly so called. See pp. 39 and 132.

† Or Paronomasia of Synonyms.

Commentary.

a. This is an example :—

भुजङ्गकुण्डली व्यक्तशशिशुभ्रांशुशीतगुः ।
जगन्त्यपि सदाऽपायादव्याच्चेतोहरः शिवः ॥

(He who has a serpent for his earring, *on whose head* is manifest the moon with the camphor-white rays, may the heart-ravishing S'iva ever preserve the worlds !)

How it belongs to both word and sense.

Here the *compounded* words भुजङ्ग-कुण्डली for example, seeming at first sight *both* to mean a serpent, bear the appearance of being tautological, but afterwards they come to convey a distinct sense, viz., 'one who wears a serpent for an earring.' In पायादव्यात् the ornament consists in *the seeming tautology* of an action, for the *seeming verb* पायात् terminates in being recognized as अपायात् *the* अ *having coalesced in sandhi, or combination, with the* आ *of* सदा. Of the words भुजङ्ग-कुण्डली the former only admits of being exchanged *for a synonym*; of हरः शिवः the latter only, and both of शशिशुभ्रांशु. In the sentence भाति सदाऽनत्याऽगः* '(A mountain shines by never bowing),' neither of the seeming words दान and त्यागः can be exchanged. Thus the figure in question is an ornament both of word and sense, inasmuch as it can partially endure an exchange of words.

Text.

Alliteration.

No. 633. A similarity of sounds, notwithstanding a difference in the vowels, is what is called Anuprása, or Alliteration.

Commentary.

a. A similarity in mere vowels, not being striking, is not counted *an embellishment.*

b. Anuprása (*anu* + *pra* + *ása* from *as* to throw) *means etymologically*, a throwing or setting together *of words* in an excellent manner favourably to flavour.

* Wrongly divided in Roer's edition—भाति सदा न त्यागः

TEXT.

Single Alliteration.

No. 634 The Chheka, or Single Alliteration, is a similarity *occurring* once and in more than one way among a collection of consonants.

COMMENTARY.

a. The Chheka—*i. e.* the Chhekánuprása.

b. 'In more then one way'—*i. e.* both in the nature *of the sound* and in the order *of their succession.* The similarity, for instance, in रसः सरः with a difference of order is not the subject of this ornament.

c. This is an example of my revered father's:—

आदाय बकुलगन्धानन्धीकुर्वन् पदे पदे भ्रमरान्।
अयमेति मन्दमन्दं कावेरीवारिपावनः पवनः॥

(Wafting the perfumes of the Vakula,* intoxicating the bees at every step, here blows softly and slowly the purifying breeze from the *holy* waters of the Káverí).

There is here the recurrence of two combined consonants in गन्धानन्धी of two separate in वेरी-वारि, and of many, in पावनः पवनः

d. 'Chheka' means skilful, and as being used by them, this figure *is called* the Chhekánúprása, or the 'Alliteration of the skilful.'

TEXT.

Harmonious Alliteration.

No. 635. Similarity among a number of consononts in one way or that occurring more than once (which distinguishes it from the above ornament) and in more than one way, or the same single consonant recurring even once is termed Vṛittyanuprása, or Harmonious Alliteration.

COMMENTARY.

a. 'In one way'—*i. e.* in nature only and not in order too. 'In more than one way'—*i. e.* in order as well as in nature. In the expression 'even once' by the word 'even' is implied 'also more than once if possible.'

b. The following is an example:—

उन्मीलन्मधुगन्धलुब्धमधुपव्याधूतचूताङ्कुर-
क्रीडत्कोकिलकाकलीकलकलैरुद्गीर्णकर्णज्वराः।
नीयन्ते पथिकैः कथं कथमपि ध्यानावधानक्षण-
प्राप्तप्राणसमासमागमरसोल्लासैरमी वासराः॥

* Mimusops Elongi. *Wilson.*

(Hardly and with difficulty are passed these days by the wandering *lovers*, enjoying the fancied bliss of the company of their sweethearts obtained but in the *transient* moments of mediative vision—*these vernal days* when the ear is tormented with the sweet confusiou of the warbles of kokilas sporting on the mango sprays, which are shaken by bees allured by the scent of the overflowing honey).

In this *example* the two (र) and (स) are similar in one way only, their order not being the same. In the second line of the stanza the consonants क and ल recur more than once and in the same order; in the first line the letter न recurs once and ष more than once.

c. An arrangement of letters ministering to the heightening of flavour is termed 'vṛitti' (*i. e.* style adapted to the sentiment) *and the present ornament is called* 'Vrittyánuprása' since it consists in an excellent disposition of words in conformity with that arrangement.

TEXT.

No. 636. When there is a similarity among consonants alone, as being pronounced by the same organ of speech, such as the palate, the teeth or the like, this is styled S'rutyanuprása. or Melodious Alliteration.

Melodious Alliteration.

COMMENTARY.

a. For example :—

दृशा दग्धं मनसिजं जीवयन्ति दृशैव याः ।
विरूपाक्षस्य जयिनी स्ताःस्तुमो वामलोचनाः ॥

(Them who with a look recall to life the mind-born god who was burnt by a look—we glorify the fair-eyed *women* the conquerors of the fierce-eyed divinity *Siva*).

Here, *in the words* जीवयन्ति याः and जयिनीः the consonants ज and य being uttered from the same part *of the mouth, viz.*, the palate, are similar. Similarly might it be exemplified of the gutturals, dentals, &c. And this is named S'rutyanuprása because of its being extremely delightful to the ear (s'ruti) of the man of taste.

TEXT.

No. 637. If a consonant, its predicament unaltered, together with the foregoing vowel, is repeated at the end *of words or lines*, it is termed Antyánuprása, or Final Alliteration.

Final Alliteration or Rhyme.

COMMENTARY.

a. 'Its predicament unaltered'—*i. e.* joined, as the case may be, with an anuswára, visarga, vowel or another consonant.

b. And this *figure* is generally to be used at the end of verses or of words. Coming at the end of verses, this is illustrated in *the following stanza of* mine :—

केशः काशस्तवकविकासः कायः प्रकटितकरभविलासः ।
चक्षुर्दग्धवराटककल्पं त्यजति न चेतः काममनल्पम् ॥

(The hair bears the appearance of a bunch of the *Kása* grass :* the body, *bent down and hunch-backed,* displays the beauty of a young camel's frame : the eyes are facsimiles of a burnt *cowri :* yet the heart quits not its exorbitant desires.)

c. Coming at the end of words, this figure is instanced in मन्दं हसन्तः पुलकं वहन्त इत्यादि.

(Sweetly smiling, with their hairs erect with joy, &c.)

TEXT.

No. 638. A repetition of sound and sense when there is a difference in the mere purport, is spoken of as the Láṭánuprása.

Láṭánuprása.

COMMENTARY.

a. For example :—

स्मेरराजीवनयने नयने किं निमीलिते ।
पश्य निर्ज्जितकन्दर्पं कन्दर्पवशगं प्रियं ॥

(Why hast thou closed thine eyes, fair lady with eyes like the smiling lotus ? Behold thy love who surpasses Cupid, by Cupid brought to subjection.)

Here though the meanings of the case-endings *of the repeated words* are different, yet the more important ideas of the concrete objects, conveyed by their crude portions, are the same, hence there is here a case of the Láṭánuprása.

b. In the example—"His eyes are eyes indeed in whose presence will be this fair-faced one," the second 'eyes' differs in meaning simply in being designed to imply a possession of such attributes as good fortune or the like. *This, then, is also an instance of the*

* Saccharum spontaneum. *Wilson.*

same ornament though assuming here the character of what, in Greek Rhetoric, is designated Ploke, πλόκη.

c. Or to take another example:—

यस्य न सविधे दयिता दवदहनस्तुहिनदीधितिस्तस्य।
यस्य च सविधे दयिता दवदहनस्तुहिनदोधितिस्तस्य ॥

(To him who has not his love by him, the cool-beamed *moon* is a conflagration, and to *him who* has his love by him a conflagration is the cool-beamed *moon.*)

In this example we have a repetition of many words.

d. This figure is termed Láṭánuprása from its being generally liked by the people *of the country* Láṭa.*

TEXT.

No. 639. Anuprása (Alliteration) then is fivefold.

COMMENTARY.

a. **The text is clear.**

TEXT.

No. 640. The repetition, in the same order, of a collection of vowels and consonants, the sense, where there is one, being different, is styled Yamaka, or Rhyme.

The Yamaka.

COMMENTARY.

a. In this *ornament* both the sounds repeated are sometimes significant and sometimes meaningless; sometimes one of them has a meaning and the other, none: hence is the clause 'where there is one' inserted *in the text.* 'In the same order'—this implies that such repetitions as दमो मोद have no connection *with the present figure.*

b. And this figure, consisting of the repetition of a word, a line, a half stanza and a stanza is abundantly divisable, because of the numerous ways in which the repetition of a word &c., may be made.

c. A part only is exemplified *as follows*:—

नवपलाशपलाशवनं पुरः स्फुटपरागपरागतपङ्कजं ।
मृदुलतान्तलतान्तमलोकयत् स सुरभिं सुरभिं सुमनोभरैः ॥

* The upper part of the Dekhin, *Lár* or *Larice.* *Wilson.*

(He saw before him the spring, fragrant with an exuberance of flowers, under whose influence the Palás'a* forest had assumed a fresh foliage, the lotus was filled with manifest pollen and the tender ends of plants were fading).

Here we have the repetition of words. In पलाश पलाश as also in सुरभिं सुरभिं both the sounds repeated are significant, in लतान्त लतान्त the former is meaningless; in पराग पराग the latter *bears no sense.* Similarly might the other cases be exemplified.

d. According to the rule, *viz.*, "ड and ल, व and ब, ल and र are to be held the same *letter* in the Rhyme or the like," there is no violation of this figure *in this verse of Kálidása* भुजलतां जडतामबलाजनः।

TEXT.

No. 641. When one construes a speech of another in a sense different from what is intended, by a Paronomasia or a change of voice, it is termed Vakrokti or the Crooked Speech, and is twofold according *as it is founded on the one or the other.*

Crooked Speech.

COMMENTARY.

a. 'Twofold' as being Paronomastic Crooked Speech and Accentual Crooked Speech.

b. For examples *of these two kinds* in their order :—

'के यूयं'—'स्थल एव सम्प्रतिवयं'—'प्रश्नो विशेषाश्रयः'
'किं ब्रूते विहगः सवा फणिपति र्यत्रास्ति सुप्तो हरिः'।
'वामा यूय'-'महो विडम्बरसिकः कीदृक् स्मरो वर्त्तते
येनास्मासु विवेकशून्यमनसः पुंस्वेव योषिद्भ्रमः'॥

"Who are you?'—*playing upon the word* क *which means water also, the addressees reply*—'Forsooth, we are on the ground just now.' 'Nay *my* question is touching the particularity (*vis'esha of your caste or country.*' 'What says the bird (*vi*) or the lord of the serpents (*s'esha*) on whom Vishnu is sleeping?'—'You are perverse (*vámá*)—'Aha, how fond is cupid of deluding people—this man, robbed of all discrimination, mistakes us men for women (*vámá*)!"

Here in the word *vis'esha* there is a 'Paronomasia with division,' as *vis'esha*, divided into *vi* and *s'esha* comes to be connected with the

* Butea frondosa. *Wilson.*

two meanings of 'bird' and 'serpent.' In the other instances there is that 'without division.'

"In the season noisy with the Kokila's warbles and delightful with the blooming mango plants, her heart grieves not (*na dúyate*) to have abandoned her offending *lover*."

Here the negative (*na*) used in the sense of denial by one of the fair friends of the lady, is by another constructed into an affirmative signification through an *interrogative* change of voice, thus—'*Grieves not her heart?*—it DOES.'

TEXT.

No. 642. When a sentence is formed of words which are the same in a variety of tongues, it is named Bháshásama, or Linguistic Sameness.

Linguistic Sameness.

COMMENTARY.

a. For instance *this stanza* of mine :—

मञ्जुलमणिमञ्जीरे कलगम्भीरे विहारसरसीतीरे।
विरसासि केलिकीरे किमालि धीरे च गन्धसारसमीरे॥

(Dost thou, fair friend, take no delight *now* in the charming anklet of gems sounding with deep melody, in the border of the pleasure-lake, in thy fondled parrot, or in the gentle breeze wafting the perfume of sandal?)

This stanza is the same in the Sanskrit, Prákrit, S'aurasení, Práchí, Avantí, Nágara, and Apabhrans'a, *tongues.*

b. In such a sentence, however, as "Sarasam kaiṇa kavvam" (Sweet is the poem of the poet), though the word *sarasam* is the same in Sanskrit and Prákrit, it is no ornament, for the sameness does not pervade the whole sentence and is therefore not striking.

TEXT.

No. 643. When more than one sense is conveyed by *distinct* words coalescing *into identity*, it is termed Paronomasia or Coalescence (S'lesha.) And this is eightfold according to the coalescence of Letters, Affixes, Genders, Verbal Bases, Inflected Words, Inflections, Numbers and Tongues.

Paronomasia or Coalescence.

COMMENTARY.

a. For examples in their order :—

प्रतिकूलतामुपगते हि विधौ विफलत्वमेति बहुसाधनता ।
अवलम्बनाय दिनभर्तुरभून्न पतिष्यतः करसहस्रमपि ॥

[When Fate (or the moon) stands in opposition, an abundance of resources becomes fruitless: the Lord of day while falling, could not be held up by a thousand rays.]

Here in *vidhau* there is a coalescence of the LETTERS *i* and *u* of the words *vidhi* (fate) and *vidhu* (moon), these letters being changed into *au* in the locative.

b. किरणा हरिणाङ्कस्य दक्षिणश्च समीरणः ।
कान्तोत्सङ्गजुषां नूनं सर्व एव सुधाकिरः ॥

(The beams of the moon, the breeze of the Southern quarter—all shed ambrosia to those who are seated in the lap of their beloved.)

We have here *the coalescence* of the *kwip* and *ka* AFFIXES* in *sudhákirah* (ambrosia-shedding), *kirah as plural being formed by the addition of the former to the verbal root kṛi, and, as singular, by that of the latter.* Besides, there is also here a coalescence of NUMBERS from the singular and plural numbers assuming the same form in *sarva*† and *sudhâkirah.*

c. विकसन्नेत्रनीलाब्जे तथा तन्व्याः स्तनद्वयी ।
तव दत्तां सदा मोदं लसत्तरलहारिणी ॥

(Those charmingly bright and tremulous eyes of the slender-bodied *lady* that shine like blue lotuses, and those breasts with the bright and tremulous necklace—may they ever be a source of delight to thee !)

Here we have a coalescence of the neuter and feminine genders in *the epithet lasat-tarala-háriṇí* which, as neuter dual, applies to *vikasan-netra-nílábje* (eyes shining like blue lotuses); and, as feminine singular, to *stanadwayí* (couple of breasts). There is also a coalescence of numbers *in the said word and dattám, which latter in the "Parasmai-pada" is the dual imperative of dá (to give), and, in the "Atmane-pada" the singular imperative of the same verb.*

* Both of these form participal adjectives.

† *Sarve* (plural) and *sarvah* (singular) coalesce into *sarva* before *eva*, according to the rules of 'Sandhi'.

d. अयं सर्वाणि शास्त्राणि हृदि ज्ञेषु च वक्ष्यति ।
सामर्थ्यकृदमित्राणां मित्राणाञ्च नृपात्मजः ॥

(This prince will carry all scriptures in his heart and expound them to the wise, will give strength to his friends and destroy the power of his foes.)

Here we have a coalescence of the BASES *vah* (to cut) and *vach* (to tell or expound) in *vakshyati*, and of *kṛit* (to cut) and *kṛi* (to do) in *sámarthyakṛit* (creator, or destroyer of strength.)

e. पृथुकार्त्तस्वरपात्रं भूषितनिःशेषपरिजनं देव ।
विलसत्करेणुगहनं सम्प्रति सममावयोः सदनम् ॥

(Our houses, O king, are now *literally* alike—*mine* filled with the distressful cries of children, *thine* with vessels of massive gold: *mine* with the whole family lying on the ground, *thine* with unnumbered attendants decorated; *mine* with holes filled with heaps of dust, *thine* thronged with majestic elephants.)

Here there is a coalescence of INFLECTED WORDS *(pada)*, not of mere bases, for when the compounds are analysed *in relation to either of the two meanings*, the inflections and composition (*samása*) *in each compound* are, *in the case of one sense*, different *from those in the case of the other: that is to say, not only do different bases coalesce into identity but different case-endings and different varieties of Composition.**

f. And so—

नीतानामाकुलीभावं लुब्धैर्भूरिशिलीमुखैः ।
सदृशे वनवृद्धानां कमलानां तदीक्षणे ॥

[Her eyes are like lotuses full grown in water, agitated by greedy swarms of bees; or (as the same words import) they are like the eyes of wild deer, overwhelmed with a multitude of arrows *shot* by the *eager* hunters.]

Here, although there is a coalescence in the words *lubdha* (greedy or hunter) and *s'ilímukha* (bee or arrow), there is *admitted* the coalescence of BASES *only*, because of the sameness of the inflections in either of the coalescent words. Otherwise, *i. e. if we do not recognize a coalesence of bases in such cases as this*, we should have to hold a coalescence of inflected words in every case.

* For instance, the Bahuvríhi and Tatpurusha in pṛithukártaswarapátram.

g. सर्वस्वं हर सर्वस्य त्वं भवच्छेदतत्परः ।
नयोपकारसाम्मुख्यमायासि तनुवर्त्तनम् ॥

[O Hara (S'iva) thou art my all, and busy art thou in liberating all creatures from this *miserable* mundane existence; and thou manifestest thyself in a corporeal form, the very presence of virtue and beneficence.*]

Here in the case of one sense, '*Hara*' is an address of S'íva and the inflection is nominal; in the other case it is formed from the root *hṛi* (to plunder) by a verbal inflection. So there is here a coalescence of INFLECTIONS; similarly in *bhava* &c. And this sort, though included under the coalescence of AFFIXES, is separately mentioned from its peculiar strikingness, arising from the circumstance of its belonging to inflected forms of nouns and verbs which cannot be obtained by the addition of other affixes *than those that take the name of inflection.*

h. महदे सुरसन्धम्मे तमव समासङ्गमागमाहरणे ।
हर बहुसरणं तं चित्तमोहमवसर उमे सहसा ॥

(O thou Light-bestowing Umá, foster in me that fondness for the acquirement of knowledge, wished for *even* by the gods, and destroy that mental delusion that, on every occasion, creeps through many *an object.*)

As Mahárásḥṭrí this is turned into Sanskrit thus :—

मह्यं देहि रसं धर्म्मे तमोवशामाशां संसाराद्धर नः ।
हरवधु शरणं त्वं चित्तमोहोऽपसरतु मे सहसा ॥

(Give me, O consort of S'iva, a love of virtue and destroy our fondness for the world that is born of ignorance. Thou art my refuge, O goddess! May my mental darkness be at once removed!)

Here there is a coalescence of *the two distinct tongues*, Sanskrit and Mahárásḥṭrí.

* For men are thus enabled to purify themselves by contemplating thee, who in thy true spiritual nature art beyond human conception. The following amiable advice of a demon to his son is the other import of the stanza!—

"Plunder thou the whole property of all, let murder be thy chief business, drive off benevolence from thy presence and carry on a trade of *perpetual* persecution."

TEXT.

No. 644. This (Paronomasia), again, is threefold *viz.*, (1) that 'with division,' (2) 'without division' and (3) consisting of both these sorts *combined.*

The three sorts of Paronomasia.

COMMENTARY.

a. These three divisions are to be recognized, according to propriety, under the said eight varieties. Or we may exemplify *the first two sorts in the following stanza:—*

येन ध्वस्तमनोभवेन बलिजित्कायः पुरास्त्रीकृतो
यश्चोद्वृत्तभुजङ्गहारवलयो गङ्गांच योऽधारयत्।
यस्याहुः शशिमच्छिरो हर इति स्तुत्यं च नामामराः
पायात् स स्वयमन्धकक्षयकरस्त्वां सर्वदोमाधवः॥

(May the Lord of Umá ever preserve thee!—He who destroyed the demon Andhaka and the deity of love, who of old made a weapon of Vishṇu's body, who wears huge serpents for his necklace and bracelets, who bore on his head Gangá *descending from the heavens,* whose head the deities declare ornamented with the moon and whose adorable name they celebrate as 'Hara.')*

Here there is a 'coalescence with division' in *yena dhwastamanobhavena* (which, in the case of the other sense, is to be differently divided thus—*yena dhwastam anah abhavena*); and one 'without division' in *Andhaka-kshaya-karah.* The third variety consisting of those 'with division' and 'without division'—for these may be combined in the same instance—is not separately exemplified, for fear of swelling the work.

b. Here some say—"the only case of the Paronomasia of words is the 'Paronomasia with division' wherein two words that are distinct, as being pronounced by distinct efforts through a difference of accent in the shape of the acute or the like, coalesce in analogy to the lac and wood. Whilst that 'without division' is no other than a Paronomasia of Sense. In this the meanings coalesce, or are bound together, analogously to a couple of fruits supported by the same footstalk; for the word, *in relation to both the senses,* is one and the same, as being pronounced by one and the same effort from the

* A similar representation of Vishṇu is the other import, which need not be rendered here.

identity of the accent. *And our opinion that these two kinds, with and without division, are Paronomasiæ respectively of word and sense is reasonable indeed,* for an ornament is the ornament of what it is set or founded on: the ornamented and the ornament being recognized, as in every day life, as the place a ' what is placed."

c. This others do not admit. For here, *in the province of poetical criticism,* the division of Suggestion, Subordinate Suggestion (see Chap. IV), Faults Excellences and Ornaments as belonging to a word or sense s regulated by their conformity with the word or sense in their presence and absence, *or, in other words, by the circumstance of their appearing and disappearing with the word or sense.* Nor is the word *Andhaka,* for instance, in *Andhaka-kshaya-karah** identical *in conveying the two meanings of the demon so called and the Yádava family,* for it is a maxim that a word differs from a difference of sense. Besides, since in the case *of a 'Paronomasia without division'* it is the word that is suggested by the poet's genius as the principal means of producing a striking effect, it is no other than an ornament of word. And this strikingness is wanting in a composition of two dissimilar words, and it is the strikingness that is reckoned as an embellishment. If the figure in question be held an ornament of sense because of its having an eye to the sense, then even such ornaments as Alliteration and the like would have to be ranked as ornaments of sense, for they too, as being intended for *the heightening of* the flavour, look to the sense. If you count it an ornament of sense, from the word's being pronounced by one and the same effort, then in such a case as '*pratikúlatámupagate hi vidhau*' (see § 643 *a*) you would be forced to admit an ornament of sense notwithstanding the difference of words. Hence both the cases *of Paronomasia, with and without division,* must be *classed as* ornaments of word.

d. Where, however, the Paronomasia is not destroyed even by an exchange of words, there it is a case of Paronomasia of sense; as—

"From a slight cause they rise and from a slight cause they fall: O how exactly similar are the conditions of the wicked and the extremity of a balance."

* See the foregoing example.

c. It is the opinion of some that since this figure (Paronomasia) cannot have a subject distinct from that of other ornaments, and since the ornaments co-existing with it, mentioned as they are by the sage afterwards, frustrate or nullify it, it is to be recognized as the means of the perception of those ornaments. *The point* is thus discussed *by them :* In such an ornament as the Modal Metaphor (see § 703) or Indirect Description (see § 706), the second sense not being intended to be expressed *but to be suggested,* there is not even a shadow of Paronomasia. Even in such a Paronomastic Metaphor as that in the expression *Vidvanmánasa-hañsa* (Thou swan of that Mánasa lake—the mind of the learned) though the word *mánasa* bears the meanings both of mind and the lake so named, the Paronomasia is nullified by the Metaphor, for the sense of the lake being what the word *mánasa* ultimately terminates in is the principal *signification:* and in Paronomasia both the meanings have an equal prominence. In such a Semblance of Contradiction as that in "*Sannihita-bálándhakárá bhásvanmúrtih*" (She of the radiant form accompanied with the darkness of the hair ; or, she of the solar form accompanied with new-born darkness) there is no Paronomasia, for the incongruous sense which is just perceived is not fully developed. So in the Semblance of Tautology (§ 632). Now *the above ornaments being dismissed as not properly co-existent with Paronomasia, we arrive at certain others which do co-exist with it.* For example: The figure Equal Pairing* (see § 695) does exist in "*Yena dhavastamanobhavena*" &c. (§ 644. *a*) and "*Nítánám,*" &c. (§ 643, *f.*), as with the same facts (*viz* 'preserving thee' and 'resembling the eyes,' respectively) are associated two distinct representations both connected with the subject matter in the one case, and both unconnected with the subject-matter in the other.

स्वेच्छोपजातविषयोऽपि न याति वक्तुं
देहीति मार्गणशतैश्च ददाति दुःखं ।
मोहात् समुत्क्षिपति जीवनमप्यकाण्डे
कष्टं प्रसूनविशिखः प्रभुरल्पबुद्धिः ॥

* This and some other renderings of names of Indian figures of speech I have adopted from Mr. Griffith's paper on "the Figures of Indian Poetical Rhetoric as illustrated in the Bhaṭṭi Kávya" appended to his 'Specimens of old Indian Poetry.'

"The God of the flowery shafts and the master with a little mind are *equally* troublesome. *The one*, while he himself has made a person the object *of desire*, goes not *to him* to speak *in behalf of the party inflamed by him*, nay torments him with hundreds of arrows, *perhaps* in envy of his body—*himself having none, nor stops here*, but distracts him and untimely wrests his life. *The other*, while his will can command all wealth, is never disposed to say 'give,' and gives only pain on a hundred importunities, and under a mental delusion or groundless suspicion violently deprives men of their lives."

Here we have the *ornament called* Illuminator (see § 696), since two persons, one (Káma) not connected with the subject-matter, the other (a little-minded master) connected with it, are associated with attributes *verbally* the same. In such *an example* as "*Sakalakalam purametajjátam samprati sudhañs'u-vimbam*" (The city with its tumultuous noise,—or as the same words import—full in all its digits, has now become the lunar orb) there exists the ornament of Simile. Now as Paronomasia cannot possibly exist apart from *one of* these *figures* and as these may exist apart from Paronomasia, and since the latter *co-existing as it does with some of these figures*, is felt to have a stronger strikingness, such cases properly go under the designation of Paronomasia, otherwise the designation would be altogether abolished.

f. To this we say: It is not true that Paronomasia has not a province distinct from that of other ornaments. For in "*Yena dhvasta*" &c. (§ 644 *a.*) it HAS a distinct subject, the figure of Equal Pairing (§ 695) in which BOTH the senses are not, as a rule, intended to be expressed, having no place in it. Now, *for the sake of including the Equal Pairing in the present example*, if it be determined that of the two deities represented, Mádhava and Umádhava, only one is intended to be actually mentioned, the other would needs have to be *held as* hinted at, *and thus it would no longer be a case of Paronomasia.** Moreover in the Equal Pairing a single attribute only is apprehended as connected with more than one subject, whilst here more than one subject is apprehended as associated with distinct

* An equal prominence of the two meanings being its condition.

attributes. Nor in such a case as "*Sakala &c.*" (§ *e.*) is the Paronomasia the source of the apprehension of the simile, for on this supposition, the Complete Simile (§ 648) would be without a subject. Should you say there is such a subject of the Complete Simile as 'this face is charming like the lotus,' I would reply—no, for if in '*Sakala &c.*' there is no *real* simile because there is a Paronomasia of words, what fault has the Paronomasia of sense committed in such an expression as 'charming'* *so as not to preclude, in this case too, a recognition of the simile.* The truth is that a verbal resemblance as well as one of quality or action may be the basis of a simile according to the direction of Rudraṭa: 'The Simile and the Conjunction (see § 739) are both clearly ornaments of sense but they may also be founded on a mere verbal resemblance.'

g. 'But then,' our opponent might further object, 'a sameness of quality or action alone is the proper basis of a simile, the resemblance in such a case being real; whilst a verbal sameness is not a reasonable support for the ornament, the resemblace here being unreal. Consequently the sameness of quality or action alone, not a verbal resemblance as in "*Sakala &c.*," is the proper subject of the Complete Simile, the Paronomasia of sense being set aside from such cases and *virtually from all cases*, seeing that otherwise there would be no room for the Complete Simile.'

h. *I would again reply :* No; for the unqualified definition of a Similitude that it is a community of attribute *or circumstance* is not exclusive of verbal sameness. And if in a case of verbal sameness the community, not being real, does not produce a Simile, then how in such an expression as "*Vidvanmánasa*" (§ *e.*), does the attribution of the nature of a lake to the mind (figured as a place) *founded merely on the verbal identity of* "*mánasa*" *(mind)* and "*mánasa*" (*the lake Mánasa*), become the occasion for the metaphor in the shape of ascribing the nature of a swan to the king? Moreover if the simile is to be admitted only in the case of a real resemblance, then why do you too recognize a Frustrated Simile in such a case as

* The reader must note a nice distinction here, before he can understand the passage. The charmingness of the face and that of the lotus are not one, nor even exactly similar, but are identified, by a Paronomasia of sense, into a point of resemblance, in the comparison of the two objects.

'*Sakala &c.*' (§ *e*)? Further it is the Paronomasia that sustains the similitude, not that the similitude sustains the Paronomasia, for the similitude is impossible prior to the Paronomastic composition. So it is proper that the ornament recognized or marked out in such cases be the simile, which is the principal,—according to the maxim that designations are made after what is chief.

i. 'But,' *it might be further objected,* 'in the province of the ornaments of word there is not admitted the Commixture (see § 757) *of figures* as principal and sub-ordinate, how then is it here maintained in respect of the Paronomasia and Simile?' I would reply—no, that non-admission respects only such figures as the Alliteration or the like, where a reference to the sense is wanting. Similarly is it to be understood of such ornaments as the Illuminatof (§ 696) and the like, *when founded upon a verbal similitude, that it is these* that are the principal, the Paronomasia *being subservient thereto.*

j. To anticipate an error:

सत्पक्षा मधुरगिरः प्रसाधिताशा मदोद्धतारम्भाः ।
निपतन्ति धार्तराष्ट्राः कालवशान्मेदिनीपृष्ठे ॥

("The well-winged, sweet-voiced swans *(hañsa)*, under the influence of the season, are now descending upon the plains, ornamenting the quarters, and uttering loud cries of joy." Or "The sons of Dhárṭaráshṭra, of agreeable discourse and of proudly valiant undertakings, who are assisted by noble partisans, who have won all the quarters of the earth, now by fate's command fall *dead* upon the ground.")

Here the words '*dhártaráshṭráh &c.*' being restricted to the signification of 'swan' &c. by the description of the autumn which is in hand, the sense of 'Duryodhana' &c. is a suggestion of matter, originating in the power of the words (see chap. VI, § 257). And here since the second representation resulting from the present composition is meant only to be hinted *as the subject-matter of the drama,* a comparison is not intended, and so there is neither the suggestion of a Simile nor a Paronomasia. Thus *our present subject is* all clear *now.*

TEXT.

No. 645. When the letters, *under a particular disposition,* induce

The Fancy Ornament. the shape of the lotus &c., it is termed the Fancy Ornament (Chitra).

Commentary.

a. By the '&c.' are implied a sword, a drum, a wheel, the *Gomútriká** and others.

b. The letters, though striking through that particular disposition of them in writing, being tropically identified with the *vocal* letters striking by means of that particular *succession in which they come in* contact with the ether of the ear, it is reckoned an ornament of word.

c. Among its *many* varieties, the composition of the lotus is instanced in *this couplet of* mine :—

मारमासुषमा चारुरुचा मारवधूत्तमा ।
मात्तधूर्त्ततमावासा सा वामा मेऽस्तु मा रमा ॥

(May that lovely lady be mine, who equals Káma's mother—*Lakshmí*, in beauty, who in fair radiance, excels his consort—I care not for Fortune, no I never care for that goddess, who takes her dwelling with the vilest rogues.)

This Composition of an octopetalous lotus has its letters, *or rather syllables*, in the primary quarters coalescent by exit and entrance, but not so in the secondary quarters, the syllable of the pericarp, *which is repeated eight times*, being of course coalescent.† Similarly may the composition of the sword &c. be inferred.

* According to the *Sarasvatí-kanṭhábharaṇa* (another Rhetorical work) the undulating flow of a cow's urine is what is meant here.

† This requires explanation. First draw a lotus of eight petals pointing respectively to the eight quarters. Begin with reading and writing the first syllable मा (*má*) in the seed-vessel, go out into the eastern petal with the next two syllables रमा (*ra-má*), then enter, at its point, the south-eastern petal, with the next two syllables सुष (*su-sha*), then come back to मा (*má*) in the seed-vessel, make your exit by the southern petal, with चारु (*chá-ru*) return the same way, with रुचा (*ru-chá*), to मा (*má*), and so on reading two syllables in each petal, but repeating them inversely in the four primary ones till you make your final entrance into the seed-vessel through the same petal (the eastern) that you first started from.

Text.

No. 646. The Enigma *(Prahelikâ)*, which, being opposed to flavour, is no ornament in poetry, *being useless and ugly* as a hump *on the human body*, is not dwelt upon here. It consists merely in a turn of words, in the shape of the want and addition of a syllable, &c.

Enigma.

Commentary.

a. The expression 'in the shape of the want and addition of a syllable' implies three varieties of the enigma, viz. (1) with a syllable wanting, (2) with a syllable added, and (3) with a syllable wanting and a syllable added. For example:—

कूजन्ति कोकिलाः साले यौवने फुल्लमम्बुजं।
किं करोतु कुरङ्गाक्षी वदनेन निपीड़िता॥

(The kokils warble on the mango tree, the lotus blooms in the water: what may the fawn-eyed lady do, oppressed as she is by love?*)

Here '*sále*' being said for '*rasále*,' the *syllable* '*ra*' is wanting; '*yau*' is added in '*yauvane*' which is read instead of '*vane*,' '*ma*' is omitted and '*va*' added in *vadanena* used in place of '*madanena*.'

b. By the '&c.' (in the text) is meant the concealment of a verb, a case or the like. Of these the concealment of a verb, as:—

पाण्डवानां सभामध्ये दुर्य्योधन उपागतः।
तस्मै गाञ्च हिरण्यञ्च सर्व्वाण्याभरणानि च।

(In the midst of the assembly of the Páṇḍavas, came Duryodhana: to him land and gold and all ornaments.)

Here the verb '*aduh*' (they gave) is concealed in '*duryodhanah*' which is to be analysed into '*aduh yah adhanah*;' *the enigma being explained—Any pauper that entered the assembly of the Páṇḍavas, they gave him land &c.* So in the other *varieties*.

c. Now the occasion having arrived for treating of the ornaments of sense, and those that are founded on similitude, as being the

* Rendered according to the riddle it would read thus: "The kokils warble on the Sál tree, the lotus blooms in youth: what may the fawn-eyed lady do, distressed as she is by the face."

principal, having to be defined first, he begins with stating the ornament of Simile, which, even of these, forms the essence.

TEXT.

No. 647. A resemblance between two things, EXPRESSED by a SINGLE sentence, and unaccompanied with a contrast *or difference*, is *termed* Simile.

Simile.

COMMENTARY.

a. In the Metaphor (*rúpaka*—§ 669) and the like the resemblance is suggested; in the Dissimilitude or Contrast (§ 700) the difference too is expressed; in the Reciprocal Simile (see § 667) there are employed two sentences; and in the Comparison Absolute (§ 666) there is only one object compared, *i. e. compared to itself.* Thus we see the difference of the present Ornament.

TEXT.

No. 648. That is Complete, in which the common attribute, the words implying comparison, the object compared and that compared to, are *all* expressed.

Simile Complete.

COMMENTARY.

a. 'That'—*i. e.* the Simile. The 'common attribute,' *i. e.*, the quality or action of two objects which occasions their similitude, such as charmingness or the like.—'Words implying comparison' such as '*iva*' (as) or the like.—'The object compared, *i. e.* a face, for instance. 'The object compared to'—for example, the moon.

TEXT.

No. 649. That again is Direct (s'rautí) in which *the comparison is expressed by* such words as '*yathá*,' '*iva*,' '*vá*' (all answering to the English *as*) or by the affix '*-vat*' as equivalent to '*iva*;' Indirect (árthi) when such words as '*tulya*' (equal) '*samána*' (like) &c., are employed, or the affix '*-vat*' in the sense of 'equal.'

Direct, and Indirect Simile.

COMMENTARY.

a. Though the particles '*yathá*,' '*iva*,' '*vá*,' &c., *or the English* '*as*' are equivalent to the terms '*tulya*' (like) &c. used in the other sort of Simile, yet since they at the very hearing convey the notion of the relation of similarity between the objects compared together, their employ-

makes a Simile direct. So in the employment of '*-vat*,' when affixed *locatively or possessively* in the sense of '*iva*' (as) according to *Páṇini's rule* "*Tatra tasyeva* (V., 1, 116)."

The terms 'like' &c., on the other hand, rest with the object compared, as in 'The face is like the lotus;' or with the object to which the comparison is made, as in 'The lotus is the like of the face;' or with both, as in 'The lotus and the face are alike:' so it is through our looking after their *implied* sense that these words come to express a comparison and consequently their use makes a Simile indirect, or virtual (*árthí*).* So in the case of the employment of '*-vat*' in the sense of 'like' according to the rule "*Tena tulya*" &c., (Pánini V, 1, 115).

TEXT.

No. 649.† The two *kinds are possible* in a nominal affix (taddhita), in a compound, and in a sentence *or phrase*.

a. 'The two *kinds*'—i. e. the Direct and the Indirect.

b. For example:

सौरभमम्भोरुहवन्मुखस्य कुम्भाविव स्तनौ पीनौ ।
हृदयं मदयति वदनं तव शरदिन्दुर्यथा बाले ॥

(The fragrance of thy mouth is as-*the-odour-of*-the lotus, thy breasts are plump as-jars, and thy countenance, O girl, gladdens the heart as the autumnal moon.)

Here, '*ambhoruha-vat*,' '*kumbháviva*,' and '*s'aradinduryathá*' are respective instances of the three varieties of the direct *Simile*.

मधुरः सुधावदधरः पल्लवतुल्योऽतिपेलवः पाणिः ।
चकितमृगलोचनाभ्यां सदृशी चपले च लोचने तस्याः ॥

* The particles '*iva*' &c., implying, as they do, nothing else but resemblance in the abstract, directly express a comparison. While the words 'like,' 'equal,' &c. being concrete terms do not directly convey the abstract notion of resemblance, but through calling up the idea of *something resembling*, which has to be apprehended in identity with what they are put in apposition to (*viz.*, any one of the objects compared together or both), before the comparison can be perceived.

† This number is, by mistake, repeated in Dr. Röer's edition of the original.

(Sweet like-ambrosia is her under-lip, soft like-the-tender-leaf is her hand, and her eyes are tremulous like those of the frightened deer.)

Here the Indirect Simile, in its three kinds, is respectively exemplified in '*sudhá-vat,*' '*pallava-tulyah*' and '*chakita-mṛigalochanábhyáñ sadṛis'í.*'

TEXT.

Three-fold subdivision of Direct and Indirect Simile.

No. 650. Thus the complete Simile is sixfold.

COMMENTARY.

a. *The text* is clear.

TEXT.

Simile Elliptical and its two divisions into Direct and Indirect.

No. 651. It is Elliptical when one, two, or three of *the four* beginning with the 'common attribute' (see § 648) are omitted, and this also, like the former (the Complete Simile) is Direct or Indirect.

COMMENTARY.

a. 'This'—the Elliptical.—He states its varieties.

TEXT.

No. 652. This, in the omission of the attribute, is like the complete, save *that* the Direct *is not possible* in a nominal affix.

COMMENTARY.

a. 'This'—the Elliptical Simile—, 'in the omission of the attribute'—i. e. of the common quality or action, 'is like the complete,' that is to say, it is sixfold in the aforesaid manner, but the Direct not being possible in a nominal affix, it is, *in fact*, fivefold.

b. For example:

मुखमिन्दुर्यथा पाणिः पल्लवेन समः प्रिये ।
वाचः सुधा इवोष्ठस्ते विम्बतुल्यो मनोऽश्मवत् ॥

(Thy face, my love, is as the moon, thy hand is equal to the tender-leaf, thy words are as-nectar, thy lips are like-the-vimba-fruit, but stone-like is thy heart.)

TEXT.

No. 653. *This* again may be five-fold, being possible in the two sorts of *the affix* '*kyach*' respectively applied in the sense of position and object, in *the affix* '*kyan*,'* and in *the adverbial affix* '*ṇamul*' added in an active or passive sense.

Simile Elliptical, omitting the common attribute, is five fold.

COMMENTARY.

a. 'The Elliptical Simile, in the omission of the common attribute'—*these words* are to be supplied *in the present text from the foregoing one.*

b. The *kyach, kyan*, and *ṇamul are named yiṇ, ṇáyi*, and *ṇam* in the technicality of *the* Kalápa *grammar.*

c. For examples in their order :—

अन्तःपुरीयसि रणेषु, सुतीयसि त्वं
पौरं जनं, तव सदा रमणीयते श्रीः ।
दृष्टः प्रियाभिरमृतद्युतिदर्शमिन्द्र-
सञ्चारमत्र भुवि सञ्चरसि क्षितीश ॥

[In the battle-field thou actest as if thou wert in thy *Zenana*, and thou treatest the people of thy city as if they were thy sons; Fortune behaves as a wife towards thee, and looked upon by thy beloved ladies as the Nectar-beamed *moon*, thou walkest upon the earth, O monarch, like the Royal God (Indra) himself.]

Here the points of resemblance are omitted, *viz.* the circumstance of being a place for pleasant sports, in *the phrase* '*antahpuríyasi*,' and (the king's) being full of loving-kindness. Similarly in the other *expressions of comparison.*

And in these *varieties*, because of the absence of the words *yathá* &c., and *tulya* &c., we have not to consider such specialities as *that of being of* the Direct sort or the like.

Some instance these as cases of the omission of *the affix* '-*vat*' expressive of comparison. This is not right, for the *affixes kyan* &c., also, being added in the sense of *vat* imply comparison. Nor should it be said that the *affixes kyan* &c., cannot well imply comparison

* These two affixes are for forming verbs from nouns, to imply comparison. The words thus formed answer to such expressions in English as 'out-heroding,' 'hectoring' &c.

because, as being affixes, they are not independently expressive, and *such words of comparison as* 'iva' &c., are not employed in these cases. For the same might be said of *the affix* '*kalpap*' and others *which are allowed to be expressive of comparison.* Nor *will it avail to argue that* the '*kalpap*' &c., as being equivalent to '*iva*' &c., are expressive of comparison and that the '*kyan*' &c. are only suggestive *of it,* for it is not certain that even '*iva*' *&c.*, are expressive. Or granting that the '*kalpap*' &c., are expressive, there can be no difference between the affixes of the '-vat' class and those of the 'kyan' class, according to either of the two opinions touching affixes, viz. (1) 'The inflected word in its integrity is expressive,' and (2) 'The base and the affix have each its own signification.' As to the assertion of some that the affixes of the class of '-vat' are directed *by Páṇini* to be employed in the sense of '-iva' and the like, whilst 'kyan' &c. are, in the meaning of 'behaviour'—this too is wrong, for 'kyan' &c., do not simply imply behaviour, but similar behaviour. So the Elliptical is thus tenfold, when the attribute is omitted.

Text.

Simile Elliptical, twofold, when the comparison is omitted.

No. 654. It is twofold, in the omission of the object compared to,—being possible in a phrase and a compound.

Commentary.

a. For example :

" Naught exists equal to her face in charmingness, or like-to-her-eyes."

Here, objects answering to the face and eyes being hinted at, *but, of course, as inferior to them in charmingness,* we have an instance of the object compared to being omitted.

b. And in this very stanza, on our reading '*mukhaṅ yathedam*' instead of '*mukhena sadṛisam,*' and '*dṛigiva*' instead of '*nayana-tulyam,*' we should have the direct sort : thus though, the two divisions of the present variety being subdivisible into the direct and the indirect, we obtain four sorts, yet after the manner of the ancients we have spoken of it as of two sorts only.

TEXT.

It is two-fold, when the likeness is not distinctly expressed.

No. 655. In the omission of the *word or affix* expressive of comparison, it is two-fold, being possible in a compound or the '*kwip*' affix.*

COMMENTARY.

a. For examples in their order :—

"*He* acts the ass *(gardabhati)*, loudly and hoarsely screaming before the great."

Here '*kwip*' expressive of comparison is omitted in '*gardabhati.*' It should not, however, be supposed that the object of comparison too is omitted here, inasmuch as it is indicated by the expression 'screaming.'

"The face of the fawn-eyed one is moon-enchanting."

TEXT.

It is two-fold when the common attribute and the comparison are omitted.

No. 656. It is twofold, in the omission of the *common* attribute and the object compared to,—*being possible* in a compound and a phrase.

COMMENTARY.

a. We shall have examples of these two *varieties* by our reading 'in the world' in place of 'in charmingness' in the sentence beginning 'Naught exists' (see §654. *a*).

TEXT.

It is two-fold, when the attribute and the word of comparison are omitted.

No. 657. In the omission of the attribute and the word of comparison, it is twofold, according as it occurs in the '*kwip*' *affix*, or a compound.

* The difference between this and the affix '*kyan*' (§ 653), which also is added to an object of comparison in the nominative case, lies in the circumstance of the former leaving no sign of itself in the verb formed by its addition; as *gardabhati* 'he asses.' This still more corresponds to the English 'hectoring.'

COMMENTARY.

a. For example :—"Her lotus-face shines like the moon (vidhavati)." Here in '*vidhavati*' there is the *grammatical* rejection of the '*kwip*' affix signifying comparison and of the point of resemblance, viz. 'charmingness.' But some, *recognizing a distinct division of the Elliptical Simile arising from the omission of an affix*, instance the present example as an illustration of the same. 'Lotus-face' is an example of the present variety residing in a compound.

TEXT.

It is single, when the object of comparison is omitted.

No. 658. In the omission of what is compared, it is single, occurring in the '*kyach*' *affix*.

COMMENTARY.

a. For example :—

"With eyes flashing at the sight of the foeman's valour, and with his rod-like hand bristling with the sword, he behaves (sahasráyudhíyati) *in the battlefield* as if he wielded a thousand weapons."

Here the object compared, viz. 'himself,' is omitted, for the expression '*sahasráyudhíyati*' is to be interpreted 'behaves HIMSELF like one with a thousand arms.' For the reasons already stated (§653 *e*) there is no omission here of the term of comparison. Here some say, the word '*sahasráyudhíyati*' being derived from *sahasráyudha*, or one associated with a thousand arms, and interpreted 'he acts like such a one,' we have here the omission of the object compared, not in the shape of 'himself,' but of the particular action of the hero which is not literally mentioned, but simply figured by the expression '*sahasráyudhíyati*.' This view of the case cannot endure a discussion, since the employment of '*kyach*' *with the nominal base* signifying an agent is opposed to the rule *of Paṇini*.

TEXT.

Simile omitting the attribute and the object compared.

No. 659. *We have* another sort in the omission of the attribute and the object compared.

COMMENTARY.

a. For example :—

"As thy fame is diffused, all the seas act the ocean of milk (kshírodíyanti)."

Here *the nominal verb 'kshírodíyanti' being explained* 'they behave themselves like the milky ocean,' we have the omission of 'themselves' the thing compared, and of 'whiteness' the common attribute.

TEXT.

Simile omitting three of the ingredients of comparison.

No. 660. When three *of the four essentials of comparison* (§648) are omitted, it (the Elliptical) is possible in a compound.

COMMENTARY.

a. As—"The stag-eyed one shines." Here the compound '*stag-eyed*' being explained—'She whose eyes are tremulous like those of a stag,' there is an omission of the word expressive of comparison, the common attribute, and the object compared to.

TEXT.

Thus Simile is of 27 kinds.

No. 661. Thus the divisions of the Simile amount to twenty-seven.

COMMENTARY.

a. The sixfold Complete and the twenty-one sorts of the Elliptical, combined, make up twenty-seven kinds of the Simile.

b. Among these divisions of the Simile, he now explains a peculiarity of those in which the common attribute is not omitted.

TEXT.

Simile of the Type and the Antitype.

No. 662. The common attribute, or point of resemblance, is sometimes (generically) one and the same in both the objects of comparison, and sometimes distinct. When the points of resemblance are distinct, they correspond to each other as the type and the antitype, or they may be merely verbally different.

COMMENTARY.

a. Among these *cases*, that where *the point of resemblance* is the same, has already been illustrated in the stanza beginning with "Sweet like ambrosia is her underlip (§649 *b*)."

b. The case of the Type and the Antitype is instanced *in the following stanza of the Raghu-vañs'a*:—

"He covered the earth with their (the Persians') bearded heads, severed by the lance, as with honey-combs teeming with bees."

Here *the epithet* 'bearded' is represented by 'teeming with bees,' analogously to the ornament of Exemplification (Drishṭánta §698).

c. When the difference lies merely in words, we have the following example:—

"The slender-bodied lady, as her eyes expanded upon me like a full-blown blue lotus, told me the whole of the secret purpose that lay in her heart."

Here the 'expansion' and the 'full-blowing' though identical, are expressed by a difference of words, as is the case in the Typical Comparison (Prativastúpamá—§ 697).

TEXT.

Partial Simile.

No. 663. Partial Simile (*ekades'a-vivartiní upamá*) is when the resemblance is expressed and implied.

COMMENTARY.

a. As—

"Lake-beauties, at every step, shine with blue lotuses as with eyes, with water-lilies as with faces, and with Brahmany ducks as with breasts."

Here the resemblance of the eyes &c., to the blue lotus &c., is expressed, and that of lake-beauties, or beautiful lakes, to fair women is implied.

TEXT.

Girdle of Similes.

No. 664. If an object of comparison is turned, further and further, into what is compared to, it is termed the Girdle of Similes.

COMMENTARY.

a. As in the following description of Autumn:—

"The swan, in its white lustre, resembles the moon; lovely women, in their charming gait, resemble the swan; the waters, in their delightful touch, resemble lovely women; and the heavens, in their clearness, resemble the waters."

TEXT.

String of Similes.

No. 665. The Garland, or String of Similes is, when we have several comparisons of the same object.

COMMENTARY.

a. For example :—

" As a lake with the lotus *is pleasant ;* as night *is delightful* with the moon ; as a fair woman, *ornamented* with youth, *is charming ;* so Fortune attended with Virtue ravishes the heart."

b. We sometimes find both the objects of comparison connected with the subject-matter *as in the succeeding stanza* :

" On the arrival of Autumn, the swan shines *bright* like the Moon, the waters are *as clear* as the heavens, and the stars *glitter* pure like the water-lilies."

c. " Princely treasures, by princes presented, shine in the house of this monarch, as (those) born of the Celestial Tree, in Indra's palace."

Here we have a case of the Simile of Intimation *(ákshepopamá)*, since by the ' treasures,' which are the object of comparison, are intimated the treasures compared to,—through the expression ' as (those) born of the Celestial Tree.' In this very example, since the sense of ' in the house' is repeated by ' in (Indra's) palace,' we have also the Simile of Repetition. These and such others have not been *regularly* defined *here*, for a thousand such varieties might be made out.

TEXT.

Comparison Absolute.

No. 666. When the same object is in the predicament of what is compared and what is compared to, *that is to say when a thing is compared to itself*, it is Comparison Absolute.

COMMENTARY.

a. The comparison, as we gather from the context, *is to be expressed* by a single sentence.

For example :—

" When Autumn had begun to manifest itself, the lotus *blushed* like the lotus, the waters *shone* like themselves, and *now* resembling *none but* herself, beamed forth the unslumbering Moon."

Here the self-comparison of the lotus, &c., is figuratively intended to intimate that they have not their like. The province of this *ornament* is distinct from the Láṭánuprása (§ 638), since, *in this, we may, without repeating the word expressive of the object of self-comparison, preserve the figure in the above stanza by the words*—'rájívamiva páthojam,' &c. (the lotus is like the water-born). The employment, however, of the same word is better, as being suitable *for letting one readily understand the identity of the object.* As has been said:

'In the Comparison Absolute, a sameness of terms used from its expediency, is only accidental, whilst in the *Láṭánuprása* it is essentially necessary.'

TEXT.

Reciprocal Comparison. No. 667. This when alternated between two things is held Reciprocal Comparison.*

COMMENTARY.

a. 'This' i. e. 'the predicament of what is compared and what is compared to,'—*supplied from the foregoing text.*

b. *This interchange of comparisons must* of course *be expressed* by a couple of sentences.

c. This is an example:—

"Ever, *O king*, shines thy intellect like thy fortune and thy fortune like thy intellect, thy beauty like thy frame and thy frame like thy beauty, thy firmness like the earth thou rulest, and this *again* like thy firmness *itself.*"

Here what is purported is that there is nothing ELSE equal to the prosperity, &c., of the king.

TEXT.

Reminiscence. No. 668. A recollection of an object, *arising* from the perception of *something* like *to it*, is termed Reminiscence.

* The commentator adds, as a condition, the sameness of the point of resemblance in each of the two comparisons involved in this figure. The following, for instance, is no example of it:—

पल्लवमिवारुणं करतलं करतलमिव कोमलं पल्लवम् ।

COMMENTARY.

a. As :—

" Seeing this lotus beautiful with the sporting wagtail, I recollect that fair face of her with the tremulous eyes."

b. This is not the ornament in the stanza beginning 'O how well I recollect that ever-smiling face of the lotus-eyed one' (§ 190 *a.*), the recollection, here, being raised without the cognizance of resemblance.

c. Rághavánanda, the great minister, however, would have the figure of Reminiscence, even where the recollection *arises* from dissimilarity or contrast. Here follows his own example of the same :—

" Whenever Sítá, tender like the s'irísha *flower*; on the mountains experienced hundreds of hardships, Ráma shedding tears, called to mind the unnumbered felicities she enjoyed at home."

TEXT.

No. 669. The Metaphor consists in the superimposition of a fancied character upon an object unconcealed or uncovered *by negation*.

Metaphor.

COMMENTARY.

a. By *the qualification* 'fancied,' *the present ornament* is distinguished from the figure of Commutation (see § 679). This point we will discuss when we come to speak of that ornament.—" Unconcealed," this is for distinguishing it from the ornament of Concealment (see § 683 and 684).

TEXT.

Its three varieties.

No. 670. This is threefold, according as it is Consequential, Entire, or Deficient.

COMMENTARY.

a. 'This' i. e. the Metaphor.

b. Of these divisions:

TEXT.

No. 671. The Consequential is when a superimposition, undetermined *by a resemblance,* is the cause of another, and (1) rests, or (2) does not rest, upon a Paronomasia. It is fourfold as each *of the two cases* occurs singly or serially.

The Consequential Metaphor, four-fold.

COMMENTARY.

a. Of these the Single Consequential resting upon a Paronomasia, as :—

" Blessing to thy arm, great monarch Nṛisiṅha, mighty controller of the world—arm that, in war, is the Monster of Darkness (Ráhu*) to that full moon—the entire assemblage of princes *hostile to thee (Rája-maṇḍala).*"

Here the superimposition, *viz.* that of the nature of the lunar orb upon the assemblage of princes, by the paronomastic expression *rája-maṇḍala,*† is the occasion of ascribing the character of Ráhu to the arm of the king.

b. The Serial *Consequential resting upon a Paronomasia,* as :—

"Unique thou art, O king, upon the earth—the Lord of day in causing the expansion of the lotus (with which by means of the pun‡ is identified 'the acquirement of fortune')—the God of wind in constantly stirring (in being the resort of the good)—the thunderbolt of Indra *in cleaving* the mountains (the *hostile* princes)."

Here the acquirement of fortune is intended to be understood in identity with the blooming of the lotus, the attendance of the good with perpetual stirring, the princes with the mountains. Thus this series of fancied superimpositions or attributions of characters are the occasion of the ascribing of the nature of the sun &c., to the king.

c. The Single *Consequential* not resting upon a Paronomasia ; as :—

" May the four cloud-dark hands of Hari, rough by the stroke of the string of his horny bow, preserve you,—hands that are the pillars to the Dome of the Triple World."

Here the attribution of the character of a dome to the triple world is the occasion of ascribing the nature of a pillar to the hands of Vishṇu.

d. The Serial ; as :—

" That white umbrella of the royal Deity of Love, or the ornamental

* The demon of the ascending node that, by endeavouring to devour the sun and moon, causes their eclipse :—

† *Rájan* means both a king and the moon.

‡ 'Padmodaya' being separable both into *padma-udaya* and *padmá-udaya* and *padma* meaning 'lotus' and *padmá,* fortune.' So for the other puns.

mark of sandal in fair Firmament's *forehead*, or the white lotus of the Celestial lake,—the orb of the Moon—shines bright like a large lump of camphor."

Here the ascribing of royalty, &c., to Cupid &c., is the occasion of superimposing the character or nature of an umbrella &c., upon the lunar orb.

e. With respect to these *four examples of the Consequential Metaphor*, it is the opinion of some (—the reverse of mine—) that the speaking of the arm of the king, &c., under the character of Ráhu, &c., is the occasion of investing the assemblage of princes, &c., with the nature of the lunar orb, &c.

TEXT.

The Entire Metaphor and its two divisions.

No. 672. If a principal object is metaphorically figured or represented, together with those subordinate, it is Entire Metaphor (see § 670), and either (1) dwells in all of the objects, or (2) resides in a part.

COMMENTARY.

a. Of these *two sorts*:—

TEXT.

The Entire Metaphor complete.

No. 673. The First is held to be when all the *constituent* metaphors* *are expressed.*

COMMENTARY.

a. 'The First'—i. e. what dwells in all of the objects. For example:—

"That *benign* dark cloud—Kṛishṇa disappeared, having thus rained the nectarine water of his words upon the deities—the corn withered by the drought of Rávaṇa's *destructive tyranny*."

Here the nature of a cloud being attributed to Kṛishṇa, his words &c., are represented under the metaphor of nectarine water, &c.

TEXT.

The Entire Metaphor, residing in a part.

No. 674. It (see § 672) is said to 'reside in a part' when any is understood.

COMMENTARY.

a. 'Any'—i. e. any of the *constituent* metaphors.—The following is an example:—

* In the original 'áropya' (what is to be superimposed).

"What clusters of bees—eyes of people—would not drink of that blooming face of her, richly filled with beauty's honey?"

Here the attribution of *the nature of* honey &c. to beauty &c. is expressed, and that of the nature of a lotus to the face is implied. The present is no case of the Partial Simile (see § 663), as the attribute of bloomingness chiefly, or literally, resides in a lotus the nature of which is superimposed *upon the face*, whilst to the latter it belongs only metaphorically.

TEXT.

Deficient Metaphor its twofold division into Serial and Single.

No. 675. If *a principal object* (see § 675) is ALONE figured, it is Deficient Metaphor, which too is twofold, being (1) Serial, or (2) Single.

COMMENTARY.

a. Of these *two species*, the Deficient Metaphor Serial is instanced thus:—

"She of the lotus eyes is the very skill of the Divine Maker in creating, the Moon-shine to the world's eyes, the pleasure-house of the incorporeal one (Káma)!"

b. Single, as:—

"When a servant commits offence, the master's kicking *him* is but proper, so it is not for that I grieve, my fair lady, but that thy tender foot is pricked by the points of those thorns—the hard shoots of my hairs that stand erect *at the thrilling touch*, this is my *sore* distress."

TEXT.

Thus Metaphor is eightfold.

No. 676. Thus of the Metaphor there are eight kinds—

COMMENTARY.

a. Conclude *the text by the words*—'spoken of by the ancients.'

b. Sometimes the Consequential Metaphor (§ 671) too dwells in a part; as:—

"That Guard *(sauvidalla)* of Earth—the sword of that Indra of men, triumphs in war."

Here the implied attribution of the nature of a queen to the earth is the occasion of ascribing the nature of a guard to the sword. An instance of this sort occurring serially also like the former sorts is to be searched out by the reader for himself.

TEXT.

The Entire Metaphor founded sometimes on Paronomasia.

No. 677. We sometimes see even in the Entire Metaphor that the images are founded upon a Paronomasia.

COMMENTARY.

a. Of *the new* sorts *thus obtained* I shall exemplify 'that dwelling in a part' (§ 674) resting on a Paronomasia, by *the following stanza of* mine :—

"Lo! the Nectar-beamed *moon* having laid his hands (or rays—*kara*) on the breast of the Eastern Mountain from which the vesture of thick darkness has fallen off, kisses the face *(mukha)* of Indra's Quarter with sparkling lily-eyes."

b. 'That dwelling in all the objects' (§ 673) would be exemplified by reading in this very *stanza* '*chuchumbe haridabalá-mukhamindu-náyakena*' instead of '*vichumbati,* &c.' *or by our adding in the English the words* '*the lover*' *and* '*that lady*' *before* '*the Nectar-beamed Moon,* *and* '*Indra's Quarter*' *respectively.*

c. The present is not a case of the Paronomastic Consequential (§ 671), for in that figure e. g. '*Bhúbhṛidávalidambholi*' (the thunder-bolt to the mountains—the princes) without speaking of the princes under the *punning* figure of mountains, the representation of the monarch in question under the character of the thunder-bolt would be, from the absence of resemblance, altogether absurd. 'How then would you admit the Consequential in such an expression as *Padmo-daya-dinádhis'a,* when a comparison between the king and the sun is possible, founded upon *the common attribute of* glory?'—Say not so, for the resemblance of the king to the sun as arising from glory is indeed manifest but not intended in the example, *padmodaya* (or the Paronomastic identity of the acquirement of fortune and the blooming of the lotus,) being what is meant as the common attribute of the two. Whilst here in the example under the text, the *propor-tionate* similarity of the mountain, for instance, to the *female* breast, in bulkiness and height, being clearly evident, it is no case of the Paronomastic Consequenstial.

d. Sometimes the Metaphor is found WITHOUT A COMPOUND. For instance "Thy face, O deer-eyed, is lotus, not otherwise."

e. Sometimes it is used WITHOUT AN APPOSITION; as, "The Creator formed here a line of bees under (the shape of) the eye-brow (bhrúlatayá)."

f. Sometimes, UNDER A NEGATION OF THE ATTRIBUTE FIGURED; as:—

"They who *inspired* with foolish hopes, have served the princes of this Iron Age—the sandy desert for the water of goodness, the aërial wall for the *ornamental* pictures of noble deeds, the fourteenth night of the dark fortnight for the moon-shine of merit, the very elegance of the dog's tail in respect of rectitude,—for these *hard but vain toilers*, how much ability would there be required to serve the God of the trident (S'iva) who is to be obtained by faith alone?"

g. The stanza is mine.—Among the metaphors exemplified *under the foregoing texts*, though some are founded upon a Paronomasia of words, they are counted as ornaments of sense, as being species of the Metaphor. Thus is it to be understood with respect to ornaments to be spoken of.

TEXT.

Metaphor Extraordinary.

No. 678. A Metaphor in which the excellence rises to an excessive or extraordinary degree is *termed* even so.

COMMENTARY.

a. 'Even so,' *i. e.* is named Metaphor of Extraordinary Excellence. For example, *the following stanza of* mine.

"This face is the moon herself without the spot; the under-lip is a *vimba* fruit ripened in a long time, the receptacle of nectar; these eyes are lotuses blooming day and night with a superior beauty; and the body is a sea of charms exceedingly delightful to one who immerses himself into it."

Here the excellence is extraordinary from the circumstances of being devoid of spot, &c.

TEXT.

Commutation; Appositional or Non-appositional.

No. 679. When what is superimposed is identified with the subject *of superimposition* and serves the purpose in hand, it is Commutation *(pariṇáma)* and is twofold as being Appositional or Non-appositional.

COMMENTARY.

a. *This figure is termed* Commutation, as the object superimposed is commuted into the nature of the subject of superimposition.—For example :—

" Of a smile she made a present to me who had arrived from a distance, and an embrace with the pressure of the breast was the wager laid by her in gaming."

In other, *or ordinary*, cases, a present and a wager are in the shape of clothes, ornaments or the like, whilst in the present case of entertaining a lover and gaming *with him*, they take the shapes of a smile and an embrace. Here in the first half *of the stanza* the figure is used without an apposition, and in the second with an apposition.

b. In the Metaphor, as for instance in the sentence 'I see the moon-face,' the superimposed moon serves only to embellish *the expression*, but has no subserviency to the *act of* seeing which is in question. Whilst here *in Commutation*, the present, for instance, is identical with the subject of *superimposition, viz. the lady's smile*, and is subservient to her, showing regard to her lover which forms the theme *of the first half*. Hence it is that in the Metaphor what is superimposed is to be construed as merely characterizing, or distinguishing *the subject*, and in the present figure, as being identical with it.

c. In the stanza beginning with "When a servant commits offence" (§675 *b.*) the ornament is Metaphor not Commutation, as the act of piercing the foot, done by the thorn, is not in question, for such an act could never be intended towards the consummation of a proposed object or effect.

d. This ornament too, like the Metaphor, is found with the excellence heightened to an extraordinary degree (see §678) ; as :—

" Where (in the Himálaya) the herbs *luminous* at night, shooting their rays into the interior of cavern-houses, become (or act as) hymenean lamps, unfed by oil, to the foresters enjoying the company of their consorts."

Here the lamps in the shape of the herbs are subservient to the removal of darkness, which removal is favourable to enjoyment, and is the principal matter in hand. Because of their being unfed by oil, they have an excellence heightened to an extraordinary degree.

TEXT.

No. 680. When an object under description is poetically suspected to be something else it is *called* a Doubt. It is threefold, as being (1) Pure, or (2) Containing a certainty, or (3) Ending in a certainty.

Doubt; its three varieties.

COMMENTARY.

a. It is Pure when it terminates in doubt; as:—

"Is this a new Sprout, that from an exuberance of juice has burst forth from the tree of youthfulness, or is this a Wave of the Sea of charms overflowing its banks, or is this the Chastising Rod of the Deity of love, eager to expound his doctrines to men agitated by fancy."

b. The sort 'containing a certainty' results when there is a doubt at the beginning and another at the end, but certainty in the middle; as:—

"'Is this the God of day?—he rises in a chariot with seven horses. Is this Fire? Certainly, it does not traverse in all directions *at once.* Is this Yama himself? He, again, rides on a buffalo,'—thus do thy foemen entertain doubts, seeing thee, *O monarch*, in battle."

Here in the middle there is the certainty of its not being the sun &c., *that are exerting their destructive power.* Were there the certainty of the royal *hero*, there would not arise a second or third suspicion.

c. When there is a doubt at the beginning but a certainty at the end, it is the sort called 'ending in a certainty.' For example:—

"'Is this a lotus *shining* nigh in the lake?—or the face of a youthful lady?'—thus did somebody, after doubting for a moment, attain certainty, by means of those gestures of loving indifference unknown to the companions of the crane *(i. e. lotuses which are produced in a lake, the border of which is frequented by the bird.)*

d. If such a doubt be not raised by a poetical fancy, as in the question 'Is it a post or a man?' it does not produce the ornament in question.

e. "To whose mind does not the doubt suggest itself—'does it exist or does it not?'—with respect to that waist of thine, lady of the lotus eyes, oppressed with the weight of thy breasts?"

The ornament here is the Hyperbole *(atisayokti)*, the proper subject of the present ornament being a suspecting of an object of comparison to be what it is intended to be compared to.

TEXT.

No. 681. The Mistaker is the thinking, from resemblance, of an object to be what it is not—suggested by poetical fancy.

The Mistaker.

COMMENTARY.

a. For example :—

"The simple cowherd, under an illusion of milk, places his jars beneath the cows ; fair ones put the blue lotus to their ear, *for ornament*, mistaking it for the white water-lily ; the mountain girl plucks the jujube fruit, fancying it to be a custard apple : who is there in whose mind the profuse beams of the moon do not cause a delusion ?"

b. An illusion caused by the nature of things is not the subject of the present ornament, such as the illusion of silver in the mother-o'-pearl, nor an illusion not arising from resemblance, as in the following example :—

"In a choice between her association and separation, her separation is to be preferred to her association. In union there is but she alone, but in separation the triple world is full of her."

TEXT.

No. 682. The description of one, under a variety of characters, arising (1) from a difference of perceivers or (2) from a difference of peculiarities, is termed Representation.

Representation; its two kinds.

COMMENTARY.

a. For examples in their order :—

"The Deity was apprehended as their beloved by the cowherdesses, as a child by the old, as their lord by the gods, as Náráyaṇa (the Universal Soul) by the devotees, as the Absolute by those who practised abstract devotion."

Here the taste &c. of the cowherdesses and others are the respective occasions of the manifold representation of the same Deity as associated with the several attributes. As they have said : 'The cognizance of one and the same object, determined, as it is, by a consideration of any of its particular attributes, differs according to the taste, the purpose, or the habit *of the perceiver*.'

b. In the present example, the state or nature of being beloved &c., ascribed to the Deity (Krishṇa), being real, and the perceivers being different, the ornament is not that of the Garland of Metaphors (§ 675 *a*), nor the Mistaker (§ 681), nor a Hyperbole consisting in *making* a distinction where there is none (§ 694 *e*). In the last ornament, as in *the example* "Strange indeed is the beauty of her body" (§ 694 *e*), the objects *of description viz.*, beauty, &c., are *falsely* represented as distinct, but here the state of being beloved &c., are not falsely ascribed to the Deity by the cowherdesses &c., inasmuch as the character of being beloved, for instance, did belong to him at the time.

c. Some say that this figure invariably derives its strikingness from another ornament, and that in the said example there is a Hyperbole, inasmuch as *Krishṇa, though really one and the same*, is represented as distinct, *with respect to the several beholders*, under the character of one beloved or the like, which is intended to be exclusive of those of a child &c. But notwithstanding the presence of this ornament (*Hyperbole*), the peculiar strikingness resulting in a distinction of perception, from a difference of the perceivers, constitutes the distinct figure named Representation.

d. The passage in the description of the country called S'ríkaṇṭha—"*It was fancied to be* an adamantine frame by those that had gone *to it* for refuge, the ethereal void by the *chátakas* &c.,"is an instance of the present ornament, distinct from Hyperbole, it being here associated with the figure of Metaphor. Strictly, however, in the *clause* beginning with 'Ethereal void' they would have the ornament Mistaker not Metaphor, for the superimposition *of a character*, only when preceded by an apprehension of its distinction *from what it is imposed upon*, constitutes the Metaphor or the like, founded, as it is, upon the Qualitative Indication (see § 18). As the venerable Váchaspati Mis'ra, in his gloss on the commentary of the S'áríraka Mímáṅsá, says—"A wòrd *implying something to be compared to* is used to signify or describe something else *(i. e. the object of comparison)* with reference to some implied attribute *common to the significations of both the words.* When, in such an employment of a word, the speaker and hearer have the right apprehension, *i. e. the understanding of resemblance*, it is qualitative, *or founded upon a common quality*, and is preceded by a conception of the distinction *of the two objects.*" Now here in the description of the country S'ríkaṇṭha, the imposition *upon it* of the nature of the ethereal void on the part of the *chátakas* is occasioned by mistake. In the same passage, *further on*—" a sacred grove by the ascetics, a place of amours by the courtezans," we have an instance of the association of the figure of Commutation (§ 679).

e. " In thy deep solemnity *(gámbhírya)* thou art the ocean, in thy gravity a mountain"—in such an example as this, the distinction of the OBJECTS *viz.* the qualities of solemnity &c., is the occasion of the manifold representation *of the same man, the former sort resting upon a* SUBJECTIVE *distinction, the distinction of the cognising persons not of attributes cognised.*

f. " He is grave (or Bṛihaspati—*guru*) in speech, broad *(pṛithu)* of breast and white (or *Arjuna*) in fame"—this is a case of this *sort,* distinct from the Metaphor, Hyperbole founded upon a Paronomasia being the ornament connected here.

TEXT.

No. 683. The denial of the real *nature of a thing* and the ascription of an alien, *or imaginary, character, constitute the figure of* Concealment.

Concealment.

COMMENTARY.

a. This is twofold, the superimposition, *or the attribution of a fancied character,* being sometimes preceded by the denial *of the real nature,* and sometimes the denial being preceded by the superimposition. For examples *of the two sorts* in their order :—

" This is not the sphere of ether but the ocean ; these are not stars but fragments of fresh foam ; this is not the moon, but the Royal Serpent (S'esha) coiled ; and that is not a black spot but the Foe of Mura (Vishṇú) reclining."

" Lo ! the orb of the cool-rayed *luminary,* shining like a lump of foam, kisses the crest of the Western Mountain, bearing the smoke, under the disguise of the manifest black spot, of the fire of love kindled during the night."

b. This stanza is mine.—Similarly a negation of the real character is to be understood under such a form as *the following* :—

" The ocean shines in the shape of the heavens, and the stars are the foam thereof."

Text.

No. 684. If having somehow given expression to some secret object, one should construe *his words* differently, either by a Paronomasia or otherwise, it too is Concealment.

Another variety of Concealment.

Commentary.

a. By a Paronomasia, as :—

" 'In the season of clouds it is really impossible to remain without a husband (or without falling—*apatitayá).*' " 'Art thou troubled, fickle woman ?'—'No, no, dear friend, the way is slippery.' "

Here the woman, having at first said 'without a husband' in the expression *apatitayá*, construes it otherwise *than was her real meaning* into 'without falling.'

b. Without a Paronomasia ; as :—

" 'What creeper is this here before me that clings not close to the tree, with its body agitated by the wind ?' 'Dost thou, fair friend, call to mind thy festive dalliance with thy lover ?' 'No, no, I just described a feature of the rainy season.' "

c. In the Crooked Speech (§ 641), a different construction is given to another's speech, and here to one's own ; so it is distinct too from that ornament. It is distinct too from the Dissembler (see §749), for the secrecy is first expressed by the person who *afterwards* conceals it.

Text.

No. 685. Certainty, again, is the establishing of the real, having denied the foreign, or fancied, *character*.

Certainty.

Commentary.

a. 'Certainty' is the name of the present ornament.—The foreign, *i. e.* what is superimposed.—For example, my own *couplet* :

" It is a face, not the lake-born *flower* (red lotus), these are eyes, not blue lotuses ; rove not, honey-maker, fruitlessly here by the side of the fair-eyed *lady*."

b. Or, for example :—

"It is a garland of lotus-stalks on my breast not the Chief of serpents; it is a string of blue lotus-leaves round my neck not that sheen of poison; it is not ashes but the *cooling* dust of sandal that besmears my body, separated as I am from my love. Strike me not, Bodiless Deity (Káma) mistaking me for S'iva *thy foe*—wherefore rushest thou at me with anger?"

c. This is not 'Doubt ending in certainty' (§ 680 *c*) since in that figure, the suspicion and the certainty *successively* reside in the same subject. Here the suspicion belongs to the black bee, for instance, and the certainty to the lover. Nay the black bee has no suspicion, inasmuch as the bee's approaching so near would be possible, only when its cognition has not more than one alternative, *that is, when it does not waver between two thoughts, but is* single-minded *and certain.* 'Well then let it be the Mistaker (§ 681).' Granting that the bee &c., was under a mistake, it is felt by the man of taste that it is not the mistake that causes surprise *in the present examples*, but the peculiar manner in which the lover &c. express themselves. Besides even if it be not really meant that the bee or the like did fly towards the face of the fair woman or was under any mistake, such a sort of speech would be quite possible, simply as a compliment to one beloved &c. Nor is the figure *in our present examples* a metaphor implied, inasmuch as the face *for instance*, is not cognised under the character of a lotus, *that character being expressly denied.* Nor is it Concealment (§ 683), *the real nature of* the thing under description not being denied. Thus, in reality, this ornament is distinct from those spoken of by the ancients. This figure does not belong to such a speech as 'This is mother-o'-pearl not silver' addressed to somebody bending towards a pearl oyster under the notion of its being silver, *such a speech* being wanting in strikingness, *the essence of an embellishment.*

Text.

No. 686. The Poetical Fancy is the imagining of an object under the character of another. As being Expressed or Understood, this is first held twofold. The Expressed is when the particle '*iva*' (as) &c. are employed, the other, when they are not used. Since in each of these sorts, a Genus, a Quality, an Action, or a

Poetical Fancy, thirty-two fold.

Substance may be fancied, the figure becomes eightfold. In each *of these eight sorts* again, the fancy being (1) Positive or (2) Negative, and the occasion *of the fancy* being in the shape of (3) a Quality or (4) an Action, they become thirty-two fold.

COMMENTARY

a. Of these, the Expressed Poetical Fancy is partially exemplified as follows :—

"The thigh of the fawn-eyed one with the skirt of her raiment fluttering upon it, shines as if it were Cupid's triumphal column of gold, bearing his banner."

As *the term* 'triumphal column' denotes many *objects, or is a generic appellation,* we have here the Poetical Fancy of a Genus.

b. "Knowledge attended with sober silence, *or with an abstinence from pedantic speech,* power accompanied with forgiveness, and liberality associated with the reverse of vaunting—his virtues, occasioning, as they did, other virtues, were, as it were, generative."

Here we have a Quality, *viz.* generativeness, *fancied.*

c. "The sound of thy march, O Sultan,* bathes, as it were, in Ganga's water,—guilty of causing the abortion of thy foemen's wives."

Here we have an Action—'bathes.'

d. "The face of the deer-eyed one shines as if it were another full moon."

The word 'moon,' signifying, as it does, an individual, is denotative of a substance *or a concrete object. So here we have the Poetical Fancy of a Substance.*

e. These examples are when the Fancy is Positive (see Text). We have the following example when it is Negative :—

"Alas, the cheeks of this *lady,* so fair, have attained to this thinness, as if not seeing each other."

Here in 'not seeing' we have the negation of an action. So in other cases.

f. The Occasion, as being in the shape of a quality or an action (see Text,) is exemplified in 'The sound of thy march &c.' where the quality of being guilty is the occasion of the Fancy, or in 'Alas,

* In the original *suratráṇa,* which the scholiast so interprets.

the cheeks of this lady, &c.' where the occasion is an action, *viz.*, attaining to thinness. So in other cases.

g. The Implied Poetical Fancy, as :—

"The breasts of the slender-bodied *lady* show not their faces (or nipples, which are of a dark colour and therefore as it were concealed) from shame that they gave no room (*so plump and so close they are*) to the excellent (or stringed—*guṇi**) pearl necklace."

Here we have Poetical Fancy implied, from the absence of 'as' or the like in connection with 'shame,' thus 'as if from shame, &c.'. Similarly in other cases.

h. 'But then,' somebody might object, 'on the occasion of discussing Suggestion, you declared the capability of all the Figures being suggested, why again do you assert particularly here of Poetical Fancy that it may be implied. I answer,—in such a case of Suggested Poetical Fancy as the following :—

"O fortunate youth, she, not obtaining a place in thy heart filled with a thousand fair women, emaciates, day by day, her frame, making that her only business." The sentence is logically complete even apart from the Fancy† ; whilst here *in the present example* the sentence is complete as to its sense only under a Fancy, that is, when 'as if' is understood, thus '*as if* from the shame,' inasmuch as the breasts could not be *really* ashamed. Thus the Suggested, and the Implied Poetical Fancy are distinct.

i. Among these *kinds of Poetical Fancy*, he mentions some peculiarities among the sixteen sorts of the Expressed Poetical Fancy:

TEXT.

No. 687. Of these the Expressed sorts again are with the exception of that of Substance (§ 686), each threefold, as pertaining to (1) a Nature, (2) an Effect, and (3) a Cause.

Sub-divisions of Expressed Poetical Fancy.

COMMENTARY.

a. 'Of these' *i. e.* among the said divisions of the Expressed, and Implied Poetical Fancy. Of the sixteen sorts of the Expressed

* *Guṇa* means both a string and a good quality.

† Which is, that the lady grows thin as if to get room in the heart of the youth.

Poetical Fancy, the twelve belonging to the three *subjects—Genus, Quality, Action* (§ 686), being each threefold as respecting a Nature, a Fruit, or a Purpose, and a Cause, we have thirty-six sub-divisions. These, combined with the four kinds pertaining to a Substance, which can be fancied only in itself,* make up forty sub-divisions.

b. Of these the Poetical Fancy of a Nature; e. g. those of the nature of a genus and a quality are respectively instanced in '—as if it were Cupid's triumphal column' (§ 686 *a*) and '—as it were generative' (§ 686 *b*) in the foregoing examples.

c. The Poetical Fancy of a Fruit, or Purpose, as:—

"The swift-going *arrow* shot by Ráma, having pierced the heart of Rávaṇa, entered the earth as if to tell the agreeable tidings to the Serpents *dwelling in the infernal regions.*"

Here by the expression 'to tell,' a fruit, in the shape of an action, has been figured, of the arrow's entering the earth.

d. The Poetical Fancy of a Cause, as:

"This is the spot where, searching for thee, I saw an anklet fallen on the ground, holding deep silence, as if from the sorrow of separation from thy lotus-foot"

Here the quality, or attribute, of sorrow is fancied as a cause.

Text.

No. 688. Of these, the sorts pertaining to a Nature are *again* twofold, according as the Occasion *of the fancy* is mentioned or not mentioned.

Further sub-divisions of the above.

Commentary.

a. Among these forty sorts, the sixteen pertaining to a nature are sub-divided into thirty-two, according to the mentioning or not mentioning of the occasion of the Fancy. So there are altogether fifty-six sorts of Expressed Poetical Fancy. Of these we have the sort MENTIONING the occasion, in the foregoing example '—bathes as it were' (§ 686 *c.*) where the occasion of the Fancy—the being guilty, is mentioned. When it is NOT MENTIONED we have the example 'as

* For, says the scholiast, a substance or rather an object denoted by a proper name, does not give rise to poetical surprise, if fancied as the fruit or cause of a certain event.

if it were another moon' (§ 686 *d.*) where the excess of the peculiar beauty or the like is not mentioned.

b. In the Fancy of a Cause or of a Fruit, the Occasion must, as a matter of course, be mentioned.* For if the Occasion, *viz.*, 'holding silence,' of the fancy—'as if from the sorrow of separation,' and 'entering the earth' of 'as if to tell, &c.,' be not mentioned, the sentences would be unconnected or absurd.

c. He states the peculiarities of the sixteen sorts of the Implied.

TEXT.

Sub-divisions of Implied Poetical Fancy.

No. 689. The divisions of the Implied *Poetical Fancy* may each pertain to a fruit or a cause.

COMMENTARY.

a. As, in the preceding example "The breasts of the slender-bodied lady" &c. (§ 686 *g.*) we have a cause fancied in 'as if from shame.'

b. In this (Implied Poetical Fancy) too it is impossible that the occasion should not be mentioned, since if *the particle* 'as' &c. *implying a fancy* be not employed and the occasion not mentioned, it would be impossible for the reader to recognize the Fancy.

c. Nor is the fancy of Nature (*i. e.* irrespective Nature § 687) possible in the present variety. For in the fancy of a nature which consists in the identification of another concrete object *with the subject of description*, if 'as' &c. be not used and an epithet be added to the character fancied, we should call it a Hyperbole; as "This king is another Indra." And if no epithet be added, we should have a Metaphor, as 'The king is Indra.' So the Implied Poetical Fancy is thus thirty-two-fold.

TEXT.

Other two aspects of Poetical Fancy.

No. 690. These, again, are each twofold, according as the subject *of the fancy* is mentioned or not.

* In the fancy of a Cause, observes the commentator, the Occasion is the fruit or consequence of what is fancied, and in the Fancy of a Fruit, the Occasion is the cause or reason of what is fancied.

COMMENTARY.

a. 'These' *i. e.* the said varieties of Poetical Fancy. When the subject is mentioned, take the example "The thigh of the fawn-eyed one &c." (§ 686 *a.*) When it is not mentioned, take the following words of Pradyumna in *my drama* Prabhávatí:

"Now the thick darkness, covering over every region of space, has sunk the world, as it were, in a sea of black collyrium;* has filled it, as it were, with particles of musk; has overspread it, as it were, with Tamála trees; has invested it, as it were, with black wrappers."

Here the subject, *viz.* the being pervaded, of the Fancy of being sunk in collyrium is not mentioned. Or, for example, "Darkness besmears, as it were, our bodies; the heavens, as it were, rain collyrium." Here the subject pervasion, of the fancy of darkness besmearing *our bodies* is not mentioned, as also the falling of darkness, the subject of the raining of collyrium.

The Occasions of the two cases of Poetical Fancy *in the present example*, are respectively the excess and the pouring down of darkness.† Some, however, say "The subject is darkness itself which is not an agent of the act of besmearing; the fancy is its being such an agent; and the occasion is the pervasion. Similarly are the heavens, as the supposed agent of the act of raining, the subject of the Fancy."

TEXT.

Poetical Fancy founded upon another ornament.

No. 691. This (Poetical Fancy) when arising from another ornament, is more striking.

COMMENTARY.

a. Among such *cases*, Poetical Fancy founded upon Concealment is exemplified *in the following stanza of* mine:—

"The flood of beauty of the fair-eyed one, incapable of being contained in her body, falls overflowing, under the disguise of tears, as her eyes are pained by the smoke of the fire kindled by the oblation of ghee."

* *Literally* has associated the world, as it were, with large quantities of collyrium.

† This explanation, says the annotator, is according to those who hold that darkness is a substance.

b. *Poetical Fancy* based upon a Paronomastic (§ 643) Occasion; as—

"The pearls, we believe, that issued from the narrow womb of the oyster, have attained this their fair quality (or string—*guna*) from dwelling on the charming conch-like neck of this lotus-eyed *damsel.*"

Here the Paronomasia in *the word* guna (*which means both a string and good quality*) is the occasion of the Fancy of a Cause (§ 687 *d.*) *contained in the clause* '(as if) from dwelling on the conch-like neck.' Here 'we believe' is the expression denotative of the Fancy. Similarly—

TEXT.

No. 692. 'Methinks,' 'I suspect,' 'of a certainty,' 'perhaps,' 'surely' and such other *expressions are used.*

COMMENTARY.

a. Sometimes we have a Poetical Fancy beginning with a Simile, as:—

"The Foe of Mura (Vishṇu) saw, on the other side of the sea, series of woods abounding with dark-green Palás'a trees, which looked like confervæ thrown every moment upon the shore by thousands of surges."

Here since the word *ábhá** implies a comparison, there is a simile in the beginning, but in the end there is Poetical Fancy, inasmuch as the existence of confervæ on the sea-shore is imagined as probable, notwithstanding its impossibility. Similarly is it to be understood in the description *of the emaciation* of certain love-lorn *ladies,* 'Their bracelets were turned into armlets;' as also in such an instance as 'The side-glance of her with eyes large like those of a deer acts the part of a blooming blue lotus in her ear.' (In these two examples the ornament begins with seeming to be a Simile, but terminates with being recognized as a Poetical Fancy, inasmuch as the bracelet and the side-glance are not compared to an armlet and a blue lotus respectively, but are fancied as if they were actually so.)

* The word means 'appearance' but it is used in comparative compounds to denote 'like appearance.'

b. In the figure of the Mistaker, as in "The simple cowherds &c." (§ 681 *a.*) the deluded cowherds have no consciousness of the moon-light, the subject *of their mistaken* notion of milk*, for it is this *supposed fact* that the poet founds his description upon. But in the present ornament, the person who entertains the fancy has a cognition of the subject *of his fancy*, i. e., *of the distinctive nature of what he invests with an imaginary character.* This is what makes their difference. In the Doubt (§ 680), both the alternatives are cognized as equally prominent, whilst here one of the alternatives is more powerful and is in the shape of a (fancied) probability, *or an undetermined cognition.* In the Hyperbole (§ 693) the unreality of the character fancied is apprehended AFTER *the sense of the sentence* is understood, and here, at the very time of the sense being understood.

c. "Has darkness coloured black the various trees and hills, or has it brought down the heavens, or has it screened them over? Has it levelled the earth in its uneven portions, or has it fastened together† all the regions of space?"

Some recognize here the ornament of Doubt, inasmuch as the trees pervaded by darkness are suspected to be coloured, and so on. This *opinion* is not *right*, for the Doubt consists in the cognizance of the same object under more than one alternative equally prominent; whilst here the pervasion of the trees, *hills*, &c., *by darkness*, is not one and the same pervasion, *but is conceived as distinct and various pervasions as distinguished and individualised by the several objects with each of which it comes, as it were, in separate contact;* and besides, the 'pervasion' or the like is swallowed up by the idea of 'colouring' &c., which alone are prominent. Others say that the present is a distinct kind of the ornament of Doubt, though having one of the alternatives more prominent, because it has the beauty of uncertainty. This too is not right. Since the apprehension of a thing, (the real nature of which is, as it were, swallowed up,) under an identity with

* The Figures termed Doubt and Mistaker respectively are sufficiently explained by their designation. It will help the reader in understanding the distinctive nature of the present figure (Poetical Fancy) to say that it similarly answers to probability. The name might, indeed, be rendered Probability, or Poetical Probability.

† The commentator reads here *saṇhṛitáh* 'destroyed' instead of *saṇhaláh.*

something else is *what is styled* Fancy; and as this evidently exists in the present case, being implied by the particle *nu* as well as by *iva,* the ornament ought to be the Poetical Fancy. Enough of inventing distinct species of the Doubt that are no where to be found.

d. "This that in the midst of the moon spreads the charms of a flake of cloud—people call a hare: to me *it appears* not so. I believe the moon to be marked by the black scars of the wound caused by the darting meteor-glances of the young women distressed by the separation from thy foemen, *their lords.*"

Here, since notwithstanding the use of the expression 'Methinks' ('*manye*' *implying a fancy*) (§ 692), we do not recognize a fancy as defined before, we have a mere conjecture, not a Poetical Fancy attended with Concealment (§ 683).

TEXT.

Hyperbole. No. 693. When the Introsusception is complete, it is styled Hyperbole.

COMMENTARY.

a. When a subjective *fancy,* having swallowed up, or altogether taken in, the object, is apprehended as identical with it, it is Introsusception. This *introsusception* is incomplete* in the Poetical Fancy, where the subjective *notion* is expressed with uncertainty. Whilst in the present ornament it being conceived with certainty, *the introsusception* is complete.

b. In the Poetical Fancy, the swallowing up of the object (vishaya)† is by simply reducing it to a subordinate condition, and so may it be also here, as in—'The face is a second moon.' As has been said, "Be the object mentioned or not, if it is simply reduced to a subordinate condition, the learned declare it to be swallowed."

* *Sádhya*—'to be completed.'

† This word was rendered 'subject' or 'subject of the fancy,' under the foregoing text, but it seems better here to adhere to its strict philosophical signification of 'object' as contradistinguished from '*vishayin*' (subject). See the beginning of S'añkara's commentary on the Vedánta Sútras

TEXT.

No. 694. This is five-fold, as there is a denial of distinction where there is a distinction *in reality*, a negation of connection where there is a connection; and *vice versâ*; and as the sequence in a causation is inverted.

Five varieties of Hyperbole.

COMMENTARY.

a. *Vice versâ i. e. implying* a distinction where there is identity and a connection where there is none.—'This' *i. e.* the Hyperbole.

b. Of these *Divisions*, an Identification where there is a Distinction is exemplified in *the following stanza* of mine:—

"How is it that the peacock's tail shines above; and beneath it, the lunar digit of the eighth night; next to it a tremulous couple of blue lotuses; below it the *Tila* flower, and still lower a tender leaf?"

Here we have the introsusception of the tresses of a beloved woman in the peacock's tail with which they are identified.

c. Or, for instance, "Holding deep silence as if from the sorrow of separation"—(§ 687 *d.*) The silence belonging to a sentient creature is one thing, and the stillness pertaining to an object unthinking is another. The two states, though distinct, are identified here.

d. Similarly in *the line* "In her youth, her lover is flushed (—with love, *rága-bhák*) together with the *soft* petal of her under-lip"—the *rága* of the under-lip is its redness and the *rága* of the lover is his love: these two *conditions* are identified.

e. A Distinction where there is an Identity; as—

"Strange* indeed is the beauty of her body, strange are the riches of the fragrance *breathed by* her: the charmingness of her with eyes like the lotus-petal is altogether extraordinary."

f. A Denial of connection where there is a connection, as—

"Was it the moon, the source of lovely radiance, that was the Creator in forming her; or was it Káma himself ever devoted to love; or was it the Season of Flowers (Spring)? How indeed could the Ancient Saint (Brahmá), cold by studying the Veda, with his mind turned away from objects of sense, create this heart-ravishing form?"

* Literally—'other.'

Here, although the Creator, the Ancient of days, is connected with the formation *of the lady*, there is a denial of His connection.

g. A Connection implied where there is really none ; as—

"If, on the orb of the moon, were fixed a couple of blue lotuses, then indeed might her face with the fair eyes be compared."

Here a connection, unreal, is fancied by means of a supposition brought in by the force of the word 'if.'

h. And the inversion of the sequence in a causation (§ 694) is two-fold, as the effect may be supposed to precede the cause or to co-exist with it. For examples in their order :—

"The hearts of the deer-eyed ladies were agitated by fancy, even before the beauty of the blossoming Vakula and blooming Mango *manifested itself.*"

"Simultaneously did he of the elephant's *majestic* gait tread both the paternal throne and the dominions of other rulers."

i. With reference to the present *figure*, some say "The ordinary, or only mundane, excellence belonging to the *lady's* tresses (§ 624 *b.*), for instance, is fancied as being super-mundane, *and it is such a fancy that constitutes the introsusception in the present ornament.* If, on the contrary, the introsusception of the tresses be *held to consist in their being fancied* under the character of the peacock's tail,* the definition of the figure (§ 693) would not include, *as it ought to do*, such instances as, 'Strange is the beauty of her body &c.' (§ 694 *e.*)." This is not right. For here too, the lady's beauty which is NOT *generically* different *from that of other women*, is fancied as different. To make the case still more clear, if we substitute '*anyadiva*' for '*anyadeva*' *and read in the translation* '*Her beauty is, as it were, quite apart from that of other women, &c.*' we should *indisputably* have an incomplete introsusception, and so a Poetical Fancy (§ 686) would be admitted. In the example beginning 'The hearts of the deer-eyed ladies' (§ 694 *h*), the beauty of the *Vakula* &c., though coming first, is fancied as coming afterwards, and so here too, on the employment of the parti-

* Here in Röer's edition of the original, supply the following and cancel ऽन्या before -ङ्गीक्रियते, and remove the inverted commas after it :—

अन्यदेवाङ्गलावण्यमित्यादिप्रकारेष्वव्याप्तिर्लक्षणस्येति"। तत्र यत्रापि ह्यनन्यदङ्गलावण्यमन्यत्वेनाध्यवसीयते। तथा ह्यन्यदेवेति स्थानेऽन्यदिवेति पाठेऽध्यवसायस्य साध्यत्वमित्युत्प्रेक्षा

cle '*iva*' (as if), we should have the Poetical Fancy. Similarly *is it to be understood* of the other examples.

TEXT.

Equal Pairing.

No. 695. When objects in hand or others are associated with one and the same attribute it is Equal Pairing.

COMMENTARY.

a. 'Others'—*i. e.* those that are not in hand, *or unconnected with the subject.*

b. 'Attribute'—*i. e.* Quality or Action.

c. *The following are* examples—

"Unguents *of Sandal*, *white* flowers, and candles, and fair ones indignant against their lords were, by that *darksome* time (evening), lighted up, and Love awoke that had long fallen asleep."

Here the description of darkness is in question, and the unguents &c connected therewith, are associated with the same action of lighting up.

"Who, that has perceived the softness of thy body, feels not the hardness of the jasmine, the lunar streak, and the plantain?"

Here the jasmine &c., that are unconnected with the subject, are associated with the same quality of hardness.

d. Similarly:—

"Charity from Affluence, Truth from Speech, Fame and Piety from Life, Beneficence to others from the Body—from unsubstantial *things, man* ought to extract substantial *good.*"

Here Charity &c., which are in the objective case, are associated with the same quality of substantialness, as also with the same action of extracting.

TEXT.

The Illuminator.

No. 696. When a thing connected with the subject, and another unconnected with it, *are associated with the same attribute*, it is termed the Illuminator; or when the same Case is connected with more than one Verb.

COMMENTARY.

a. For examples *of these two sorts of the Illuminator* in their order:—

"From a pride of power, he (S'is'upála), desirous of victory, oppresses the world now, as of old: the chaste wife and unchanging Nature come to the man even in succeeding births."

Here there is an association with the same action of accompanying, of unchanging Nature, which is connected with the subject, and the chaste wife who is not connected.

"When thou, life's lord, hast come to a distance, she, poor woman, pierced by the shaft of Love, rises up fitfully and lies down and comes to thy dwelling-house, goes out and laughs and sighs!"

The stanza is mine. Here the same heroine is connected with the many actions of rising up &c.

b. In the present *Figure,* the three varieties, arising from the Quality or the Action being expressed in the beginning, middle or end, have not been *formally* defined, inasmuch as a thousand such varieties are possible in every ornament.

TEXT.

Typical Comparison.

No. 697. Typical Comparison is when in sentences or descriptions, of which the correspondence is implied, the same common attribute is differently expressed.

COMMENTARY.

a. For Example:—

"Glorious art thou, daughter of Vidarbha, thou that by noble qualities hast attracted even the lord of Nishadha: what greater praise can be *bestowed* upon the Moon-light than that it agitates even the Ocean?"

Here the actions of 'attracting' and 'agitating,' though the same, are expressed by a difference of words, in order to avoid a repetition.

b. This Figure is also found in a series; as—

"Glorious indeed is the sun, pure the moon, the mirror is by nature brilliant, S'iva's mountain (Kailása) is closely akin to S'iva's laughter, and the virtuous man is essentially fair."*

"* Full many a gem of purest ray serene,
The dark unfathom'd caves of ocean bear:
Full many a flower is born to blush unseen
And waste its sweetness on the desert air." *Gray.*

This stanza, in connection with the succeeding, may be given as twice instancing this Figure.

Here the words 'glorious,' 'pure,' &c., are the same in *their ultimate* meaning.

c. *The same figure* under a negation of attribute; as—

"The *chakorís* alone are expert in the act of drinking the moonlight: none, but the fair ones of Avantí, are skilled in the pranks of love."

TEXT.

Exemplification. No. 698. But Exemplification is the reflective representation of a SIMILAR attribute.

COMMENTARY.

a. 'Similar'—this distinguishes it from the Typical Comparison (§ 697).

b. This figure too is twofold, being founded upon a similarity or contrast. For examples in their order:—

"A good poet's song, though its merits have not been examined, pours a flood of honey into the ear: A wreath of jasmine ravishes the sight, though its fragrance has not been perceived."

"The stag-eyed lady ceases to feel the torments of Love when thou art seen: The assemblage of water-lilies has been seen to droop, when the moon has not risen."

c. How can my heart, the affections of which are enchained to Vasantalekhá alone, turn to other lovely women? Does the bee, eager for the honey of the blooming jasmine, seek any other plant?"

The stanza is mine. Here since the phrases 'how can my heart turn?' and '(does the bee) seek any other plant?' terminate in conveying the same sense, we have but the Typical Comparison. Whilst in the example *of the present Figure*, the pouring of honey into the ear and the ravishing of the sight are similar, not the same.

d. When between the significations of a couple of sentences, one of which illustrates the other, there is the relation of genus and species, we have *the ornament termed* Transition (*arthántara-nyása*—§ 709). Such being not the case in the Typical Comparison and the Exemplification, they are distinct *figures*.

TEXT.

No. 699. When a possible, or, as is sometimes the case, even an impossible connection of things implies a relation of type and prototype, it is Illustration.

Illustration.

COMMENTARY.

a. Of the *two sorts implied in the text*, we have Illustration under a Possible Connection of Things exemplified in the following lines :

" 'Who that vainly torments creatures in this mundane sphere enjoys prosperity for a long time?'—telling this, the Sun, in a day, then reached the Western Mountain."

Here the connection of the sun, as the agent, in the act of intimating such a fact, is possible, inasmuch as the circumstance of his setting in the Western Mountain is capable of making such an intimation. And this connection implies the relation of a Type and Prototype between the sun's setting and the falling into adversity of those who oppress others.

b. The Illustration under an Impossible Connection of Things is twofold as being conveyed by one or more sentences. Of these, that conveyed by a single sentence ; as—

" Her sidelong darting glance bears the loveliness of the blue lotus-garland ; her under-lip, the fairness of the tender leaf ; her face, the radiance of the moon."

Here the impossibility of the darting glance, for instance, bearing the loveliness of the blue lotus-garland—for how can a thing bear the property of another?—suggests a loveliness like thereto, and implies the relation of a Type and Prototype between the wreath of blue lotuses and the darting of a side-glance.

c. Or, for example :—

" At thy march, O Chief of monarchs, the face and feet of thy foeman's fair ladies forsook the fairness of the moon and the gait of the royal swan."

Here the setting aside, by the *fair ones'* feet, of the gait of the royal swan, with which they have no connection, being absurd, the connection is FANCIED, but this fancied connection being *actually* impossible implies a gait similar to that of the royal swan.

d. The same in more than one sentence (see § *b.*) ; as—

" The saint, who wishes to make this unfeignedly lovely frame fit for penance, surely resolves to cut the *S'amí* plant with the edge of the blue-lotus-leaf."*

* In the Sanskrit, the relative and correlative clauses are always separate and are therefore here reckoned as distinct sentences.

Here the connection of identity between the significations of the sentences, respectively marked by the Relative *yad* and the Demonstrative *tad*, i. e. of the relative and correlative clauses, being absurd, terminates in the relation of type and prototype, thus—The desire of making such a frame fit for penance answers to the desire of cutting the *S'amí* plant with the edge of the leaf of the blue lotus-leaf.

e. Or, if you refuse to count the relative and correlative clauses as distinct sentences (?)—take the following example :

" By my eagerness to secure the pleasures of the world, I have made my life void of fruits: Alas! I have sold the ***invaluable chintámaṇi*** at the price of glass."

Here the ultimate meaning is, that the wasting of life in pursuit of worldly enjoyments is like the selling of the *Chintámaṇi* at the price of glass.

Similarly—

f. " The sun-born race, and the intellect of small compass *to describe it*—how vast the disparity! Ready am I, through folly, to pass, by means of a raft, the impassable ocean!"

The ultimate meaning, here, is that the description of the solar race, by my intellect, corresponds to the crossing of the ocean by a raft.

g. This variety may be also when the impossibility consists in a circumstance of an object compared, when said to belong to what is compared to, as—

" What sweetness was experienced in the under-lip of the deer-eyed lady—that same sweetness has been relished by the tasteful in the juice of the grape."

Here the attribute of sweetness, belonging to the under-lip which is in question, being impossible in the grape-juice, the sense, as before, terminates in similarity.

h. This occurs also in a series; as—

" Thou throwest a parrot at the teeth of a cat, thou committest a deer into the mouth of a hyena, thou drivest a horse upon the horns of a buffalo, setting thy heart on the enjoyments *of the world*."

i. In the present ornament we have not the consummation of the sense of the sentence, or sentences, apart from the intimation of the relation of Type and Prototype, whilst in the Exemplification (§ 698) we apprehend that relation from the context, after the complete meanings of the sentences have been understood. Nor is the present Figure the same with the Natural Inference (see § 737), since in the latter, as in the example "Lo! the necklace rolls on the breasts of the fair ones," &c., (§ 737 *h.*), the meaning does not terminate in a comparison.

Text.

Contrast, or Dissimilitude; forty-eight varieties.

No. 700. When an object compared to another (1) excels or (2) falls short of it, it is Contrast, or Dissimilitude. This is single when the occasion is mentioned, and threefold when it is not mentioned. These four sorts are again sub-divided into twelve, from the idea of resemblance being conveyed by a word (i. e. directly see § 649), by the sense (indirectly), or by intimation, and since *each of these twelve sorts may consist even of* a Paronomasia (§ 643), they become twenty-four. Each of the *two cases* thus containing twenty-four sorts, the Figure, on the whole, comprises forty-eight varieties.

Commentary.

a. The 'occasion' in the case of the object compared excelling that compared to, is the point of superiority belonging to the former and the point of inferiority belonging to the latter. When both of these are mentioned, there is one variety, and when one or both of these are omitted, there are three varieties. Thus the figure being fourfold, we have again twelve varieties, the relation of the compared, and the compared to, being expressed *directly* by the word, or indirectly through the sense, or being intimated. The twelve varieties being in the form 'even of a Paronomasia,' that is to say, occurring apart from a Paronomasia *as well as in a Paronomasia,* are sub-divided into twenty-four. In the same manner, the Figure (Dissimilitude) containing twenty-four sorts when the object compared is inferior to that compared to, it comprises altogether forty-eight varieties.

b. For example :—

"Her stainless face is not as (yathá) the sullied moon."

Here both the circumstances, *viz.* the stainlessness belonging to the object compared and the stainedness belonging to the object compared to, are mentioned. The comparison is Direct from the employment of the word *yathá'* (as). In this very example, instead of 'not as the stained moon' (न कलङ्की विधुर्यथा) if we read 'not like the stained moon' (न कलङ्किविधूपमम्) we should have an Indirect comparison, and if we read 'triumphs over the stained moon,' we should have an Intimated comparison from the absence, both of 'as' &c. and 'like' &c. the only terms that abstractly or concretely DENOTE similitude. In this very example again, on leaving out the word 'stainless,' there would be *the case of* an omission of the circumstance of superiority (stainlessness) residing in the object compared; on leaving out the word 'stained,' we should have *the case of* the omission of the circumstance of inferiority residing in the object compared to; and if we leave out both words, we should have the case in which both the circumstances are omitted.

c. This Figure in a Paronomasia; as—

अतिगाढगुणायाश्च नाब्जवद्भङ्गुरा गुणाः ।

[The excellences (guṇa) of her with substantial merits are not as the frail fibres (*guṇa*) of the lotus.]

Here there is a Direct Comparison, from the employment of the affix '*-vat*' in the sense of '*iva*,' and both the points of superiority and inferiority are mentioned, and the term '*guṇa*' (meaning an excellence or a fibre) is paronomastic. The other varieties under this division are to be understood in the foregoing manner.

d. These (the preceding) are examples of the case where the object compared excels that compared to. The case in which the former falls short of the latter is, in part, exemplified in the following stanza:—

"The moon, waning, waxes again, ever and anon: forbear fair lady, be gracious; youth, when gone, is never to come back again!"

e. With reference to this stanza, some say: "Since the instability of youth, which is the object compared, is greater in this example, the clause 'or *vice versâ*' is not required in the definition given by a certain author viz.—'The Contrast is when what is compared is greater than what is compared to, or *vice versâ*'." This opinion cannot bear a discussion, for what is meant by being greater or less is nothing but superiority or inferiority, and in the present example it is evident that youth is inferior to the moon, in *point of stability*. Admitting however, that my opponent's view may, in a manner, hold good in the present instance, how is he to deal with such a one as—

"Hanúmat and others illumined the messenger's passage by their fame's white lustre, but I, by my foemen's *brilliant* laugh!"?

So the clause 'or falls short of it' was properly inserted in the text.

Text.

No. 701. When a single expression, by the force of a term denoting simultaneity or conjunction, signifies two facts, it is Connected Description (*sahokti*), provided that a Hyperbole (§ 693) is what it is founded upon.

Connected Description.

Commentary.

a. The Hyperbole, again, must, in the present *figure,* be based (1) upon the introsusception *of an object* into an identity *with another*, or (2) upon the inversion of the sequence in a causation (see § 694). That based upon an introsusception under identity, again, may rest upon a Paronomasia, or otherwise. For examples in their order:—

b. "In her youth, her lover is flushed (with love—*rágabhák*), together with the petal of her under-lip."

Here there is a Paronomasia in the term *rága* (see § 964 *d*).

c. "The beams of the nectar-rayed *luminary* shoot through every direction—awakening love along with the assemblage of the water-lilies, dispelling firmness of mind along with the thick shades *of the night*, and closing the heart (in the contemplation of the beloved one) along with the multitudes of lotuses."

The stanza is mine. Here the 'awakening' &c., are distinct, from the distinction of what they pertain to,*—not merely under a Paronomasia *as in the foregoing example where the two* LITERAL *senses of 'rága'—'redness' and 'affection' are identified.*

d. The following are examples of the second division of the Connected Description, or that founded upon a Hyperbole consisting in the inversion of the sequence in a causation:—

"Together with the king, she fell upon the ground—her conscious-

* Thus; in relation to love, 'awakening' (उल्लास) is 'exciting' and in relation to the assemblage of water-lilies, it is 'expanding'. These two significations, by the help of the phrase 'along with,' are identified by *similitude* not by a pun. So for the other participles.

ness taken away by a deep swoon, as the spark of a lamp falls with the dropping oil.*"

e. This *Figure* is also possible in a series; as in the preceding example—" The beams of the nectar-rayed luminary" &c.

f. In such a sentence as "Ráma, together with Lakshmaṇa, went to the thick forests," there is not this figure, from its not being based upon a Hyperbole.†

Text.

No. 702. The Speech of Absence (*vinokti*) is when a thing, in the absence of another, is represented as (1) not disagreeable or (2) disagreeable.‡

Speech of Absence.

Commentary.

a. 'Not disagreeable'—not unsightly. Thus though the ultimate meaning of the phrase is 'agreeable,' yet the expressing of the quality of agreeableness through the negation of that of disagreeableness is intended to import that the *apparent* disagreeableness or loss of beauty of the object of description is the fault of the presence of another object, the former being indeed essentially fair. For example :—

b. "In the absence of the season of clouds, the moon obtained its unslumbering state (or shone forth in its native brilliance); in the absence of summer's *burning* heat, the woods put on their *native* charms."§

c. The case where a thing is represented as disagreeable or not pleasant; as—

"Well hast thou done, following thy lord that transcends all people: What is Day-beauty without the Sun; what is Night without the Moon?"

* The commentator mistakes this for the similar stanza in the Raghuvans'a, describing the swoon of Aja at the sudden death of Indumatí his wife, of which the present is an exact counterpart.

† The commentator justly asserts the propriety of admitting this ornament wherever this mode of speech may be striking, even apart from a Hyperbole, and cites the following line from the Kávya-prakás'a—सह मणिवलयैर्बाष्पधारा गलन्ति ।

‡ Read नासाध्वन्यत् for न साध्वन्यत् in Roer's edition of the original.

§ Lit.—became delightful.

d. "The days of the Lotus have passed in vain; it saw not the orb of the Cool-beamed Luminary: Fruitless too was the birth of the Moon who never beheld the Lotus awakened."

There is a particular strikingness, in this *stanza*, from the reciprocation of the Speech of Absence. Although the very particle '*viná*,' (without) is not used here, yet the ornament is no other than the Speech of Absence, inasmuch as the sense of '*viná*,' 'absence' or 'want,' is implied. Similarly is it to be understood that the Figure of Connected Description (§ 701) may occur without the actual employment of the word '*saha*,' the meaning of it being implied.

TEXT.

Modal Metaphor, threefold.

No. 703. The Modal Metaphor (*Samásokti**) is when the behaviour *or character* of another is ascribed to the subject of description, from a sameness of (1) Action, (2) Sex (or gender), or (3) Attribute.

COMMENTARY.

a. Of the three sorts *thus obtained*, the ascription of the behaviour of one not in question to the subject of description, from a sameness of ACTION is exemplified as follows:—

"Happy indeed art thou, Wind of the Malaya mountain, who forcibly embracest every part of the frame of the Lotus-eyed lady, having shaken off the vesture of those breasts that bear the beauty of a couple of golden jars."

Here we have the attribution of the behaviour of a rough lover to the wind.

b. From a sameness of sex, or gender; as:—

"How can the lofty-minded man think of woman, when he has not satisfied his desire of victory? The Sun *(ravih)* woos not *fair* Evening *(sandhyá)*, without having careered, in triumph, over the whole world."

Here the characters of the lover and the beloved *are ascribed* to the sun and evening, simply because of *the words* being respectively of the masculine and feminine gender.

* Lit. 'a speech of brevity.' The figure answers to the English Personification, except that it includes its reverse, or the attribution of the character of an inanimate thing to a sentient creature.

c. The sameness of ATTRIBUTE may be in three ways, (1) from a Paronomasia, (2) from Community, or (3) as implying a Resemblance.

d. Of these *three cases, the following stanza* of mine illustrates that *in which the sameness of attribute is* based upon a Paronomasia :—

विकसितमुखीं रागासङ्गाद्गलत्तिमिरावृतिं
दिनकरकरस्पृष्टामैन्द्रीं निरीक्ष्य दिशं पुरः ।
जरठलवलीपाण्डुच्छायो भृशं कलुषान्तरः
श्रयति हरितं हन्त प्राचेतसीं तुहिनद्युतिः ॥

[Alas! the Luminary of the dewy beams resorts to Varuṇa's Quarter (the West), very gloomy at heart and pale like an old *lavalí* plant, as he beholds the East* with a smiling face, with the mantle of darkness falling off, from the rosy light *of dawn* (or warmth of affection,)—touched by the rays (or hands) of the Lord of day.]

Here the words मुख (face or extremity), राग (redness or affection) &c., are Paronomastic. In this *example,* even on our turning one portion into a metaphor, by reading तिमिरांशुकाम् (vesture of darkness) instead of तिमिरावृतिम् (cover of darkness), we should still have the Modal Metaphor, not the Partial Metaphor (§674). For, in that case, the figuring of darkness as vesture would, from their evident resemblance as covering, rest in itself, independent of the help of any other *metaphor* (the metaphorical figuring of the East, for instance, as a woman) ;† so it could not preclude our recognition of *the figure as* the Modal Metaphor. Where, however, the thing figured and the thing figuring it, or that with which it is metaphorically identified, do not bear an evident resemblance, there indeed the metaphor being absurd or unintelligible apart from another metaphor, we have to recognize an implied metaphor in another part of the description, though none be expressed. The following, for instance, is a case of the Partial Metaphor :—

* Lit. Indra's Quarter.

† That is to say, we should not be necessitated to recognize an implied metaphor (*rúpaka*), technically so called, in any of the other parts of the description, by the single metaphorical expression, which may stand quite apart and independent.

"The Army (*sená**) of his foeman, as *the monarch*, in that retreat of love†—the field of battle—holds in his hand the *fair* Sword (*maṇḍalágralatá*), turns away from him, though at first passionately eager to meet him."

Here the resemblance between the battle-field and the retreat of love is not evident.

e. In those instances too, where there is an expressed figuring of several objects, bearing evident resemblance *to those under the character of which they are poetically disguised*, and an implied figuring of only one portion, we have but the Partial Metaphor, inasmuch as the cognition of the metaphor, being copious or diffusive, prevails over that of the Modal Metaphor. 'But then there is a clear resemblance between the battle-field and the retreat of love, in both of which the hero moves with ease.' Truly said,—there is *a clear resemblance*, but dependent upon a consideration of the meaning of the *whole* sentence, not independently; for a battle-field and a retreat of love are not both, from their nature, places of easy loitering, as a face and the moon are from their nature charming.

f. From a Community (see § *c.*); as:—

"The Lotus smiled (or, was expanded—*smerá*), on the rise of the Lord of day,—with the bee charmed with the native fragrance, melodiously humming."

Here the Lotus, under the common epithet‡ 'with the bee charmed &c.,' is recognized under the character of a woman, by reason of the attribution of the action of smiling which belongs only to a human being: for without this attribution, it would be impossible to recognize the behaviour of a woman merely from a community of epithet.§

g. The circumstance of *the common qualification* implying a re-

* Both of these words being feminine, Maṇḍalágralatá is represented as the rival of Sená.

† In the original अन्तःपुर—inner apartment or the apartment of women.

‡ I. e. the epithet equally applicable to a woman, for, as the Commentator observes, 'native fragrance' is such a thing as is frequently ascribed to the breath of a fair woman.

§ So, adds the Commentator, a common epithet, accompanied with the ascription of a peculiar attribute, is, in fact, the condition of the present division of the figure.

semblance (§*c.*) again, is possible in three ways, according as a Simile, a Metaphor, or a Commixture* *of the two* is included.

h. Of these *three cases*, that implying a Simile is thus exemplified:—

दन्तप्रभापुष्पचिता पाणिपल्लवशोभिनी ।
केशपाशालिवृन्देन सुवेशा हरिणेक्षणा ॥

"With those flowers—the beams of the *bright* teeth, with those tender leaves—the hands, with that swarm of bees—the *dark* tresses, shines that deer-eyed lady in her beautiful dress."

Here by reason of the qualification 'in her beautiful dress,' the composition of the epithet *danta-prabhá-pushpa-chitá* ('with those flowers' &c.,) *for example*, is at first, to be interpreted to imply a Simile *danta-prabháh pushpániva* (the beams of her teeth are like flowers). Afterwards another way of analysing the compound being resorted to, *viz. danta-prabhá-sadṛis'aih pushpais' chitá*† ('abounding with flowers looking like the beams of teeth'), we recognize the deer-eyed lady in the character of a creeper, by virtue of the qualifications, which (as shown in one instance) are equally applicable, *by a simple turn of interpretation*, both to the lady and a creeper.

i. When a Metaphor is implied, we have the example *of the stanza* beginning 'what clusters of bees—eyes of people'—(§674).

j. The *common qualification* implying a Commixture (§*g.*); as, for instance, if we read परीता (encircled '*with that swarm &c.*') instead of सुवेशा ('in her beautiful dress') in the stanza beginning दन्तप्रभापुष्प—(§*h*), we have to resort to a Commixture, from the absence of any means of, *or criterion for, settling that* a Simile or a Metaphor *is the ornament used here.* The other way of analysing the compounds, according to which the lady is recognized as a creeper, *has been shown* before.

k. Of these *three cases*, there is the Modal Metaphor in the first and third, according to those who hold that a Simile and a Commix-

* The Commixture, or confusion, of two or more figures, as also their Conjunction, or independent co-existence, in the same passage are counted as distinct ornaments (see §755 and 756).

† This is *madhya-pada-lopí samása* (composition omitting a middle term), as *abhijnána-S'akuntalá.*

ture cannot be partial; whilst the second is but an instance of the Partial Metaphor. On consideration, however, it would appear proper to recognize no other than the figure of Partial Simile in the first case. Otherwise, in such an instance as—

"Autumn, bearing on (her) pale cloud-breast *(payodhara)* the bow of Indra (the rainbow) resembling the fresh wound of the nail, and delighting (or making clear of clouds*) the branded (or spotted—*sakalaṇka*) moon, increased the distress (or heat—*tápa*†) of the sun,"—how should we recognize the autumn as behaving like a woman, when the breast of a woman bearing the rainbow resembling a fresh wound of the nail is impossible?

l. "But then," as *somebody might object*, "the nature of what is compared to *(upamána)*, though, *according to the letter*, belonging to the wound of the nail, ought, in consideration of the things *(i. e. the spirit of the description)*, to be transferred to the rainbow; just as the *Vaidik* injunction of oblation, *the proper object of which is ghee*, is transferred to curd in such *a representation* as 'He makes an oblation of curd,' when, in the absence of ghee, an offering cannot otherwise be made. Thus *the clause in question* will be understood to imply 'Bearing the fresh wound of the nail resembling (or rather simulating) the bow of Indra."'

m. I answer—No, it is better to admit the Partial Simile here than to resort to such a far-fetched interpretation, in maintaining *that the Modal Metaphor is the ornament employed*. Granting, however, that this figure may somehow be recognized in the present example, we have no alternative *but the admission of the Partial Simile* in the example beginning 'Lake-beauties at every step.—' Besides how can the Modal Metaphor, which consists in the attribution of the behaviour *of an animated being to an inanimate thing or vice versâ*, have room in the Simile which conveys no idea of such action? To this effect it has been said: 'Since in the Simile, neither the *identical* action nor the nature *of the object compared to* is understood *to be attributed to that compared*, there is no *such thing as a* Modal Meta-

* My MS. probably rightly reads प्रसादयन्ती instead of प्रमोदयन्ती the reading in Roer's edition.

† Roer wrongly reads पापम्.

phor resting upon a Simile,* but *what is wrongly* reckoned as such is evidently the Partial Simile. Thus the possibility of a Partial Simile and a Partial Metaphor being recognized, it is logically established that the Modal Metaphor has no room in a Commixture founded in the two former figures, and so, *in fact*, the Modal Metaphor does not admit of being sustained by an epithet implying a comparison. It is therefore two-fold in the employment of a common qualification, as resting upon a Paronomastic, or a common epithet; and two-fold as founded upon the sameness of Action or Gender (see text and §c.) So the Modal Metaphor comprises four varieties, of each of which the attribution of behaviour, is the *essential* constituent.

n. This attribution of behaviour, again, is four-fold, according as the action of a being or thing pertaining to the ordinary world, or to science, is ascribed to another of the same sphere, or as the action of an object of the ordinary world is ascribed to one belonging to Science, or *vice versâ*. Of these *two classes of beings*, that of the ordinary world is numerous, from the difference of Relish, (or the variety of the sentiments which the constituents of the class are respectively capable of exciting) &c. Numerous likewise are the entities pertaining to science, such as those known in the sciences of Logic, Medicine, Astronomy, &c. In this manner the Modal Metaphor is divisible into many sorts, of whch a portion is exemplified as follows :—

o. In the stanza beginning "Happy, indeed, art thou, Wind of the Malaya mountain," we have the attribution of the action., &c., of a violent lover, a being of the ordinary world, to another being of the ordinary world—*the Malaya wind.*

p. यैरेकरूपमखिलास्वपि वृत्तिषु त्वां
पश्यद्भिरव्ययमसंख्यतया प्रवृत्तं ।
लोपः कृतः किल परत्वजुषो विभक्ते-
स्तैर्लक्षणं तव कृतं ध्रुवमेव मन्ये ॥†

(They, I believe, have indeed obtained a sure knowledge of Thee, who, seeing thee the One unchangeable in all things, not to be exhaus-

* Here, instead of तन्नौपम्यं समासोक्तिः read तन्नौपम्यसमासोक्तिः in Roer's edition of the text.

† The meaning of the stanza, according to the signification of the grammatical terms used here, need not be rendered.

ted, though infinitely energizing, have lost, O Supreme, all notions of duality.)

Here the properties of things, dealt with in the science of Grammar, are ascribed to the Being (God) known in the Scriptures. Similarly in other cases.

q. In the Metaphor, a thing not in question, by bringing in its own nature, covers over the nature of what is in question; whilst here, the former, by an attribution of its own character, distinguishes the latter from its original character, without hiding its real nature. It is for this reason that they speak of 'the ascription of behaviour' not 'the attribution of nature' *in defining the present figure.* In the Suggestion of Simile and in the Paronomasia of Sense (§ 705), the resemblance of the qualified too is implied, but here that of the attribute alone. In the Indirect Description, the being or thing in question is intimated, but in this figure, one not in question. Such is the distinction.

TEXT.

The Insinuator.

No. 704. A speech with a number* of significant epithets is held the Insinuator (*parikara*).

COMMENTARY.

a. As :—" Ho ! monarch of Anga, commander of the forces, derider of Drona—Karna, do save this Duhs'ásana from Bhíma."†

TEXT.

Paronomasia.

No. 705. Paronomasia is the expression of more than one meaning by words naturally, or literally, bearing one signification.

a. 'Naturally bearing one signification'—this distinguishes the present figure from the Paronomasia of Words (see § 643). The term 'expression' *discriminates it* from a Suggestion.

b. For example :—

* The plural number, implying more than two, in the original, is, as the scholiast observes, purposely employed.

† A'swatthámá, in the Veṇí-Sañhára, by these insinuations cries shame to Karṇa unable to defend Duhs'ásana, though he bragged much of his power and derided his superiors.

प्रवर्त्तयन् क्रियाः साध्वीर्मालिन्यं हरितां हरन्।
महसा भूयसा दीप्तो विराजति विभाकरः ॥*

[" Occasioning the performance of good works, and dispelling the gloom of all quarters, the sun or the king, (vibhákara) shines resplendent with excessive glory."]

Here in the absence of such *means of* determination as the circumstances of the case or the like (see § 25 *a*), both a king and the sun are expressly meant (see § 25 *e*).

Text.

Indirect Description, five-fold.

No. 706. When (1) a particular from a general, or (2) a general from a particular, (3) a cause from an effect, or (4) an effect from a cause, or (5) a thing similar from what resembles it, is understood, each of the former being in question, and the latter not so, it is Indirect Description, and is thus five-fold.

Commentary.

a. For examples in their order :—

" A man that can be at ease even under an insult— better than he is the dust, that, struck with the foot, rises up and sits upon the head."

Here a 'man' in general, is spoken of, when *those in whose mouth is put the stanza* mean themselves in particular,—thus 'Even the dust is better than WE.'

b. " If this wreath *of flowers* is destructive of life, why does it not kill me, when placed on my bosom? Even poison may sometimes be ambrosia, and ambrosia poison, by the will of the Lord!"

Here, the particular *things, poison and ambrosia*, are spoken of, whilst an injurious thing doing good and a beneficial thing doing evil, by the will of God, is what is intended in general. And so we have here *the figure of* Transition (see §709) based upon Indirect Description.

* The words *málinya* (gloom), *mahas* (glory) &c., literally or primarily mean only 'darkness' 'brilliance' &c., respectively, but secondarily 'sadness,' 'great prowess' &c. The word *vibhákara,* however, as the scholiast observes, literally denotes both the sun and a king, and hence the present is but a mixed example.

c. In the Exemplification (see § 698), a notorious* object only is employed as a type, and since poison and ambrosia respectively turning into ambrosia and poison have not been experienced, that ornament has no place in the present example.

d. "Alas, in the presence of Sítá, the moon is, as it were, besmeared with lamp-black; the eyes of does appear to have become motionless; the redness of the *vidruma* leaf seems faint and the lustre of gold gloomy; the notes of the female cuckoo seem to speak the harshness of her throat, and the long tail of the peacock displays but its blemishes."

Here from the fancied effects of the moon being besmeared with lamp-black &c., is understood the cause, *viz.*, the pre-eminent beauty of the face &c., which is in question.

e. "The deer-eyed lady, when I said to her 'I depart,' heaved a swelling sigh, and glancing at me side-wise with one of her eyes suffused with tears, spoke, in sad pleasantry, to the fondly nourished fawn—'Do thou now fix on my dear ladies that fondness thou hast felt for me.'"

Here the cause, *the lady's intimation that she would die*, is mentioned, when the effect, the prevention of the lover's departure, is in question.

f. When one thing being in question,† another like to it is described, the figure is twofold, as being founded upon a Paronomasia or on simple resemblance. *The variety* founded upon a Paronomasia again is twofold, according as there is a Paronomasia in the epithet alone as in the Modal Metaphor, or as there is a Paronomasia in the qualified word too as in the figure of Paronomasia itself. For examples in their order:

g. सहकारः सदामोदो वसन्तश्रीसमन्वितः।
समुज्ज्वलरुचिः श्रीमान् प्रभूतोत्कलिकाकुलः ॥‡

("The Mango tree, fair and fragrant, adorned with vernal graces and covered with exuberant blossoms, shines in resplendent beauty.")

* Here, in Roer's edition, read प्रख्यातं for प्रस्थानं.

† For ऽप्रस्तुते read प्रस्तुते in Roer's edition.

‡ The epithets सदामोदः, वसन्तश्रीसमन्वितः and प्रभूतोत्कलिकाकुलः mean also respectively 'ever gay,' 'dressed in vernal attire,' and 'agitated with powerful love.'

Here a lover, the subject of discourse, is understood, by means of the epithets alone, from the description of a mango tree which is not in question.

h. पुंस्त्वादपि प्रविचलेद्यदि यद्यधोऽपि
यायाद्यदि प्रणयने न महानपि स्यात् ।
अभ्युद्धरेत् तदपि विश्वमितीदृशीयं
केनापि दिक् प्रकटिता पुरुषोत्तमेन ॥

("Though departing from the state of a male, *as he did when he assumed the form of a beautiful woman to charm the demons to destruction*, though going down *to the infernal regions, as he did to raise up the earth submerged under water*, though becoming low *of stature as a dwarf* to beg *of the demon Balin* land *measured by three paces of his—paces which, to the demon's astonishment, measured the triple world*—yet preserving the universe—such are the *marvellous* ways made out by that indescribable Purushottama.)

Here from the qualified word too, *viz.*, *purushottama*, *which is* paronomastic, is first understood Vishṇu, because of its ordinary usage *in that sense.* From this, some personage, intended to be described, is understood.

i. Indirect Description founded on mere resemblance, as—

"There is *but* one young pigeon and a hundred hungry hawks are flying towards it; the heavens are fenceless; good gods! Divine mercy is the *only* refuge."

Here from the pigeon which is not in question, is understood somebody, the subject of discourse, *whom a great number of men are bent upon persecuting.*

j. This *figure* also occurs sometimes under a contrast; as—

"Happy, indeed, are the winds of the woods, cooled by contact with lotus-*lakes*, that touch, unobstructed, Ráma of the *indívara's** dark *and lovely* complexion."

Here, the subject of discourse, *oneself*, is understood under this contrast, *viz.*—'The winds are happy whilst I am unfortunate.'

k. The figure *again* is three-fold, according as what is expressed is possible, impossible, or both. Of these three cases, that of a possibility is illustrated by the above examples.

* A sort of lotus of a dark-blue colour.—This is Da'saratha's speech, says the commentator.

l. The case of impossibility ; as—

" I am a *kokila* and your honour is a crow : blackness is common to both of us. But those who can appreciate soft melody will tell the difference."

Here, the dialogue* of a crow and a *kokila* is impossible, unless we superimpose upon them the characters intended, *viz.*, *those of two men externally alike but different as to their internal qualities.*

m. The case of both *a possibility and impossibility combined ;* as—

अन्तश्छिद्राणि भूयांसि कण्टका बहवो बहिः ।
कथं कमलनालस्य मा भूवन् भङ्गुरा गुणाः ॥

[" Why should not the fibres (or reputation) of the lotus-stalk be fragile (or short-lived), that has so many holes (or failings) within and so many thorns (or foes) without ?"]

Here without understanding some person, as the subject of discourse, under the character of the lotus stalk, it is impossible that the internal holes thereof should be the cause of making the fibres fragile, but it is possible in the case of the thorns *which can rend the fibres.* Thus we have both *a possibility and impossibility combined.*

n. That variety of this figure, which, under a Paronomasia, intimates an object, by describing one similar to it (§ *f*), is distinct from a Suggestion of Matter founded upon the power of Words (see § 257 *b.*), inasmuch as it, like the Modal Metaphor (§ 703), has for its life an ascription of behaviour. In the suggestion of a simile, an object NOT in question is intimated, and in the Modal Metaphor and Paronomasia, both what is, and what is not, in question, are expressed. *Thus the present figure is distinct.*

TEXT.

Artful Praise.

No. 707. When from blame and praise expressed, are understood praise and blame respectively, it is termed Artful Praise *(vyája-stuti).*

COMMENTARY.

a. When praise is understood from *apparent* blame, the etymology of the term 'vyája-stuti' is to be explained thus 'vyájena stutih,' or

* For वाकोवाक्यं read वाकोपवाक्यं in Roer's edition.

praise BY an artifice; and when blame is understood from *an apparent* praise, it is to be interpreted 'vyája-rúpá stutih' or praise CONSISTING in an artifice or trick.

b. For examples in their order:—

"With pearl-necklaces on their breasts (but, under the pun,—with breasts divested of ornaments), with the hairs of their bodies erect (with their bodies covered with thorns), the women of thy enemies, O king, have become as secure (widowed) at thy anger as ever."*

The stanza is mine.

c. "This, O Cloud, is but a false encomium I have bestowed upon thee—'thy waters are the life of the world.' But this indeed is a great praise to thee, that thou renderest assistance to the Lord of Justice (Yama—the god of death), by killing the way-farers *separated from their beloved.*"

TEXT.

Periphrasis.

No. 708. Periphrasis is when the fact to be intimated is expressed by a turn of speech.

COMMENTARY.

a. For example:—

"—Whose troops in the Garden of Bliss *(nandana)* touched, with contempt, the flower-bunches of the *Párijáta* tree,—fondly cherished for the adornment of 'Sachí's tresses."

Here, what is in question and to be intimated, *viz.* the fact, in the shape of a cause, of Indra's Heaven being conquered by Hayagriva, is expressed through the effect *viz.*, the troops scornfully touching the flower-bunches of the *Párijáta*,—for the purpose of giving particular strikingness to the description. Nor is it that variety of the Indirect Description in which a cause is understood from an effect (§ 706 *d.*), since in that the effect is not in question, whilst in the present figure the effect equally with the cause is in question, as indicating the greatness of the power of the subject of description.

* Here, observes the commentator, the apparent blame of the king consists in representing him as causing pain to women, and the praise intimated is that he is victorious over his enemies.

b. Similarly :—

"He restored to the fair ladies of his foemen their necklaces without the binding thread, as he caused tears to trickle down their breasts in drops large like pearls."

Here the effect—the tears of the enemies, as indicating the great prowess of the king who is the subject of description, is as much connected with the question as the intimated cause—the killing of the enemies: so the figure is no other than the Periphrasis.

c. '"The princess, O king, does not teach me to speak; the queens too are silent; feed me, hump-backed girl; are not the princes and ministers taking their food yet?'—thus, the royal parrot of the enemy's palace, let loose from the cage by the passengers, speaks, one by one, to the pictured personages in the empty turret."

Here the *cause of this state of things* is in question, what is meant to be said being—'The enemies have suddenly fled away, having heard your majesty was ready to march.' *With respect to the present example, cited in the Kávyaprakása in illustration of the Indirect Description*, some say that the effect too is in question, as being fit to be described *in connection with the subject-matter, the cause.* Others, however, declare that the figure is no other than the Indirect Description, inasmuch as the inexpressibly *great* prowess of *the monarch* in question is understood from the account of the royal parrot, *which is not connected with the subject.*

Text.

Transition, eight-fold.

No. 709. When a general is strengthened by a particular or a particular by a general, and when an effect is justified by a cause, or *vice versá*,—either under a correspondence or a contrast—, it is Transition *(arthántara-nyása)*, and is thus eight-fold.

Commentary.

a. For examples in their order :—

"The meanest creature, assisted by one that is great, attains to the consummation of a deed. The rivulet of the mountain, united with a great river, reaches the *mighty* ocean."

Here, the generality, implied in the first half *of the stanza*, is confirmed by a particular *illustration*, implied in the second half.

b. " Thus having discoursed in words that did not exceed the sense, Mádhava (Krishna) ceased ; for the great are, by nature, of measured speech."

c. " Be firm, O Earth ! O Serpent sustain her ; thou, Royal Tortoise, uphold them both ; ye Elephants of the Quarters, exert your energy to support the three—my venerable *brother* is about to string Mahádeva's *mighty* bow !"

Here, the cause, or occasion, *viz.*, the stringing of Mahádeva's bow is what justifies the effect or consequence, *viz.*, earth exerting herself to be firm, &c.

d. In the stanza—" One ought not to perform an act rashly : indiscretion is the great resting-place of evils. And Prosperity, attracted by merit, chooses, of her own accord, the man who does prudently"—the effect, *viz.*, Prosperity's choosing *the prudent man*—justifies the cause, *viz.*, the opposite of heedless proceeding, or prudence. These are examples *of the cases resting* upon Correspondence (see text).

e. The cases of Contrast ; as—

" Served, as he is, thus, *by us Deities*, he (the demon Táraka) still torments the triple world : It is evil requital, not beneficence, that pacifies the wicked soul."

Here a particular is strengthened by a general, under a contrast. Similarly of others.

Text.

Poetical Reason.

No. 710. When a reason is implied in (1) a sentence or (2) a word, it is termed Poetical Reason.

Commentary.

a. Of these, the case of *a reason* being implied in a sentence ; as—

" The blue lotus, which was like thy eyes in loveliness, is *now* sunk under water ; that moon, my love, which imitated the fairness of thy face, is mantled over by clouds ; those royal swans too are gone *(to the mánasa lake)* whose pace resembled thine—alas ! the gods would not suffer me to derive a consolation even from thy similitudes—*in this season of rains so tormenting to separated lovers.*"

Here, the sentences forming the *first* three lines *of the stanza* imply reason for *what is affirmed in* the fourth line—' alas ! the gods' &c.

b. The case of *a reason* implied in a word ; e. g. *the following couplet of* mine :—

" S'iva, afraid of the immense weight, bears not the Ganges on his head, muddy as it is with the heaps of dust raised by the multitude of thy horses (त्वद्वाजिराजिनिर्धूतधूलीपटलपङ्किलां)."

Here, the one *compound* word, forming the first half, implies a reason for what is expressed by the second half.

c. The reason expressed by more than one word ; as *in the following example of* mine :—

' O Sire, Gangá who flows through three ways *only*, (or Heaven, Earth and Pátála), conceals herself, through shame, on Mahádeva's head, as she beholds the river *formed* of the waters *poured* in thy donations, streaming through innumerable passages (पश्यन्त्यसङ्ख्यपथगां त्वद्दानजलवाहिनीं)."

d. Some writers, it is to be observed here, do not admit those cases of the Transition (§709 *c.* and *d.*) which rest upon the relation of causation, because, *they suppose*, they are superseded by the Poetical Reason residing in a Sentence. (§710 *a.*) This *opinion* is not right. For here *in the province of Poetry*, Reason is three-fold, as being Informative, Completive and Justificative (or Confirmative.) Of these *three sorts*, the Informative Reason is the subject of the figure of Inference, the Completive of the Poetical Reason, and the Justificative of the Transition : thus the Transition founded upon a causation is evidently distinct from the Poetical Reason. To illustrate : In the stanza beginning " The blue lotus—" (§710 *a*), the sentences forming the first three lines are *indispensably* wanted for the *completion of the sense*, inasmuch as, without them, the sentence constituting the fourth line would be incomplete in its signification and therefore absurd. Whilst in the stanza beginning " One ought not to perform an act rashly" (§709 *d.*) the prohibition of heedlessly acting is fully intelligible in itself as being complete in its signification, just in the manner of a counsel such as—" Never ought any one to associate, I tell your honour the truth, with the wicked, who are busy in working harm to their fellow creatures." The circumstance, *added in the stanza*, of Prosperity's choosing the discreet, only confirms or justifies *the prohibition, without being needed to be mentioned in order to the completion of its sense.* So the Transition resting upon a causation is clearly distinct from the Poetical Reason.

e. " Hara (Mahádeva), for fear of the immense weight, bears not the Ganges on his head: for it is muddy with the heaps of dust raised by the multitude of thy horses."

Here, we have not the ornament in question, since the reason is made as clear, by the use of the particle '*hi*' (for), as if we were to employ the formal expression *pankilatwát* (from its being muddy), and it is strikingness that is the essence of ornament.

TEXT.

Inference.

No. 711. The notion, expressed in a peculiarly striking manner, of a thing established by proof, is termed Inference.

COMMENTARY.

a For example:—

" I believe, in the heart of this fair lady shines the moon-face of her beloved: for in the diffusive beams burst out, all her limbs look pale, and those lotuses, her eyes, are closed."

Here the strikingness has its original in the metaphor.

b. Or we may take the following example:—

" Wherever falls the sight of women, there fall sharpened arrows; hence, I infer, Cupid runs before them with his bow furnished with shafts."

Here the strikingness rests upon the boldness of the poet's speech. In the figure of Poetical Fancy, the notion is attended with uncertainty, whilst in the present ornament it is attended with certainty, this is what makes their difference.

TEXT.

The Cause.

No. 712. When a cause is represented in identity with the effect, it is *termed* the Cause (*hetu*).

COMMENTARY.

a. As in my couplet beginning " She is the ecstasy of youthfulness"* (Chap. III §131 *a.*) the heroine, the cause of subjugation, is represented as the very subjugation *of the minds of young men.* In the expressions 'ecstasy' and 'laugh,' however, the ornament rests upon an introsusception (see §693 and 694).†

TEXT.

The Favourable.

No. 713. The Favourable *(anukúla)* is when unfavourableness turns into a favour.

COMMENTARY.

a. For example:—

" When thou art angry, lady of the slender frame, wound him with thy nails, and tie his neck tight, with those *fair* cords, thy hands."‡

The peculiar strikingness *of such a mode of speech* is properly counted as a distinct ornament, since it is perceived altogether different from all other figures.

TEXT.

Hint, two-fold.

No. 714. When something, really intended to be said, is apparently suppressed or denied, for the purpose of conveying a particular meaning, it is termed Hint (ákshepa),§ and is two-fold as pertaining to what is about to be said or what has been said.

COMMENTARY.

a. Of these *two cases*, that pertaining to what is about to be said, has two varieties, inasmuch as some thing, wholly and summarily hinted at may be suppressed, or something may be partially mentioned and partially omitted. The case pertaining to what has been said, admits of two sub-divisions, inasmuch as the very character of a thing may be denied, or as the speaker may pretend to negative, or cancel, what he has already spoken. Thus the Hint has four varieties.

* " She is the ecstasy of youthfulness—the laugh of the abundance of excessive beauty—the ornament of the face of the earth—the subjugation of the minds of the young men."

† The sentence is obscure in the original, and the scholiast, who mistakes even the name—*hetu*—of the figure to be *abhidhá-hetu*, gives an absurd interpretation of it.

‡ So in Romeo and Juliet:

"Jul. Then have my lips the sin that they have took.
Rom. Sin from my lips? O trespass sweetly urg'd!
Give me my sin again."

§ *Paralipsis* in Greek Rhetoric.

b. For examples in their order :—

" I would say something for the sake of my dear lady, pierced with a hundred shafts of Cupid—do thou, friend, stay here for a moment—nay, nay, what shall I say to one whose heart is devoid of compassion !"

Here the *pangs of* separation, felt by the female friend *of the speaker*, are hinted at in general, but the particulars, which were about to be spoken of, are suppressed.

c. " In separation from thee, the stag-eyed lady, beholding now the new jasmine expanded, is, of a certainty, alas !—but oh, enough of such a cursed discourse."

Here the portion 'to die' is omitted.

d. " My boy, I am no go-between, my business is not to say that thou art beloved. She dies, and thine will be the disgrace—these words of righteousness are what I have to say."

Here the character of a thing, *or rather a person,* is denied—that of the go-between.

e. " How can she of the slender frame pass the night in separation from thee—nay what is the use of talking to thee who art of so cruel a purpose ?"

Here the very fact of speaking is, as it were, negatived.

f. In the first example, the particular meaning conveyed (see text) is 'My friend is sure to die ;' in the second, what is particularly intimated, is the impossibility of speaking further or the like ; in the third, speaking the truth in spite of being a go-between ; and in the fourth, excess of misery. It is not to be supposed that a PROPER negation of what has been, *or is about to be,* said is what constitutes the present figure, for the SEMBLANCE of a denial is the essence of it.

TEXT.

Another Hint.

No. 715. Another figure, *also termed Hint*, is held, likewise, to be an apparent permission of something, *really* unwished for.

COMMENTARY.

a. 'Likewise'—for the purpose of conveying a particular meaning, as in the preceding *ornament.*

b. For example :—

"Depart, my love, if thou art resolved to go—auspicious be thy paths, and may I be born again in the place where thou hast gone!"

Here the permission of going, which is so much unwished for, failing as it does, terminates in prohibition; and the particular meaning conveyed, is that the addressee ought ENTIRELY to desist from going.

TEXT.

Peculiar Causation.

No. 716. When an effect is said to arise without a cause, it is Peculiar Causation, and is two-fold, according as the occasion is, or is not, mentioned.

COMMENTARY.

a. The production of an effect, though represented as being without the *supposed sole* cause, must depend upon some other cause. This distinct cause, or occasion, as it is sometimes mentioned and sometimes omitted, makes the figure two-fold. For example:—

"In youth, the waist of the fair-browed lady is slender, though she has never toiled, her eyes are tremulous, but she is not affrighted, her body is heart-ravishing, yet it is not ornamented."

Here the occasion, viz. youth, is mentioned. In this very example *if we leave out* '*in youth*' by reading *vapur bháti mṛigí-dris'ah*' (the body of the deer-eyed lady shines) instead of '*vapur vayasi subhruvah*' (in youth the body of the fair-browed lady), we should have the case of the Occasion being omitted.

TEXT.

Peculiar Allegation.

No. 717. When, in spite of the existence of a cause, there is an absence of the effect, it is Peculiar Allegation, and is likewise two-fold.

COMMENTARY.

a. 'Likewise'—that is to say, as the Occasion is, or is not, mentioned. Of these, the case in which the Occasion is mentioned; as—

"Truly great are they, who though rich, are free from haughtines, though young, are not fickle, and though possessed of power, do not give way to heedlessness *in the exercise of it.*"

Here the Occasion, *viz.* true greatness, is mentioned. In this *very stanza* if, for the fourth line *mahá-mahima-s'álinah* (truly great are they), we read *kiyantah santi bhútale* (few there are on earth), the Occasion would be omitted.

b. The case in which the occasion is inconceivable, being only a variety of that in which it is omitted, is not separately mentioned. The following is an example :—

" He of the flowery bow conquers the three worlds, alone,—whose power was not destroyed by Mahádeva, though he destroyed his body."

Here the cause of his power not being destroyed, notwithstanding the destruction of the body of *Káma*, is inconceivable.

c. In the present *figure*, an effect is also intimated to be absent, by means of representing something as present, which is opposed to it. So also in the Peculiar Causation (§ 716), a cause is represented to be absent through speaking of something, opposed to it, as present. Thus *in the stanza (given under* §2. o, *Chap. I. &* § 187, *Chap. III.*), there is Peculiar Causation, because of the representation of circumstances opposed to the cause of longing, *which yet is ascribed to the heroine*—circumstances such as are implied in 'The bridegroom is the very youth who embraced me before marriage' &c.;* and there is the Peculiar Allegation, inasmuch as the lady is described as longing, whilst longing is opposed to the effect expected to be produced by such a cause as the circumstance of her gaining that very person for her bridegroom who enjoyed her before marriage.

Thus there is in this example the Commixture (see §757) of Peculiar Causation and Peculiar Allegation. A pure example of such a modification of the figure is to be sought out *by the reader for himself.*

TEXT.

Contradiction ; its ten forms.

No. 718. When there is an apparent incongruity between a genus and *any of* the four beginning with genus (i. e. genus, quality, action and substance) ; between a quality and *any of* the three beginning with quality ; between an action and another action or a substance, or between two substances—it is Contradiction, *occurring* in *these* ten forms.

* Substitute this clause for 'There is that very husband who gained me as a girl' in the stanza in question. This mistake was overlooked by me, in revising Dr. Ballantyne's translation.

COMMENTARY.

a. For examples in their order :—

" Separated from thee, the wind of the Malaya mountain is to her a conflagration ; the beams of the moon are impregnated with heat ; even the hum of the bee pierces her heart ; even the lotus-leaf is to her the summer sun."

b. " O king, the hands of the wives of the Twice-born (Bráhmans), hardened by the constant rub of the pestle and by manifold household work are, whilst thou reignest, soft like the lake-born flower (lotus)."

c. " Though Self-existent, yet Thou art born, though devoid of passion, Thou destroyest thy foes (the Demons), though in Thy *deepest* sleep, Thou art awake—is there the being who knows Thee in truth ?"

d. " To the deer-eyed lady, separated as she was from the lap of her beloved, the Lord of Night (moon), in his complete glory, was full of burning poison."*

e. " O ! this form, ecstatic to my eyes but hard to obtain even through imagination, O ! the one with drunken eyes gladdens my heart yet torments it."

f. " S'iva, afraid of the immense weight," &c.

g. In the stanza beginning " To the deer-eyed lady," if, in the fourth line, *instead of 'full of burning poison,'* we read 'the mid-day sun,' we shall have the Contradiction of Substances.

h. In the example beginning 'Separated from thee,—' 'the wind' &c., which, as denoting many individuals, are generic terms, seem, at first sight, to contradict 'a conflagration,' 'heat,' 'piercing the heart' and 'the sun,' which, respectively, are a genus, a quality, an action and a substance. The apparent contradiction is explained by the fact that the state of things was caused by separation.

i. In the example beginning 'Though Self-existent,—' the quality of self-existence &c. is opposed to the action of being born &c., *and the seeming contradiction* is explained by the greatness of the power of God, *who, though unborn, can manifest himself as a human being born and so forth.*

* The Miltonic representation of the Deity "Dark with excessive light" should, perhaps, be ranked under this variety of the figure, i. e. the Contradiction of Quality and Substance.

j. In the verses commencing "S iva, afraid of the immense weight,' the contradiction may be expressed thus: 'S'iva himself, who ever bears the Ganges on his head, ceases to bear it &c.'; and the boldness with which poets are privileged to speak is the explanation of it. The other *illustrations* are clear.

k. In the Peculiar Causation, an effect only, as represented without a cause, is seemingly incongruous; in the Peculiar Allegation, a cause only, without an effect; and in the present figure, both the things *represented* are apparently contradicted by each other. Such is the difference.

TEXT.

Disconnection. No. 719. When a cause and the effect are represented as locally separated, it is Disconnection.

COMMENTARY.

a. For example:—

"She is a girl, but it is our minds that want manly boldness; she is a woman, but it is we that are timid; she bears a couple of plump and lofty breasts, but it is we that are oppressed; she is charged with the weight of fleshy thighs, but it is we that are unable to move—marvellous it is that the faults belonging to another have deprived us of power."

b. This figure being counted as an exception, the ornament of Contradiction (§718) is left to rest in the mutual inconsistency of two things residing in the same place.

TEXT.

Incongruity. No. 720. When the *respective* qualities or actions of a cause and its effect are opposed to each other; or when an endeavour becomes fruitless and brings an evil result; or when there is an association of two incongruous things—it is held Incongruity.

COMMENTARY.

a. For examples in their order:—

"His sword, wonderful to say, dark as it is like the Tamála tree, in every battle, having obtained contact with his hand, engenders, at the very moment, a fame white as the autumnal moon, glorifying the triple world!"

Here, we have white fame arising from the dark sword, figured as the cause,—in opposition to the rule or theory that the qualities of the effect conform to those of the cause.

b. "O thou with eyes like the blue lotus-leaf, how ecstatic is the joy thou givest, yet Separation which has its origin in thyself—how fiercely it burns my frame!"

Here we have burning Separation originating in a joy-exciting cause, *viz.*, a woman.

c. "This ocean is a store-house of gems, so I resorted to it in the hope of obtaining treasures, but treasures far from obtaining, my mouth was filled with salt-water."

Here, not only is the desired wealth not obtained, but, on the contrary, the mouth is filled with salt-water.

d. "The woods with barks of trees for ornament, and the glory of royalty admired even by Indra—how vast the disparity. Ah! how hard it is to bear the dealings of Fate, evil-disposed as he ever is."*

We have, here, the association of the woods and royal glory. The stanza is mine.

e. Or for example:—

"He, the Sleeper on the Ocean (Vishṇu), whose vast belly drank up the worlds at the consummation of the ages—that Deity was drunk in by one of the fair ones of the city, with a corner of one of her eyes, languid in love!"†

TEXT.

The Equal.

No. 721. The Equal is the commendation of an object fitly united *with another*.

* The commentator does not admit this as a proper example of the fourth variety of the figure, contending that Ráma, the subject of the stanza, was not a king when he went to the woods. The author, however, perhaps means to intimate that majesty was the hero's by nature, though he was not, at the time, inaugurated a king.

† Mallinátha, in commenting on this stanza (Mágha, xiii, 40), characterizes the figure as the Exceeding (see §723), and in so doing differs with the author of the Kávya-prakás'a as well as with that of the present work.

COMMENTARY.

a. For example:—

"The moon-light has been wedded to the deer-marked luminary (moon), freed from clouds; Jahnu's daughter (Gangá) has come down to meet worthy Ocean'—such were the words—harsh to the ear of the other monarchs—that the citizens, with one voice, spoke, glad at the union of that couple of equal worth."

TEXT.

The Strange. No. 722. The Strange is, when, for the attainment of an object, one acts contrarily *to it*.

COMMENTARY.

a. For example:—

"For the purpose of being elevated, he bows down; for the sake of his life, he parts with it altogether; for the sake of happiness, he subjects himself to misery—who is there a greater fool than the servant?"

TEXT.

The Exceeding. No. 723. When of the container and the contained, one is represented as vaster than the other, it is termed the Exceeding.

COMMENTARY.

a. The case when the Container is vaster; as:—

"How shall we better describe the vastness of the Ocean than by saying that Vishṇu sleeps upon him—obscure, having thrown the worlds into his belly."

The case when the Contáined is vaster; as:—

b. "The Foe of Kaiṭabha (Vishṇu) could not contain within himself the flood of joy caused by the advent of the holy saint—He in whose *divine* person the worlds did freely abide, when, at the consummation of a cosmic cycle, he had withdrawn within himself all the created souls."

TEXT.

The Reciprocal. No. 724. The Reciprocal is when two things do the same act to each other.

COMMENTARY.

a. For example:—

"She of the slender frame is graced by thee, and thou art graced by her: The night gives glory to the moon, and the moon lends lustre to the night."

TEXT.

No. 725. When something that depends on another is represented as existing without it; or when one object is spoken of as being present in many places simultaneously; or when somebody, in doing an act, unexpectedly does another act, either unconnected with the subject, or otherwise; it is the Extraordinary, and is thus three-fold.

The Extraordinary; its three forms.

COMMENTARY.

a. For examples in their order:—

"Who would not glorify the poets, whose discourse—though they have gone to heaven—graced with infinite beauties—delights the world, generation after generation, until the end of creation?"

b "In the forest, by the river's side, in the mountain cave,—*every where* do thy foemen see thee standing in front, terrible like Death!"

c. "Wife, minister, confidant, beloved disciple in the charming arts,—say, what has not merciless Death deprived me of, in depriving me of thee?" *Raghuvan's'a.*

TEXT.

No. 726. The Frustration is when by the same means that one employed in bringing a thing to a particular state, another brings it to an opposite one.

Frustration.

COMMENTARY.

a. For example, the stanza beginning 'Them, who with a look.'* (§ 636 *a.*)

* "Them, who, with a look, recall to life the Mind-born God, who was burnt by a look—we glorify the fair-eyed *women*, the conquerors of the Fierce-eyed Divinity (S'iva)."

TEXT.

A second kind of the above.

No. 727. Or when the contrary of a certain act is justified *by the same reason*, with facility.

COMMENTARY.

a. *Supply* 'It is the same Frustration.'

b. *For example* :—

" 'Stay here, my love ; after but a few days I shall speed to be here again—*stay here*, for thou art tender and canst not bear toil.'—'Tenderness, fair youth, is rather a reason for my going with thee, for tender, as I am, I shall not endure the terrible pangs of separation'."

Here, the hero mentions the tenderness of the heroine as a reason against her accompanying him, and the heroine, on the other hand, makes it, with still more facility, a reason for the same.

TEXT.

The Garland of Causes.

No. 728. When something mentioned first is spoken of as the cause of what follows, and this again of what comes next, and so on, it is the Garland of Causes.

COMMENTARY.

a. For example :—

" Knowledge is acquired from association with the learned ; meekness from knowledge ; the affection of the people from meekness ; and what *is it that is* not *obtainable* from the affection of the people ?"

TEXT.

The Serial Illuminator.

No. 729. The Serial Illuminator, again, is when a number of objects is, in succession, connected with the same attribute.

COMMENTARY.

a. For example :—

" When thou didst come to fight, the bow obtained the arrows ; the arrows, the foeman's head ; the foeman's head, the Earth ; she again, thee ; and thou, *immortal* fame."

Here the action of obtaining is the attribute.

TEXT.

No. 730. When what is mentioned first is qualified, (1) affirmatively, or (2) negatively, by what follows, and this again by what comes next, and so on, it is the Necklace, and is thus two-fold.

The Necklace, two-fold.

COMMENTARY.

a. For examples in their order :—

"—When (in Autumn) the lake *is adorned* with the expanded lotus, and the lotus *is* associated with the bee, the bee *is perpetually* humming and the humming is attended with the excitement of love."

b. "There was not a lake that was not graced with fair lotuses, there was not a lotus in which there reposed not a bee, there was not a bee which hummed not melodiously, there was not a hum that ravished not the heart."

c. Sometimes the qualified, too, is found successively to be affirmed or denied as qualification ;* as—

"The lakes are pure, the lotuses bloom in the lakes, the bees fly to the lotuses, the musical hum is now uttered by the bees."

So also in the case of a denial.

TEXT.

No. 731. A succession of things, gradually rising in excellence, is termed the Climax (sára).

The Climax.

COMMENTARY.

a. For example :—

"The most important thing in the requisites of royalty is a kingdom ; in a kingdom, a capital ; in a capital, a palace ; in a palace, a couch ; in a couch, a fair woman, the whole property of Love."

TEXT.

No. 732. The Relative Order is when a reference is made respectively to what have been mentioned.

The Relative Order.

COMMENTARY.

a. For example :—

"'They bloom :' 'Pluck them with thy nails.' 'It blows :' 'Hedge

* The reader will observe that the term 'qualified' (विशेष्य) is here used in the sense of *subject* and 'qualification' to denote a member of the predicate.

it with the skirts of thy garment.' 'They enter the garden:' 'Scare them away with the tinkling of thy bracelets.'—thus, fortunate youth, do the female friends of thy love separated from thee, talk to each other by hints, touching the *vanjula* flowers, the southern breeze and the *kokila*."*

TEXT.

No. 733. When the same object (1) is, or (3) is made to be, in many places, in succession; or when many objects (2) are, or (4) are made to be, in the same place, in succession,—it is termed the Sequence *(paryáya)*.

The Sequence.

COMMENTARY.

a. For examples in their order:—

"Reposing for a moment on the *thick* eye-lashes, striking the *delicate* lips, split by the fall upon the breasts, rolling down the dimples in the skin—thus gradually did the first rain-drops reach the navel of Umá."

b. "Wolves, crows and jackals run in thy foeman's city, where walked gay women once, languid with the weight of hips."

c. "That hand, the fingers of which were cut by the handling of the *sharp-edged* sprouts of the sacred grass (kus'a), she made a friend to the rosary—kept off from the under-lip which she had ceased to colour, *kept off* from the play-ball reddened by the unguent of her breasts."

d. "Thy foemen's wives now let fall thick drops of tears on those breasts where rolled the pure pearl necklace."

e. In these varieties, the Place or Places is either one or are several, and so also the Placed. To illustrate. In the stanza beginning 'Reposing for a moment,' the rain-drops are gradually in the places—eye-lashes &c.—which are several. In the example commencing 'Wolves, crows and jackals,' the 'wolves' &c., the placed, were successively in the foeman's city, which is one place. So of the rest.

* So in Shakespear's Comedy of Errors, Act II, Scene 2nd.

"The time was once when thou, unurg'd, wouldst vow
That never words were music to thine ear,
That never object pleasing in thine eye,
That never touch well welcome to thy hand,
That never meat sweet savour'd in thy taste,
Unless, I spake, or looked, or touched, or carv'd to thee."

f. Since in the present figure one object is *represented to be* in many places only in consecution, it is distinct from the Extraordinary (§725); and it is different from the Return (§734), because of the absence of an exchange.

TEXT.

The Return.

No. 734. The Return (*parivrittih*) is the exchange of a thing for what is (1) equal, (2) lesser or (3) greater.

COMMENTARY.

a. For examples in their order :—

"The fawn-eyed lady gave a glance and took my heart, whilst I gave my heart but got the fever of love."

Here, in the first half there is an exchange for the like, and in the second half, for what is lesser.

b. "The old Jatáyuh, translated to heaven—wherefore should we lament him now, who, at the price of a decrepit body, bought a fame lustrous like the light of the moon?"

Here we have an exchange for what is greater.

TEXT.

Special Mention.

No. 735. When with, or without a query, something is affirmed for the denial, expressed or understood, of something else similar to it, it is Special Mention (*parisan'khyá*).

COMMENTARY.

a. For examples in their order :—

"What is a lasting ornament here below?—fame, not a gem. What is to be practised?—good deed done by the great, not a crime. What is an eye unobstructed?—the intellect not the *corporal* eye. And who is there besides thee who knows to discriminate good and evil?"

Here, a gem &c., which are to be rejected *or denied as an ornament &c.*, are mentioned.

b. "What is ever to be practised?—virtue; what is to be earnestly sought?—the company of the good. Who is to be meditated upon?—the Lord Vishṇu. What is to be desired?—the supreme abode, *or final beatitude.*"

Here what are to be rejected, *viz.*, sin &c., are understood. In these two examples, *the declaration* is preceded by a query.

c. When it is not preceded by a query, we have the following examples:—

" Devotion to God not to Mammon; addiction to Scripture not to woman, the weapon of Love; regard for fame not for the body are often found in the great."

d. " His strength was for the purpose of quelling the fear of the oppressed, his great learning was for the sake of honouring the learned —not the wealth alone but the perfections too of that sovereign were for the sake of others."

e. When founded upon a Paronomasia, it is peculiarly striking; e. g. " When that king, the conqueror of the world, was protecting the earth, the mixture of colours (or classes—वर्ण) was in painting, the want of the string (or merits—गुण) was in bows" &c.

TEXT.

No. 736. The Reply is when a question is inferred from an answer; or, the questions being given, when there is a number of answers, unlooked for.

The Reply.

COMMENTARY.

a. For examples, *the following verses of* mine:—

" My mother-in law has lost her sight, my husband is gone far away and I am a solitary girl: how canst thou stay here?"*

From *this is* understood a traveller having asked for lodging.

b. " What is *most* odd?—the decree of destiny. What is to be sought out?—a man appreciating merit. What is the source of bliss? —a good wife. What is hard to be won?—a wicked man."

This is distinct from the Special Mention, because, here, other things of a similar nature are not intended to be disowned, *or denied*

* The author probably means to represent the girl as tempting the traveller as we infer from similar stanzas of such indirect import. The strikingness of this example, if there is any in it, as well as of that given in the *Kávya-prakás'a,* rests upon the indirect way in which the speaker, in either case, expresses his or her meaning, and is quite independent of the inference on our part of a query or request previously made. I do not see why it should be counted a figure at all. It is indeed strange to find the author of the *Kávya-prakás'a* admitting this figure of speech, when he is unwilling to recognise such a figure as the Cause (*hetu*), that comes under the English Metonymy, and perceives no strikingness in such an example of it as 'The Spring, the *joy* of the *kokila,* has arrived.'

as possessing the respective predicates. Nor is the first case of the present figure the same with the Inference (§711), since that is recognized only when what is inferred and the ground of inference, or the reason, are both mentioned,—*and here the query is not mentioned.* Nor is it Poetical Reason (§ 710), for the reply is not the source of the question.*

TEXT.

No. 737. When according to the Maxim of the Stick and the Cake, a fact is concluded from another, it is held the Necessary Conclusion (arthá patti).

The Necessary Conclusion.

COMMENTARY.

a. The Maxim of the Stick and the Cake is one by which, a truth or fact being given, another truth or fact comes in through a necessary connection; for example, it being admitted that a mouse has eaten up a portion of a stick, the fact of its having eaten the cake connected therewith, comes in as a matter of course.

b. The figure has two varieties, inasmuch as from a fact connected with the subject-matter, there comes in one unconnected with it, or *vice versâ.*

c. For examples in their order:—

"Lo! the Necklace rolls on the round breasts of the fawn-eyed ladies. When such is the condition even of the pearls, free (*muktá*) *as they are called,* of what consequence are we, the slaves of love?"

d. "Forsaking his native fortitude, he bewailed, with his voice choked by weeping. Even iron, heated to excess, becomes soft, why speak we then of mortals *melting under affliction?*"

e. In the present ornament, there is a peculiar strikingness when the Necessary Connection is founded upon a Paronomasia, as in the

* The Kávya-prakás'a, whom the present work literally follows here, has, it seems to me, failed to elucidate the distinction between the two figures. The following is the proper explanation: In the Poetical Reason, an epithet, a clause, or a whole sentence is used *by the poet as implying a reason or ground for an assertion or representation made by himself;* whilst in the present figure the *whole* of what has been said by the poet serves as a reason for the *reader* in inferring a query supposed by the poet. The difference from the inference too is not rightly marked.

example "Lo! ·the Necklace," &c. This figure is not identical with the Inference (§ 711), since the Necessary Connection has not the nature of a mere Relation, *established by experience.**

TEXT.

No. 738. The Alternative is an ingenious opposition of two things of equal probability.

The Alternative.

COMMENTARY.

a. For example; "Bend ye your heads or your bows; make our authority or your bow-strings the ornaments of your ears, *i. e. yield to our authority or draw your bows.*"†

Here the bending of the heads and that of the bows are opposed to each other, being respectively marks of peace and war, which it is impossible to resort to at the same time. And this opposition terminates in the having recourse to one of the alternatives. The facts are equally probable, inasmuch as the bending of the bows and that of the heads are alike looked for *by the speaker*, through a pride of prowess. The ingenuity of the speech consists in its implying a comparison; so also in the sentence 'Make our authority or your bow-strings the ornaments of your ears.' Similarly in the sentence "May the eyes or the body of Vishnu effect (*kurutám*) the cure of your worldly distresses," the ingenuity consists in the use of the Paronomasia *in 'kurutám' which, in one voice, is singular, and in another, dual. In the sentence* 'Let wealth acquired be given away to a Divinity or a Brahman, there is no ornament, because of the absence of ingenuity.

TEXT.

No. 739. The Conjunction is (1) when notwithstanding the existence of one cause sufficient to bring about an effect, there are represented others producing the same, according to the Maxim of the Thresh-

The Conjunction.

* We have here the recognition of necessary, or intuitive, truths, as contradistinguished from those established by experience.

† So Satan exhorts the fallen angels—'Awake, arise, or be for ever fallen.'

ing-floor and the Pigeons ; or (2) when two qualities or actions, or a quality and an action are simultaneously produced.

COMMENTARY.

a. For example, *take the following stanza of* mine :—

"Thou wast, O gentle Zephyr, begotten by the Mountain of the Sandal ; pre-eminent art thou in the world in mild complaisance (or southernness—*dákshiṇya*), and intimate art thou with the holy waters of Godávarí—if thou, alas! even thou dost burn my whole frame like a fierce conflagration, what shall I say to the black *kokila*, savage and intoxicated as he is?"

Here, notwithstanding the existence of one cause, *viz.*, the circumstance of being begotten by the Mountain of the Sandal, for *the effect of* burning, other causes such as the circumstance of coming from the South &c., are mentioned. All these causes being good things (since they are a source of delight to all, excepting the separated lover), we have in the above example a Combination of Good Things. In the fourth line of the same stanza, wherein the bad things such as madness &c., are joined together, we have a Combination of Bad Things.

b. To exemplify the Combination of Good and Bad Things.

"The moon dimmed by the day, a lovely woman whose youth has departed, a lake bereft of its lotuses, a fair form with an unlettered tongue, a master devoted to Mammon, a good man in perpetual misery, a wicked person seated in the court of a king—these seven are sore afflictions to my heart."

With respect to this example, some say that there is here the Combination of Good and Bad Things, inasmuch as the moon &c., are good and a wicked man is bad. Others, however, declare the same characteristic to rest upon the circumstance of the moon being by nature fair, and the dimness, *with which it is associated*, being foul. For, *they contend justly*, the strikingness of the example rests upon this peculiar way of pointing to the impropriety of *such foul states as* dimness &c., coming upon such good things as the moon &c. Besides, all the seven being summed up as afflictions by the sentence—'These seven are sore afflictions to my heart,' the clause 'a wicked person seated in the court of a king' bears the character of a fault, because of its violating the uniformity *of the representation* (see Chap. VII § 575, bb), in each of the other instances the subject, *and not the predicate*, being a good person or thing.

c. In the present ornament, all the causes are jointly introduced just as pigeons alight together upon a threshing-floor; whilst in the figure Convenience, notwithstanding the existence of a cause sufficient for the production of an effect, another cause is represented as operating BY CHANCE.

d. "No sooner had thy eyes, youthful lady, become red than the face of thy beloved became gloomy; no sooner, fair friend, hadst thou bent down thy head than the fire of love blazed up in his heart."

Here, in the first half there is a simultaneity of Qualities; in the second, that of Actions.

e. When a Quality and Action are simultaneous, take the following example:—

"No sooner, king of kings, had thy eyes, those fair brethren to the white lily, become, on a sudden, dismal towards thy foemen, than the fierce glances of *fell* Adversity distinctly fell on their frames."

f. We also see this figure respecting one and the same subject; as in "He brandishes his sword and diffuses his glory."* It is not an instance of the Illuminator, (see § 696), since these varieties of the Conjunction implying the simultaneity of quality and action, are, as a rule,† founded upon a Hyperbole consisting in the inversion of the necessary sequence of a cause and an effect; whilst the Illuminator has not for its foundation a Hyperbole.

* Cæsar made himself the subject of this variety of the figure when he wrote "I came, I saw, I conquered;" to which Shakespear has supplied the following humorous counterpart, illustrating the figure in a series:—

'—For your brother and my sister no sooner met, but they looked; no sooner looked, but they loved; no sooner loved, but they sighed; no sooner sighed but they asked one another the reason; no sooner knew the reason, but they sought the remedy:" *As You Like It*, Act V, Scene II.

† Here in the original, instead of समुच्चयप्रकाराऽनियमेन, as read in Roer's edition, read समुच्चयप्रकारा नियमेन, though my own MS. sanctions the former by inserting the mark ऽ of a rejected अ.

TEXT.

No. 740. The Convenience is when what is to be effected becomes easy through the accidental operation of another agency.

The Convenience.

COMMENTARY.

a. For example:—

"As I was about to fall at her feet to quell her indignation, happily, for my good, rose the roar of the clouds."

TEXT.

No. 741. The Rivalry *(pratyaníka)* is when somebody, unable to avenge himself on his enemy, is *represented as* doing harm to what has a connection with him, which only proves his superiority.*

The Rivalry.

COMMENTARY.

a. 'His'—i. e. the enemy's.—For example the following couplet of mine:—

"'She of the slender waist has vanquished my waist with hers'—so thinking, the lion breaks the protuberances of the elephant's head that resemble the jar-like breasts of the lady."

TEXT.

No. 742. When things to which a comparison is generally made are (1) themselves turned into objects of comparison, or (2) declared to be useless, it is termed the Converse *(pratípa.)*

The Converse.

COMMENTARY.

a. For examples in their order:—

"The blue lotus, which was like thy eyes in loveliness, is *now* sunk in water" &c. (see § 710. *a.*)

b. "When there is that face, all discourse of the moon is closed; alas! for gold, when there is that radiance; if there are those eyes, the blue lotusus are lost; that smile existing, what is nectar; fie! to *proud* Cupid's bow, if there are those eye-brows—nay why talk we

* Röer erringly blends this with the foregoing Commentary.

so much when it is true that the Maker's rule of creation is opposed to superfluities."

Here the radiance of the moon &c., being eclipsed by that of the face &c., the former are rendered useless.

TEXT.

No. 743. When the pre-eminence of an object, greatly excelling *in some quality*, being at first declared, another is compared to it, it too is termed the Converse.

A second sort of the Converse.

COMMENTARY.

a. For example :—

"Be not proud, *O destructive* Poison, to think that thou art the chief of direful things. Are there not in this world the words of the wicked as malign as thyself?"

In the first line *of the stanza, i. e. in the clause* '*Thou art the chief of direful things,*' the pre-eminence of the object is declared, *though in evilness.* When it is not declared, we have not this ornament; as in such a sentence as 'Like Brahmá speaks the Brahman.'

TEXT.

No. 744. The Lost (*mílita*) is when something is spoken of as concealed in another of a like quality.

The Lost.

COMMENTARY.

a. The thing of a like quality may be either inherent or borrowed.

b. For examples in their order :—

"Saraswatí saw not the mark on Vishnu's bosom of the musk that had perfumed Lakshmí's (her rival's) breasts—lost as it was in his lustre that shone like the dark-blue lotus."

Here, the dark-blue lustre is inherent in the person of the Divinity.

c. "In that *city* the faces of fair women, reddened, as they ever were, with the ray of the ruby earring, excited no mistrust, even when glowing in anger, in the hearts of the youthful lovers."

Here, the redness of the ruby earring is borrowed in the face.

TEXT.

No 745. The Sameness is when something in question is spoken of as having become identical with, or undistinguishable from, something else, through a likeness of properties.

The Sameness.

COMMENTARY.

a. For example :—

" Fair women resorting to their beloved, went securely, undistinguished in the moon-light—their tresses covered with jasmines and their bodies anointed with bright sandal."

b. In the Lost we have the eclipse of an object of an inferior quality by one of a superior quality ; whilst in the present figure there is an absence of discrimination on account of both the objects possessing like properties.

TEXT.

No. 746. The Borrower (*tadguṇa*) is when an object is represented as quitting its own quality and assuming an excellent one.

The Borrower.

COMMENTARY.

a. For example :—

" He spoke and the gleams of his radiant teeth whitened those honey-lickers—*the black-bees*—that hovered round that *blooming* lotus disguised as his face."

In the Lost, something in question is covered over by another, whilst in this figure, the quality of another is recognized as superinduced upon it.

TEXT.

No. 747. The Non-borrower is when something (in question) does not assume the quality of another, though there is a reason *for it.*

The Non-borrower.

COMMENTARY.

a For example :—

" How is it alas! that, seated in my heart glowing with ardent love, thou, though white with goodness, dost not reflect the glow?"*

b. Or for example :—

" White are the waters of Gangá and black are those of Yamuná—dipping in both, O royal swan, thy whiteness is the same—it increases not, nor does it decrease."

In the former *example*, the beloved person, spoken of as 'white with goodness,' does not glow† *with answering love*, though it is proper that he should do so, having come in contact with an excessively glowing heart.‡ In the latter example, though there is an Indirect Description (see §706), *and the swan, therefore, absolutely speaking, is not the proper subject of the description*, yet it is a thing in question, in comparison with Gangá and Yamuná, *which are still more remote from the real subject, viz., a person of a steady character.*§ The swan, in spite of its contact with Gangá and Yamuná, takes not the colour of either.

c. This figure is distinct from the Peculiar Allegation (see §717), being founded upon the peculiarly striking circumstance of not assuming a quality, *or colour ;* and it is different from the Incongruity (§720), because a distinct colour is not said to be produced.

TEXT.

The Subtle.

No. 748. When a delicate circumstance, indicated by (1) some appearance or (2) gesture, is intimated by any hint, it is termed the Subtle (*súkshma*).

COMMENTARY.

a. 'Delicate'—i. e. not to be understood by one of a dull apprehension.

* This is not a literal rendering of the original stanza, in which the figure rests upon the use of the word *rága* which means both 'love' and 'redness.'

† *Lit.* Does not become red or affectionate.

‡ Lit. Excessively red or affectionate heart.

§ This remark is with reference to the qualification, bracketed in the translation of the Text, which our author intends to be supplied from Text No. 745. The qualification however seems needless and is virtually annulled by the first example of the present figure given in the *Kávyaprakás'a.* Our author indeed modifies the example (*see* §*a*) to reconcile it to the qualification, though he forgot it while illustrating the foregoing figure, for the black-bees there spoken of are certainly not things in question.

b. Of the two cases, that of Appearance; as:—

"Some female friend, observing the saffron ointment on the lady's neck divided by the continuous flow of heat-drops oozing from her face, drew, with a smile, the figure of a sword in her hand to intimate her masculineness."

Here the masculine action of a woman, indicated by the division of the saffron, is intimated by another, by drawing in her hand the figure of a sword, which is the token of a man.

c. The case of Gesture; as:—

"Perceiving that her lover had his mind *anxious* about the time of assignation, the quick-witted dame closed the lotus-flower with which she was playing—whilst her laughing eye conveyed to it the import."

Here, the time of meeting which the lover inquired for by straining his eyebrows &c., is intimated by the close of the lotus which takes place at night.

TEXT.

No. 749. The Dissembler (*vyájokti*) is the artful concealment of a thing, though discovered.

The Dissembler.

COMMENTARY.

a. For example:—

"May S'iva preserve you!—that Deity who—as the Mountain-king joined his daughter's hand with his, in wedlock—thrilled by the touch and troubled by the distraction of his attention from the various ceremonials of marriage, cried out 'Oh! how cold are the hands of the Mountain of Snow,' and was beheld with a smile by the troops of the Divine Mothers standing in a circle in the inner apartment of Himálaya."

b. It is not the first Concealment (see §683), as the object is not mentioned by the person who conceals it. Its difference from the second Concealment has been shown on the occasion of speaking of that ornament.

TEXT.

The Description of Nature.

No. 750. The Description of Nature (*swabhávokti*) is the description of such peculiar action or appearance of an object as is not easily perceived.

COMMENTARY.

a. 'Not easily perceived'—*i. e.* perceived by the poet alone.—'An object'—such as a boy or the like.—'Peculiar action or appearance'—*i. e.* such as characteristically belong to the object.

b. Take the following example of mine :—

"Lo! the angry hyena, with red and swollen eyes, scaring away the animals all around with his howling roar, traverses from forest to forest—behold, he lashes the earth repeatedly with his tail, rests upon it *for a moment* with his *hind* feet, then on a sudden shrinking into himself, he springs with fierce velocity in the air."

TEXT.

Vision.

No. 751. When (1) a wonderful object,* or (2) something past or future, is represented as if it were present, it is termed the Vision (*bhávika*).

COMMENTARY.

a. For example :—

"Victorious is that prince of ascetics—Agastya of the mighty soul—who, in the hollow of one of his hands, saw the divine Fish and Tortoise (incarnations of Vishṇu), *as he drank up the ocean in one handful of water.*"

b. Or for example :—

"*Methinks* I see thy eyes with the black collyrium that was there; I *seem to* perceive thy form with that profusion of ornaments that is yet to adorn it."

c. This figure is not one with the Merit named Perspicuity (see Chap. VII, 611), for the latter does not cause a thing past or future†

* This variety is not recognized in the *Kávya-prakás'a*, being our author's own invention, and an unreasonable one too, for it is either included in the second variety or has no meaning at all.

† 'Or a wonderful object'—adds the Commentator.

to seem as if it were present. Nor is it the Marvellous flavour (see Chap III § 37), for it occasions no wonder.* Nor is it the ornament of Hyperbole, because it implies no introsusception (see § 693). Nor is it the Mistaker, for what is past or future is mentioned as past or future. Nor is it the Description of Nature, for this consists in a faithful representation of the nice characteristics of a natural object, whilst the present figure rests upon the peculiarly remarkable circumstance of an object (*really past or future*) seeming to be present. If, however, in the description of the nature of an object, the above peculiarity does occur, then there is a Commixture of the two *figures*.

d. "Who is he that, without an umbrella, seems as if he were surrounded with white umbrellas; who is he that, without a *chámara*, is ever fanned with the *chámar* of *flickering* graces?"

There is not the present figure in the above example, inasmuch as what appears in itself to be present is here described. As the figure in question consists in *an object's* seeming to be present THROUGH the description,† it has its proper place there where something not actually seeming to be present is so represented; as in the example '*Methinks* I see thy eyes with the black collyrium that was there' &c.

TEXT.

No. 752. The description of super-mundane prosperity is termed the Exalted, or an action of one that is great, *represented* collaterally to the subject in hand.

The Exalted.

* Read अहेतुत्वात् for हेतुत्वात् in Röer's edition of the text. It indeed seems odd to speak of the representation of a wonderful object causing no wonder.

† Cancel here the stop (।) after स्वरूपत्वात् in Röer's edition of the text. The translation is according to the reading of my MS. *viz.* यत् पुनरप्रत्यक्षायमाणस्यैव वर्णने प्रत्यक्षायमाणत्वं &c. which, cannot but be preferred to Röer's reading, *viz.* यत् पुनः प्रत्यक्षायमाणस्यापि वर्णने प्रत्यक्षायमाणत्वं &c., which is simply unintelligible, and makes a distinction without a difference. The commentator seems indeed to support it and toils hard to make out a sense, but to no purpose.

COMMENTARY.

a. For examples in their order :—

"There, the pleasure-gardens are fed by the waters oozing from the roofs of the Lunar Stone (*s'as'ánkopala*) by the fall of moon-light —roofs that leave the sphere of the clouds beneath."

b. "Used to the slumber of blessedness after the consummation of a cosmic cycle, the Lord sleeps here (on the ocean), having destroyed the worlds—hymned by the First Maker (Brahmá) seated on the lotus that has risen from His navel."

TEXT.

The Impassioned, the Lovely, the Impetuous and the Allayment.

No 753. When (1) a Flavour (chap. III. § 32), or (2) an Incomplete Flavour (chap. III, § 245), or (3) Semblances thereof (§ 247), or (4) the Quelling of a sentiment (§ 249. *a*) are reduced to a subordinate condition, then they become Ornaments and are respectively termed the Impassioned (*rasavat*), the Lovely (*preyah*), the Impetuous (*úrjaswi*) and the Allayment (samáhita).*

COMMENTARY.

a. 'Semblances thereof'—*i. e.* the semblance of Flavour and Incomplete Flavour. Of these *four kinds of embellishment*, the *Rasavat* (Impassioned) is so called from the association of *rasa*, Flavour, or passion.

b. For example—"This is that hand" &c. (see § 266 *b.*)

Here, the erotic is subordinate to the pathetic. So also of other Flavours.

c. The *Preyah* (Lovely) is *so named* from being loved by the best *of critics*. For example, the following stanza of mine :

"With eyes half-closed, in which the eye-balls were languid and motionless, with her soft creeper-like arms gently loosened as they clasped my neck, with her round cheeks suffused with heat-drops—

* These four figures have quite different definitions in the *Kávyá-dars'a* of Dandin and the *samáhita* there is what our author has denominated *samádhi*. The *Kávya-prakásá* does not recognize these ornaments nor the succeeding three

that fair one as I remember ever and anon, my heart obtains no tranquillity."

Here 'Love in union' (see chap. III, § 225) is subordinate to the sentiment named Reminiscence or Recollection (§190), and this again to 'love in separation' § 212).

d. The *U'rjaswi* (Impetuous) is so designated from its implying *úrjas* or impetuosity, in doing an improper deed. For example :—

" The savages of the forests, *now* betaking themselves to all the charming arts—*singing*, *dancing &c.*—enjoy thy foemen's ladies, having abandoned their own consorts."

Here the Semblance of the Erotic is subordinate to the sentiment of Love having a king for its object. So of the Semblance of an Incomplete Flavour.

e. 'Allayment' denotes 'giving up,' or rather, '*quelling.*'—For example :—

" That pride of thy foemen which perpetually manifested itself in continuous blandishments of the sword, in frowns, in threats and in shouts of defiance, has gone—we know not where—at the very sight of thy eyes."

Here the quelling of the sentiment named Pride is subordinate to the sentiment of Love having for its object a king.

Text.

Excitement, Conjunction and Commixture of Sentiments.

No. 754. And when there is an 'excitement' of a sentiment and a 'conjunction' and a 'commixture' of sentiments (see chap. III § 249) *in a subordinate condition*, they are entitled the same.

Commentary.

a. 'Entitled the same.' *i. e.* the ornaments are named the Excitement of a Sentiment, the Conjunction of Sentiments, and the Commixture of Sentiments. For examples in their order :—

b. " Busy as they were in their carousal in company of their friends, those foemen of thine were reduced to a miserable condition, having somehow heard thy name."

Here Terror, &c., *the sentiments excited*, are subordinate to the sentiment of Love having a king for its object.

c. "Longing for union with him who was her lord in her former birth, but modestly *seated* by the side of her female friend—may Párvatí ever preserve us!"

Here the conjunction of Longing and Modesty is subordinate to the sentiment of Love having a divinity for its object.

d. "'O we may be seen. Move off, thou wicked man. Why am I in a hurry? Nay, I am a maiden. Do thou give me the support of thy arm. Alas! alas! for this transgression *of the bounds of modesty*. Where dost thou go?'—thus—bearing fruits and tender leaves upon *which she lives*—the daughter of thy foeman *now* abiding in a forest, speaks to somebody, O thou *victorious* monarch of the earth."

Here the Commixture of Apprehension, Resentment,* Equanimity, Recollection, Weariness, Depression, Awaking† and Longing is subordinate to the sentiment of Love having a king for its object.

e. With respect to these *ornaments, viz. the Impassioned &c.* some people say—'What subserve Flavour &c. by means of embellishing the form of sense or sound are alone ornaments. But Flavour &c., being what are subserved by sense and sound, they cannot properly be ornaments.' Others however affirm that the designation of Ornament given to such representations, merely because of their subserving Flavour &c., is tropical and is to be assented to, in compliance with ancient custom. Others assert that, strictly speaking, an ornament, such as a Metaphor or the like, is what simply subserves Flavour &c., and the circumstance of its embellishing the sense &c. is *of no importance*, being analogous to the nipple attached to the neck of a she-goat, *which serves no end*. But those who have

* असूया in the original, which means 'envy' or 'malice' (see § 196), but अमर्ष ('resentment' or 'indignation') incomprehensively rendered by Dr. Ballantyne into 'impatience of opposition' (see § 184), is evidently the sentiment described here.

† The Commentator observes, with reference to the example, that excessive fatigue had brought a transient slumber on the maiden who, waking, regrets that she had passed beyond the bounds of feminine modesty by leaning upon the arm of a man.

thoroughly considered the matter are of opinion that a Flavour or the like which has become subordinate and which is itself subserved by word and sense that suggest it, properly obtains the denomination of Ornament, subserving, as it does, the Flavour or the like that is principal, through embellishing the words and the sense *that suggest the latter.* In the Modal Metaphor (see § 703), it is the behaviour merely of a lover or the like that constitutes the ornament, not the Relish *that is derivable from the representation*, because *being itself ultimate*, it wants the said condition *of assisting a principal Flavour through ornamenting the words and sense suggestive thereof.* Hence it is that the author of the 'Dhwani' has declared—'In that piece of poetry where a Flavour or the like is subordinate to another Flavour or a sense that is principal, the *former* Flavour or the like, is, in my opinion, an Ornament.' If the character of an ornament should be constituted by the circumstance of merely subserving the Flavour or the like, then it might be claimed even by plain or direct expressions or ideas, *and there are such capable of exciting poetical relish.* Similarly is refuted the opinion of those that affirm that the ornaments Impassioned &c. are, when the Flavour or the like is principal, and that when it is subordinate, there is the second ornament named Exalted.

TEXT.

The Conjunction and the Commixture.

No. 755. If any of these very ornaments (*that we have treated of in this chapter*) are united together, then there arise two distinct ornaments, *viz.* the Conjunction and the Commixture.

COMMENTARY.

a. As material ornaments, when united together, obtain a distinct beauty, and are consequently counted as one distinct ornament, so the poetical embellishments that have been defined, when united together, become distinct ornaments and are designated the Conjunction and the Commixture. Of these—

TEXT.

The Conjunction, defined.

No. 756. The existence of these independently of each other is termed the Conjunction.

COMMENTARY.

a. 'Of these' *i. e.* of ornaments of word and those of sense.—For example:—

देवः पायादपायान्नः स्मेरेन्दीवरलोचनः ।
संसारध्वान्तविध्वंसहंसः कंसनिषूदनः ॥

(May Kaṅsa's Destroyer—the Deity of the smiling lotus-eyes—preserve us from destruction—the Glorious Sun in annihilating the darkness of the world.)

We have a Rhyme in *páyádapáyát* and an Alliteration in the line beginning *saṅsára;* so there is the Conjunction of two ornaments of word. In the second quarter of the verse, *viz.* '*the Deity of the smiling lotus-eyes*' there is a Simile and in the second half, a Metaphor; thus we have the Conjunction of two ornaments of sense. Both these Conjunctions residing in the same verse, we have here the distinct ornament of the Conjunction of the ornaments of word and sense.

TEXT.

The Commixture, defined.

No. 757. The Commixture again is, when of two or more ornaments united, (1) one is principal and the others are subordinate to it,* or (2) when they reside in the same place, or (3) when there is a dubiousness about them—being *thus* threefold.

COMMENTARY.

a. The case of the Principal and Subordinate Ornaments; as—

"Under the form, methinks, of that mantling silk-white slough that had slipped, through the force of pulling, from the body of the royal Serpent (Vásuki, employed as the string), long did love-quick Mandákiní cling to his feet† (in kneading them), as if to remove the pain that Ocean had suffered in the churning."

* The *Kavya-prakás'a*, with much greater convenience, holds this variety to consist in the *mutual* subserviency of ornaments. Our author's illustrations imply that one of the ornaments in such cases is ultimately the principal, the others being subordinate, or subservient, to it.

† Or—with reference to the actual fact—*to a part* of the ocean, which the word पाद also means, according to the Commentator.

Here, the nature of Mandákiní (the celestial Ganges) is superimposed upon the slough, the real nature whereof is denied, so we have the Concealment (§683). This is subordinate to Paronomasia or Coalescence (see §643), inasmuch as it gives rise to, *or implies*, the verbal identification of the actual fact of Mandákiní's* clinging to a portion of the *personified* ocean, with clinging to its feet (by means of the pun in the word *páda* which means 'part' as well as 'foot'). The Paronomasia is subordinate to the Hyperbole (§693) consisting in the said identification. The Hyperbole is subordinate to the Poetical Fancy (§686) contained in the clause—'as if to remove the pain that Ocean had suffered in the churning.' The Poetical Fancy is subservient to the Modal Metaphor (§703), inasmuch as it implies Ocean and Mandákiní behaving *respectively* like a male and a female personage.

b. Or for example :—

"Fair Evening glows (with passion or redness—*anurága*) and Day is *ever* before her, still,—O wonderful is the decree of fate—they are never united."

Here the Modal Metaphor is subordinate to the Peculiar Allegation (see §717).

c. The Commixture of Dubiousness; as—

"Lo !† the Lunar Orb shines in the sky, dispersing the outspreading gloom, causing exquisite joy to the eyes."

Here, it is dubious whether there is a Hyperbole in the shape of the introsusception of a fair face into the moon ; or a Metaphor consisting in the superimposition of the nature of the moon *upon a face* intimated by *the pronoun* 'this;' or an Equal Pairing (§695), a face (intimated by 'this') and the lunar orb being both subjects of discourse and associated with the same attribute of destroying (internal or external) gloom &c.; or an Illuminator (§696), the moon not being in question; or a Modal Metaphor (§703), the face being not in question and understood from a sameness of attribute; or an Indirect Description (§706), the face being in question, and understood through the description of the moon which is not in question; or a Periphrasis (§708), the time (night) that excites love being meant to be described through the description of the moon, *the rise*

* Or, rather, the slough's, feigned as such. | † *Literally* 'this' (idam.)

of which is the effect thereof. Thus there being a doubtful possibility of each of these several ornaments, we have here the Commixture of Dubiousness.

d. Or, to take another example (*—if our dubious fancies with respect to the former one seem too far-fetched—*) in the sentence "I see the moon-face," it is doubtful whether there is a Simile, it being meant that the face is LIKE the moon; or a Metaphor, the meaning being that it IS the moon.

e. When, however, there is a reason for one of the ornaments, and another, against the others, or one only of such two reasons, there the doubt does not exist. For example, in *the sentence* "He kisses the moon-face," kissing being consistent with a face and inconsistent with the moon, it is a reason for our recognizing a Simile here, and against our admitting a Metaphor. In the example "The moon-face shines," the attribute of shiningness is a reason for the Metaphor, but being tropically possible in a face, it is not against the Simile. In the sentence "Lakshmí (Prosperity), O royal Náráyaṇa, embraces thee firmly," a woman's embrace of one LIKE her lord being improper, the embrace of a king, *as such*, by Lakshmí is impossible and so thwarts a Simile, but the embrace of Náráyaṇa (her lord) being possible, there is a Metaphor: *that is to say, the king is not* LIKENED *to Náráyaṇa but* IDENTIFIED *with him.* Similarly in 'The lotus-face of the fawn-eyed lady shines with tremulous eyes,' the eye, which is possible (only) in a face, indicates a Simile and thwarts a Metaphor, being impossible in a lotus. So in such a phrase as सुन्दरं वदनाम्बुजं (the beautiful lotus-face) where the common attribute (*viz.* beauty) is mentioned, since the compound वदनाम्बुजं (lotus-face) cannot imply a similitude, according to the grammatical rule उपमितं व्याघ्रादिभिः सामान्याप्रयोगे, *Paṇini* II, 1, 56, S. K. p. 356, (A word donoting an object compared is compounded with *vyághra &c.*, when the common attribute is not mentioned), the Simile is debarred, and consequently the compound implies a Metaphor, as belonging to that class which begins with the word *mayúra-vyaṇsaka* (*Pán.* II, 1, 72, S. K. p. 336).

f. The *case of the* Residence of Ornaments in the Same Place, or the Identical Position, is exemplified in the following stanza of mine:—

कटाक्षेणापीषत् क्षणमपि निरीक्षेत यदि सा
सदानन्दः सान्द्रः स्फुरति पिहिताशेषविषयः ।
सरोमाञ्चोदञ्चत्कुचकलशनिर्भिन्नवसनः
परीरम्भारम्भः क इव भविताऽम्भोरुहदृशः ॥

(If even for a moment she glances at me with the corner of her eye, ecstatic joy bursts forth in my heart and shuts out *the consciousness of* all external objects. What raptures then would flow from the embrace of her of the lotus-eyes, while the vesture falls off from those swelling breasts that quiver *with joy.*)

Here the Chhekánuprása contained in कटाक्षेणापीषत्क्षणमपि, and the Vṛittyanuprása, consisting in the compounded letters क्ष (k-sh) occurring twice in this phrase and once in निरीक्षेत, have an identical position. So also there is in this very example the identical position of Alliteration and Necessary Conclusion (§737). Or, for instance, in the phrase संसारध्वान्तविध्वंस &c. (§756*a.*), there is the identical position of Metaphor and Alliteration. Or, for instance in कुरवका रवकारणतां ययुः, रवका रवका form one Rhyme (§640), and वकार वकार another; so there is the identical position of two Rhymes.

g. Or for example :—

"Festively do the peacocks with out-stretched necks dance in these days, noisy with the roar of fresh clouds, and gloomy like the traveller's heart (or with travellers for spectators—पहिअसामाइएसु)"

Here, in the same position, *viz.*, the word पहिअ-सामाइएसु, there are the Simile पथिक-श्यामायितेषु (gloomy like the traveller), and the Metaphor पथिक-सामाजिकेषु (with travellers for spectators).*

* The Commentator rightly considers the above example as an instance of the Commixture of Dubiousness, not of the Commixture of the Identical Position, inasmuch as the Prákṛit expression पहिअ-सामाइएसु does not admit of the two interpretations simultaneously or positively, but alternatively or dubiously. He, evidently reading पओहररसितेसु instead of—सीतेसु and णच्चइ instead of सोहइ, renders the couplet into Sanskrit thus :—

अभिनवपयोदरसितेषु पथिकश्यामायितेषु (पथिकसामाजिकेषु) दिवसेषु ।
नृत्यति (उत्सवायते) प्रसारितग्रीवाणां नृत्यं मयूरवृन्दानाम् ॥

The term सामाजिक, applied to the travellers, implies a Metaphor, inasmuch as it properly means one of an audience at some *regular* festivity, such as a dramatic entertainment. The peacock's dance is no festivity in the proper

Intelligent readers, do you, with ease, acquire a knowledge of the principles of *poetical* composition in their integrity, by the perusal of this Mirror of Composition, the work of S'rí Vis'wanátha Kavirája, the son of the glorious moon among the poets, S'ri Chandra-S'ekhara.

As long as Lakshmí, whose face resembles the unclouded moon, adorns the lap of Náráyaṇá, so long may this work be celebrated in the world, rejoicing the mind of the poets!

Here ends the 10th chapter of the Mirror of Composition.

sense of the word,—none, at all events, to the separated lover, to whom every merry sight is a source of pain.

It would not be uninteresting to illustrate some of these mixed ornaments by an English example:

"Ye ice-falls! ye that from the mountain's brow
Adown enormous ravines slope amain—
Torrents, methinks, that heard a mighty voice,
And stopped at once amidst their maddest plunge!
Motionless torrents! silent cataracts!"—*Coleridge.*

In the 3rd and 4th lines, there is a Modal Metaphor (§ 703), subserved by a Poetical Fancy (§ 686). In the last line, there is a Commixture, called Identical Position, of a Hyperbole (§ 697) and a Contradiction (§ 718). If we may look upon these five lines as forming one piece of poetry, there is here a Conjunction (§ 756) of these two Commixtures.

THE END.